Educational Foundations:
Diverse Histories, Diverse Perspectives

INTRODUCTION

Educational Foundations is a unique new text that puts diversity issues at the core of its foundations content. As today's classrooms become increasingly diverse — culturally, linguistically, and academically — student teachers need to be aware of (1) cultural factors that influence schooling practices today, (2) the changing nature of teaching and learning, and (3) the history and contemporary structures of the American education system.

The ultimate objectives of Educational Foundations are to provide student teachers with readings relevant to contemporary school instruction and to enhance their professional discourse as well.

SPECIAL FEATURES IN THIS TEXT

Each chapter begins with the **First Person** feature — an engaging, personal account of the author's experiences as a student and classroom teacher. These narratives establish a personal and professional connection for readers to consider as they delve into each chapter.

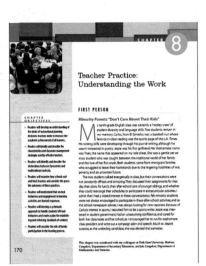

> I loved [the First Person stories]. I found [that] most of them offered a personal glimpse—a human interaction if you will—that many textbooks lack.
>
> — Amy Laible, Bucks County Community College

I am a big believer in students working to decode their own identities and the ways those identities are wrapped up in social and cultural practices. Students will find the Pause and Reflect sections quite useful as they begin work on this project.

— Mark Malaby,
Ball State University

SPECIAL FEATURES . . .

From **Preservice to Practice** highlights real teachers and educational scenarios in today's schools. This feature brings the themes and concepts of chapter material to life and allows readers to explore the multiple perspectives of K–12 students. **Questions for Reflection** at the end of the feature encourage students to think critically about the topic being addressed in the section.

For Your Consideration boxes provide Web addresses that offer supplementary information on topics presented in each chapter.

Pause and Reflect sections appear throughout each chapter to help students make the connection between chapter content and their own perceptions and personal experiences.

For Your CONSIDERATION

Visit the Educational Testing Service, Praxis Test website at **http://www.ets.org/portal/site/ets**. What kinds of review, test preparation, and study strategies are recommended? What suggestions are offered to reduce test anxiety?

PAUSE & REFLECT

Idealism and realism reflect teacher-centered philosophical approaches to curriculum and instruction. As you develop your own philosophy, how do these perspectives apply to skills-based or content-specific instruction at the elementary or secondary grade levels? How can either philosophy influence students' problem-solving skills?

Connecting to CL Video Cases features direct students to the website to view the Education Video Cases. Viewing the cases online and reading this feature box will help students make the connection between foundation content and the real-life classroom.

> *I believe the 'Connecting to CL Video Cases' section is an excellent addition to introduce real-life situations and use them for discussion of the topics introduced in the chapters. The instructors and students can do a lot with it, really.*
>
> — **Ahmad Sultan, University of Wisconsin-Stevens Point**

End-of-Chapter Activities include

- A general Chapter Summary
- Discussion Questions
- Activities to further engage students with the materials
- Website addresses that provide links to additional readings and resources

UNIQUE COVERAGE

Go to these chapters for answers to the following questions and more.

Chapter 4, Equity and Educational Practice:

- How does poverty affect public schools in regions across the United States?
- What are the educational outcomes and graduation rates of students from low socioeconomic backgrounds and communities?
- How can teachers apply the Funds of Knowledge approach to parent outreach and curriculum development?

Chapter 11, Teaching English Language Learners: Bilingual and English as a Second Language Efforts

- What are your beliefs about English language learners?
- What are the strategies and challenges in the assessment, identification, and placement of ELLs in school programs?
- What are the complexities and challenges that ELLs face related to their identities in schools?

Chapter 12, Globalization and Schooling: Education at the Crossroads

- What educational approaches and initiatives are being implemented beyond the United States' borders?
- What are the different perspectives that inform the definition of globalization?
- How does education in the United States compare and contrast with education in international settings, including Japan, Mexico, and Iraq?

COMPLETE PACKAGE FOR INSTRUCTORS AND STUDENTS

Instructor Resources

The **Instructor Website** provides instructors with access to the Instructor's Resource Manual, PowerPoint Presentations for each chapter, a correlation chart connecting the text content to national standards, and all student materials.

The **Digital Instructor's Resource Manual,** located at the Instructor Website, contains

- Sample syllabi
- Student objectives
- Chapter overviews
- Supplementary lecture and discussion topics
- Class activities
- Assessment questions
- Selected references and Web resources

Diploma Testing (powered by Diploma) is a flexible testing program that allows instructors to create, edit, customize and deliver multiple types of tests via print, network server, or the Web.

Eduspace®, Cengage Learning's Complete Course Management System, is a customizable, powerful, and interactive platform that enables instructors to create all or part of their courses online using the widely recognized tools of Blackboard™ and text-specific content from Educational Foundations:

- Video cases
- Teacher Disposition tool
- Grade book
- Homework
- End of chapter activities

Student Resources

The **Student Website** provides students with additional case studies, homework, and Web links from each chapter. It also houses the Cengage Learning Video Cases, four- to six-minute video modules that present actual classroom scenarios. Each case contains reflection questions, bonus videos, classroom artifacts, teacher interviews, and key terms to enhance the viewing experience.

Educational Foundations

Educational Foundations:

Diverse Histories, Diverse Perspectives

Grace Huerta
Utah State University

WADSWORTH
CENGAGE Learning

Australia • Brazil • Japan • Korea • Mexico • Singapore • Spain • United Kingdom • United States

WADSWORTH
CENGAGE Learning™

Educational Foundations: Diverse Histories, Diverse Perspectives
Grace Huerta

Publisher: Patricia Coryell

Sponsoring Editor: Shani Fisher

Marketing Manager: Amy Whitaker

Development Editor: Julia Giannotti

Senior Project Editor: Rosemary Winfield

Art and Design Manager: Jill Haber

Cover Design Director: Tony Saizon

Photo Editor: Jennifer Meyer Dare

Composition Buyer: Chuck Dutton

New Title Project Manager: Priscilla Manchester

Editorial Assistant: Amanda Nietzel

Marketing Assistant: Samantha Abrams

Editorial Assistant: Paola Moll

Cover: Sewn Faces, copyright © 2007 Elizabeth Rosen.

Credits continue on page C-1, which constitutes an extension of the copyright page.

For product information and technology assistance, contact us at
Cengage Learning Customer & Sales Support, 1-800-354-9706

For permission to use material from this text or product, submit all requests online at **www.cengage.com/permissions**
Further permissions questions can be emailed to
permissionrequest@cengage.com

Library of Congress Control Number: 2007931441

ISBN-13: 978-0-618-56255-8

ISBN-10: 0-618-56255-9

Wadsworth
20 Channel Center Street
Boston, MA 02210
USA

Cengage Learning is a leading provider of customized learning solutions with office locations around the globe, including Singapore, the United Kingdom, Australia, Mexico, Brazil, and Japan. Locate your local office at **www.cengage.com/global**

Cengage Learning products are represented in Canada by Nelson Education, Ltd.

To learn more about Wadsworth, visit **www.cengage.com/wadsworth**

Purchase any of our products at your local college store or at our preferred online store **www.cengagebrain.com**

Printed in the United States of America
2 3 4 5 6 7 14 13 12 11 10

Dedication

This book is dedicated to the memory of my parents, Maria Luisa Huerta and George Sanchez Huerta, who provided the tools for me to withstand prejudice and the opportunity to attend college. Their experiences, sacrifices, wisdom, and selflessness continue to inspire my brothers and me daily. I also wish to thank my familia, LAF, and dear friends in Alaska, California, Oregon, New Mexico, Washington, and Utah, whose joy and generosity helped make this project happen.

BRIEF CONTENTS

Contents **viii**

Preface **xv**

PART 1 A Foundational Framework

CHAPTER 1 Historical Perspectives Informing the Schooling of a Diverse
Society: A Legacy of Inclusion and Exclusion **2**

CHAPTER 2 Educational Philosophy **31**

PART 2 The Teaching Profession: Our Callings, Our Challenges

CHAPTER 3 Entering the Teaching Profession **60**

CHAPTER 4 Equity and Educational Practice **81**

PART 3 School Structure, Finance, and Public School Law

CHAPTER 5 School Governance and Community Ties **104**

CHAPTER 6 Paying the Bills: School Funding **124**

CHAPTER 7 Public School Law **144**

PART 4 Educators in Action: The Local Classroom, the Global Classroom

CHAPTER 8 Teacher Practice: Understanding the Work **170**

CHAPTER 9 Understanding Assessment **199**

CHAPTER 10 Exploring the Relationship Between American Culture and Education **222**

CHAPTER 11 Teaching English Language Learners: Bilingual and English as
a Second Language Efforts **240**

CHAPTER 12 Globalization and Schooling **264**

Glossary **G-1**

Credits **C-1**

Index **I-1**

CONTENTS

Brief Contents   **vii**

Preface   **xv**

PART 1

A Foundational Framework

CHAPTER 1 Historical Perspectives Informing the Schooling of a Diverse Society: A Legacy of Inclusion and Exclusion   2

First Person: Anyone Can Make It in America, but Not Alone 2

Greek Influences on American Education 5
  Makeup of Greek Society 5
  Education in Greece 5

An Education Program for a New Country.......... 8
  European Influences on Early American Education 8
  The Vision of Thomas Jefferson 9
  Horace Mann and the Emergence of the Public Schools 10

FROM PRESERVICE TO PRACTICE: Schools Are for Everyone 11

The Education of Immigrants: A Historical Overview 12
  Assimilating Immigrant Children 12
  Early Resistance to Assimilation in the Schools 13

For Your Consideration 14

Immigration in a Contemporary Context 14
  The Complexities Associated with Immigration 15

  Educational Achievement of Immigrant Students 15
  Maintaining Cultural Identity 16

FROM PRESERVICE TO PRACTICE: Walkout! 17

The Legacy of Educational Exclusion: African Americans, American Indians, Mexican Americans, and Asian Americans 18
  Early African American Education 18
  Early American Indian Education 20
  Early Mexican American Education 21
  Early Asian American Education 22

PAUSE AND REFLECT 24

Arab Americans Seeking Understanding amid the Stereotypes 24
For Your Consideration 25
  Arab Americans: Immigration and Changing Demographics 25
For Your Consideration 26
  Arab American Education 26

FROM PRESERVICE TO PRACTICE: Anti-Arab Discrimination: What Teachers Can Do 26

Summary 28

CHAPTER 2 Educational Philosophy   31

First Person: Making Time to Care About Philosophy: Connections to Practice and Social Justice 31

The Role of Philosophy in the Teaching Profession 32
  Fundamental Philosophical Positions 33
  Teacher-Centered Philosophies 33

PAUSE AND REFLECT 35

FROM PRESERVICE TO PRACTICE: Philosophies in the Classroom 36

PAUSE AND REFLECT 38
  Student-Centered Philosophies 38

For Your Consideration 40

Connecting to the Cengage Learning Video Cases 40

FROM PRESERVICE TO PRACTICE: Social Reconstructivism in Action 42

PAUSE AND REFLECT 44

Leaders Whose Educational Philosophies Cross and Blur Borders 44

Mary Wollstonecraft: Advocate for Women's Rights and Education   44

Mohandas Gandhi: Education for Life, Through Life   46

W. E. B. Du Bois: Merging Social Justice and Higher Education   49

Gloria Anzaldúa: Crossing Borderlands   53

PAUSE AND REFLECT   55

FROM PRESERVICE TO PRACTICE: Now Consider and Compose Your Own Teaching Philosophy   56

Summary   56

PART 2 The Teaching Profession: Our Callings, Our Challenges

CHAPTER 3   Entering the Teaching Profession   **60**

First Person: Anyone Can Teach: The Default Major   60

The Important Role of Teachers in a Democratic Society 61
 Who Are Today's American Teachers?   62
 Women and Minorities in the Teaching Profession   62

FROM PRESERVICE TO PRACTICE: Cows and a Career   63

The Process: Securing Licensure and Certification 64
 Alternative Routes to Licensure   64

FROM PRESERVICE TO PRACTICE: Alternative Licensure Program Model, San Juan Board of Cooperative Educational Services (BOCES), San Juan, Colorado   66

FROM PRESERVICE TO PRACTICE: To License or Not to License? That Is the Question   67

Expectations of Teachers: Tenure and Evaluation 67
 Securing Tenure   67
 Competency Testing: The Certification Process   67

FROM PRESERVICE TO PRACTICE: Praxis Overview   68

For Your Consideration   69

Educational Reform's Impact on the Teaching Profession Today 69
 The No Child Left Behind Act   69

Connecting to the Cengage Learning Video Cases   70

NCLB and High Stakes Testing 70

FROM PRESERVICE TO PRACTICE: Meeting the Challenges of NCLB   71
 Implications for Teachers   72
 The Function of Unions   72
 National Education Association   72
 American Federation of Teachers   72

For Your Consideration   73
 Teacher Salaries   73

PAUSE AND REFLECT   76

The Education Job Market: Projected Needs and Recruitment Strategies 76
 Antidote to Early Burnout: New-Teacher Induction or Mentoring Programs   77

FROM PRESERVICE TO PRACTICE: Why Do Teachers Leave the Profession?   77

PAUSE AND REFLECT   78

New-Teacher Induction Programs: Inconsistencies 78

Summary   79

CHAPTER 4   Equity and Educational Practice   **81**

First Person: Minority Communities "Don't Care About Kids" and Other Myths   81

What Is Equal Opportunity? 83

PAUSE AND REFLECT   84

Poverty, Segregated Communities, and Segregated Schools 84
 Poverty and Minority Students   84
 Poverty in Inner Cities   85

FROM PRESERVICE TO PRACTICE: Advocate for Educational Equity: Jonathan Kozol 85

Regional Diversity in Public Schools 86

For Your Consideration 87

Low-Income Status and Free Lunch 88

FROM PRESERVICE TO PRACTICE: Where Should I Teach? 88

Social and Educational Outcomes of Desegregation 89

PAUSE AND REFLECT 90

Intersections Between Educational Practice and Socioeconomic Status 90

Ability Grouping and Tracking of Students 90

Advantages of Students with a High Socioeconomic Background 91

For Your Consideration 92

Dropout Rates and Their Relationship to Poverty, Segregation, and Race 92

FROM PRESERVICE TO PRACTICE: Empowerment of a Dropout 93

The No Child Left Behind Act and Education Equity 94

Implications for Educators 94

Making Decisions About Employment 94

Dealing with Classroom Size 94

Effects of Ability Grouping and Tracking 95

Bring Communities Together 95

PAUSE AND REFLECT 96

Engaging Family and Community 96

Funds of Knowledge 96

FROM PRESERVICE TO PRACTICE: Excerpts from Martha Tenery's Home Visit: La Visita 97

Using Funds of Knowledge in the Classroom 98

Connecting to the Cengage Learning Video Cases 99

Summary 99

PART 3

School Structure, Finance, and Public School Law

CHAPTER 5   School Governance and Community Ties   **104**

First Person: We Don't Care About the Politics! 104

Federal Role: U.S. Department of Education and Political Contexts 106

PAUSE AND REFLECT 108

The Role of the State Board of Education and Office of Education 108

FROM PRESERVICE TO PRACTICE: Do Medical Inaccuracies in Abstinence-Only Programs Put Youth at Risk? 108

Local Control: School Districts, School Boards, and Departments of Education 111

For Your Consideration 112

The Role of the Local School Board 112

PAUSE AND REFLECT 114

The Role of the Superintendent and Local District Office 114

The Role of Principals 115

FROM PRESERVICE TO PRACTICE: Principals in Transition 116

School Structures, School Choices 116

For Your Consideration 117

Privatization of Public Schools: Charter Schools 117

For Your Consideration 119

Charter, School Choice, and Voucher Initiatives: Controversial Implications 119

PAUSE AND REFLECT 120

The Home School Movement 120

For Your Consideration 121

CHAPTER 6   Paying the Bills: School Funding   124

First Person: Unequal Funding Equals Unequal Schools 124

Education Funding: A Historical Overview 125
School Finance: A Reflection of Early American Values 126
Establishing New Schools in a New Country 126

PAUSE AND REFLECT 126

Federal Educational Initiatives: New Responsibilities 127

Contemporary Finance Systems 128
Education of Mentally Retarded Children Act 128
Breaking Ground: The Elementary and Secondary Education Act 128

For Your Consideration 130
Social Needs and Federal Policy Responses 130

FROM PRESERVICE TO PRACTICE: Grant Writing and Salvaging Savage Inequalities 131
Standards-Based Accountability and Federal Funding 131
The Impact of the No Child Left Behind Act on School Funding 131

State Funding of the Public Schools: Taxation 132
The History of Taxation 132

FROM PRESERVICE TO PRACTICE: Limited Funds and the Competition for Resources 133

PAUSE AND REFLECT 134
Types of Taxes That Generate School Funding 134

For Your Consideration 136
Other Views of Educational Finance and Taxes 136

Funding Schools Equitably 136
For Your Consideration 139
Charter and Private School Funding: School Choice 139
Should Public Funds Be Used to Finance Private Schools? 140

PAUSE AND REFLECT 140

The Impact of Changing Demographics on School Finance 140

CHAPTER 7   Public School Law   144

First Person: Following the Law: Did I Do My Job? 144

Teachers and the Law: An Introduction 145

Securing Employment, Securing a Contract 147
Terms of a Contract 148

FROM PRESERVICE TO PRACTICE: Missouri Supreme Court Hears Oral Arguments in Case About Public-Sector Collective-Bargaining Rights 148

For Your Consideration 149
Breach of Contract 149

PAUSE AND REFLECT 150
The Importance of Being Tenured 150
How Teachers Achieve Tenure 150

FROM PRESERVICE TO PRACTICE: Earning Tenure 151

PAUSE AND REFLECT 152
Termination of Tenured and of Nontenured Teachers 152

Losing a Job: Contributing Factors Regarding Dismissal 153
What Does It Mean to be Incompetent? 153
Other Causes for Termination 153

FROM PRESERVICE TO PRACTICE: New Jersey Teacher Tenure Laws Make Removal of a Teacher Complicated and Costly 154

For Your Consideration 155

Teachers' Rights and Liability Issues 155
When Are Teachers Negligent? 155
Liability and Child Abuse 156

FROM PRESERVICE TO PRACTICE: Breaking Up a Fight 157

Teachers' Private Lives 158
Teacher's Rights 159
Academic Freedom 159
Religion and Education 160

FROM PRESERVICE TO PRACTICE: Florida Student Sues Principal and School Board for Not Allowing Gay–Straight Alliance Club to Meet   161

What Can and What Cannot Be Taught? 162
Teaching Evolution   162
Sex and AIDS/HIV Education in the Public Schools   163

Students' Rights..165
Free Speech   165
Student Records   165
Search and Seizure   165

PRESERVICE TO PRACTICE: Illinois High School Association Considers Random Steroid Testing   166
Pending Issues   166

PART 4 Educators in Action: The Local Classroom, The Global Classroom

CHAPTER 8   Teacher Practice: Understanding the Work   170

First Person: Minority Parents "Don't Care About Their Kids"   170

Effective Teaching: Characteristics, Theory, and Strategies 171
Personal Traits   172

For Your Consideration   172
Characteristics of Caring Teachers   172

Understanding Ability Differences: Multiple Intelligences 173

FROM PRESERVICE TO PRACTICE: Is Loving Kids Enough to Be an Effective Teacher?   174

PAUSE AND REFLECT   179

Understanding Sorting and Tracking 179

PAUSE AND REFLECT   180
The Impact of Tracking on Diverse Learners   180
Challenges to the Implementation of Detracking   181

For Your Consideration   181

Linking Theory and Practice 181

FROM PRESERVICE TO PRACTICE: Theory to Practice   182
What Is Scaffolding?   183
Points to Consider When Implementing Instructional Scaffolding   183

The Eurocentric and Inclusive Curricula........... 184

FROM PRESERVICE TO PRACTICE: Chicano Students Challenge Inequities and the Curriculum: The 1968 East Los Angeles Blowouts   186

PAUSE AND REFLECT   187

Who Is Responsible for Students' Classroom Behavior?..188
Twelve Classroom Management Strategies to Keep in Mind   188

Connecting to the Cengage Learning Video Cases   191

Parental Involvement in the Learning Process ... 192
Framing Parent Involvement   192

Connecting to the Cengage Learning Video Cases   193

FROM PRESERVICE TO PRACTICE: Ten Ways for Parents to Help Elementary Teachers by Mimi Doe   194
Engaging Families with the Curriculum Through Funds of Knowledge   195

Connecting to the Cengage Learning Video Cases   196

CHAPTER 9   Understanding Assessment   199

First Person: Teaching to the Test   199

History of Student Assessment Strategies......... 200

PAUSE AND REFLECT   201

The Identification of Goals and Objectives...... 201

FROM PRESERVICE TO PRACTICE: An Authentic Assessment Toolbox   202

Connecting to the Cengage Learning Video Cases   204

The Politicization of National and State Assessment Standards 204

For Your Consideration   205
National Organizations Generating Content-Area Standards   205

What Knowledge Is Measured and How 206

PAUSE AND REFLECT   207

Assessment Instruments Commonly Used:
Strengths and Weaknesses 208
Paper and Pencil Tests   208
Rubrics   208
Portfolios   209

FROM PRESERVICE TO PRACTICE: A Sample Book Review
Rubric   209

Connecting to the Cengage Learning Video Cases   210
Student Portfolio Night   211

FROM PRESERVICE TO PRACTICE: Blackstone Valley Tech High
School Electronic Portfolio Guidelines   211
Planning and Evaluation of Portfolios   212

The Impact of Standardized Test Outcomes
on Teachers 213
Students' Test Scores and Changes
in Curriculum   213
The No Child Left Behind Act and Its Effect on
Teacher Certification   213

FROM PRESERVICE TO PRACTICE: A Teacher's Union Position on
Assessment   214

FROM PRESERVICE TO PRACTICE: Highly Qualified or
Stigmatized?   215

The Impact of Standardized Test Outcomes
on Diverse Learners 215
English Language Learners (ELLs)   216
Students with Special Needs   217
Students of Poverty   217

Alternative Assessment Strategies 218

CHAPTER 10 Exploring the Relationship Between American Culture and Education

222

First Person: Is a Culturally Relevant Curriculum Just
About Celebrating Holidays?   222

What Is Culture? 224

FROM PRESERVICE TO PRACTICE: Critical Literacies   226
Differences Are Not Deficits   226

For Your Consideration   227
The Enculturative and Acculturative Processes
of Schooling   228

Connecting to the Cengage Learning Video Cases   229

American Cultural Values 229

For Your Consideration   230
Judging Success: Material Well-Being   230
On Work, Time, and Money   231
On Effort   232

PAUSE AND REFLECT   232

PAUSE AND REFLECT   233

American Culture and Egalitarianism 233

For Your Consideration   234
Bringing Cultures Together   234

Connecting to the Cengage Learning Video Cases   235

FROM PRESERVICE TO PRACTICE: Cultural Teaching and
the Tamalera   236

CHAPTER 11 Teaching English Language Learners: Bilingual and English as a Second Language Efforts

240

First Person: Success Story: Vicki and Ruben's Sixth-
Grade Year   240

PAUSE AND REFLECT   242

Different Roads to Different Outcomes:
Choices in Language Education 242

PAUSE AND REFLECT   243

The Story: History, Politics, and Law 243
A Surprisingly Multilingual History   244
Changing Policies but an Unchanging Focus
on English   246
The Law: What We Must Provide English
Language Learners   246

PAUSE AND REFLECT   247

Ideologies: How Do We Think About
English Language Learners? 247

PAUSE AND REFLECT   249

The Theories: How Should We Teach
English Language Learners? 249

Connecting to the Cengage Learning Video Cases   250

The Programs: A Largely Monolingual Tale 250
    Sheltered Programs   251
    Pullout ESL Programs   251
    Bilingual Education   252

PAUSE AND REFLECT   253

FROM PRESERVICE TO PRACTICE: Language Gains,
Language Losses   254

Curriculum: What Should We Teach
English Language Learners? 256

For Your Consideration   256

Assessment: How Do We Know What
English Language Learners Know? 256

PAUSE AND REFLECT   258

Karen: Hybrid Identity 258

PAUSE AND REFLECT   260

CHAPTER 12 Globalization and Schooling

264

**First Person: Computer Labs, School Cafeterias,
and the Global Economy: A Healthy Mix?**   264

Considering Education Beyond Our Borders ... 265

Understanding the Global Community 266
    What Is Globalization?   266
    Other Meanings That Circulate in the Public
    Discourse Regarding Globalization   266
    Why Should Teachers Be Concerned About
    This Perspective on Globalization?   267

PAUSE AND REFLECT   268

What Is Global Education? 268

For Your Consideration   269

Understanding Comparative Education 270
    Japanese Schooling and Structure   270
    Mexican Schooling and Structure   271
    Iraqi Schooling Post-9/11   272

FROM PRESERVICE TO PRACTICE: USAID in Action   273

Glossary   **G-1**

Credits   **C-1**

Index   **I-1**

First Person: First to College

Each chapter in this text begins with a first-person narrative describing my experiences in the community as well as in public school and university classrooms. It is my hope that these narratives help frame the themes and content of each chapter with personal and professional points of view. Because I am the first person in my family to graduate from college, working with and helping the next generation to have similar opportunities are important parts of my own teaching philosophy.

Even though my father did not attend college, I can recall his vision for me. When I was a kid, we would walk thorough the Los Angeles campus of the University of Southern California and collect aluminum cans to sell for extra cash for the familia prior to football games. He told me repeatedly, "Someday you are going to go to this school. Someday you are going to be a Trojan." I didn't know at the time what that meant, but I did understand that being on the USC campus represented something powerful to him, as well as to my mom.

Another powerful memory of those walks during the late 1960s and early 1970s was the journey to get to the campus. On game days and nights, the parking lots were packed. We often parked for free a mile or so away at the Department of Motor Vehicles. We had to walk under the Harbor freeway, Interstate 110, to get to the USC campus and the grounds of the Los Angeles Memorial Coliseum. Night games were scary to me because of the darkness and the homeless people we passed on the streets and under the freeway who slept in cardboard refrigerator boxes and burned trash to keep warm. My father would say, "Don't worry, mija [my daughter]. You won't ever have to sleep in a box. I'll make sure of that." But I remember those sad and haunted faces. I also remember that my dad, as well as my mom, kept their word, even though we too needed the extra money we earned from picking up and selling aluminum cans.

Eventually, I was accepted to USC as a music major and even joined the marching band. I attended games and performed many times in the coliseum while my parents were in the stands during my four years at school. But I will never forget my dad's words, his vision, the picking up of cans, and especially the faces of the homeless. When I became a teacher, I was aware that not everyone would have the opportunities that I had. And yet I became a teacher because I thought I could become part of a system that needs to hold true to the commitment of giving everyone the opportunity to live, enjoy, and contribute to life outside the fragility of a cardboard box.

Text Rationale and Goals

Today, I write this preface having just concluded another semester of teaching a multicultural educational foundations class and working with a caseload of ESL student teachers in the local public secondary schools. My students and I are relieved that we made it through a busy semester of relationship building, challenging readings (including sample chapters from this book), assignments, multimedia projects, survival techniques, and yes, tensions. But I believe we produced exciting ideas about teaching and learning that we will carry with us when we work with the next generation of students in our classrooms.

Over the course of several years as an educational foundations instructor, I have tried a variety of textbooks, course readers, handouts, and trade books. As I reviewed possible foundations books to use as part of my instruction, I found that many lacked depth about diversity issues. This was ironic, given the increasingly diverse public schools in which teachers now serve in such places as Iowa, Illinois, North Carolina, Utah, Wisconsin, as well as in Arizona, California, New Mexico, Florida, Georgia, and New York. In fact, the discussion of diversity issues in these texts were often limited to sidebar feature boxes or trivialized within the narrative. My students were bored by page after page of educational philosophy and history and freely expressed this sentiment in their evaluations.

As a result, I adopted texts that were generally intended for stand-alone multicultural education courses. However, these texts also had their limitations. A faculty member within my department complained that my classes did not address foundation course content—without ever talking to me or observing my course! He believed that our graduates did not understand what a comprehensive high school was. While I questioned his comment, especially regarding this particular example, I did reflect on his critique, as well of those of my students, who now complained, "There's too much diversity in this class!" In response, I felt the need to think about writing a textbook that merged both foundational and diversity content for prospective teachers to consider as they prepared to enter the teaching profession.

My approach to educational foundations here explores

- The interrelationship between historical events and the structure of the contemporary American education system,
- The changing nature of teaching and learning, and
- The cultural factors and implications that influence schooling practices as we know them today.

My goals in this text also are to help preservice teachers explore

- *The historical antecedents that inform how educators have served diverse learners,*
- *The social, political, and global issues that affect the profession, and*
- *The ways that teaching approaches combined with collaborations within the community at large can help foster student achievement and parent involvement.*

Today, teaching remains a complex line of work and service. Teacher shortages in the states of California, Florida, Illinois, Nevada, New York, and Texas (to name a few) are now compounded by the pressures associated with bureaucracy and standardized testing. Euro-American teachers from suburban or rural homogeneous states are being recruited to work in culturally and linguistically diverse, urban school environments. To meet this demand for teachers, public and private teacher-training institutions are offering year-round courses through a variety of delivery systems, including distance and electronic media, paid internships, paraprofessional programs, extensive summer coursework, and alternative licensure plans.

Faced with this urgent need for teachers, a textbook must relate directly to the needs of the K–12 classroom. And the linchpin of teacher-preparation coursework is a foundations text that focuses on the integration of diversity issues throughout its basic content. *Educational Foundations: Diverse Histories, Diverse Perspectives* does this by providing students with readings and activities that examine the educational concerns and practices that are relevant to contemporary school instruction.

Organization of the Text

This educational foundations textbook serves the needs of universities and colleges that offer teacher-preparation coursework with an emphasis on educational foundations *and* multicultural education in a single course:

- Chapter 1 traces the history of American education and its role in our democratic society. In its historical overview of education, particular attention is given to the education of minority groups in America.
- Chapter 2 provides an overview of educational philosophy from historical, contemporary, and multiple perspectives.
- Chapters 3 and 4 discuss the nature of the teaching profession and the pursuit of educational equity.
- Chapters 5, 6, 7, and 8 provide an analysis of educational governance and structure, school funding plans, public school law, and guidelines for teachers. The impact of power relations on national, state, and local school structures is analyzed with special attention given to such initiatives as the No Child Left Behind Act and teacher-education standards.
- Chapters 9, 10, 11, and 12 focus on the practice of teaching, with discussions of classroom management, assessment, culture, English language learners, and the effects of globalization on schooling. These chapters examine how the American education system might transform itself through the practices of its own teachers (with careful and methodical classroom management, instructional planning, and alternative assessment approaches), meet the needs of English language learners, and engage with community and families through an understanding of their funds of knowledge. Finally, I also explore the impact of globalization in classrooms beyond U.S. borders and social contexts.

Textbook Features

- Each chapter begins with a narrative called *First Person*. In these narratives, my coauthors and I describe our experiences in diverse communities and classrooms that are relevant to the specific chapter themes. These narratives aim to establish a personal and professional connection for readers to consider as they delve into each chapter.
- The chapters also include case studies called *From Preservice to Practice*. With this feature, I describe educational scenarios that embrace broader learning communities, welcome various sources of knowledge, encourage teacher collaboration, promote student inquiry through application, and explore multiple perspectives of K–12 students.
- Each chapter also includes a *Connecting to the Cengage Learning Video Cases* resource. This feature connects the concepts of the online CL video cases to the themes of this textbook. Students can go online to view the cases and then make the connection to what they just read in the book.
- *For Your Consideration* boxes throughout the text refer students to important online resources that relate to textbook concepts.

- Another feature, *Pause and Reflect*, poses questions to readers as they relate to the chapter content and to their future careers in education.
- At the end of each chapter, I also pose *discussion questions*, suggest *activities*, and recommend *websites* and *references* for readers to reflect on and consult as they conduct their own research into teaching approaches and curriculum design.

Ancillaries

Accompanying this text are the following ancillaries:

Instructor Resources

- An Online *Instructor's Resource Manual* contains sample syllabi, chapter outlines, discussion topics, student projects, homework assignments, and other teaching tips.
- The *Diploma Testing CD* offers a computerized test bank with multiple-choice questions, short-answer questions, and essay questions for each chapter.
- The *Instructor Website* features the *Online IRM and PowerPoint Slides*.
- Cengage Learning's powerful, customizable, and interactive online learning tool, *Eduspace*, offers a convenient, user-friendly platform to manage, customize, create, and deliver course materials online. In addition to its gradebook, discussion board, and other course-management tools, Eduspace provides text-specific interactive components such as videos, reflective journal questions, test items, and additional materials to aid students in studying and reflecting on what they have learned.
- The books in the *Cengage Learning Guide Series* are brief paperbacks that examine important topics such as "Diversity in the Classroom," "Classroom Assessment," "Inclusion," "Technology Tools," "Teacher Reflection," "Motivation," and "Differentiated Instruction" in more depth. These are available as paperback books or online eBooks.

Student Resources

- *CL Video Cases* are available online and organized by topic. Each case is a four- to six-minute module. The video files present actual classroom scenarios that depict the complex problems and opportunities that teachers face every day. The video clips are accompanied by artifacts to provide background information and allow preservice teachers to experience true classroom dilemmas in their multiple dimensions.
- The *Student Website* offers additional tools to help students connect with the textbook material. Features include ACE self-quizzes, a review of key topics in each chapter, glossary flashcards, and the CL Video Cases.

A Note to Students

As this book finds its way out of your backpack and is cracked open under a good reading light, it is going to provide you with some insights that are relevant to your future career as a professional teacher. Being a college student does entail a certain amount of financial sacrifice. Tacos for dinner or Top Ramen? Should I buy this textbook, try to "wing it" with a copy on reserve, or share with a friend? Whatever mode of information transmission you decide on, I do hope this book is read. In other words, *I hope it does not become the best book you never read.*

To become a professional teacher requires a level of commitment that equals that of other professions. In-service teachers are often quick to comment that the profession is disrespected, underpaid, and threatened by outsiders who demand that higher standards be met. Yet we must look at how seriously we take our profession and how seriously we take our professional preparation. Each teacher education class that you take will require you to maintain your commitment to that training over the course of a lifetime, just as we would expect that of medical and law students who also give service to our country.

Whatever way you take possession of the book, *read it*. Just as with other college textbooks, you are not required to agree with its content. Consider the ideas that the readings introduce. Reflect on and anticipate the ways that the content adds to your professional teacher discourse. I invite you to paint the book with your highlighters, to scribble over the text you disagree with, to pose questions in the margins, and to throw down exclamation points if the content inspires you. Email and dialogue with the authors if you like. Check out the video case studies that take you inside to the classroom.

You are about to begin to shape your own professional views on education and to collaborate with your colleagues in ways that enhance your own views as well as theirs.

Acknowledgments

A number of reviewers made key contributions to the organization and content of this edition. Special thanks to contributors Barbara Cangelosi, James Cangelosi, Tricia Gallagher-Geurtsen, and Ruth Struyk and to the reviewers:

Charles Alberti, *Bemidji State University*

Gaylia Borror, *Winona State University–Rochester*

Carolyn M. Bowden, *Salisbury University*

Ginny A. Buckner, *Montgomery College*

Mary Kennedy Carter, *Hofstra University*

James Codling, *Mississippi State*

Barry S. Davidson, *Troy University*

Isolete De Almeida, *Cameron University*

Francine L. DeFrance, *Cerritos College*

Martin Eigenberger, *University of Wisconsin, Parkside*

Sherell M. Fuller, *University of North Carolina at Charlotte*

Judith Glies, *New Jersey City University*

Tim Green, *California State University, Fullerton*

Janice Hardesty, *Concordia University*

Peter A. Hessling, *North Carolina State University*

Sharon Hobbs, *University of Montana, Billings*

Patrick Johnson, *Dowling College*

Marion Johnstun, *Brigham Young University of Idaho*

Amy P. Laible, *Holy Family University, Bucks County Community College*

Mark Malaby, *Ball State University*

Harrison Means, *University of Nebraska Omaha*

Janet Medina, *McDaniel College*

Cindy Melton, *Mississippi College*

Michael Parrella, *Queens College*

Eugene Provenzo, *University of Miami*

Adah Ward Randolph, *Ohio University*

Maria Elena Reyes, *University of Alaska, Fairbanks*

Tim Simpson, *Morehead State*

Trae Stewart, *University of Central Florida*

Ahmad Sultan, *University of Wisconsin–Stevens Point*

Guy Wall, *Indiana University Southeast*

John Weaver, *Georgia Southern*

Tony Williams, *Marshall University*

Janice L. Wright, *Prince George Community College*

Educational Foundations

1

A Foundational Framework

CHAPTERS

1 Historical Perspectives Informing the Schooling of a Diverse Society: A Legacy of Inclusion and Exclusion

2 Educational Philosophy

Historical Perspectives Informing the Schooling of a Diverse Society: A Legacy of Inclusion and Exclusion

CHAPTER OBJECTIVES

- Readers will be introduced to the contributions of the Greeks and Europeans to philosophy and to our concepts of civic duty and schooling.

- Readers will understand how American educational goals were heavily influenced by the third president of the United States, Thomas Jefferson, and by the senator, social reformer, and educator Horace Mann.

- Readers will explore the educational histories of African Americans, Native Americans, Mexican Americans, and Asian Americans in the United States.

- Readers will understand the impact of immigration on the nature of public schooling today.

FIRST PERSON

Anyone Can Make It in America, but Not Alone

In this textbook, I begin each chapter with a personal narrative to help frame the content with examples from my own experiences relevant to education, teaching, and community life. I began my career 20 years ago after having attended both Catholic and public schools within diverse communities in Los Angeles County. Neither of my parents was able to attend college. In fact, my mother, having grown up in the mining town of Silver City, New Mexico, attended a segregated Mexican grade school up to the eighth grade. Yes, my maternal grandparents were among those who provided cheap immigrant mine labor and housecleaning.

In 1932, my father moved from San Antonio, Texas (where his mother attended a Spanish-language Catholic school), to California, where he attended Roosevelt High School in East Los Angeles when the school population was predominantly Jewish American. My parents' first language, Spanish, was not allowed in the schools they attended, and neither had the opportunity to attend college. They recall being hit by their teachers or having their mouths "washed out with soap" if they got caught speaking Spanish.

Nevertheless, my "produce man" father and "household manager" mom were able to provide my three brothers and me with motivation and "just enough" opportunities to receive the sampling of college experience that helped prepare us for future careers. Although I was the only member of my family to formally finish college and complete a PhD (in educational policy), today all of my brothers have succeeded in business or in civil service fields.

The personal sacrifices my parents made were simple, yet solidifying for us as a Mexican American family living in Los Angeles during the 1960s and 1970s. My brothers and I were able to attend school- and community-based activities, such as after-school sports, to go occasionally to YMCA summer camp, or to take $5 music lessons. Inside our rental houses in L.A. could be found newspapers, library cards, a phonograph that played 33s and 78s, a little sewing machine, an even smaller black-and-white TV, a used Sears washer, and at any given time, a dog or a cat.

We also had, of course, culture and familia. Spanish was often in the air, especially when my parents sought to teach us something valuable or when they tried to conceal secrets. Spanish was the language of grandparents, uncles, aunts, and extended families. Canciones Mexicanos, mariachi music, and even the bossa novas of Brazilian Antonio Carlos Jobim were the soundtracks of many family gatherings. Holidays and birthdays were made festive by tamale making and champurrado (a thick, Mexican hot chocolate) tasted from a clay pot, homemade chili salsa critiqued by the family experts, and the secret ingredients of homemade chorizo seldom divulged to outsiders. As a child, I also remember my mother chastising my brothers and me for not speaking enough Spanish in the house.

There was politica, as well. My father and uncles all served in the U.S. military during World War II or in Korea and were proud and saddened by their experiences. We were all labor union families whose youngest members all aspired to join a union. During the civil rights movement and the Vietnam War, our families lived mostly among African Americans and other Mexican Americans. As a child, I recall seeing in the distance the smoke from the Watts Riots in South Central L.A. I remember driving past the burned-out remains of the Silver Dollar Saloon, where *Los Angeles Times* journalist Ruben Salazar was killed by L.A. county sheriffs as he reported about the Vietnam protest during the Chicano Moratorium. I remember feeling afraid of these things as a child—but also being curious why they were happening. Our families protected us from being directly involved in these contexts, and yet, at the same time, even as kids, we knew that somehow we already were.

Initially, schooling meant discipline. During my early years at Transfiguration Catholic School, we were uniformed, held to strict classroom management by black and white nuns and lay teachers and taught to read, write, study our catechism and, yes, confess our sins. This school was located in South Central L.A., where the vast majority of students were African American. Later, we would move to a small suburb east of East L.A., Alhambra, whose public school populations were increasingly Latina/o but mostly white. Playgrounds were definitely better than my South Central school, with a grass field, basketball courts with chain nets, and an asphalt kickball diamond. There were more books to read and a once-a-week music program. A separate school auditorium was a huge, amazing space to me, as were school cafeterias with stainless steel counters.

With the exception of two Japanese American teachers, all of my instructors were Euro-American during my middle and high school years. Meanwhile, the Alhambra community became increasingly Latina/o and Asian—the result of "brown" and "yellow" flight from neighboring East L.A. and Monterey Park.

Gang activity emerged, and one of my brothers got recruited. My mother steamed and threatened to leave the house if my brother did not change. A brush with the law and a graze of a bullet eased his engagement with the gang per se, although he befriended a member or two. A boy nicknamed Mosca ("Fly") was my favorite among my brother's friends. He was always kind to this pesky kid sister, was unfailingly friendly, and talked to me about school. He had dropped out and was desperate to find a job.

My white teachers dispensed a fairly conventional high school curriculum that is mirrored today in the schools I now observe with my own student teachers. However, because of the diverse environments where I grew up, I was also exposed to what Gloria Ladsen-Billings refers to as culturally relevant pedagogy taught by culturally sensitive teachers. One English teacher, Cheryl Sylanski, took a particular interest in my writing about my familia. She introduced me to multicultural texts and advocated for my inclusion in the senior AP English class. She tutored me after school, while encouraging my participation in the student newspaper. I spent much time in the library researching, interacting with my community, practicing interviewing, writing, and building my self-esteem. My school did not have any other additional resources, although at the time, I did not know what I was missing.

Although my parents did not understand everything that was taking place at the high school, my mother attended open house while my father worked at the market. And yet, my dad always talked to me about attending college, even though he did not really know what it would cost or what it entailed. With help from my English, teacher, Cheryl, and a Latina/o Mentor Program at the University of Southern California, I applied and was admitted. Supported by state and school scholarships and whatever funds my parents could contribute, I completed my English degree there and went on to earn a master's in English and a teaching credential from California State University of Los Angeles. After nine years teaching high school English, transitional English, and journalism in L.A. county high schools, I went on to pursue doctoral studies at Arizona State University.

Today, I am an associate professor in the College of Education, Department of Secondary Education at Utah State University, in Logan, Utah. Like many other minority faculty members in smaller universities across the country, I am the first Latina to have earned tenure in our department, at a university that is over 100 years old.

I know I am the beneficiary of a larger common-school movement, in a republic that historically sought to educate a citizenry for literacy, civic responsibility, economic sustainability, and, yes, cultural reproduction. I am also the beneficiary of the advocacy and commitment of families, activists, legal scholars, and educators. For many of these individuals, the sacrifice and struggle evidenced in their life contexts did not result in the kind of progress they might have liked to see in their own lifetime.

As a result of my life experiences so far, I begin this educational foundations book with a question I have often been asked: "How did you make it?" This is a question relevant not only to you as a college student with your own lived experiences, but also to your future students as they pursue equal educational opportunities and, ultimately, college, careers, and a place in the world where they can contribute positively to the lives of others.

When I reflect on my own educational experiences and resiliency, I must first acknowledge that we do not do it alone. Together, families, educators, and community activists can recognize the importance of maintaining a cultural identity meaningful to the students we teach. They can model research and identify historical antecedents relevant to educational empowerment of all learners. And these efforts can ultimately help educators to generate strategies that deconstruct institutional and instructional practices that impede our ability to provide equitable educational opportunities for all learners. It is my hope that as you read about the historical foundations of education within the diverse contexts of contemporary community life, you will see how educators have been, and must always be, frontrunners in a shared pursuit of educational equity.

An important step in understanding contemporary American education is understanding its history. This chapter will give you an overview of influences on education that have brought us to where we are today. This chapter doesn't go into as much detail as the timeline shown in Figure 1.1, but as you read this and future chapters, please refer to Figure 1.1 regularly and consider these two questions: (1) Which historical events or contributors do you feel have had the most impact on education today? (2) Which trends and controversies continue to be debated by contemporary educational leaders and why?

Greek Influences on American Education

How has education in America's democratic society been influenced by ancient Greek culture? Consider the following overview, and refer to Figure 1.1 for an overview of education.

Makeup of Greek Society

In the fifth century BC, the city of Athens was home not only to Greek citizens but also to slaves (traded from the East), metics (neither slaves nor citizens, but immigrants), and children. With little trade taking place at the time, agriculture was the predominant economic activity. Slaves and metics provided the field labor. Thus, separate economic classes emerged. Among the weathy, citizenship was soon a prized societal distinction. Citizenship was based on gender (male), adulthood, and place of birth (Athens). Once a man was identified as a citizen, he could become a voting member of the Athenian assembly. One citizen in eight could attend assembly meetings, debate the issues that arose, and vote on local proposals (Tozer et al., 2006). All others were excluded from voting.

This kind of democracy reflected both the vision of freedom and the struggle for inclusion in the process, given one's socioeconomic class, ethnicity, and gender. Women were not allowed to take part in political life and were expected to manage childrearing and household chores. The ownership of slaves, either by individuals or by the state, would prove to have a tremendous impact on the country's economy. A similar scenario was to emerge 2,000 years later in America, as the states struggled to maintain a labor force at the expense of human chattel.

Education in Greece

Male Athenians who held citizenship also had the right to an education. The Greeks believed that the curriculum must focus on the development of both the mind and the body. Males between the ages of 6 and 14 could attend elementary or primary school, where they studied literature, music, and gymnastics. Private, secondary education was extended to those 14 to 18 years old, where they studied philosophy and dialectics (that is, discussion and debate). Slaves and females could not attend

Prehistory

Before the written word, humans learn by example and by word of mouth.

3000 BC

Priests in Egypt teach religion, writing, and sciences in temple schools.

2000 BC

China establishes the first formal schools.

1500 BC

Priests in India teach religion, writing, philosophy, and sciences.

850 BC

Homer writes *The Illiad* and *The Odyssey*, which teaches Greek history and mythology. In Greece, most men have access to teachers.

560 BC

Gautama Siddhartha (563–483? BC), Indian philosopher and founder of Buddhism, teaches that people can eliminate suffering by practicing morality, mastery of the mind, and wisdom.

550 BC

Confucius (Kung Fu-tse) (551–479 BC) teaches in China, emphasizing virtue, family, and justice.

400 BC

In Greece, Sophists teach argument through logic. Socrates (470?–399 BC), the founder of Western philosophy, teaches in Athens' public squares using questions (Socratic method)

to examine moral issues and search for truth. His technique is the foundation of the scientific method.

387 and 355 BC

In Athens, Aristotle's student Plato (427?–347 BC) establishes a school called the Academy. Plato's student Aristotle (384–322) also establishes a school in Athens. Both schools focus on truth. Plato writes *The Republic*, outlining his vision of a perfect society and education based on social standing. Aristotle will become the tutor of Alexander the Great.

70s–43 BC

In Rome, Cicero (106–43 BC) says that education should be broad in art and sciences.

AD 20s

Mostly in Galilee (today Israel), Jesus (c. 4 BC–AD 29) uses parables to teach self-sacrifice, service to others, and humility.

AD 60s–100

In Rome, Quintilian (c. AD 35–c.100) says that education should be based on a student's ability to learn.

AD 105

Paper is invented in China.

AD 500

In India, Nalanda University is the largest resident place of learning in history up to this point (10,000 students).

AD 849

The University of Magnaura is founded in Constantinople.

AD 1000

In Persia (today Iran), Ibn-Sina (Avicenna) (AD 980–1037)

writes on philosophy. His *The Canon of Medicine* was a standard medical text in European universities for nearly five centuries.

1100

The Scholastics help bridge differences between purely religious teachings and philosophical and scientific thinking.

1100–1250

Universities are founded in Bologna (1088), Paris (1150), Oxford (1196), and Cambridge (1209).

1450

The printing press is invented. Books become more available to some people, and literacy improves.

1499

In Rotterdam, Desiderius Erasmus (1466–1536) begins to research ancient documents and advises teachers to think about literature, not just read or memorize it.

1500–1700

The Renaissance is a period of renewed interest in learning, especially in Italy. A few more women begin to pursue education. Important texts in mathematics are translated into ordinary language, which leads to developments in science.

1517

The Reformation improves literacy as Bibles are printed in local languages.

FIGURE 1.1

Education Timeline: Exploring Historical Themes

Source: Retrieved March 19, 2007, from http://www.worldwidelearn.com/education-timeline/education-timeline.htm.

1592

In England, Shakespeare writes plays. The theater allows philosophical ideas to be taught to both literate and illiterate audiences.

1609

In Italy, Galileo Galilei (1564–1642) invents the telescope, states that the sun is the center of the universe, and is denounced by the Roman Catholic Church as a danger to the faith. He is ordered not to teach his findings.

1620s

The slide rule is invented, making math easier.

1659

The Czech educator John Comenius (1592–1670) writes the first picture book for children and travels in northern Europe encouraging teachers to make classrooms more interesting.

1690

The English philosopher John Locke (1632–1704) argues that we are born with blank minds and education should develop them, beginning in early childhood.

1770s

Americans Thomas Jefferson (1743–1826) and Benjamin Franklin (1706–1770) claim that education is important for all citizens of a new nation.

1799

Johann Pestalozzi (1746–1827), a Swiss educator, establishes schools thoughout Switzerland and Germany that use "object lessons," the senses, and expression to help children learn.

1837

Friedrich Froebel (1782–1852) opens a Play and Activity Institute in Bad Blankenburg, as a place where young children can learn before entering elementary school. It is the first kindergarten.

1852

Massachusetts, led by Horace Mann (1796–1859), establishes the first all-free education in the United States.

Mid-1800s

Most European governments establish formal education policies and plans for the general population.

1880s

In Great Britain, naturalist Charles Darwin's (1809–1882) theories of evolution are incorporated into education by the philosopher Herbert Spencer (1820–1903).

1905

The first standardized test of intelligence is developed by French psychologist Alfred Binet (1857–1911).

1918

All U.S. states require free education.

1920s

The Italian physician and educator, Maria Monessori (1870–1952), develops methods to teach young

children using practical, sensory, and formal skills that influence kindergartens and preschools.

1930s

Radio begins to broadcast a variety of educational programs.

1954

The U.S. Supreme Court mandates racial integration in U.S. schools in the case of *Brown v. Board of Education of Topeka*.

1950s

Television beings to broadcast a variety of educational programs.

1960s

Multimedia devices (slides, filmstrips, tape recordings) are commonly used in classrooms.

1970s

Home schooling begins to regain popularity when some parents object to federal laws that prevent the practice of religion in classrooms.

Early 1980s

Videocasette recorders make video learning common.

Late 1980s

Apple and IBM computers begin to appear in schools.

1991

Charter schools emerge in Minnesota and soon in other states.

Late 1990s–Present

The Internet makes information and communication available instantly. Universities offer degree programs online.

school but could receive tutoring for the purposes of home-schooling young children under their care. By the age of 20, Greeks were also required to participate in military training.

The study of the arts in primary school reveals the Greeks' support of a life grounded in an appreciation of aesthetics, drama, music, poetry, and leisure. A student of Socrates and teacher of Aristotle, the Greek scholar Plato (c. 427–347 BC), maintained in his academy of higher learning and philosophy that an education driven primarily by the pursuit of money was no education at all. Plato's position on the nature of wisdom and reflection also exposes the division of labor present in Greek society that afforded affluent males the time and opportunity to pursue a liberal education.

Thus, the educational vision embraced by the Greeks reflects a curriculum that focused on the mind, the body, and civic duty. At the same time, however, schooling was available only to affluent, male Athenians. This reflects the presence of exclusionary educational practices in feudal Europe, where different populations, certain classes, and women did not have equal access to education. It also suggests the assumption that not all members of society possessed the intellectual capacity to participate in the state and city governance and in power sharing.

Access to formal education was available only to those who were deemed worthy of it. As we consider the influence of European culture on the development of education in the United States today, we can begin to understand some of the complexities associated with providing equitable schooling to all of its citizens—complexities that have persisted since well before the birth of Christ.

PAUSE & REFLECT

Consider the features of a Greek education. As you read this chapter, consider what characteristics it shares with the American education system today. How does it differ? Think about the relationship between education and citizenship today.

An Education Program for a New Country

The new government had established a Constitution and a Bill of Rights, but groundwork was needed to develop an education program for its citizens. Although locally controlled New England town schools, **parochial schools** in the mid-Atlantic states, and private tutors provided an education for the children of plantation owners, a new educational infrastructure was needed to reflect the philosophy of the new country.

European Influences on Early American Education

During the eighteenth century, a period known as the **Enlightenment,** theorists argued that the order of the universe could simply not be explained as the single achievement of a paternal God, who, during times of great historical conflict, would intervene to save humankind. The **Age of Reason** theorists, such as Swiss philosopher Jean-Jacques Rousseau (1712–1778) and the French philosopher François Marie Arouet, also known as Voltaire (1694–1778), acknowledged the presence of an objective deity. But they also maintained that people had the intellectual capacity to think for themselves and use their reason to reshape the world for its own better-ment (Becker, 1932). An important proponent of the power of human reason was Thomas Jefferson (1743–1826), third president of the United States, the principal author of the Declaration of Independence, and founder of the University of Virginia.

Along with his colleague Benjamin Franklin, Jefferson felt that the power of reason, manifested through research, implementation of the scientific method, data collection, and analysis, would reveal the fundamental principles of natural law and the human experience.

Jefferson's interest in the Age of Reason had tremendous ramifications for the development of a national curriculum. Philosophers' interests were piqued as they studied anthropology, botany, chemistry, geology, and physics. Jefferson himself was intrigued by what lay beyond the Mississippi River (indeed, it was he who commissioned Lewis and Clark's expedition west).

This emerging interest in the sciences conflicted with traditional approaches to knowledge construction and what should be included within a school curriculum. Leaders of parochial town schools insisted on a curriculum that focused on the Bible, church theology, Latin, and Greek. They maintained that the human fall from grace required a response from church and state leadership and that such leader-ship and authority should not be undermined.

Nevertheless, the period of the Enlightenment influenced inquiry in other fields of study as the new American society developed. Thus, the emergence of the social sciences, such as economics, political science, and sociology, became important in the understanding of human interactions and the perfection of the institutions they sought to create. For example, Jefferson argued that this new society should no longer be governed by familial monarchs and established churches, who had earlier been assumed to rule by God-given right. Jefferson advocated the separation of church and state, arguing in his 1779 Bill for Establishing Religious Freedom that "civil rights have no dependence on our religious opinions."

PAUSE & REFLECT

In what ways do states and schools today address the origin of the universe and humankind, both controversial topics posed during the period of the Enlighten-ment and the Age of Reason? How do teachers introduce evolution into the curriculum today?

The Vision of Thomas Jefferson

Jefferson was heavily influenced by the English philosopher John Locke's (1632–1704) *Second Treatise on Government*, which expressed Locke's belief that everyone had the same capacity to acquire knowledge. Thus, Jefferson reasoned, if all citizens had equal access to an education, a select few could be elected to represent them in a government for a specific duration of time. In his 1779 Bill for the More General Dif-fusion of Knowledge, Jefferson maintained that a state system of schools should provide three years of free education of white, nonslave youth. The best of these stu-dents would be selected to continue school at state expense. From this group, the elite would be chosen to train to become leaders within the democracy. However, families would bear the expense if they wished to continue their children's education.

Jefferson's educational goals included such features as a state-supported and locally controlled school infrastructure whose curriculum focused on literacy, particularly reading, history, and mathematics; a school system that identified, selected, and trained leaders in higher-education settings; and schools whose education programs promoted and protected individual liberties. In essence, schooling would help prepare children for American citizenship.

Certainly, paradoxes emerged in Jefferson's education plan. American Indian and African American children were not included in his vision of who could attend this new school system. In fact, while he argued against the slave trade, Jefferson continued to own slaves, whom he felt were cognitively and spiritually inferior to Euro-Americans (Takaki, 1993). Female students could attend school for only three years; furthering their education would not be considered.

Jefferson's plan elicited questions that still resonate today. What would be the criteria for the identification and selection of those students chosen to continue their education for future leadership positions? In what way would such a selection process be equitable? Would this process ensure excellence? These questions persist as we strive to provide equal educational opportunities for underrepresented university students, while at the same time seeking to identify and admit those students predicted to be "our best and our brightest."

As it happened, Jefferson's bill was defeated in the Virginia state assembly. Nevertheless, the bill articulated who is responsible for American education and set the stage for state and local funding of the public schools. Following the defeat, Jefferson turned his attention to higher education, in hopes that he could build support for state-sponsored elementary and public schools by pursuing a different, top-down strategy. By 1818, Jefferson chaired a commission to develop his plan and choose a location for the University of Virginia. His plan included a curriculum, criteria for faculty selection, and architectural designs for such campus facilities as classrooms, libraries, and housing. In 1825, the University of Virginia welcomed its first class of 30 students, with Jefferson dedicating the institution as one determined "to follow the truth wherever it may lead" (Cunningham, 1987).

Horace Mann and the Emergence of the Public Schools

Common schools, or what we now refer to as public schools, began to formally take shape in American during the late 1830s. Horace Mann, a Massachusetts senator, lawyer, and educator, was a proponent of the common-school movement and saw its establishment as a way to institutionalize equal educational opportunity for all, particularly following the Civil War. Using a portion of federal funds that compensated the states for their participation in the War of 1812, Mann's home state of Massachusetts established a statewide common-school fund that would be supplemented with local taxes. Using the momentum of James G. Carter's "An Act Relating to Common Schools," Massachusetts also created its own state board of education (Messerli, 1972).

Mann left his position in the state senate to become the first secretary of the Massachusetts Board of Education. Considered to be the one of the leaders of the common-school movement, Mann traveled across the state to gain public support for common schools and argued vigorously for their renovation, an expanded curriculum, and the rejection of corporal punishment. He also advocated for the establishment of teacher training in "normal," or "model," schools and stressed the need for increased status and pay for female and male teachers. At the time, men were paid under $16 a month, and women earned no more than $8 a month (Messerli, 1972).

Mann's educational vision built on that of Thomas Jefferson. In addition to endorsing the importance of schools in developing an educated and literate citizenry for future leadership roles in service to society, Mann extended this goal to include the need for education to help increase the economic strength of the country.

Unlike Jefferson, Mann believed that slave children should have access to an education. In his efforts on behalf of admitting African Americans to common schools, Mann believed that such schools must serve as societal equalizers to help reduce class and racial conflicts (Messerli, 1972). Politically, Mann (as a member of the 1850 U.S House of Representatives) went on to vote against the Fugitive Slave Act (which sanctioned the arrest of runaway slaves for return to their masters). Nor did Mann support expansion of slavery in the West.

A coalition builder, Mann sought to establish a common school that all students could attend, not just the elite as he observed in Europe. Students from diverse backgrounds were welcome in schools where the curriculum included not only reading, writing, mathematics, and history but art, health, music, and geography as well.

From PRESERVICE to PRACTICE

Schools Are for Everyone

Ruth Reynolds, a second-grade elementary school teacher, was asked by her principal to take on a new student teacher. The student teacher, Ross, was amazed to learn that Ms. Reynolds's class included a student with special needs. Martin, who had been diagnosed with autism, was mainstreamed into Ross's class for half of the day.

Martin was able to decode letters and to speak simple sentences, but he did not socialize much with his peers. He stared into space during those group activities that were part of the classroom instruction. Ms. Reynolds worked one-on-one with Martin when he appeared withdrawn. Ross worried about the isolation of the student and felt he shouldn't be in the class. Ross expressed this belief to Ms. Reynolds. She encouraged Ross to get acquainted with Martin's family when they met with the special education teacher and discussed his individualized education plan, or IEP.

When Ross attended this meeting with Martin's parents, the special education teacher, and Ms. Reynolds, he learned about the progress Martin had made over the past year and a half. His parents were thrilled that he spent a bit more time with his peers and that his vocabulary had slowly increased, one word at a time. He had also begun to read and articulate letters, and, soon thereafter, words. They recognized that Martin had trouble recognizing and displaying body language and physical cues. But everyone agreed that being mainstreamed for part of the day had enhanced his progress.

At once, Ross began to feel guilty about his attitude toward Martin. He realized that learning in the company of his peers in the general education classroom, rather than being taught in an isolated setting, was critical to Martin's progress and participation in society. Suddenly, the importance of a free and public education for all Americans had new meaning for Ross, beyond the theory he had read in his educational foundations class. "So," Ross nodded to himself, "this is what equal access to education is all about."

Questions for Reflection

1. Why did Ross feel that Martin should not be mainstreamed? What changed his opinion?
2. Horace Mann felt that everyone should have equal educational opportunities and access to a balanced curriculum. What do you think his response would have been regarding special education students?

Such a curriculum, Mann hoped, would prepare students for citizenship, equip them to work to support a family, and provide the state and local districts with a tax base to fund education. It is worth noting that Mann's common-school curriculum did not include the use of texts that supported "any religious sect" (Messerli, 1972). Although he believed that the schools should instill in their students such moral values as honesty, diligence, and respect for truth and justice, Mann convinced his religiously diverse constituents that only "common Christian values" should be addressed in classrooms, not those specific to a particular religious institution's belief system (Gutek, 2005).

In the end, Mann's role in the development of the common school, the predecessor of today's public school, institutionalized the idea that developing an educated society could take place in a formal setting beyond Jefferson's selective three-year plan. Structurally, the school systems would reflect the collaboration between state and locally controlled school districts now funded by taxes. Later, Mann's educational goal—developing a citizenry who would contribute to their country's economic viability—would evolve into the framework for a common, capitalistic country whose domination would continue to move westward.

The Education of Immigrants: A Historical Overview

As education in America continued to evolve, the United States continued to welcome European immigrants to its ever-expanding borders, and with such growth emerged a foreshadowing of concerns about how schools and educators would respond to their newest community members. Such responses would not occur in simple isolation but, rather, would reflect the political, cultural, and philosophical landscapes colliding in a new America. Schools became the arenas where these collisions of culture, language, traditions, and religions would take place. And schools were the places where an American dominant national identity would be shaped.

During the mid-1800s, immigrants became associated with what white Anglo-Saxon Protestants referred to as the strange, the deviant, the poor, the criminal, and the Catholic (Kaestle, 1983). Such a view represented an educational belief that teachers needed to provide immigrant students with the moral character they apparently lacked. This is not to claim that all immigrant families accepted this focus on the **assimilation** process during the nineteenth century. In fact, some communities balked at the **acculturative** nature of public schooling and chose to enroll their children in parochial schools (Kaestle, 1983).

Immigrants rights march in Salt Lake City, 2006.

Assimilating Immigrant Children

With the continued influx of southern and eastern Europeans seeking work in United States cities during the late 1800s, the public school leaders continued their quest to assimilate immigrant children. The curriculum that previously addressed reading, writing, history, and mathematics now also included such topics as citizenship, accentless English, diet, dress, hygiene, manners, and patriotism (Brumberg, 1986; Tyack, 1974). This kind of curriculum, it can be argued, went beyond simply introducing immigrant children to

American culture and aspired to transform larger community identities through the use of social control.

Such educational historians as Steven Brumberg argue that some immigrant families, such as eastern European Jews, supported these Americanization strategies so that they could participate in a complicated new environment. And today, as well, some immigrant families appear to accept the acculturative nature of the public schools, at least to the extent that these schools offer immigrant children equal opportunities to pursue higher education and well-paying jobs (Huerta & Coles-Ritchie, 2004).

As the 1800s progressed, the nature and extent of assimilation and accommodation of immigrants in the public schools continued to differ regionally. In the Midwest, with concentrations of immigrants living in rural communities, it was not uncommon for teachers to be employed who spoke the native languages of their students—in this case, German. Given the influence of the immigrants in such communities, it was not unusual for administrators to "look the other way" when languages other than English were used in the classroom, in hopes that students would eventually assimilate into the English-only common-school classroom (Kaestle, 1983). However, accommodations were made only for German speakers, who represented the predominant language group who attended elementary public schools in the late 1880s.

Early Resistance to Assimilation in the Schools

Some English-speaking communities resisted bilingual practices in the community and in the schools. Parents resented the fact that their English-speaking children were being taught in German, and as a result, district lines were redrawn. In addition, English-only legislation was introduced in such states as Missouri (Jorgenson, 1987). By 1914 an ongoing debate continued in urban St. Louis regarding German instruction in the elementary schools. Administrators maintained that such instruction should be used only as a transition to the full delivery of an English-only curriculum.

Ironically, community concerns about the continued use of German in the common schools reflect many of today's arguments against bilingual education: expense, special services afforded to immigrants, the "disuniting" of America, and the emergence of a curriculum focused entirely on the assimilation process (Schlossman, 1983).

In the early 1900s, another dimension of immigrant education emerged. Even though first-generation, northern European immigrant children accepted the conformity imposed by the American public school curriculum, this was not necessarily the case for second-generation immigrants. In fact, Irish-Catholic families questioned the Protestant-dominated curriculum and faculty who promoted a socialization that was not inclusive of religious and cultural perspectives. This gave rise to increased enrollment in parochial schools, not only for Catholics and Protestants but for German and Slavic immigrant children as well. These schools sought to promote religious, ethnic, and linguistic traditions and the skills that could lead to economic empowerment (Olneck, 2004).

Immigrant educational research also established the presence of "culturally responsive schools" during the 1900s (Sanders, 1977). For example, some public schools sought to meet the needs of German-speaking communities by addressing German-language issues. Also, parochial school enrollment increased in such cities as Chicago, as immigrant populations continued to grow.

However, with the coming of 1882, 1921 and 1924 federal legislation that established immigration quotas based on national origins, America began to see a decrease in ethnically cohesive communities that maintained their native languages and traditions (Sanders, 1977). Accommodations for immigrant students in the common schools diminished, because the belief that prevailed at the time—and persists in some quarters today—was that any use of a language other than English in the classroom would inhibit students' ability to develop fluency in English. It was also believed that English-only instruction would facilitate assimilation and allegiance to American culture.

The need to provide English-language instruction waned during the 1920s and 1930s as immigration decreased. Many second-generation students who adopted Americanized ways soon became teachers (Berrol, 1978). Following passage of the 1965 Immigration Reform Act (which abolished quotas based on national origins and established a preference for relatives of U.S. residents and citizens), immigrant education was subsumed by larger societal concerns regarding the civil rights movement and the education of American-born minority groups.

Early proponents of what is now referred to as multicultural education pursued a curriculum that reflected an analysis of knowledge construction, introduced multiple perspectives and contributions, sought to reduce prejudice, and implemented equitable school policies that ultimately would help empower all students (Banks, 2004). At present, these educational efforts that are often associated with multicultural education also include English as a second language (ESL) and bilingual education, programs that seek to meet the linguistic needs of immigrant students.

For Your CONSIDERATION

Visit the Library of Congress, American Memory website at **http://memory.loc.gov/ammem/index.html.** Explore the experiences of America's early immigrants. Investigate across-the-curriculum lesson plans created by teachers using primary sources from the Library of Congress.

Immigration in a Contemporary Context

Today, educational approaches such as bilingual education and English as a second language are challenged by some American conservatives, who argue that diversity in education fosters immigrant disloyalty and acts as a divisive influence in American society. In addition, some educational researchers have found that these program interventions literally "pull out" and isolate immigrant students from the "standard" academic program. They believe that these program models serve only to maintain negative teacher and community beliefs about immigrant student status (Gibson, 1988).

Educators and immigrant families also worry that these educational programs are not well conceived and implemented. As a result, such programs, and the students who attend them, are often seriously **marginalized** on campus. This status, critics contend, is demonstrated by a less rigorous and inequitable curriculum. Furthermore, some parents feel their children are transitioned too slowly out of the ineffective programs (Gibson, 1988). At the same time, other researchers have found that successful program models, such as bilingual education, newcomer programs, immigrant parent outreach strategies, integrated academic core curriculum design, and ongoing teacher training, have resulted in increased academic resilience and enhanced performance by English language learners (Valdes, 1996).

The Complexities Associated with Immigration

Such ambiguity and complexity represent the challenges associated with understanding and articulating new goals and strategies for immigrant education within the contemporary contexts of the twenty-first century. The changing patterns of and reasons for migration differ tremendously from those of early American immigrants who settled here voluntarily (Ogbu, 1991). Immigration patterns continue to evolve. For example, in the decades between 1821 and 1920, immigrants from Austria, Hungary, Ireland, Italy, the United Kingdom, and the Soviet Union arrived in the United States (U.S. Department of Justice, 1994). However, from 1942 to 1964, immigrants from Africa, Asia, and Latin America replaced those from Western Europe.

In 1943, an emergency wartime agreement between the United States and Mexico called the Mexican Farm Labor Supply Program and the Mexican Labor Agreement, and also known as the **Bracero Act** (from the Spanish word *brazo*, meaning "arm"), allowed the legal entry of temporary agricultural and railroad workers into the United States. The Bracero Program was sanctioned by Congress to meet the labor shortage occasioned by World War II.

Immigration laws were again amended in 1965. As a result, immigration increased at rates higher than those of the 1920s. The Immigration Act of 1990 resulted in an increase in skilled immigrant workers and family members from a greater variety of countries (U.S. Commission on Immigration Reform, 1997). In 1993, the percentage of the immigrant population increased to 8.6 percent, concentrated, but not limited to, cities located in California, Florida, Illinois, New York, and Texas (Jacobson, 1997).

From 1994 to 1996, Mexico, China, India, the Phillippines, Korea, and Vietnam represented the greatest contributing countries (Jacobson, 1997). Why do such shifts occur? In 1999, the United Nations found that tremendous economic disparities are the primary cause for immigration. This clearly extends beyond the drive for religious freedom that was the colonists' major impetus when America was first settled in the 1660s. Factors contributing to twentieth-century immigration include (1) political conflicts along race, class, and religious lines; (2) the disenfranchisement of minority groups; (3) the collapse of the governance of nations/states, and (4) the absence of security regarding human rights and environmental protections (United Nations, 1999). Other factors include the migration of agricultural workers and the destabilizing impact of multinational corporations that transfer labor to other countries.

As a result, immigration to the United States is ongoing and dramatic, just as it always has been. These changing migration patterns resulted in a 1994 school enrollment that was nearly 25 percent culturally and linguistically diverse, and this diverse student population was predominantly Asian and Latina/o (U.S. Department of Education, 1999). Certainly, this percentage has increased in the years since then and will continue to increase in the twenty-first century.

Educational Achievement of Immigrant Students

The immigrant experience holds tremendous implications for the educational achievement of new immigrants. How American public schools have accepted immigrant children has historically rested on the terms set by early leaders who envisioned the classroom as a place where children learned how to be "American." Given the ongoing nature of American immigration, educators have struggled to find the best way to teach reading, writing, history, mathematics, and science in an effort to ensure that students were prepared to engage in civic participation and attain economic success.

Historical outcomes related to the academic achievement of immigrant students remain mixed, and they are often misrepresented in the press. Asian "model minority" immigrant students who excel in math and science and obtain admission to high-profile Ivy League schools are contrasted with hasty generalizations about low standardized test scores and high dropout rates of African American, American Indian, and Latina/o student populations. Research that finds differential academic outcomes by ethnic group members in specific content areas is generally overlooked (Lee, 1996).

What educational research does reveal is that today, a number of factors affect the academic achievement of different immigrant groups. These factors include the economic status of immigrant families, the nature and extent of parents' and children's schooling, recency of immigration, levels of literacy in the native language and English, parental expectations, and number of hours spent on homework (Kao et al., 1996).

Of equal importance are the factors associated with school structures and policies and the discord evident between school culture and the home cultures of immigrant students.

As noted in the earlier discussion of immigrant education, the cultural traditions, language, family loyalty, religion, beliefs, values, and expectations that are important in their lives both before and after immigration have an extraordinary impact on the educational and social mobility of immigrant students now attending schools in the United States.

Maintaining Cultural Identity

Immigrant students today struggle with the acculturation and assimilation **process**, much as early American immigrants did. However, many early immigrants eventually assimilated or accepted the dominant culture's traditions, language, and behaviors while distancing themselves from their own cultures. They believed that assimilating would bring them social mobility, economic opportunities, and an enhanced American cultural status.

Contemporary educational research challenges this belief. As students acculturate and acquire the dominant culture's norms, beliefs, and actions, they now do so under specific conditions and settings for particular purposes. This "selective acculturation" or "accommodation without assimilation" (A. Portes & Rumbaut, 2001; Gibson, 1988) enables immigrant families to engage in American economic, educational, and social structures while maintaining their cultural cohesiveness, language, beliefs, and behaviors, as well as parental roles of authority (Lee, 1996).

Maintaining cultural identity can result in different educational outcomes for different students, and some of these outcomes may not be positive (Valenzuela, 1999). As Rumbaut (1995) found, this is contingent on "the specific nature, content and style of the minority group's perceptions and adaptive responses to their specific social and historical contexts" (pp. 65–66). The interrelationships among contemporary immigrant families, their communities, and educators are most positive when they reinforce what Coleman (1988) refers to as social capital. Social capital consists of those norms that we can share, the building of trust among community members and educators, and the reciprocal support demonstrated through the exchange of resources and opportunities that help foster the academic engagement and achievement of immigrant students (A. Portes & Rumbaut, 2001).

The maintenance of community, family, and student peer networks also helps create a climate where immigrants identify and engage in acculturative interactions that support academic success. Researchers have found that immigrant students who maintain relationships with immigrant peers (of the same ethnic group) experience more school success than those whose relationships are not so close (A. Portes & Rumbaut, 2001).

Another variable that impacts the academic achievement of immigrant students is the educational interconnection between siblings who share school knowledge, resources, and study skills strategies (Bankston, 1998; Valenzuela, 1999). And yet the fact that schools are historically bound by assimilative practices, such as English-only policies and a curriculum dominated by American cultural reproduction, makes the establishment of intergenerational relationships difficult. Thus it comes as little surprise that second- and third-generation students often resent first-generation immigrant students who resist assimilation (and vice versa).

Finally, what can research tell us today about the history of immigrant education? The affirmation of culture—based on familiarity with one's cultural history, understanding of its influence on the present, and maintenance of one's native language, all enhanced by a loyalty to community and family—has been shown to have a positive effect on the academic achievement of immigrant students (Caplan et al., 1991). This calls us to reexamine early Americans' own immigrant roots, for some such groups were *compelled* to assimilate and hence were especially vulnerable to cultural loss.

From PRESERVICE to PRACTICE

Walkout!

Gina Larkin teaches seventh-grade English as a second language (ESL) at Rocky Mountain Middle School in the state of Utah. During the congressional debates regarding immigration in 2006, her intermediate ESL students often asked her, "Why do the white kids hate us? They say we are illegal and we should go back to our country." Another student, Olivia, wanted to organize a student walkout similar to student walkouts and protests that were taking place across the nation at the height of the immigration debates.

Initially, Gina, a second-year teacher, told her students "No." She privately worried about how such a protest would be received in the community and how it would affect her tenure. On the other hand, she recognized that her students were having a difficult time in school, given all of the news focusing on the issue and the local television reports on the protests, including an especially large immigrant-rights march held in nearby Salt Lake City.

Other teachers started to discuss Olivia's interest in activism. Olivia's math teacher even challenged Gina in the faculty lounge. "You're the ESL teacher. What are you going to do about Olivia? She is a rabble-rouser and wants to organize a student protest! I think she should be suspended."

Questions for Reflection

1. What would you do if you were Gina?
2. How would you respond to a student's call for a walkout?
3. How could Gina's interests, and those of her peers, be channeled into a positive educational experience? How could faculty be involved in such a way that they would model democratic principles, rather than demonstrating polarized positions to their students?

The Legacy of Educational Exclusion: African Americans, American Indians, Mexican Americans, and Asian Americans

Since the eighteenth and nineteenth centuries, the American educational system has sought to develop a literate citizenry who would later participate in a democratic and economically successful society. Equity hinged on the notion that everyone would have an equal opportunity to compete, regardless of ethnicity, race, gender, and family wealth. Education in the common (public) schools appeared to be the best mechanism for realizing these goals. Horace Mann even argued that economic class differences would disappear if everyone had access to an education. However, this idea was not applied to such historically excluded groups as African Americans, American Indians, Mexican Americans, and Asian Americans.

Even though America aspired to these goals, the barriers presented by prejudice, discrimination, and economic disparities manifested themselves in the U.S. political and legal systems. The structures and outcomes of these systems often favored the wealthy, Anglo-Saxon Protestant who could garner power by supporting certain political candidates and campaigns or could hire even more powerful legal representation.

The common schools were envisioned to be the "great equalizers," but not yet addressed were the variables that impacted the quality of education students from diverse race, class, and gender backgrounds would receive. Affluent students could attend private or public schools and would also be exposed to a number of educational experiences and resources (i.e., comfortable housing, food, clothing, books, the arts). Poor European American students would have access to a common school experience but not much more. African Americans, American Indians, Mexican Americans, women, and the disabled would receive even less.

Early African American Education

African slaves received sporadic and informal educational opportunities prior to the beginning of the Civil War in 1861. In the 1600s, British clergy offered religious training to slaves. In Charleston, South Carolina, an African American Zion School opened in 1866. Fifteen years later, Presbyterian schools for slaves opened in Virginia. In addition, evangelical Protestantism soon blended with African religious beliefs. Charged by the biblical search for freedom, these denominational influences surfaced within various forms of the Baptist Church, including the African Methodist Episcopal Church (Gutek, 2005).

The religious experience of African families had a major educational influence on the development of leadership, established guiding values that were driven by the pursuit of freedom and by the emergence of an oral tradition as an empowerment tool. However, the sale of a family member would break up the family—a family whose marriage was not recognized by law. An extended family structure, then, became critical to assist members as they endured a life in bondage. This kinship, and religious experience, helped establish a framework for self-education, however informal.

Southern laws prohibited the establishment of schools for slaves. These laws reflected the conviction that slaves should learn only what they needed to know to perform menial labor and that this ignorance would ensure they would not be tempted by rebellion. Some slaves learned to read and write while "on the job," as they conducted the work of their masters. For others, reading was often banned. In order to circumvent this rule, Frederick Douglass bribed white children with bread in exchange for *Webster's Spelling Book* lessons (Bullock, 1967).

At times, slave owners did attempt to provide an education for some slaves through apprenticeship-like working relationships or day-to-day interactions. Historian Henry Bullock (1967) describes how some slave owners felt that the education of slaves would help equip them for eventual freedom.

By the 1800s, free African Americans and missionaries sought to establish more African schools. The most notable was established by Christopher McPherson, an African American who, in 1811, organized a school in Richmond, Virginia. Resistance to his school by white southerners resulted in the school's closure, and McPherson, deemed dangerous, was sent to an insane asylum (Berlin, 1974).

Slaveholding states, however, continued to enact laws that kept slaves from getting an education. This legislation included Missouri's 1817 law that prohibited blacks from attending schools, Virginia's 1819 law that banned reading and writing instruction for African Americans, Georgia's law forbidding a white or black person to teach an African American to read or write, and Florida's and Mississippi's 1832 denial of blacks the right to meet for the purposes of education (Woodson, 1919).

In the 1830s and 1840s, speakers such as Frederick Douglass, and publications such as William Lloyd Garrison's abolitionist magazine *The Liberator* and Harriet Beecher Stowe's novel *Uncle Tom's Cabin,* helped ignite the broader antislavery movement, particularly in terms of its expansion into the new western territories. The four violent years of the Civil War, 1861–1865, ultimately gave way to the Reconstruction period of 1865–1877. A group of "radical Republicans," despite President Abraham Lincoln's successor Andrew Johnson's veto, established the Freedmen's Bureau, whose goal was to provide equal legal, educational, and employment rights for former slaves. However, it was W. E. B. Du Bois who wrote, "Public Education for all public expense, was, in the South, a Negro idea" (quoted in Spring, 2002, p. 179). Such initiatives helped pave the way for the ratification of the Fourteenth and Fifteenth Amendments to the U.S. Constitution. These amendments required the federal government to ensure equal rights and due process for all Americans and established that everyone had the right to vote regardless of race or past servitude.

The Freedmen's Bureau schools were modeled after the New England common schools, with a curriculum, taught by white Northerners, that featured civic participation; the importance of the Republican Party and Abraham Lincoln; reading, writing, math, geography, and music; and a McGuffey reader and a Bible. The curriculum also included an "industrial" component that focused on a utilitarian labor skills relevant to mechanics, farming, and sewing. The vocational educational "track" for African Americans that was thus established would later be the focus of such colleges as the Hampton Institute, developed under the guidance of Samuel Armstrong. Armstrong influenced the educational philosophy of Booker T. Washington and his emphasis on industrial education for freed slaves. This view would later come in conflict with the educational philosophy of Du Bois, who argued for black political empowerment and civil rights through higher education.

White southerners distrusted the northern schools and their teachers. The philanthropic American Missionary Society helped to educate freed slaves in the South and supported the establishment of black secondary schools and colleges. Between 1868 and 1877, a formal common-school system operated in the military-occupied South, with the support of the Freedmen's Bureau. However, a new debate emerged: Should the schools be segregated? With the end of Reconstruction, segregated schools emerged in Alabama, Louisiana, Mississippi, North Carolina, South Carolina, Texas, and Virginia from 1873 to 1882. Racial segregation in the states and in the schools would continue until the civil rights movement of the 1950s and 1960s.

Early American Indian Education

In terms of early American perceptions of their need and capacity for education, American Indians fared no better than African Americans. Traditionally, American Indian children were taught, through observation and practice, their native languages, religions, traditions, and skills by their families, elders, and such extended community leaders as shamans, hunters, artisans, and warriors (Coleman, 1993). Like African Americans, American Indians were perceived as "savages" who lacked the "mental ability" of the white Europeans settlers and needed to be assimilated.

The eradication of American Indian culture was evidenced legislatively in 1819 when the first director of the U.S. Office of Indian Affairs, Thomas McKenney, encouraged Congress to support the Civilization Fund Act. This act provided funds to employ Christian missionaries "of good moral character, to instruct them [Indians] in the mode of agriculture suited to their situation; and for teaching their children in reading, writing and arithmetic" (in Spring, 2002, p. 147). The act also spurred the development of Catholic and Protestant mission schools.

With nineteenth-century western expansion came the displacement of numerous tribes. It was soon evident that the federal government, according to Commissioner of Indian Affairs Charles Mix, had shared too much land with the tribes—land that was needed for the white settlers moving west. Mix argued that because Indians shared this land, they would never get a sense of owning property in their own right. This became the rationale for sending American Indians to reservations, tracts of land where their languages, beliefs, and behaviors could be controlled until the deculturalization process (referred to later, in the twentieth century, as "Americanization," even in segregated settings) was complete.

Carlisle Indian School, early 1900s.

To disrupt the cultural identity of native peoples, off-reservation boarding schools were also established, beginning with the Carlisle Indian School in Carlisle, Pennsylvania, in 1879. The school motto reveals the U.S. resistance to cultural pluralism in its newly formed democratic society: "To civilize the Indian, to get him into civilization. To keep him civilized, let him stay" (in Spring, 2002, p. 148).

From 1879 to 1905, the U.S. federal government established 25 off-reservation schools. With the development of these often overcrowded boarding schools, another phase of assimilation was established, as American Indian children were now isolated from their tribal cultures, languages, communities, and families. They also were exposed to such diseases as tuberculosis. With little or no time allotted for recess, after attending class the children often performed the labor to sustain the schools. Corporal punishment, such as whippings, exposure, humiliation, and abuse were often the chosen cultural management strategies.

By 1960, American Indian activists called for educational control and self-determination. Under the administration of President John F. Kennedy, the U.S. Task Force on Indian Affairs advocated for Indian self-sufficiency and citizenship. Demonstration schools in the Southwest established the role of parent participation in schooling, with an emphasis on native culture and bilingual education.

Given the momentum of the civil rights movement, the U.S. Senate published its 1969 report "Indian Education: National Tragedy—A National Challenge," which highlighted the negative effects of forced assimilation and land loss. Other recommendations in this report resulted in the passage of a number of Indian Self-Determination and Education Assistance Acts from 1972 to 1998 and helped establish the U.S. Office of Indian Education.

The broad ramifications of these laws established Indian sovereignty, and tribes can now contract with the federal government to develop and control their own health and education programs, offer tribal educational grants, and ensure that local school boards maintain Indian representation. In pursuit of educational equity and inclusion, today American Indian educators' goals include developing reading, math, science, and technology programs, while lowering dropout rates and increasing participation in higher education.

Early Mexican American Education

Following the 1846–1848 Mexican-American War and the 1848 Treaty of Guadalupe Hidalgo, Mexico ceded to the United States the northern half of its territory, which became all of the future states of California, Nevada, and Utah; almost all of New Mexico and Arizona; and parts of Colorado and Wyoming (Acuna, 1972). Mexico received $15 million for the exchange. Mexicans who remained in the Southwest experienced the challenges that come with being a subjugated people. They lived in segregated communities, attended segregated schools, faced job discrimination, and encountered forced assimilation.

In 1849, Texas agreed to be annexed to the United States. Between 1853 and 1855, Mexicans who remained in the state were driven out of Austin; those living in the counties of Colorado and Matagorda and the city of San Antonio were physically removed in 1856 (Montejano, 1987). Racism provided a rationale for the exclusion of Mexicans in the state, as white settlers felt they were superior to "lower-class" Mexicans.

During the late 1880s and early 1900s, however, American farmers' need for agricultural labor, combined with Mexico's political and economic upheaval, resulted in the immigration of many Mexicans back to Texas and the United States. Subsequently, labor exploitation was evidenced by the low wages paid to Mexican workers (Montejano, 1987). Segregated schools were established for Mexican children. These Mexican families were perceived as lowly peons with Indian roots who were now under white authority. They were contrasted with the Spanish, Castilian families whom Anglos considered elite because they owned large cattle ranches. This "racial" distinction created another basis for discrimination, as Mexican ranch hands lived, worked, and drove cattle in segregation.

In the public schools, Mexican students were exposed to a curriculum devoid of cultural content, despite the bicultural history of the region. In a program reminiscent of the boarding school experiences of American Indians, Mexican students' native language, Spanish, was prohibited in classrooms in order to accelerate the assimilation process (Valencia, 2002). Eventually Arizona, California, Colorado, New Mexico, and Texas would implement English-only laws in the public schools. "Violators" would be subject to corporal punishment and detention classes (Valencia, 2002).

As the 1800s came to a close, Mexican Americans in California and Texas sought bilingual education, a curriculum relevant to Mexican history and traditions, and English-language instruction for their children. Private and Catholic schools provided this kind of curriculum, and some California and Texas schools did not implement the English-only laws. At the same time, parents seeking bilingual education for their children in 1863 were dissuaded from sending their children to El Paso's first public school. Four years later, Mexican Americans opened a Mexican Preparatory School (San Miguel, 1987).

The great wave of Mexican immigration between 1910 and 1929 was enticed by a U.S. labor market desperate for cheap farm labor in California and Texas. American educators wanted Mexican children to go to school so that they could be decultural-ized, while ranchers and farmers resisted because Mexican families, including children, were needed for cut-rate labor. In 1920s Texas, to make certain that a Mexican labor force would remain available, compulsory-school laws were often not enforced (San Miguel, 1987).

Segregated public schools for Mexican Americans, with their inferior buildings, lack of curriculum materials, and English-only policies, were in place throughout the 1920s. Just as in the early American Indian education experience, families who did not speak English and their children were considered foreigners until they adopted white, Anglo-Saxon Protestant values. The conduit of cultural transmission would be through the acquisition of English. If Mexican children were not exposed to the public school assimilation process and were not subject to compulsory-attendance laws, these factors ensured that the U.S. need for manual labor would be met well into the twentieth century.

School segregation in California and Texas was ultimately challenged in the state courts from 1920 to 1940. In 1946, the segregation of Mexican American students in California was found to be illegal. Challenging the status quo view that Mexican American students needed to be segregated as a consequence of their language needs, the judge concluded instead that "evidence clearly shows that Spanish-speaking children are retarded in learning English by lack of exposure to its use by segregation" (in Gonzalez, 1990). As a result, segregation based on lack of English language acquisition without an "educational justification" was deemed illegal.

A sign indicating a segregated café in Texas. In 1930, the League of United Latin American Citizens (LULAC) won its struggle to desegregate hundreds of public places throughout Texas, including restaurants, barber and beauty shops, swimming pools, restrooms, drinking fountains, and hotels. By 1931, LULAC filed a class action lawsuit to desegregate Texas schools, and the suit remained unsettled until 1948.

In Texas, the League of United Latin American Citizens (LULAC, organized between 1927 and 1929 with the merger of the Mexican American organizations known as the Order of the Sons of America, the Knights of America, and the League of Latin American Citizens) filed lawsuits against segregated Texas school districts as early as 1931. It was not until 1948, however, that the case of *Delgado v. Bastrop Independent School District* established that segregating Mexican American students on the basis of race was discriminatory and illegal. This marked an end of de jure segregation of Mexican American students in the early history of education. However, here we will explore how de facto segregation continues to affect the educational participation and outcomes of Mexican American students as we move into the twenty-first century.

Early Asian American Education

In accordance with the Naturalization Act of 1790, which allowed only whites to become naturalized citizens, Africans, American Indians, and first-generation Asian immigrants could not achieve citizenship until the law was changed in the 1950s.

Federal and state governments utilized this law to keep the country's citizenry essentially white, or what was referred to at the time as "Caucasian." Because only citizens could own property, Asians were also denied the right to own land. The law was challenged in 1855 and again in the 1920s by Asian Indians who argued that they were Caucasian and therefore should be granted citizenship. In the 1923 case of *U.S. v. Bhagat Singh Thind*, the Supreme Court ruled against the Asian Indians, acknowledging that they were Caucasian but insisting that they were not white—that is, European. The intention of the Founding Fathers, the Court ruled, was to "confer the privilege of citizenship upon the class of persons they knew as white" (in Takaki, 1989, p. 299).

Chinese immigrants ventured to the state of California during the 1850s. Seeking financial opportunity, some 16,000 Chinese immigrants mined for California gold despite poor results (Takaki, 1989). Unable to return to their native country, the Chinese took employment as builders of the transcontinental railroad (a very hazardous job) and provided labor for the agriculture industry. Like the Mexican Americans, the Chinese were paid much lower wages than whites.

In response to fear generated by the influx of the Chinese into California, Congress passed the 1882 Chinese Exclusion Act. This act prevented the immigration of the Chinese to America. With such a racist climate in place, the Chinese were also excluded from attending public schools. In 1884, a second-generation Chinese American named Mamie Tape was refused entrance into the San Francisco School District. The San Francisco School Board issued a stern resolution: "Each and every principal of each and every public school . . . [is] hereby absolutely prohibited from admitting any Mongolian child of school-able age, or otherwise, either male or female, into such school or class" (in Low, 1982, p. 48).

However, citing the Fourteenth Amendment, the U.S. Supreme Court found that the San Francisco School Board was not providing Mamie Tape with equal protection under the law. This 1885 January court decision was not received well by the California legislature, which, only 14 days later, changed its education code so that Chinese students could now attend public schools—segregated public schools. As a result, the first Chinese Primary School opened its doors in San Francisco in April 1885. Another segregated Chinese school opened in Sacramento in 1893, but the system of segregated Chinese schools was challenged and dismantled by 1905 (Takaki, 1989).

Children pledging allegiance to the United States flag at Weill Public School, San Francisco, California, prior to relocation during World War II.

The influx of Japanese immigrants into the United States during the early 1900s also caused great disdain among whites, who felt racially superior to the newcomers. Much like the Mexican Americans and Chinese Americans, the Japanese were a cheap, compliant labor force. American workers expressed jealousy and resentment of Japanese workers, who they feared would take their jobs. For their part, the Japanese held high expectations for life in America and hoped to attain citizenship and social mobility through education.

Nevertheless, in 1906 the San Francisco Board of Education again decided to segregate Asian students by creating a school only for Chinese, Japanese, and Korean children. This time, the Japanese community boycotted the school and voiced their protests in the Japanese press overseas. This caused an international dispute between the United States and Japanese governments. Threatened with federal measures by President Theodore Roosevelt, the school board relented (Spring, 2002). Racial prejudice and other forms of community segregation continued to plague Asian Americans through the world wars. But later, we would see a new "turn" as Asian students came to be categorized and stereotyped as the "model minority."

PAUSE & REFLECT

What historical events shape society's approach to the education of minority groups currently? What educational experiences do these immigrant populations share? What effect does the legacy of inequitable educational opportunities have on minority groups today?

Arab Americans Seeking Understanding amid the Stereotypes

Since the tragic events of September 11, 2001, a great deal of misunderstanding, stereotyping, and discrimination have plagued many Arab Americans and Muslims. In order to challenge these assumptions, it is important for teachers to be aware of the history, changing demographics, and educational perspectives that affect the lives of many Arab Americans today.

First, it is important to understand that not all Arabs are Muslims, nor are all Muslims of Arab descent. These terms are not interchangeable (Adeed & Smith, 1997). And yet, this assumption persists. It stems from a lack of understanding about the cultures and religions beyond Western borders. For instance, many Americans are uncertain what an Arab is. An Arab is a person who speaks Arabic, who is a member of the Semitic race, and whose roots can be traced to the Arabian Peninsula (Suleiman, 2000).

Arabs are a diverse people, representing 20 countries in three regions (the Mediterranean, Northern Africa, and the Middle East) with an estimated population of nearly 300 million (Schwartz, 1999; Elmandjra, 2004). But even though these countries have populations that are Arab, specific traditions and dialects may differ. Arabs participate in all walks of life, and very, very few fulfill the media-driven stereotypes of being terrorists or members of a wealthy, royal family whose business interests are in the oil industry. It is especially important to note that "Iranians, Turks, Armenians, Kurds, Afghans, and Pakistani are not Arabs, although they reside in the same part of the world" (Al-Hazza & Lucking, 2005, p. 4). The governments of Arab nations also differ considerably. Their structure can include republican and socialist infrastructures, or their primary leaders may be dictators and emirs (an emirate, such as those that make up the United Arab Emirates, is a sheikdom governed by an emir).

Americans are often surprised to learn that the majority of Muslims are not Arab but Indonesian. This may seem counterintuitive, given that the predominant religion in the Middle East is Islam, and the majority of Arab countries are located there. However, worldwide, only an estimated 20 percent of Arabs are Muslims (Suleiman, 2000). According to Al-Hazza & Lucking (2005), "There are also significant Arab populations of Christians, Melokites, Maronites, Jews, Druze, and Copts residing in the Middle East (p. 4)."

For Your CONSIDERATION

Visit the American-Arab Anti-Discrimination website at **http://www.adc.org/index.php?id=203.** Learn what teachers can do to challenge discrimination against Arab Americans. Download lesson plans that address Arab contributions to our global community and that challenge cultural and religious stereotyping.

Arab Americans: Immigration and Changing Demographics

Beginning in 1862, the first Arab Americans immigrated to the United States in response to the Homestead Act. Signed into law by Abraham Lincoln following the Civil War, this act turned over 270 million acres, or 10 percent of the current United States, to private citizens.

According to Orfalea (1988), the immigration of Arabs to America took place during three periods: pre–World War I (1878–1924), post–World War II (1948–1966), and 1967 to the present. The first wave of Lebanese immigrants arrived in America in the 1800s, with the hope of improving their economic status. They did not immigrate because of religious or political strife but, instead, planned to reside in the United States in order to send remittances, or funds, home (Naff, 1994).

Over time, immigrants established successful businesses and raised families. Soon generations had attended public schools and universities. Children experienced success in the classroom, while maintaining their culture at home. For example, students learned English in schools and spoke Arabic at home (Shakir, 1997). Following World War II, Arab immigration continued to increase. After the creation of Israel, displaced Palestinians traveled to America. In addition, Egyptians, Syrians, Yemenis, and Iraqis immigrated to the States in order to avoid political strife, turmoil, and war (Al-Hazza & Lucking, 2005).

By 1965, Arabs entered the country more easily, as U.S. immigration laws were relaxed. Those who made up this wave of immigrants were often college educated and conversant in English. They were considered by some to be westernized (Naff, 1994). As Al-Hazza and Lucking explain, "Many had received education abroad and decided to seek higher education in America. Many Arab professionals came to America under the auspices of the professional-preference clause (in Naff, 1983). When they arrived in America, they established churches, mosques, newspapers and meeting centers and emphasized the value of education to their children" (2005, p. 4).

The most recent U.S. Census (2000) reports that 1.2 million persons of Arab descent currently live in the United States, an increase of approximately 40 percent over the last two decades. The Lebanese make up the largest Arab American population in the United States, with numbers of 440,279. Egyptians are the second largest group of Arabs in America, with an estimated population of 143,000. Today, large Arab American populations live in five states: California, Florida, Michigan, New Jersey, and New York.

As is true of other immigrant groups residing in America today, issues related to cultural maintenance are at the forefront in Arab American communities. A reinvigorated sense of Arab identity is apparent in this interest in Arab history, Arab contributions to society, and Arabic language development, in a renewed awareness of Arab arts and cultural heritage, and in an increase in the construction of mosques. Post-9/11 discrimination against Arab Americans and Arabs has also stimulated interest in Arab and Middle Eastern studies in the public schools, as well as in colleges and universities.

For Your CONSIDERATION

Take a virtual tour of the Arab American National Museum. Visit the musuem's website at **http://www.arabamericanmuseum.org/Home.id.2.htm.** Find resources on Arab history, perspectives, and art and lesson plans relevant to the culture and contributions of Arab Americans in the United States.

Arab American Education

College graduation rates of Arab American students establish that they have been very successful in the classroom. For example, the 1990 Census Ancestry Report found that 36.3 percent of Arab Americans hold bachelor's degrees, with 15.2 percent holding graduate degrees, a higher rate than the national average for Americans, which is 20.3 percent earning bachelor's degrees and 7.2 percent earning graduate degrees (in Al-Hazza & Lucking, 2005, p. 8).

College students of Egyptian ancestry had a high rate of educational attainment as well, with 60 percent earning bachelor's degrees and 26 percent completing graduate degrees, according to the 1990 Census.

And yet, little research has been conducted on the academic achievement of K–12 Arab American students. This void in the literature may result from the fact that Arab Americans have blended quietly into American society as their immigration occurred gradually over time. The process of assimilation has also been less strident, because Arab Americans, as voluntary minorities, transitioned into American culture by their own choice (Ogbu, 1991).

In fact, a study of Arab American school children residing in three major American cities revealed that Arab American students maintained high levels of positive self-concept (Al-Khatah, 1999). However, given the horrific events of 9/11 and the subsequent wars in Afghanistan and Iraq, Arab American students remain vulnerable to new challenges associated with discrimination and stereotyping.

From PRESERVICE to PRACTICE

Anti-Arab Discrimination: What Teachers Can Do

Perhaps the most important first step is to remember to include Arab Americans and the Arab world in your multicultural curriculum. Avoid the standard laundry list ("white, black, Hispanic, Asian, Native American"), which usually includes Arab Americans as "white" but renders them culturally invisible. Persuade your colleagues and the school and/or district to make this a matter of policy.

One way to avoid excluding Arab Americans and the Arab world is for the school and the school district to create an Arab American category on data forms listing racial and ethnic categories. Federal regulations do allow this, because such data can be subsumed into the "white" category.

The Basics

Learn, read. There is no substitute for serious study. Many excellent resources are now available. Arab history and culture is an intrinsically interesting topic. Check the book catalogues on the websites of Interlink or the Washington Report on Middle East Affairs, or contact the American-Arab Anti-Discrimination Committee (ADC) Education Department.

Reach out to the Arab American community: Invite Arab American parents and others to give presentations to classes; plan field trips to Arab American community institutions. Reach out to Arab American educators. Ask ADC if there is a local ADC chapter in your community. Attend talks by Arab American speakers, films, forums, and community events. Develop relationships with Arab American community leaders. Cultural understanding is an ongoing and never-ending process. There is no substitute for personal contact.

Consciously integrate Arab materials into all classes at your school: American and world history, literature, music, geography, math and science history, government and democracy, sociology, current events, cooking, reading, and so forth.

Teach students to appreciate the Arab world as the seat of one of the great cultures when Europe was still an underdeveloped region on the periphery of world civilization. Study how the later flowering of European culture in the Middle Ages and Renaissance was made possible in part through trade, cultural contacts, and scientific links to Arab Islamic civilization. Celebrate the values cherished in the contemporary Arab world: family ties, hospitality, ethics and morality, community. There is poverty in Cairo, for example, but little street crime or violence. The streets are safer than those in many U.S. cities.

Resources

Ask the district social studies or curriculum office to review, approve, and purchase key educational resources recommended by ADC. Also, ADC offers lesson plans, articles, bibliographies, fact sheets, and other resources on its website (www.adc.org).

Problem Areas

- Use any anti-Arab incidents that occur as learning opportunities. Anti-Arab "jokes" and epithets are common problems. This often is simply hurtful adolescent frivolity. It is a chance to bring home to students the truth that personal identity is serious and that others' feelings matter and should be respected. The movement from frivolity to a deeper seriousness is one of the most important of all lessons.
- Counteract the stereotypes that children absorb from popular culture. Teach students to recognize stereotypes.

Give them an in-depth understanding of the social, cultural, and historical reality of the Arab world. Teach them critical thinking skills; prepare them to critique the rhetoric of the media, government officials, and "experts." This is basic preparation for responsible citizenship.

- Report problems and their solutions to ADC. Let others learn from your experience.
- Look at textbooks, curricula, and other resources with a critical eye to identify bias. Review library resources. Compare the coverage of the Arab world with the coverage of other regions and civilizations. Textbook critiques prepared by the Middle East Studies Association may be useful. Beware of current events periodicals that sensationalize issues. Inform ADC about problems you encounter. It may be able to help.

Other Suggestions

- Don't avoid the Middle East conflict as "too complex" or "too controversial." The Middle East is a major part of modern world history, and students need to understand the region to be responsible citizens.
- Persuade education officials to recognize Ramadan and other Muslim holidays. Allow Muslim students time off; arrange the state and school testing schedule to avoid Islamic holidays. Remember not to order pepperoni or sausage for the class pizza party.
- Write articles for educational periodicals about your experience of teaching Arab American students or about the Arab world. ADC may be able to assist you in getting them published.

Questions for Reflection

1. In what other ways do you see yourself addressing anti-Arab attitudes in the classroom and in the curriculum?
2. How can the community be involved in helping to challenge stereotypes about Arab Americans?

References

American-Arab Anti-Discrimination Committee. http://www.adc.org/index.php?id=504.

Banks, James. (1989). "Integrating the Curriculum with Ethnic Content: Approaches and Guidelines." In James A. Banks and Cherry A. Banks (Eds.), *Multicultural Education: Issues and Perspectives*. Boston: Allyn and Bacon.

Banks, James. (May 1994). "Transforming the Mainstream Curriculum." *Educational Leadership*.

SUMMARY

The educational goals of Thomas Jefferson and (later) Horace Mann offered a new society equal educational opportunity through literacy development, economic empowerment, and the tools for civic participation. But the early educational experiences of immigrants and excluded groups offer us a perspective far removed from what these educational leaders conceived. Ideas about what constituted an American citizen often devalued the cultural history, traditions, language, knowledge, and skills of Africans, American Indians, Mexicans, and Asians. Excluded from attending school or segregated at inferior schools, these groups historically received an inferior education that undermined their ability to compete with European Americans and attain comparable economic mobility. Today, another immigrant group, Arab Americans, endure stereotyping and discrimination as a result of tragic world events. In the next chapter, we will meet educational leaders and philosophers whose ideologies challenged these social restraints that linger today.

DISCUSSION QUESTIONS

1. In what ways has Thomas Jefferson influenced the development of an educational vision for the United States? How did Jefferson's own life experiences and contradictions complicate that vision?

2. How did Horace Mann extend the educational aims established by Thomas Jefferson? What educational goals did Mann feel that American schools should strive to meet?

3. Immigration is an ongoing process that continues to shape American society. How did America respond to its European immigrants during the country's early development? How has that response affected how immigrants are received today?

4. Describe how America has sought to educate minority groups. Analyze and explain how these different groups had to engage in legal challenges in order to access equal educational opportunities.

ACTIVITIES

1. Research the educational philosophies of Socrates, Plato, and Aristotle. Compare and contrast their positions on the goals of education, the curriculum, and pedagogy. What were their views concerning who had access to primary schools, as well as to the Academy?

2. Interview two science educators. How do the perspectives of the Age of Reason, and specifically the scientific method, influence their approach to teaching, learning, and curriculum development? How do these teachers balance the differing perspectives of creationism and the process of scientific inquiry?

3. Visit with two or three diverse community leaders or teachers in your town or city. Discuss with them the history of the education of minority populations in the United States. What are their views about the educational access of minority populations today? In what ways has education improved as we have pursued educational equity? What setbacks has it experienced?

WEBSITES

The History of American Education Web Project
http://www.nd.edu/~rbarger/www7/
This site provides brief overviews of the history of education, ranging from the colonial period in America to contemporary contexts. The site also includes interesting historical photographs.

League of United Latin American Citizens
http://www.lulac.org/index.html
This site provides information that its sponsors hopes will advance the educational accomplishments, economic conditions, political influence, health, and civil rights of Latina/o people in the United States.

The Learning Page: The Library of Congress, American Memory in the Classroom
http://memory.loc.gov/learn/
This site provides over 7 million historical documents, photos, maps, films, and audio recordings. It offers activities, lesson plans across the curriculum and grade levels, and links to other websites.

Migrations: A Collection of Views on Mexican Immigration to the United States, Center for Latin American Studies, University of California, Berkeley
http://ist-socrates.berkeley.edu:7001/Outreach/education/migrations2003/photos.html
This comprehensive site provides historical papers and photos about early Mexican migrant experiences.

School: The Story of American Public Education
http://www.pbs.org/kcet/publicschool/index.html
This site, maintained by the Public Broadcasting Service, reflects a four-part documentary film series that examines the history of American education, its major contributors, and its movements. Bilingual and immigrant education are also featured at this site.

The University of Southern California, Rossier School of Education, Center for Multilingual, Multicultural Research
http://www.usc.edu/dept/education/CMMR/
This website provides a wealth of research and primary documents chronicling the history of minority and immigrant education. References and full-text articles regarding the history of African American, American Indian, Asian, Polynesian, and Latina/o education are provided. Teacher education research materials and strategies for community service are also available on this extensive site.

REFERENCES

Acuna, R. (1972). *Occupied America: The Chicano's struggle toward liberation.* San Francisco: Canfield.

Adeed, P., & Smith, P. (1997). Arab Americans. In J. Banks (Ed.), *Teaching strategies for ethnic studies* (pp. 489–508). Boston: Allyn and Bacon.

Al-Hazza, T., & Lucking, R. (2005). The minority of suspicion: Arab Americans. *Multicultural Review, 14*(3), 32–38.

Al-Katah, A. (1999). In search of equity for Arab-American students in public schools of the United States. *Education, 120*(2), 254–266.

Banks, J. (2004). Multicultural education: Historical development, dimensions, and practices. In J. Banks & C Banks, C. (Eds.), *Handbook of research on multicultural education* (pp. 3–23). San Francisco: Jossey-Bass.

Bankston, C., III. (1998). Sibling cooperation and scholastic performance among Vietnamese-American secondary school students: An ethnic relations theory. *Sociological Perspectives, 41*(1), 167–184.

Becker, C. (1932). *The heavenly city of the eighteenth-century philosophers.* New Haven: Yale University Press.

Berlin, I. (1974). *Slaves without masters: The free negro in the antebellum South.* New York: Vintage.

Berrol, S. (1978). *Immigrants at school, New York City, 1898–1914.* New York: Arno Press.

Brumberg, S. E. (1986). *Going to America, going to school: The Jewish immigrant public school encounter in turn of the century New York City.* New York: Praeger.

Bullock, H. A. (1967). *A history of Negro education in the South: From 1619 to the present.* Cambridge, MA: Harvard University Press.

Caplan, N., Choy, M. H., & Whitmore, J. K. (1991). *Children of the boat people: A study of educational success.* Ann Arbor: University of Michigan Press.

Coleman, J. (1988). Social capital in the creation of human capital. *American Journal of Sociology, 94*, 95–120.

Coleman, M. C. (1993). *American Indian children at school, 1850–1930.* Jackson: University Press of Mississippi.

Cunningham, N. E. (1987). *In pursuit of reason: The life of Thomas Jefferson.* New York: Ballantine.

Elmandjra, M. (2004). How will the Arab world be able to master its own independent developments? The transnational foundation for peace and future research. Retrieved March 11, 2007, from http://www.transnational.org/Aera_Index_MiddleEast.htm

Gibson, M. (1988). *Accommodation without assimilation: Sikh immigrants in an American high school.* Ithaca, NY: Cornell University Press.

Gonzalez, G. (1990). *Chicano education in the era of segregation.* Philadelphia: Bach Institute Press.

Gutek, G. L. (2005). *Historical and philosophical foundations of education.* New Jersey: Pearson.

Huerta, G. C., & Coles-Ritchie, M. (2004). Teacher case studies of language ideologies, practice, and change: ESL programming at Cherry High School. Paper presented at the 2003 American Educational Research Association Annual meeting, San Diego, California.

Jacobson, D. (1997). *Rights across the borders: Immigration and the decline of citizenship.* Baltimore: Johns Hopkins University Press.

Jorgenson, L. (1987). *The state and the non-public school, 1825–1925*. Columbia: University of Missouri Press.

Kaestle, C. (1983). *Pillars of the republic: Common schools and American society, 1780–1860*. New York: Hill and Wang.

Kao, G., Tienda, M., & Scheider, B. (1996). Racial and ethnic variation in academic performance. In A. Pallas (Ed.), *Research in sociology of education and socialization* (vol. 2, pp. 263–297). Greenwich, CT: JAI Press.

Lee, S. J. (1996). *Unraveling the "model minority" stereotype: Listening to Asian American youth*. New York: Teachers College Press.

Low, V. (1982). *The unimpressible race: A century of educational struggle by the Chinese in San Francisco*. San Francisco: East/West Publishing.

Messerli, J. (1972). *Horace Mann: A Biography*. New York: Knopf.

Montejano, D. (1987). *Anglos and Mexicans in the making of Texas, 1836–1986*. Austin: University of Texas Press.

Naff, A. (1983). Arabs in America: A historical overview. In S. Abraham & N. Abraham (Eds.), *Arabs in the new world* (pp. 8–29). Detroit, MI: Wayne State University.

Naff, A. (1994). The early Arab immigrant experience. In E. McCarus (Ed.), *The development of Arab-American identity* (pp. 23–36). Ann Arbor: University of Michigan.

Ogbu, J. (1991). Immigrant and involuntary minorities in comparative perspective. In M. A. Gibson & J. U. Ogbu (Eds.), *Minority status and schooling: A comparative study of immigrant and involuntary minorities* (pp. 3–33). New York: Garland

Olneck, M. (2004). Immigrants and education in the public schools. In J. Banks & C. Banks (Eds.), *Handbook of research on multicultural education*. San Francisco: Jossey-Bass.

Orfalea, G. (1988). *Before the flames*. Austin: University of Texas Press.

Portes, A., & Rumbaut, R. (2001). *Legacies: The story of the immigrant second generation*. Berkeley: University of California Press.

Rumbaut, R. (1995). The new Californians: Comparative research findings on the educational progress of immigrant children. In R. Rumbaut & W. Cornelius (Eds.), *California's immigrant children: Theory, research and implications for educational policy* (pp. 17–69). San Diego: University of California at San Diego, Center for U.S.-Mexican Studies.

Sanders, J. W. (1977). *The education of an urban minority: Catholics in Chicago, 1833–1965*. New York: Oxford University Press.

San Miguel, G. (1987). *"Let all of them take heed": Mexican Americans and the campaign for educational equity in Texas, 1910–1981*. Austin: University of Texas Press.

Schlossman, S. L. (1983). Is there an American tradition of bilingual education? *German in the public elementary schools, 1840–1919. American Journal of Education, 91*(2), 139–186.

Schwartz, M. W. (1999). Introduction: The Arab immigrant experience. In M. Suleiman (Ed.), *Arabs in America* (pp. 1–25). Philadelphia: Temple University Press.

Shakir, E. (1997). *Bint Arab*. Westport, CT: Praeger.

Spring, J. (2002). *American education* (10th ed.). Boston: McGraw-Hill.

Suleiman, M. (2000). *Teaching about Arab Americans: What social studies teachers should know*. ERIC Document Reproduction Service No. ED442 714.

Takaki, R. (1989). *Strangers from a different shore: A history of Asian Americans*. New York: Penguin.

Takaki, R. (1993). *A different mirror: A history of multicultural America*. Boston: Little, Brown.

Tozer, S., Senese, G., & Violas, P. (2006). *School and society* (5th ed.). Boston: McGraw-Hill.

Tyack, D. (1974). *The one best system: A history of American urban education*. Cambridge, MA: Harvard University Press.

United Nations. (1999). *Review and the appraisal of the progress made in achieving the goals and objectives of the Programme of Action of the International Conference on Population and Development*. New York: Author.

United States Commission on Immigrant Reform. (1997). *Becoming an American: Immigration and Immigrant Policy*. Washington, DC: General Accounting Office.

United States Department of Education. (1999). *Challenging the status quo: The education record 1993–2000*. Washington, DC: U.S. Government Printing Office.

United States Department of Justice. (1994). *Statistical yearbook of the Immigration and Naturalization Service*. Washington, DC: U.S. Government Printing Office.

Valdes, G. (1996). *Con respecto: Bridging the distance between culturally diverse families and schools*. New York: Teachers College Press.

Valencia, R. (2002). The plight of Chicano students: An overview of schooling conditions and outcomes. In R. Valencia (Ed.), *Chicano school failure and success* (pp. 3–52). London: Routledge/Falmer.

Valenzuela, A. (1999). *Subtractive schooling: U.S. Mexican youth and the politics of caring*. Albany: State University of New York Press.

Woodson, C. G. (1919). *The education of the Negro prior to 1861*. Washington, DC: Associated Publishers.

Educational Philosophy

FIRST PERSON

Making Time to Care About Philosophy

Connections to Practice and Social Justice

After completing my undergraduate English degree at the USC, I began my teacher education coursework at California State University, Los Angeles. One course I was required to take was called "Educational Foundations." The textbook was a compilation of educational history, including a discussion of contemporary teacher roles, curriculum development trends, and school administrative structure. The class and its accompanying text were also dedicated to a rather lengthy examination of educational philosophy. We read extensively about such philosophers as Aristotle, Erasmus, and Plato, and our understanding of such philosophies as behaviorism, perennialism, and essentialism was tested.

In retrospect, it was amazing how quickly I became disengaged with this content. One of the reasons why it had so little relevance to me at the time was the incongruence between the curriculum and instruction I was observing in my public school clinical experiences and what I was required to study in my education program. Within the Los Angeles inner-city schools where I observed classes, tutored individual students, and would ultimately find full-time employment, the philosophical underpinnings framed in my teacher preparation coursework and demonstrated in the practices of teachers in the predominantly African American secondary schools (such as Crenshaw High School and Manual Arts High School) and in the predominantly Latina/o Roosevelt High School, held little relevance. Furthermore, the philosophical beliefs demonstrated by my teachers continued to support a "deficit theory" that maintained low expectations and translated into the placement of minority students in low academic tracks that excluded them from equitable access to a college preparatory curriculum.

CHAPTER OBJECTIVES

- Readers will become familiar with philosophies that offer a foundation for understanding different approaches to teaching and learning.

- Teacher-centered and student-centered philosophies will be introduced to help readers consider how such distinctions inform pedagogy.

- Readers will recognize the interconnections among philosophy, social change, and problem solving relevant to schooling.

- Readers will identify the contributions of educators and social justice leaders whose philosophies continue to influence the pursuit of educational equity.

- The philosophies introduced in this chapter will assist readers as they consider and develop their own educational philosophy to apply in their own classrooms.

Presently, the educational beliefs of such leaders as Thomas Jefferson and Horace Mann continue to influence classroom teachers as they deliver a curriculum focused on English literacy, American history, mathematics, and science. In addition, the administration of President George W. Bush supports an outcomes-based initiative; the No Child Left Behind Act is a mandate driven by the belief that an American labor force with skills tested in the public schools will ultimately produce workers who will serve the American economy and reproduce its culture more effectively.

However, noble philosophical beliefs once introduced in teacher education programs are often reduced to meritocractic educational policies whose primary focus is the stratification of students through the use of standardized tests, deculturalization, punitive actions, and the maintenance of academic tracks. It is now important to revisit leaders, such as Gloria Anzaldúa, W. E. B. Du Bois, Mohandas Ghandi, and Mary Wollstonecraft, whose life stories and emergent philosophies can help a new generation of educators envision innovative possibilities for all learners by affirming student identity, building communities, supporting diversity, and encouraging service to others. As student teachers develop their own educational philosophies, they will soon learn how rich their collaborations with youth will become. As Anzaldúa reminds us, "Voyager, there are no bridges, one builds them as one walks" (1983).

The Role of Philosophy in the Teaching Profession

Defining philosophy is a difficult task. The etymology of the word *philosophy* can be traced to the Greek *philo*, which means "love," and *sophos*, which means "wisdom." It can be described as a set of one's beliefs or ideas about the meaning of life or can be explained as a complex analysis regarding the nature of reality and the universe. A philosophy can also be analyzed through the lens of one's own meaning-making about knowledge, truth, and ethics.

Before entering a classroom, every educator must arrive at a philosophy that guides his or her role as a teacher. Teachers must examine the construction of knowledge, identify what knowledge they will teach, and determine how they will ultimately teach and assess that knowledge. Once a teacher understands how these variables are interrelated, this understanding can translate into an educational philosophy that influences an educator's decisions about such issues as the intent of education, what knowledge is, how that knowledge is demonstrated, and how such knowledge can reflect and serve a larger community. Thus, the intent of this chapter is threefold. First, it introduces preservice teachers to historical philosophies that influence educational practice and pedagogy. Second, the chapter provides background on leading social and political figures whose lived experiences inform new ways to examine the relationship between educational philosophy and social justice. And third, through the merger of these philosophical perspectives, preservice teachers will have an opportunity to create their own educational philosophy, using guidelines provided at the chapter's conclusion.

Fundamental Philosophical Positions

We will examine eight philosophical orientations that are especially relevant to educational policy, curriculum, and instruction: **essentialism**, **perennialism**, **behaviorism**, **idealism**, **realism**, **progressivism** (pragmatism), **social reconstruction**, and **existentialism**. Understanding these philosophies can be useful to new teachers as they begin to formulate their own educational philosophy.

The views that one holds about education are often influenced by past educational experiences, cultural and family beliefs, religion, and community values, as well as by political standpoints. These variables and others will affect the nature of your evolving educational philosophy, and the philosophies that we will discuss in this chapter will serve as a good point of departure.

Teacher-Centered Philosophies

Essentialism This teacher-centered philosophy stresses the role of the teacher in delivering a basic body of knowledge that every student should know to become a productive member of society. William Bagley, an American educator (1874–1946), stressed the idea that there is "essential" Western academic content that teachers must present to students for them to become problem solvers and moral citizens. Bagley and his organization, the Essentialistic Education Society, challenged such philosophies as progressivism, whose educational focus is on the contemporary concerns of students, and whose curriculum is driven by student-generated questions and "real-world" problem solving facilitated by a teacher. Bagley felt that both American values and student educational performance were diminished by such student-centered philosophies.

Although Bagley and his followers did not prescribe a specific body of literature to be taught in the public schools, they did believe that there are essential concepts that the curriculum must include. This belief later translated into such present-day, essentialist educational initiatives as "back-to-basics," teaching to the "core curriculum," and meeting annual performance standards as evidenced in the No Child Left Behind Act.

The complex issues and events that currently impact society—such as immigration, globalization, economic rivalries, world wars, and the threat of global terrorism—continue to result in an emphasis on essentialism in contemporary American educational policy. Essentialists believe that a singular curriculum, taught by teachers in an authority role, will help unify the country's citizenry.

A first-year teacher uses the board while conducting a math class.

One who takes this position is English professor E. D. Hirsch, Jr., of the University of Virginia. In his book *Cultural Literacy: What Every American Should Know* (1987), Hirsch maintains that there is a common body of knowledge that all citizens should be familiar with so that they can communicate with one another. According to Hirsch, the ability to share this knowledge constitutes "cultural literacy." Such essential knowledge includes concepts introduced in geography, history, literature, mathematics, philosophy, religion, science, and technology, as well as important facts, people, events, and dates related to these subject areas. Led by their teachers, students are expected to master this knowledge at each grade level, and they should not proceed to the next grade level until they have demonstrated this mastery on standardized tests. As for elective courses, essentialists believe that such classes serve only to distract students and diminish the academic standards of American schools.

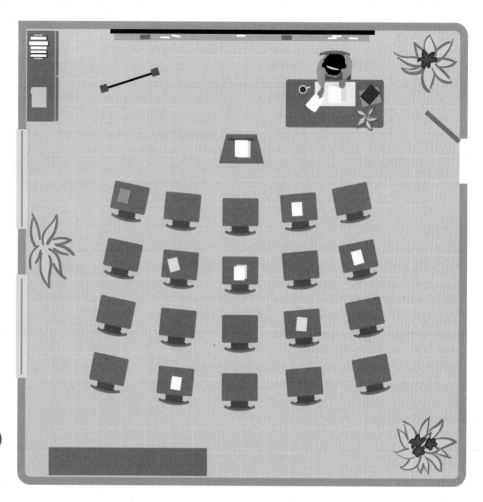

FIGURE **2.1**

**A Teacher-Centered
Classroom Design**

Critics of essentialism point out the Eurocentric nature of such a curriculum. An essentialist curriculum is generally focused on male, European contributions and does not meaningfully recognize the knowledge base and contributions of societies across the world. Instead of exposing American students to other ways of knowing, essentialists restrict the curriculum to a limited number of cultural exemplars that often lead to cultural stereotyping and overgeneralizations. Indeed, an essentialist curriculum suggests that only American and European knowledge bases are worth knowing.

Essentialists also assume that all schools and their students have equal access to schooling, resources, and quality instruction and largely overlook the diversity of American society. Communities reflect differences across language, race, class, gender, physical ability, and sexual orientation. Critics of essentialism argue that such differences need to be addressed as part of a larger school curriculum, including new assessment methods to enable students to pursue problem-solving strategies readily. Although an essentialist curriculum is useful for introducing foundational European-based curriculum concepts, critics contend that it leaves little room for cross-cultural inclusion, student discussion, and community action.

PAUSE & REFLECT

Teachers and students alike enter the classroom with their own shifting discourses, histories, lived experiences, and traditions. **Discourses** are informed by our language, cultures, institutional memberships, and social networks, which together often compete for power in society. How do you think these discourses influence the development of a teaching philosophy?

Perennialism The word *perennial* is often defined as "everlasting." Thus perennialism emphasizes the belief that Western civilization and its history embody eternal universal concepts that can provide future generations of students with a sense of reality, truth, culture, and ethics. Unlike essentialists, perennialists establish a very specific body of literature that highlights ideas, themes, principles, and questions. Perennialists argue that when students read these primary sources or "great books" from the "Western canon," they are exposed to a level of rationality introduced in the classics but often glossed over in textbooks.

Proponents of perennialism Mortimer Adler (1902–2001) and Robert Maynard Hutchins (1899–1977) endorsed the idea that truth, rationality, and religion are universal across cultures and time. People, they contended, are generally the same. Thus, as Adler argued in *The Paideia Proposal* (1982), it makes sense that all students should receive a similar education using readings in such fields as history, literature, mathematics, and science. This curriculum leaves little room for "frivolous" elective courses. Learning about the past through the study of the classics, Adler and Hutchins argued, better prepares youth to manage the future.

Presented by teachers in command of this knowledge, a perennialist curriculum would produce rational, disciplined thinkers well versed in a universal knowledge. It comes as no surprise then, that today's American secondary students are often exposed to the works of Aristotle, Dickens, Homer, Plato, and Shakespeare in their literature or Western civilization classes.

Perennialists would also argue that students lacking the discipline to study and understand these works are less intellectual than others and academically incapable of pursuing advanced study and holding future leadership positions. These students would then be identified for placement in vocational education or less rigorous academic programs. They might also be identified as "at risk" students who do not have the "moral character" to pursue a college preparatory "track" of study. Instead, their academic program may emphasize basic skills and remedial work.

The Greek philosopher Plato.

Like essentialism, perennialism remains a teacher-centered approach to learning, in which teachers transmit knowledge to students, giving students little voice. Perennialists generally believe that a contemporary curriculum is a transient one, replete with trendy, elective courses responsible for the "dumbing down" of America's youth. As a result, classes that emphasize such topics as multiculturalism, gender studies, and bilingualism violate the perennialist's vision of what kinds of Western knowledge should be valued.

Educators who espouse a strictly perennialist philosophy also subscribe to the notion that culture and knowledge are fixed entities. Such a belief does not reflect the fluid nature of language, discourse, human interactions, and evolving cultural, political, and economic contexts. Rather, a wholly perennialist curriculum dismisses other forms of knowledge construction and marginalizes other kinds of knowledge. This too, can be viewed as a disservice to students in that it does not prepare them to address multiple perspectives beyond a Eurocentric world view—perspectives especially relevant to diversity and a global society.

Behaviorism Behaviorism contends that all behavior is learned. The theory, explored through the study of behavior modification by the American psychologist B. F. Skinner (1904–1990) explains how an individual's past and present environments influence the way she or he responds and learns. Behaviorism in the classroom can play out in a number of ways. It becomes a teacher's responsibility to design and create learning environments where students can learn to their utmost potential. Teachers arrange a set of conditions and contingencies that encourage students to respond and behave in a certain way. Thus instruction from a behaviorist perspective is generally teacher-centered.

Behaviorist teachers employ instructional strategies that reinforce positive responses. Punishment for undesirable behaviors is not the focus of behaviorism. Instead, behaviorist teachers emphasize the positive in an effort to decrease misbehaviors. Teachers then must provide positive reinforcement immediately when students respond correctly.

From PRESERVICE to PRACTICE

Philosophies in the Classroom

In debating about curriculum content, teachers often talk about how philosophy informs their pedagogy. For example, some social studies teachers may be convinced that the history of European civilization must be a major focus of the curriculum. Other teachers maintain that the events surrounding 9/11 and the war in Iraq are of critical concern and should be at the center of the curriculum. Ben Chavez, a secondary school history teacher, believes that a curriculum based on a perennialist philosophy provides students with a fundamental knowledge of historical events that can also lead to an understanding of contemporary issues. Ben explained,

If I teach students about ancient Egyptian society, they assume we're just going to learn about King Tut and mummies because that is what they've learned before. So some teachers hold on to a perennialist point of view in regards to the curriculum choices they make. And of course, they may feel their curriculum choices are limited because of the pressure associated with standardized testing.

But I feel we can merge and blend philosophies together. We can introduce basic historical content to the students while infusing contemporary political

issues associated with problem solving and social reconstructivism. It doesn't have to be an either/or proposition. I can integrate perennialistic content that reflects historical perspectives, such as the history of religion and cultures in the Middle East. I can trace that history and present an overview that includes a discussion of the long-term conflicts and [of the] peace resolutions being sought in the region.

This way, I'm not just a teacher who exclusively maintains a perennialist philosophy that drives my entire curriculum. I am fluid in my approach to applying different philosophical positions in order to analyze events from an historical context as well as a contemporary one.

Questions for Reflection

1. What do you think of Ben Chavez's philosophical approach?
2. As you consider the philosophies discussed in this chapter, how do you see yourself interpreting and developing your own philosophical positions relevant to the subjects you will teach?

The focus of the behaviorist curriculum suggests that content, taught in segments, is important to learn primarily so that it will be available for future use. In other words, the learning of skills for practice and immediate display is not of great importance for a teacher who engages with behaviorist theory. Such teachers believe that students will summon the learned behavior when the appropriate situation or context arises. From the perspective of behaviorism, students do not necessarily generate knowledge. Students come to recognize learned patterns. Advocates of behaviorism support its application particularly when classroom management issues arise and negative behaviors impede the learning process.

Idealism According to the philosophy of idealism, reality exists primarily within our own mind and consciousness. The Greek philosopher Plato (427–347 BC) held the view that idealism, as generated by one's own search for truth, social justice, and aesthetics, would help propel the advancement of knowledge in a society. To pursue knowledge from within, he believed, would lead us away from responding only to what was visibly and physically tangible. In this way, Plato asserted, we would become more engaged with the search for more complex thoughts, such as the analysis of a fair and just government.

From an educational viewpoint, idealism is framed by the perspective that reality is a world free from change; it is a world grounded by universal truths and perfect ideas. Therefore, knowledge is created when ideas and questions emerge when we examine our own ideas critically and engage in dialogue with one another. This approach to inquiry and discussion, which is known as the Socratic method, addresses such topics as truth, life, and justice. Plato wrote numerous "dialogues" from the perspective of his own teacher, Socrates. The Socratic method continues to be used as a guide for the teaching of critical thinking and debate in the public schools today.

Plato extended his view of idealism to education. He argued that status in society should not be based on one's wealth, but instead on one's intelligence and kindness. Although he believed that everyone should have access to an education, he also realized that not everyone had the intelligence and sense of justice to provide leadership in a society. In Plato's ideal world, leaders, rich or poor, would have to prove their ability to lead with wisdom and strong morals. People who did not have those qualities would serve the community as soldiers, laborers, or merchants. Education, then, would prepare citizens for a specific role in society, as individuals pursued self-knowledge and an understanding of morality. In a contemporary context, idealism influences a perspective on education that emphasizes the sharpening of the mind and intellectual processes.

Realism Because he, unlike the idealists, believed that the real world can be researched and understood, Aristotle (384–322 BC) embraced realism, which holds that the objects we perceive in the world exist independently, outside of our own thinking or recognition. Aristotle maintained that the study of matter and knowledge can help us go beyond what we understand within our own minds. He insisted that students study the world in which they live because he believed that reality is knowable through observation. Aristotle's view established the groundwork for the development of the scientific method.

Today, the term *realism* refers to the belief that educators must provide students with the fundamental knowledge they need to survive in the natural world. This knowledge will in turn provide learners with the skills to develop and maintain a positive and successful life.

In essence, realists adhere to the belief that at birth, an individual's mind is blank. From the moment of birth, and throughout life, a variety of sensations are impressed on the brain. Through these sensations, humans learn, and knowledge develops through the learner's exposure to these sensory experiences. In the classroom, a teacher who adopts a realist philosophy will have a strong command of the subject matter. The educator may appear distant, given the emphasis on the curriculum content. Nevertheless, the teacher will strive to connect the subject matter with the lived experiences of the students. As part of the realist teacher's instructional repertoire, he or she may maintain classroom management, and promote motivation, through the use of intrinsic rewards.

Realists believe that the curriculum is best organized around specific content areas. These subjects should be presented according to developmental views of learning, where subject matter is introduced according to level of difficulty. Realists maintain that the curriculum must consist of science and mathematics, humanities and social sciences, as well as values education. Science and mathematics are emphasized in the curriculum, because realists argue that these subjects are the most important for survival in an ever-changing environment.

However, realists do not completely downplay the importance of the humanities; indeed, they agree that interactions with the social world are also critical to one's survival and development. Authoritative instructional methods may be used by a realist instructor. The teacher may ask students to recall, discuss, and analyze facts, as well as to compare and contrast examples and generate new knowledge. Assessment is an important component of realist teaching, because testing measures students' command of essential subject matter. For motivational purposes, realists believe that it is important for teachers to reward academic achievement. When teachers report the accomplishments of their learners, they reinforce what has been learned.

PAUSE & REFLECT

Idealism and realism reflect teacher-centered philosophical approaches to curriculum and instruction. As you develop your own philosophy, how do these perspectives apply to skills-based or content-specific instruction at the elementary or secondary grade levels? How can either philosophy influence students' problem-solving skills?

Student-Centered Philosophies

Other educators believe that instruction should be more student-centered. In a student-centered classroom, it is the students who determine their own learning needs, on the basis of what is relevant to them. An example of a progressive classroom is shown in Figure 2.2. How does this classroom compare to Figure 2.1? Think about your own educational experiences, and consider how teachers chart out their seating arrangements in ways that match their educational philosophies.

Utilizing new technologies, teachers introduce skills to students so that they can work on service learning projects and other areas of interest. The community and environment in which the students live generate such interests. Instead of competitive standardized testing, authentic assessment of student work is demonstrated in project portfolios, skill displays, hands-on activities, and technology projects. Student-centered educational philosophies include progressivism, social reconstruction, and existentialism, among others.

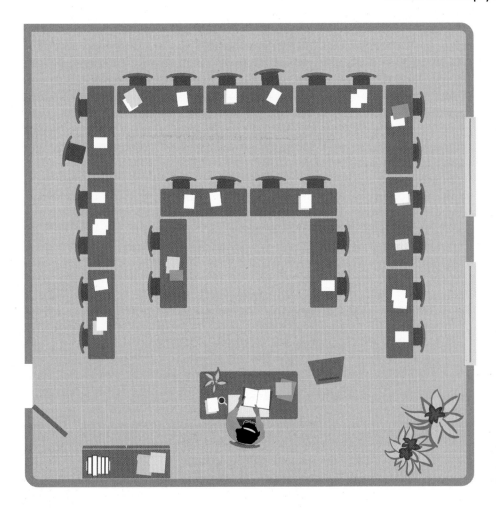

FIGURE 2.2

A Progressive, Student-Centered Classroom Design

Progressivism The philosophy of pragmatism contributes significantly to the presence of progressivism in education. Pragmatism holds that people should acquire, demonstrate, apply, and test their ideas in real-world contexts and experiments. In this way, it is possible to determine what actually works. By implementing such practical knowledge, students learn through experience and the application of skills. Thus, progressivism is the pragmatic lens that teachers use to guide students as they pose problems and design solutions. In contrast to essentialism and perennialism, a progressive curriculum is not focused on a specific set of concepts or literary canon introduced by a teacher. Instead, progressive educators encourage their students to analyze questions, subject their own ideas to scrutiny, and draw conclusions across content areas. Through the pragmatic learning of skills, the teacher facilitates this process of problem solving with the students.

The educational philosopher and psychologist John Dewey (1859–1952), long considered a founder of progressivism, essentially believed that students learn by doing—and especially by doing things that are related to their needs and interests. Basing his argument in the conviction that there is a knowable physical world, Dewey argued that students should learn the scientific method, in which they identify a problem, generate a hypothesis, consider outcomes, and test the hypothesis. Dewey tested these ideas in his own progressive laboratory school at the University of Chicago.

In addition, Dewey believed that classroom instruction was too teacher-centered and authoritarian in nature. He felt American schools need to demonstrate democratic principles. Thus, an important component of progressivism is designing the classroom in such a way that the instructor is working one-on-one with students or in small groups. Hands-on activities enable students to demonstrate their skills. Knowledge is generated and shared between teachers and students. An integrated curriculum represents the needs, interests, and experiences of the students. A single standardarized test may not be the assessment measure of choice in a progressive teacher's classroom.

Progressivism is not without its critics. Detractors argue that progressivism is too focused on learner interests, instead of concentrating on a standardized, core curriculum consisting of perennialist literature (Ravitch, 2000). Critics feel that progressivism limits the academic performance of American students, keeping them from competing successfully with learners from other countries.

For Your CONSIDERATION

Visit the Institute for Learning Technologies website at **http://www.ilt.columbia.edu/publications/dewey.html.** Here you can read the full text of John Dewey's *Democracy and Education* or excerpts from it.

Connecting to the Cengage Learning Video Cases

Middle School Science Instruction: Inquiry Learning

Watch Cengage Learning Video Case 2.1, "Middle School Science Instruction: Inquiry Learning." You will see how a middle school science teacher uses inquiry learning in teaching a lesson on the geology of the Grand Canyon. As you watch students construct knowledge through experimentation, you'll also hear the teacher's views on the benefits of inquiry learning, as well as the challenges it presents, such as general "messiness" and a need for extra planning. After viewing the Chapter 2 video case study, consider the following questions.

Video Case Study

1. How do the classroom and the lesson in this video case illustrate a progressive philosophy of learning?
2. What kinds of skills are students learning about and demonstrating in the video? How are these skills generalizable to other kinds of scientific inquiry?
3. This video represents a culminating activity that builds on students' prior knowledge. What kinds of curriculum content and skills can be introduced to students before this activity?

Student Website

Social Reconstructionism: Sparking Social Change According to the philosophy of social reconstruction, individuals are responsible for their position in life. Given this perspective, schools have the moral responsibility to prepare citizens to influence the society in ways that promote social justice and equal opportunity for all. Educational philosopher George Counts (1907–1974) maintained that social reconstructionists have the immediate charge to stimulate social change. A student of Dewey, Counts agreed with the essence of progressivism. However, he argued that educational reforms must be broader in scope in order to inspire a new social order quickly.

Influenced by the Great Depression, and later by such disturbing events as World War II and the Cold War, social reconstructionists were motivated by the belief that worldwide inequities had to be confronted immediately. The public schools provided an educational venue to pursue social change through the modeling of problem-solving strategies and social action. The role of teachers was to introduce social problems to their students, facilitate critical thinking, offer resources, and promote group resolutions.

With this emphasis on challenging social problems, social reconstructivism requires a close examination of the social structures themselves, such as government and political entities, as well as school systems. By examining societal structures, social reconstructivists analyze the very systems of which they are a part. Such an examination requires that teachers be trained in new ways, too, so that they will be prepared to address with their students such issues as racism, sexism, poverty, homelessness, unemployment, and health care. Social reconstructivist educators agree that with innovative teacher training, societal problems can be better addressed in the public schools.

Social reconstructivism requires teachers to introduce the idea that American society seeks to live up to its democratic principles. It is the teacher's role to inform students about inequities present in American society. In turn, students pose questions, identify goals and objectives, and conduct research related to problems that arise in any number of integrated academic content areas. As facilitator, the teacher helps students generate research questions, locate information sources, and analyze data in the course of preparing, for example, a well-researched project presentation or social action plan. The teacher also determines how to assess this work, in keeping with the students' project objectives.

Some educators believe that social reconstructivism does not prepare students to develop the skills needed to compete in a global society and promotes low academic expectations. Again, such a student-centered educational philosophy may result in an outcome that affects a community only to a limited extent, if at all. Without a core curriculum of study, students may be less prepared to pass grade level examinations and tests on basic skills, and they may not be prepared to compete for admission to college or to select a career. Thus social reconstructivism ultimately asks future teachers to consider whether educational goals such as skill development and social action can coexist effectively within the larger curriculum.

Existentialism: Individual Choices, Individual Learning The philosophy of existentialism has been influenced by a number of thinkers, including Søren Kierkegaard (1913–1855), Friedrich Nietzsche (1844–1900), and Jean-Paul Sartre (1905–1980). These existentialists reject the idea of a single reality that reflects one truth. To the existentialist, the physical world holds no special meaning outside the experience of the individual. All individuals create their own reality, experience their own reality, and ultimately make meaning of their own reality. Therefore, our reality is determined by our individual freedom of choice, even if we allow others to influence our choices—which is in itself a choice.

From PRESERVICE to PRACTICE

Social Reconstructivism in Action

The immigration issue in America continues to be a controversial one. Communities where a number of immigrant families work, worship, and attend school face complex challenges when seeking acceptance and access to health care, education, and housing. To better inform her students about these issues, Martha Lugo, a middle school ESL and English teacher, created a thematic unit about the history of immigration for her American-born students, as well as for her intermediate English language learners.

In particular, Mrs. Lugo was concerned about negative responses to immigration that had recently been published among the local newspaper's letters to the editor and dramatized on television. She had also overheard her native-born American students talking harshly about her ESL students, who they assumed were illegal aliens. This problem was troubling to her, and she felt she needed to address it with her students.

It was Mrs. Lugo's hope that after *all* of her students had completed an Internet research project and reviewed photographs, oral histories, and documents from the Library of Congress American Memory website (http://memory.loc.gov/ammem/index.html), they would be better informed about immigration issues. She was eager for them to display their group findings by creating poster boards to share at the school's open house.

The students were excited about what they found. They had much to communicate with one another regarding diverse families' immigration stories and the questions society continues to confront. As the students worked and learned together, Mrs. Lugo observed that with this increased level of understanding, the negative campus climate began to diminish. She admitted, "No, the negativity did not entirely go away. But at least through our approach to problem solving and student-generated research, we had a positive start. To me, this is social justice; this is social reconstructivism at work."

Questions for Reflection

1. How does Mrs. Lugo's instructional approach reflect a social reconstructivist philosophy?
2. Can you see yourself demonstrating this philosophy through your own classroom practice and community service? If so, how? And yet, in what ways is a social reconstructivist philosophy controversial in the public school classroom?

Earth science teacher Jean Hooper uses a word board to help her ninth-grade English language learners understand both new vocabulary and core curriculum content.

Existentialist thought also influences education. Students are responsible for determining what is right and what is wrong, what is valid and what is not. Thus, students determine what knowledge they want to learn on the basis of their own needs. Such knowledge is measured not by the outcomes of a test, but by the level of understanding that a student attains and recognizes personally. This focus on the development of student identity, as learners choose what kinds of educational activities they would like to pursue, is a feature of existentialism.

Unlike essentialism, with its curriculum emphasis on basic concepts, existentialism focuses on the humanities. The arts give students the opportunity to explore identity, culture, religion, values, tragedy, interrelationships, and community. Students themselves can determine what holds meaning in life.

In the existentialist classroom, students determine what strategies for engaging content and learning work best for them. Teachers collaboratively work with individual students

TABLE 2.1   Basic Philosophies Relevant to Teaching and Learning

Philosophy and Contributors	Educational Goal	Teacher's Role	Students' Role	Teaching Methods	Content Areas
Essentialism (William Bagley, E. D. Hirsch)	To acquire essential cultural literacy	To introduce a basic curriculum	To meet basic skills competencies and receive knowledge	Teacher-centered; content-area instruction	Standard curriculum for all; American focus
Perennialism (Mortimer Adler, Robert M. Hutchins)	To study Eurocentric curricula, widely accepted truths and values	To present a curriculum based on classics and essential skills	To receive knowledge and demonstrate basic skills	Teacher-centered; lecture emphasis	Sciences; social sciences; humanities
Behaviorism (B. F. Skinner)	To create environments that set the stage for effective and efficient learning	To design the learning environment and offer stimuli for conditioned responses	To become self-regulated as they respond to stimuli	Regimented instruction that provides feedback on student behavior and responses	Any that include tasks and responses that can be observed and measured
Idealism (Plato)	To learn about universal truths because reality is unchanging and fixed	To introduce fundamental ideas and discuss them with students	To learn self-discipline by studying the past	Teacher-centered, with students reporting the truths taught to them	Sciences; social sciences; humanities
Realism (Aristotle)	To observe reality (such as events and objects), regardless of human awareness	To introduce knowledge	To test and verify knowledge through skill demonstration	Student-centered; field testing of knowledge	Sciences; social sciences; humanities
Progressivism (John Dewey, Helen Parkhurst)	To have the needs and interests of students formulate the curriculum	To allow the curriculum to be driven by student debate, discussion, and demonstration	To join with teachers in integrating content-area interests, as opposed to learning subject matter in isolation	Students' establishment of their own curriculum and schedules	Sciences; social sciences; humanities
Social reconstructivism (George Counts)	To achieve socal justice with a problem-solving approach	To encourage critical thinking, build curriculum around social problems, and serve as a resource	To exercise critical thinking skills for problem solving and action	Teacher-guided inquiry and research; cooperative group work	Social sciences; sciences
Existentialism (Søren Kierkegaard, Friedrich Nietzsche, Jean-Paul Sartre)	To encourage students to exercise freedom of choice and accountability	To guide students to think for themselves	To set their own goals and become independent through self-discipline	Dialogue; problem-solving strategies with analysis of choice-making	Social sciences; humanities

on their projects in the hope of providing a stimulating learning environment. As their identities flourish, existentialist educators believe, students accept responsibility for the understanding and knowledge they have constructed.

Critics of existentialism contend that students do not have the maturity or the background to construct their own forms of knowledge. After all, individuals may not have the basic skills needed to understand what it is important for them to know, let alone what knowledge is important to the world around them. Without core curriculum foundations and the assessment of learner skills, student-centered educational philosophies will continue to be criticized for their perceived lack of academic rigor and structure.

PAUSE & REFLECT

Is it possible to have more than one philosophy? Do you agree partially with one philosophy but also disagree with another aspect of the same philosophy?

Leaders Whose Educational Philosophies Cross and Blur Borders

Such educational philosophers as Mortimer Adler, William Bagley, George Counts, and John Dewey provide a general understanding of the philosophical orientations that influence American teachers today. This is not to say that these thinkers were the only scholars to have an impact on American education. What about the leaders whose philosophies addressed the needs of learners who did not have educational access and opportunities because of their history, race, class, gender, or language? In the next section of this chapter, the life stories and educational philosophies of the social activists Mary Wollstonecraft, Mohandas Ghandi, W. E. B. Du Bois, and Gloria Anzaldúa will be examined. Consider their perspectives as you begin to construct your own teaching philosophy.

Mary Wollstonecraft: Advocate for Women's Rights and Education

Born in Spitalfields, near London, England, Mary Wollstonecraft (1759–1797) lived during a time of women's subordination, when women had little formal schooling and few career choices. Nor could women serve as legal guardians for their own children or (after marriage) hold rights to previously owned property or income. And yet, Wollstonecraft's life, spanned two liberating events in history, the American Revolution in 1776 and the French Revolution in 1789, provided the context for her pursuit of social, educational, economic, and religious freedom for British citizens, particularly women.

Challenging the conservative, aristocratic institutions of British life, the monarchy, and the Church of England, Wollstonecraft became a supporter of liberalism. In her writings, she expressed her belief that humans possess the ability to reason, pursue equity, and advance. Emboldened by the French Revolution but disturbed by the violence, she articulated, in *A Vindication of the Rights of Men* (1790), her belief that human rights for all citizens, rich and poor, should be extended to women as well as men (Wollstonecraft in Todd and Butler, 1989).

Throughout her writing, Wollstonecraft also challenged the convention that only privileged members of society could pursue an elite education. She argued that women urgently needed access to education to move away from the "doctrine of educational appropriateness, an eighteenth-century belief that kept women in subordinate roles as housekeepers and mothers. Wollstonecraft's own life experiences sensitized her to the inequities women and the poor faced. Her father struggled financially throughout his life. Succumbing to alcoholism, her father dominated and abused the family, including her passive mother (Falco, 1996). Family financial resources were provided to her brother as he pursued a career, while Wollstonecraft received none. Challenged by these experiences, Wollstonecraft was determined to resist the domination she would continue to experience throughout her life.

Finding Her Own Way With virtually no financial support from her family, Wollstonecraft had few educational and career options except serving as a governess or primary school teacher. Having secured employment as a companion to a wealthy widow, she learned about the well-heeled lifestyles of the rich and came to view them with disdain.

Drawing on her experiences as a governess, Wollstonecraft and her sisters opened a school near London in 1784. Although the school would close two years later, Wollstonecraft would soon meet other liberal thinkers who challenged the Church of England and its oppressive effects on society and, more specifically, on women. These dissenters would soon lose the right to vote and were barred from Cambridge and Oxford universities. Soon Wollstonecraft became more politically active, as she extended her views to other social struggles taking place in Europe, particularly in France.

Following the closing of her school, Wollstonecraft had no income, and to raise money, she returned to her work as a governess. But it was not long before she wearied of serving the wealthy, left this employment for good, and dedicated herself to becoming a full-time writer.

Groundbreaking Work In her first groundbreaking, nonfiction piece of writing, *Thoughts on the Education of Daughters* (1787), Wollstonecraft depicted her difficult childhood and her dissatisfaction with the status of women in society. Wollstonecraft described the importance of early childhood experiences with parents, particularly mothers, who ultimately shape the character of daughters. Wollstonecraft also explored the need for mothers to remain actively engaged in the parenting process and not to leave the responsibility to servants. (Doing so, she argued, would encourage children to develop negative behaviors that would inhibit their moral development.)

Wollstonecraft also believed that the intellectual development of daughters could be fostered only through experience, reflective reading, and shared verbal expression. She rejected the "women's literature" of the period, which often consisted of romance novels (often written by men) that stereotyped women. Instead, Wollstonecraft felt that with a formal education identical to what men received, women could arrive at a more fulfilling, intellectual understanding of their world beyond the limited roles associated with being a daughter and a wife.

By 1788, following stints as a translator and journal editor, Wollstonecraft would publish three books that explored women and familial relationships, childhood, child rearing, and education. A major theme in her work was the discussion of women's intellectual, as well as moral, development, with a special focus on the devastating effects of living in a "subordinate state" (Wollstonecraft in Todd, 1977).

In a work now viewed as one of the first feminist writings, *A Vindication of the Rights of Woman* (1792), Wollstonecraft challenged the idea of developing a national educational system designed exclusively for men. She challenged the ideas of philosopher Jean-Jacque Rousseau, who argued that women should have an education that focused on making them attractive and pleasing to their husbands. Because women were just as intelligent as men, Wollstonecraft felt they should have access to the same educational programs in the very same schools. She was convinced that women should develop their intellect and independence through a liberal, critical education to avoid becoming dependent on men. This meant a curriculum devoid of needlework, embroidery, music, and other forms of entertainment meant to impress a male audience.

Balancing Career and Family This is not to suggest that Wollstonecraft completely dismissed the importance of marriage and motherhood or of the arts. Rather, she held steadfast to the belief that both genders should have access to knowledge and an understanding of truths. Wollstonecraft rejected the limitations associated with traditional gender roles, limitations that impact women's empowerment politically and economically. And yet, Wollstonecraft supported a more traditional, gender-specific curriculum for girls from low socioeconomic backgrounds. Nevertheless, Wollstonecraft's influence on today's educational arena, ranging from such ideas as the establishment of free, government-sponsored, co-ed schools, to the inclusion of science, mathematics, writing, and physical education in the curriculum clearly were ahead of her time.

Mohandas Gandhi: Education for Life, Through Life

Social activist, political leader, lawyer, husband, father, and, to many in the world, liberator, Mohandas Gandhi (1869–1948) may not immediately come to mind as an educational philosopher. Well known as the leader of the nonviolent Indian independence movement that challenged British imperialism from 1915 to 1947, Gandhi was also instrumental in the development of an educational philosophy whose primary goal was to provide sustainable educational access and programming for the poor.

Helping to win independence from Great Britain (whose rule of India began in 1639) remains one of Gandhi's most celebrated accomplishments. But he also pursued social justice, equality, cultural affirmation, and economic empowerment through the integration of spirituality, service, and educational vision in South Africa, as well as in India.

Gandhi's Background Gandhi, however, did not grow up as an "untouchable" in India (the status assigned to members of the lowest socio-religious Hindu caste, who often labored on the streets). The son of Karmachand and Puthabai Gandhi, Gandhi was born to a merchant, or commercial, caste in Porbandar, India, where his father served as prime minister to the state prince. While his mother provided him with a deeply spiritual upbringing, Gandhi attended a college preparatory high school where he studied astronomy, chemistry, English, history, and mathematics (Chadha, 1997).

By the age of 13, Gandhi married Kasturbai Makanji, in keeping with the Hindu tradition of arranged marriage. Gandhi attended Sarmaldas College in India in 1887 and moved to England in 1888 to attend law school. Kasturbai and their son would rejoin Gandhi back in India in 1891 after he completed his studies. Kasturbai did not have a formal education and was considered by some historians to be illiterate (Chadha, 1997). Nevertheless, she worked alongside Gandhi throughout his life.

Social Justice Work Following a brief stint practicing law in the city then known as Bombay, Gandhi moved to South Africa in 1893 to work with an Indian firm. During the next eight years, Gandhi discovered the discrimination that Indians ("coloreds") and black South Africans experienced, as they faced numerous human rights violations, including denial of the right to vote, travel restrictions, and few employment opportunities. In order to challenge these laws, Gandhi organized the Natal Indian Congress, thus beginning his social justice work.

Gandhi would return to India in 1901 to open his own Bombay law office. He would continue his social activism there. However, Gandhi acknowledged that his own English education, coupled with his privileged caste status, left him out of touch with his nation's cultural identity. He would soon travel across the country, leaving his third-class train car to seek out Indian villages and Indian National Congress party leaders at stops along the way.

In the following year Gandhi was recalled to South Africa. New laws discriminating against Indians were implemented. Facing deportation if not fingerprinted and registered, Indians called on Gandhi to represent them and help organize a challenge to such policies. In response, he designed a plan to prepare Indians to confront these discriminatory laws using nonviolent methods. He drew from the work of two diverse authors, British critic and writer John Ruskin (1928-1910) and Russian novelist Leo Tolstoy (1828–1910). In their writings, both Ruskin and Tolstoy addressed the need for social justice, as well as the power of the individual to confront corrupt states through civil disobedience. In addition to his strategizing, Gandhi also published a journal entitled *Indian Opinion*, which served as an information outlet for the Indian community in South Africa, as well as abroad.

The next step in Gandhi's organizational plan was to prepare his community for nonviolent social activism. He created ashrams, or communal schools, in South Africa: the Phoenix Farm, near Durban, and the Tolstoy Farm in the Transvaal region. The children who attended the schools represented the diverse Indian community who lived on the farms—Indians from different castes and different religions who spoke a variety of languages. This set the tone for a school climate that accepted differences and embraced a common, unifying goal.

Gandhi's Educational Philosophy Instruction at the schools reflected Gandhi's educational philosophy. He believed that children should be exposed to a more holistic curriculum that included a spiritual, moral, and cultural foundation as well as an academic one. Students were taught the fundamental beliefs of their own religions, while receiving instruction in their native languages. They also learned mathematics, reading, and writing in addition to history and geography.

Another feature of Gandhi's educational philosophy focused on the development of job skills through vocational education. A keen observer of the caste system, and shaped by his own British educational experiences, Gandhi felt a deep concern for the negative misperceptions of the working class. Instead, he believed that there was much dignity associated with skilled, physical labor. Thus, at Tolstoy Farm, children learned skills associated with agriculture, arts, and crafts, and they also helped maintain the school.

Gandhi's organizing of Indians to oppose discrimination in South Africa enabled him to put into practice strategies he would later use in India. Driven by the Hindu belief in *satyagraha*, the use of one's sense of inner truth against immoral forces, Gandhi encouraged his followers to practice passive resistance and civil disobedience against injustice. However, people needed to learn about the presence of such injustices through consciousness raising. Only then could they learn to control their feelings so they would not respond to violence with violence. This model of instruction would mirror the beliefs of Henry David Thoreau—and would later influence other advocates of social justice, including Cesar Chavez, Dolores Huerta, Dr. Martin Luther King, Jr., and Nelson Mandela.

As a result of this work, by 1914 the South African government repealed a number of the anti-Indian laws that it had imposed. Gandhi returned to India in 1915 to continue the struggle for independence from the British. Once there, Gandhi used organizational and educational strategies he implemented in South Africa. Gandhi founded Satyagraha Ashram, published journals in both English and Gujarati (an Indian language), and sought to bring together diverse religious and ethnic groups living in India. Pursuing his nonviolent philosophy, Gandhi would struggle to keep the groups united, as violence erupted between Hindus and Muslims. Muslims feared the lack of self-determination in an independent India. Eventually, Pakistan would become partitioned into a Muslim state.

Nevertheless, Gandhi continued to pursue a nonviolent approach to liberation. Driven by a philosophy that valued truths universal to all religions, he believed that morality could be achieved in communities whose members were committed to serving one another. Love and service were the forces that united such communities. Communities, however, needed to be taught how to help and sustain one another, as opposed to depending on outside forces. Thus, in his ashrams, Gandhi supported a curriculum that not only focused on academic skills but also celebrated diverse cultural identities and advocated for the economic development of a socially reconstructed India.

Gandhi's Educational Vision Gandhi's educational vision confronted the problems associated with a stratified Indian population. In opposition to the colonial, elite educational system and a caste system that contributed to the illiteracy and poverty of the nation, Gandhi argued that everyone should have access to an education. Gandhi believed that all children between the ages of 6 and 14 should receive instruction that prepared them for self-determination and productive employment. Children were to be taught, in their native language, a craft or skill in a basic education plan. No longer would lower-caste children be illiterate or unproductive in a new India. Improving children's self-worth through the teaching of hands-on skills, such as the production of cotton and other agriculture products, would help build and sustain the economic development of the new country (Patel, 1953). This was at the heart of Gandhi's basic educational philosophy.

Thirty-two years later, after having served 2338 days in prison and having conducted fasts to stop the violence between competing groups, Gandhi witnessed the voluntary withdrawal of the British in 1947 (Patel, 1953). Gandhi's nonviolent strategizing and the trials of World War II both contributed to Great Britain's decision to withdraw. However, conflict and violence continued between Hindus and Muslims as India and Pakistan divided. Sadly, Ghandi would be assassinated on January 30, 1948, by a Hindu nationalist named Vinayak Godse.

Gandhi's educational vision challenged systemic discrimination while pursuing educational reforms that affirmed the dignity of disempowered communities. Over time, other educational philosophies with an emphasis on vocational skills for community development have emerged, such as those advocated by Booker T. Washington at the Tuskegee Institute.

Like all the philosophies discussed thus far, Gandhi's has its limitations. A majority of Indian children today attend traditional schools, while basic schools educate a working class (Gutek, 2005a). Educational programs designed to help sustain local economies and preserve cultural traditions have been negatively affected by the intrusion of large corporations looking to support short-term projects, using cheap labor, and profiting from deregulation and the repeal of environmental and labor laws. In the end, Gandhi's educational philosophy sought to engage social change through nonviolence, cultural acceptance, and skill development. These are goals that many educators continue to pursue today.

W. E. B. Du Bois: Merging Social Justice and Higher Education

William E. B. Du Bois (1868–1963) is considered by many to be one of America's most preeminent scholars in the fields of sociology and history. Du Bois was also a crucial catalyst for the civil rights movement, serving as one of the founding members of the National Association for the Advancement of Colored People (the NAACP) and as the editor of its journal, *The Crisis*. His educational vision for African Americans extended over the course of such historical periods as the Reconstruction and post-Reconstruction years (1877–1910).

W. E. B. Du Bois

A Complex Life Throughout his prolific career, Du Bois challenged the philosophy of accommodation and industrial or vocational training that characterized the educational belief systems of Colonel Samuel Armstrong, of Virginia's Hampton Institute, and that of his protégé, Booker T. Washington, president of the Tuskegee Institute in Alabama. Du Bois argued instead that African Americans required access to a higher education that prepared students for professional and leadership positions to raise social consciousness and, ultimately, secure voting and civil rights.

Unlike Washington, William E. B. Du Bois was born in the North, in Great Barrington, Massachusetts. His father, Alfred Du Bois, was born in Haiti, where his white grandfather was a plantation owner. Du Bois's mother, Mary Silvina Burghart, was brought from Africa to the United States by a Dutch slave trader, William Burghart.

Well established in New England, the Burghart family would witness in 1867 the marriage between Alfred and Mary. Although William was born the following year, his father soon left Massachusetts seeking work. The young family never saw Alfred again, and Mary was left to support the family. Despite experiencing a debilitating stroke, Mary raised her son and supported his educational pursuits.

Life in an Interracial Community Not surprisingly, growing up in the North was quite different from the childhood Booker T. Washington experienced in the South during the mid-1800s, having been born into slavery. After all, Du Bois's family was essentially born free. New Barrington was a community whose members included Czech, Dutch, English, and Irish immigrants (Lewis, 1993). Du Bois's family attended the First Congregationalist Church, a church whose beliefs were influenced by a Calvinist congregationalism that supported the abolitionist movement.

Living in an interracial community, Du Bois was quite successful in school. While enrolled in Great Barrington High School, he was encouraged by his principal, Frank Hosmer, to take college preparatory classes such as algebra, Greek, and Latin. In addition, the community helped open employment "doors" for him. He worked numerous part-time jobs to help his mother, who now served as a maid to white families. These jobs included working at the community grocer, assisting senior citizens, and writing for the local newspaper. At the same time, Du Bois served as coeditor of his own high school newspaper and worked on community projects that supported the local African American community.

College Life Du Bois was the first African American to graduate from his high school in 1884. In his commencement address, Du Bois described the contributions of the New England abolitionist Wendell Phillips. Although his mother encouraged Du Bois to apply to Harvard University, her 1885 death and a lack of funds made it impossible for him to pursue this goal. However, with the help of Principal Hosmer and members of the Great Barrington community, money was raised so that Du Bois would be able to attend a Congregationalist institution, Fisk University. Located in Nashville, Tennessee, this African American university, with its predominantly white faculty, introduced Du Bois to a classical curriculum that included calculus, world languages, science, philosophy, and history. While at Fisk, Du Bois also served as editor of the university newspaper.

During the summers of 1886 and 1887, Du Bois began teaching black students, ranging in age from 6 to 20, in the rural South (Lewis, 1993). Following the completion of his teacher preparation courses at Lebanon Teachers Institute, Du Bois was witness to the overwhelming poverty and inequities that African American students faced in the segregated South. What he observed there, so different from what he had witnessed in the North, had a profound effect on Du Bois's emerging educational philosophy and social activism.

Following graduation from Fisk University in 1888, Du Bois continued his studies at Harvard University, having been admitted as a junior. Scholarship funds helped support his education. At this time, Du Bois was able to study with such notable scholars as the philosopher George Santayana and the psychologist William James. In 1890, Du Bois would complete his bachelor's degree in philosophy, cum laude (Lewis, 1993).

Graduate Studies at Harvard and Beyond Du Bois continued his graduate work at Harvard, with an emphasis on history. Combining his interests in history with sociology, political science, and economics, Du Bois completed his master's degree in 1891. He would soon pursue doctoral studies in history; his dissertation was titled "The Suppression of the African Slave-Trade to the United States of America (1638–1870)."

Like many graduate students of the day, Du Bois traveled to Germany in 1892 to resume his studies. From 1892 to 1894, Du Bois attended the Friedrich Wilhelm University in Berlin on scholarship. Honing his German skills and working with leading economists, political scientists, and the renowned sociologist Max Weber, Du Bois was also introduced to the capitalist theories of Karl Marx and the dialectic philosophy of Georg Hegel. This helped Du Bois interpret historical events through the perspective of an oppositional thesis and antithesis, symbolized by past slave masters and freed slaves (Gutek, 2005b).

Although Du Bois was unable to finish his degree in Germany because of residency requirements and limited funding, he returned to Harvard in 1894 and completed his dissertation in the following year. More significantly, Du Bois would return to America with a heightened worldview. He was sensitized to global race relations, including those existing in colonized African nations. As a result, Du Bois came to believe that it was important for African Americans to become conscious of their own history, including the civil rights struggles taking place abroad as well as in the United States. Capitalism also remained a power that Africans needed to challenge, Du Bois argued, because he felt that blacks continued to be exploited economic labor sources.

Contrasting Philosophical Viewpoints It was inevitable that Du Bois's positions on these issues would clash with those held by Booker T. Washington. While Du Bois completed his studies in Germany and at Harvard, Washington's Tuskegee Institute thrived. It would become the model for numerous black colleges across the United States, all of which emphasized industrial education. With limited funding available, these historically black colleges would enlist students to "work off" their tuition by learning trades useful in the construction and maintenance of the campuses. If they developed trade and agricultural skills, Washington contended, blacks would not need to leave the South but could sustain their own economy instead of competing against whites in the North (Lewis, 1993).

However, Washington underestimated the devastating effects of racism on African Americans. Poor white farmers saw blacks as competition. The white supremacy movement gained momentum throughout the 1880s, as Jim Crow segregation laws and social Darwinism promoted the belief that whites were superior to blacks. Ku Klux Klan membership grew. Poll taxes and restrictions that tested blacks' specific knowledge of the national Constitution and of state constitutions kept thousands of blacks from voting.

Nevertheless, Washington continued to insist that blacks must accommodate whites. He believed that civil rights could not be forced but would be won eventually through struggle (Hawkins, 1962). Du Bois would challenge this view for the rest of his life through his educational endeavors, research, and activism.

New Research, New Perspectives, New Philosophy In 1896, Du Bois was invited by the University of Pennsylvania to serve as research director of a sociological study of African Americans living in Philadelphia. This comprehensive study, known as *The Philadelphia Negro*, explored family and community life, social networks, education, economics, and political participation via thousands of surveys and hundreds of interviews (Gutek, 2005b). The study, published in 1899, concluded that family relations, educational outcomes, and the economic status of African Americans were devastated by the effects of slavery and discrimination.

The study also revealed the class differences among African Americans. The small economic elite, Du Bois believed, would become "the talented tenth" who could provide leadership to the larger black community (Lewis, 1993). This elite, he felt, should have access to the best educational and professional training.

Du Bois's research findings would prove highly influential in the field of sociology and had far-reaching ramifications for the civil rights movement. In 1897, he would be offered a position at Atlanta University in Georgia, where he taught history, sociology, and economics for 13 years. It was there that he published one of his most famous works, *The Souls of Black Folks* (1903). In it, he described the lived experiences and culture of African Americans.

Du Bois would come to resent Booker T. Washington's essentialist philosophies. Although Washington once offered Du Bois a teaching position at Tuskegee, Du Bois declined. Their different backgrounds, given Washington's ties to slavery in the South, vocational education, and accommodationist views, in contrast to Du Bois's northern roots, travels, scholarly pursuits, and social activism, came to represent the diversity of the African American experience in a variety of sociocultural and poltical contexts.

The Creation of the NAACP Largely to challenge Washington's positions, Du Bois helped organize the 1905 "Niagara Movement." Its interracial members would soon form the National Negro Committee, which later reorganized into the National Association for the Advancement of Colored People (NAACP). In 1910, the group's goals were to empower African Americans through black consciousness raising, develop an educational program to inform the public about the status of African Americans, and mount a legal challenge to segregation. Du Bois's charge was to serve as editor of the NAACP journal, *The Crisis,* and function as director of publicity and research.

The activism of the NAACP, combined with the large circulation of its journal, stimulated social change. And with the onset of World Wars I and II, blacks migrated to the North to secure work. Black, urban communities soon grew in the East. African Americans voiced their rejection of racism and discrimination, especially now that so many had served in the wars overseas. By Washington's death in 1915, his views supporting passive accommodation had less influence among African Americans.

Du Bois continued to teach at Atlanta University. He published numerous works about African American cultural history and politics. Philosophically, he believed that an elite academic education was an important vehicle for the liberation of African Americans. He felt that blacks continued to be an exploited source of labor.

He would later join the American Socialist Party and participate in other political organizations. He argued that black-run cooperatives would better meet the economic needs of African Americans. Members of the NAACP disagreed with this belief. Du Bois resigned in 1934, only to return to the NAACP in 1944 and serve as director of special research. He would focus his interests on international affairs affecting Africans worldwide. Maintaining his political positions, he was accused of being a Communist sympathizer. By 1949, he was dismissed from his NAACP position. Senator Joseph McCarthy's commission would target him as a member of a "Communist front organization." But the U.S. Supreme Court found Du Bois and his colleagues innocent, ruling that the Justice Department had not proved its case.

Family and an Enduring Legacy Du Bois and his wife Nina had two children. Du Bois remarried a year after Nina's death in 1950. His second wife, Shirley Graham, like Nina, supported and contributed to the work of the social justice and civil rights movements.

Despite the Supreme Court decision, the U.S. government would deny Du Bois a passport because of his socialist beliefs. Between 1952 and 1958 he could not travel to Africa, despite the numerous invitations he received. Eventually, Du Bois was issued a passport in 1958. He would travel to the Soviet Union. In 1961, Du Bois visited Ghana at the invitation of its first president, Kwame Nkrumah. Alienated by the lingering presence of discrimination in America, Du Bois decided to stay in Ghana and continue to research and develop an African encyclopedia. In time, he would apply for citizenship in Ghana, where he passed away at the age of 95 on August 29, 1963.

Throughout Du Bois's life, he felt that only through higher education could African Americans be prepared for leadership, social activism, and political empowerment. His own research and writings reflected a social reconstructivist position, as he examined the African American experience.

Du Bois stressed that only through an elite higher education could the "talented tenth" be prepared to promote social change. Du Bois was also concerned with the education of elementary and secondary students. He was disturbed by the absence of educational equity that he observed while teaching in black public schools in the South. He felt that these students should have access to an academic curriculum, as opposed to a vocational one, which was often introduced too early in a child's educational career, Du Bois believed.

Du Bois was also one of the first advocates of an Afrocentric curriculum. He argued that American history textbooks did not educate students adequately about the contributions of other cultures. He sought to challenge the Eurocentric curriculum, through the publication of his own groundbreaking historical and sociological scholarship. Du Bois believed that such research should be included within the general curriculum, which in turn would help energize the social activism within the African American community.

Finally, Du Bois's contribution to a social reconstructivist educational philosophy included a curriculum that looked beyond American borders. Stressing the importance of pan-Africanism, Du Bois introduced a global perspective on knowledge construction that urged African Americans to become unified with Africans worldwide. He believed that African Americans should learn about the cultures, languages, and history of their brethren overseas so that students could develop a strong sense of identity and, ultimately, unite in political empowerment.

Gloria Anzaldúa: Crossing Borderlands

Gloria Evangelina Anzaldúa's (1942–2004) interdisciplinary work as a writer, feminist theorist, and social activist helped establish the presence of borderland cultural theory across a number of academic fields whose domains are significantly informed by social reconstructivist philosophy. The disciplines influenced by Anzaldúa's writings include American literature, American studies, Chicana/o and Latina/o studies, ethnic studies, feminist theory, gay and lesbian studies, and history. A versatile author, Anzaldúa also published numerous works across genres such as children's literature, interviews, poetry, literary analysis, the short story, and multicultural anthologies. In her work, she blended Mexican, Anglo, and indigenous narratives.

Anzaldúa is best known for her contributions to borderlands cultural theory, a theory especially significant to schools whose teachers (and the curricula they teach) are predominantly Euroamerican despite the presense of increasingly diverse student populations. In her historical counternarrative *Borderlands/La Frontera: The New Mestiza* (1999), Anzaldúa merges autobiography, cultural studies, reconstructivist history, poetry, and Latina/Chicana feminist theory to introduce a new borderland that describes the experience of living simultaneously among different cultures, languages, traditions, and economic classes. Anzaldúa also presents an analysis of how changing gender roles, traditions, spirituality, and languages can create new identities or cultural hybridity—identities different from the labels, categorization, and expectations we are quick to place on "others."

Understanding Borderland Theory In borderland theory, Anzaldúa extends the existentialist philosophical position. Students must not limit their understanding of themselves and their educational needs to, say, a simple binary scheme that essentializes. For example, a student should not be compelled to pursue an academic curriculum on the one hand or a vocational, working-class course of study on the other. Nor should an American-born student and an immigrant, ESL student be forced to compete for educational resources. Instead, Anzaldúa offers historical counternarratives that ask readers to examine more accurately where we come from; to study the shift of cultural, gender, and class traditions and outcomes influenced by the powerful; and to explore how these understandings can help renew our pursuit of social justice through the creation of a new, inclusive education— across communities and across symbolic, psychological borders.

Living and Writing on the Borderlands Anzaldúa was born in the Rio Grande Valley, in the small town of Hargill, south Texas, in 1942. She was the eldest of Urbano and Amalia Anzaldúa's six children. Anzaldúa refers to her life on the border between the United States and Mexico as "una herida abierta" (an open wound). Following the death of her father, 15-year-old Anzaldúa and her family worked the fields of Arkansas and Texas. She continued her education and became one of the first rural Mexican American women to complete a bachelor's degree from Pan American University. Anzaldúa went on to earn her master's degree in English and education at the University of Texas, Austin.

Following her interests in education and social activism, Anzaldúa taught children of migrant workers before moving to California in the late 1970s. By 1979, Anzaldúa was lecturing at San Francisco State while pursuing Chicano and feminist studies. Continuing a lifetime of writing, she published a number of works and garnered such writing awards as the Before Columbus Foundation American Book Award, a National Endowment of the Arts Fiction Award, an American Studies Association Lifetime Achievement Award, and the Lesbian Rights Award.

In addition, her *Borderlands/La Frontera: The New Mestiza* (1987) was named one of the "100 Best Books of the Century" by both *Hungry Mind Review* and *Utne Reader*. Anzaldúa also pursued her doctorate at the University of California, Santa Cruz. However, in May 2004, nearing the completion of her dissertation, Anzaldúa died from complications of diabetes at the age of 61.

Challenging Academia Although Anzaldúa opted not to work continuously within a university system (except for selected teaching assignments and speaking engagements), her impact on educational philosophy has been profound. In her celebrated book *Borderlands*, Anzaldúa writes, "the borderlands are physically present whenever two or more cultures edge each other, where people of different races occupy the same territory, where lower, middle, and upper classes touch, where the space between individuals shrinks with intimacy" (1999, p. 19). Anzaldúa's autobiographical and historical writings, or autohistorias, challenge the Eurocentric, erased histories that the traditional American history curriculum offers. Anzaldúa also articulated the hybridity of Mexican/Mestiza/indigenous identity through the lens of working-class, immigrant women whose cultures are often rejected, whose labor is exploited, and who are "separated from our identity and our history" (1999, p.30).

Like Du Bois's call for Pan-Africanism and the need to bring together marginalized communities at times historically opposed to one another, Anzaldúa's *Borderlands* calls for the reestablishment of the cultural and linguistic bonds between Mexicans, Mexican Americans (Chicana/os) and Indians of the Americas. The bilingual titles and themes of several of her books, such as *Making Face, Making Soul/ Haciendo Caras: Creative and Critical Perspectives by Feminists-of-Color* (1990), two bilingual children's books, *Friends from the Other Side/Amigos del Otro Lado* (1993) and *Prietita and the Ghost Woman/ Prietita y la Llorona* (1995) and *Interviews/Entrevistas* (2000), demonstrate her interest in the cross-cultural and intergenerational merging of peoples whose histories and commitment to serving one another are much more powerful than their present-day dissonance.

The Blending of Cultures, Languages, and Philosophies In Anzaldúa's texts, the preconquest Aztec language, Nahuatl, blends with English and Spanish. All of the languages coexist and validate one another. This linguistic position challenges educational philosophies informed by perennialism and essentialism, which emphasize classical texts and content and seldom include or affirm the languages and contributions of Latin American cultures. In fact, the emphasis on bilingual skill development and the use of bilingual texts in public schools today is often co-opted by English-only advocacy, assimilationist policies, and standardized testing.

Like Wollstonecraft, Anzaldúa stressed the importance of educational access for women of color. Challenging the few life options that women, particularly minority women, could experience, Anzaldúa confronts her family's Mexican American expectations (pp. 39):

> For a woman of my culture there used to be only three directions she could turn: to the church as a nun, to the streets as a prostitute, or to the home as a mother. Today some of us have a fourth choice: entering the world by way of education and career and becoming self-antonomous persons. (1987)

This theme of empowerment and defying categorization was initially introduced by Anzaldúa in *Borderlands*. In an earlier groundbreaking multicultural feminist anthology (coedited with Cherríe Moraga), *This Bridge Called My Back: Writings by Radical Women of Color* (1981), and later in *this bridge we call home: radical visions for transformation* (2002), (coedited with Ana Louise Keating), Anzaldúa sought to disrupt identity classification, essentialism, and exclusion. She was acutely aware that all cultures, from within, are subject to such conflicts as sexism, racism, and homophobia. She argued that living with, writing about, and engaging in discourse about these paradoxes is an active part of cultural life on the borderlands—a life that changes. This belief resonates with a progressive educational philosophy in that students are encouraged to engage in a similar discourse, to ask questions, pursue study, and pose new critical questions about events that inform the larger society (Elenes, 2003).

Anzaldúa believed that feminists of all colors and social justice activists must acknowledge and confront their racism, sexism, homophobia, and other desconocimientos (intentional and unintentional ignorance or lack of awareness). And much like Gandhi, Anzaldúa felt that such views should be challenged without rejecting the people who held them.

Anzaldúa demonstrated this belief at the 1990 National Women's Studies Association conference in Akron, Ohio. Frustrated by the organization's racism and other desconocimientos, many women of color left the conference proceedings. Anzaldúa understood this decision. However, she chose to remain at the conference, becoming what she would later describe as a nepantlera, a visionary, cultural worker. Moving within and among multiple cultural worlds, Anzaldúa explained, nepantleras use this motion to carefully listen to all parties without retreating into their own cultural group. In this way, Anzaldúa maintained, groups could discuss unworkable positions with one another to identify those positions that might be workable. New alliances could be forged without falling back on insularity and divisiveness.

PAUSE & REFLECT

Which of the foregoing leaders and their philosophies can you relate to the most? Why? How did these social advocates challenge the traditional philosophies associated with early educators? In what ways can these leaders' perspectives influence the development of your own teaching philosophy?

From PRESERVICE to PRACTICE

Now Consider and Compose Your Own Teaching Philosophy

Why do teachers need to articulate their philosophy of teaching? What purposes does a teaching philosophy serve? Many teachers have found that the process of identifying a personal philosophy of teaching and continuously examining, applying, and revising this philosophy through teaching can lead to improved instruction and professional and personal growth.

In his book *The Skillful Teacher* (1990), Stephen Brookfield points out that the development of a teaching philosophy can be used for both personal and pedagogical purposes:

- Personal purpose: "A distinctive organizing vision—a clear picture of why you are doing what you are doing that you can call up at points of crisis—is crucial to your personal sanity and morale."
- Pedagogical purpose: "Teaching is about making some kind of dent in the world so that the world is different than it was before you practiced your craft. Knowing clearly what kind of dent you want to make in the world means that you must continually ask yourself the most fundamental evaluative question of all: What effect am I having on students and on their learning?"

There is no right or wrong way to write a philosophy statement, which is why it is so challenging for most people to write one. You may decide to write in prose, use famous quotations, create visuals, use a question/answer format, etc. It is generally 1 or 2 pages in length.

Use present tense, in most cases. Writing in the first person is most common and is the easiest for your audience to read.

Most teaching philosophies avoid excessive use of technical terms and favor language and concepts that can be broadly understood. A general rule is that the statement should be written with the audience in mind. It may be helpful to have someone from your field read your statement and give you some guidance on any discipline-specific jargon and on issues to include or exclude.

Include teaching strategies and methods to help people "see" you in the classroom. By including very specific examples of teaching strategies, assignments, discussions, hands-on activities, and technology, you can give your readers a mental "peek" into your classroom. Help them visualize what you do in the classroom and the exchange between you and your students. For example, can your readers picture the learning environment you create for your students?

Make it memorable and unique. What is going to set you apart? What brings a teaching philosophy to life is the extent to which it creates a vivid portrait of a person who is intentional about teaching practices and committed to his or her career.

"Own" your philosophy. By writing about *your* experiences and *your* philosophical beliefs, you "own" those statements and appear more open to new and different ideas about teaching. Even in your own experience, you make choices about the best teaching methods for different courses, content, and objectives.

Read sample teaching philosophies at The Ohio State University, Developing a Teaching Portfolio webpage at http://ftad.osu.edu/portfolio/philosophy/Philosophy.html.

Source: The Ohio State University, http://ftad.osu.edu/portfolio/philosophy/Philosophy.html

SUMMARY

Resonating with the philosophies of progressivism and social reconstructivism, Anzaldúa's borderland theory reflects a pursuit of social justice, critical thinking, and problem solving relevant to education today. As future educators consider which philosophies will best inform their professional practice, we can certainly reflect on the life work of such leaders as Gloria Anzaldúa, W. E. B. Du Bois, Mohandas Ghandi, and Mary Wollstonecraft, who, in their unique contexts, pursued innovative ways of thinking about education, identity, inclusion, and service to new communities of learners.

1. Compare and contrast perennialist and essentialist approaches to curriculum development. What are the strengths and weaknesses of each?

2. Describe the differences between teacher-centered and student-centered educational philosophies. In what different kinds of instructional situations do you think teacher-centered and student-centered philosophies are effective for guiding instruction?

3. Teachers must often confront philosophical differences when working together. What would you do if colleagues in your department wanted to focus on an essentialist curriculum plan while your students were eager to participate in community service activities, along the lines of social reconstructionism?

4. Describe the philosophies of Wollstonecraft, Du Bois, Ghandi, and Anzaldúa. Explain how their philosophies are relevant to education and schooling today.

1. Interview two or three of your professors in your major field of study. Ask them to describe their own educational philosophy and to explain how their philosophy influences their instruction strategies and curriculum design.

2. Read one or two primary documents by Anzaldúa, Du Bois, Ghandi, or Wollstonecraft. Using examples from these works, describe how such philosophies as essentialism or social reconstructivism emerge from their writings.

3. Research Plato's development and use of the Socratic method. Conduct a role play in this class in which you model use of the Socratic method to try to resolve a conflict that is often in the news today.

The Official Mahatma Gandhi eArchive and Reference Library
http://www.mahatma.org.in/index.jsp
This site includes writings, opinion essays, and poems by Mahatma Gandhi. Multimedia presentations are also available on this site, as well as video and audio recordings.

The Philosophy Pages
http://www.philosophypages.com/index.htm
This webpage offers students information about Western philosophers. Also included are a survey and timeline of the history of Western philosophy, biographies of major philosophers, a dictionary of philosophical terms, and basic principles of logic. Additional links are provided.

Stanford Encyclopedia of Philosophy
http://plato.stanford.edu/index.html
This webpage offers comprehensive biographies of philosophers and their contributions to our global society. The site also explores philosophical concepts, arguments, and analysis.

University of Texas, Austin: Benson Latin America Collection, Anzaldúa Archives
http://www.lib.utexas.edu/benson/archives/ma_manuscripts.html
This site will soon house the manuscripts of Gloria Anzaldúa's published works, including *Borderlands/La Frontera* and her "Prieta" stories, as well as unpublished manuscripts, notebooks, correspondence, lectures, and audio and video interviews.

W. E. B. Du Bois Research Center for African and African American Research at Harvard University
http://dubois.fas.harvard.edu/index.html
The comprehensive webpage is dedicated to the spirit and work of Dr. Du Bois. The center provides links to research and community outreach activities relevant to Africans and African Americans.

REFERENCES

Adler, M. (1982). *The Paideia proposal: An educational manifesto*. New York: Macmillan.

Anzaldua, G. (1983). *This bridge called my back: Writings by radical women of color*. San Francisco: Aunt Lute Books.

Anzaldua, G. (1999). *Borderlands/la frontera: The new mestiza* (2nd ed.). San Francisco: Aunt Lute Books.

Chadha, Y. (1997). *Gandhi: A life*. New York: Wiley.

Elenes, C. A. (2003). Reclaiming the borderlands: Chicana/o identity, difference, and critical pedagogy. In A. Darder, M. Baltodano, & R. Torres (Eds.), *The critical pedagogy reader* (pp. 191–210). New York: RoutledgeFalmer.

Falco, M. (1996). *Feminist interpretations of Mary Wollstonecraft*. University Park: Pennsylvania State University Press.

Gandhi, M. K. (1947). *India of my dreams*. Ahmedabad: Navajivan.

Gutek, G. L. (2005a). Mohandas Gandhi: Father of Indian independence. In *Historical and philosophical foundations of education* (pp. 378–394). New Jersey: Pearson.

Gutek, G. L. (2005b). W. E. B. Du Bois: Scholar and activist for African American rights. In *Historical and philosophical foundations of education* (pp. 408–417). New Jersey: Pearson.

Hawkins, H. (1962). *Booker T. Washington and his critics*. Boston: Heath.

Lewis, D. L. (1993). *W. E. B. Du Bois: Biography of a race, 1868–1919*. New York: Holt.

Patel, M. (1953). *The educational philosophy of Mahatma Gandhi*. Ahmedabad: Navajivan.

Ravitch, D. (2000). *Left back: A century of failed school reforms*. New York: Simon & Schuster.

Todd, J. M. (1977). *A Wollstonecraft anthology*. Bloomington: Indiana University Press.

Todd, J. M., & Butler, M. (1989). A vindication of the rights of men. In J. Todd & M. Butler (Eds.), *The works of Mary Wollstonecraft*. New York: New York University Press.

2

The Teaching Profession: Our Callings, Our Challenges

CHAPTERS

3 Entering the Teaching Profession

4 Equity and Educational Practice

Entering the Teaching Profession

CHAPTER OBJECTIVES

- Readers will identify the role that contemporary teachers play in the ongoing support of democratic principles in America's public schools.

- Readers will trace the factors that influence teacher licensure and certification in the United States.

- As educational reforms increase, readers will recognize how such movements affect teacher evaluation and the tenure process.

- Readers will analyze the goals and functions of teachers' unions.

- Given the high rates of beginning teacher attrition, readers will become familiar with model programs and strategies to help support new teachers during their early years in the profession.

FIRST PERSON

Anyone Can Teach:

The Default Major

During my undergraduate years, my goal was to become a fiction writer. Thanks to the connections I made with my own high school English teachers and our shared love of literature, I had the passion the writing profession required. Once I declared my major in English, however, I found the critical writing standards for the coursework to be much more rigorous than such course titles as Contemporary American Short Stories, Shakespeare's Comedies, and Adolescent Literature had led me to expect. My creative writing classes still captivated me, classes where I could write to my heart's content—until that heart was broken by the merciless critiques I received from my professors and peers.

In writing draft after draft of paper after paper, I soon came to realize that writing is a lonely endeavor. As my graduation date came near, I also started to worry about what on earth I would do for a living. How would I pay rent or cover my student loans? What about my car and insurance payments? I still felt an attraction to what I envisioned as the "writing lifestyle," but such a lifestyle started to lose its luster when interest rates rose and loan deferment applications started to pile up.

It soon became apparent to me and the other English majors among my friends that the term *realistic* would become one we would use often in discussing our plans for the future. Perhaps pursuing a teaching certificate and licensure would not be so bad, we thought. We could inspire young literature students to write, just as we were inspired by our teachers. Our students would certainly love reading what we loved to read. They would thrive in the late hours as they composed their own great poetry and penned essays that solved social problems. And teaching wouldn't interfere with the completion of our own prospective writing projects.

But what did we really know about the teaching profession? Just because we attended school ourselves and were engaged in the study of writing, did we really understand the ramifications of selecting education as a career? After all, we had to be "realistic." We had to be honest with ourselves and admit that perhaps, to our inner horror, we might not have the skills, the talent, the persistence, and the breaks ever to see our names on the *New York Times* bestseller list. So teaching was our default major. Teaching was our "back-up."

As I took part in the teacher preparation program, I was soon fascinated by the teachers and students I observed in my clinical or practicum experiences. Some educators would demonstrate and reproduce instructional strategies that were driven by a perennialistic philosophy and quickly alienated students. Other educators would introduce a social reconstructivist philosophy where each student had an equal opportunity to address and study social problems from a variety of viewpoints without fear of being silenced. This was democracy at work.

During the course of my teacher preparation program and fieldwork, assumptions about the profession continued to break down. Whereas I had believed that most English teachers would be consumed by their own writing goals, I soon learned that few had time to write. After school, they graded essays, prepared for the next day's lessons, participated in extracurricular activities, or raced home to spend time with their own families. Others scrambled to attend union meetings in order to discuss health benefits. I was especially shocked to learn that some teachers rushed away so they could get to their second job on time because they struggled to make ends meet.

As for summers, most teachers used this time to "recharge" or to take another job. This period of recharge was considered by many veteran teachers I met during my training to be a critical part of the academic year. My mentor teachers used their summers to generate new ideas, seek out new readings, and prepare innovative strategies to better motivate their students.

Many tenured, as well as untenured, teachers pursued professional development activities. They took graduate courses about classroom management, team teaching, or parent outreach or studied the latest in technology. Others attended workshops about union negotiations, the core curriculum, and how to address the latest educational reforms. In essence, what I learned during my teacher preparation program was that I knew little about the teaching profession and the students I would serve beyond my content area. In this chapter, I explore the distinctive features of one of the most important professions our society offers today—features that changed my "default major" into the most important career choice of my life.

The Important Role of Teachers in a Democratic Society

As noted in Chapter 1, Thomas Jefferson envisioned a state-supported and locally controlled educational infrastructure whose curriculum focused on literacy, history, and mathematics; a school system that identified, selected, and trained leaders; and a nation whose education programs promoted and protected individual liberties. In other words, schools and their teachers prepared children for American citizenship and participation in a democratic society. However, in the twenty-first century, we see the role of teachers changing. They not only provide subject-area instruction to students but also offer counseling, test-taking strategies, technology education, and job training, all the while performing administrative duties, completing program evaluations, meeting teacher licensure requirements, engaging in community outreach activities, and mentoring novice teachers.

Given such a full plate, why would anyone want to become a teacher today? Some educators-to-be have always felt an affinity, a special connection, with the teaching profession as a result of personal experiences, family traditions, or a commitment to serving youth. For others, the decision to become a teacher is an uncertain one, given the other career possibilities and turns that life has to offer. Rarely do we associate entering the teaching profession with a commitment of service to a democratic nation. And yet, when we revisit the histories of past leaders both within and across borders, we can better understand their pursuit of educational opportunity, as they keep in sight humankind's inherent equality.

Perhaps you have decided to enter the profession because you enjoyed your school days. Maybe you despised those days and now are eager to "right some wrongs." Or, simply enough, you love young people and your major field of study, and as a result, the teaching profession calls to you. Whatever our reason for entering the profession, we must also consider our commitment to supporting a democracy—a democracy whose Constitution inspires us to provide equal educational opportunity for all. Through teaching, we hope to demonstrate to all of our students that they are equally valued, and thus, they must be equally taught. This done, ensuring and maintaining equal opportunity for our students in order for them to succeed remains one of the most important charges of the teaching profession.

How do we know we have achieved this goal? By empowering our students with a skill, a problem solving strategy, or a knowledge base that helps them move on to other skill levels, or actions that ultimately can enable them to help others in the future.

Who Are Today's American Teachers?

Teachers reflect an interesting profile of the American workforce. Ninety percent of the 3.5 million U.S. teachers taught in public schools in 2000 (Hussar & Gerald, 2001). Public school teachers represent 2.1 percent of the United States workforce, and yet they make up only 52.1 percent of an entire school staff that includes administrators, counselors, specialists, secretaries, and custodians (NCES, 1997).

With the increase in the K–12 student population and continued calls for smaller class sizes, the need for public school teachers will increase. Until the year 2009, projections suggest that the need for new teachers will increase each year by 4 percent (Hussar & Gerald, 2001). In addition, because 65 percent of the teachers had 10 or more years of experience, this older workforce has to be replaced by more than 200,000 new teachers by 2010 (Bradley, 2000a).

Women and Minorities in the Teaching Profession

As history demonstrates, the teaching profession consists predominantly of women, with females representing 75 percent of elementary, early childhood, and secondary education teachers (NCES, 1997). Male teachers represent the highest percentages of secondary teachers in math, science, and social studies, and women teachers dominate the elementary, language arts, and special education ranks.

Despite the fact that public school populations reflect the increasingly diverse population of the nation, the teacher workforce continues to be 85 percent white, Euro-American. African American teachers represent 7 percent of the workforce; Latina/o teachers represent 4 percent, Asian Americans represent 1 percent, and American Indians represent 0.05 percent of the teacher workforce (NEA, 2001).

It has also been estimated that whereas minority teachers make up only 12 percent of the teacher workforce, one-third of the U.S. youth of school age are members of minority groups (Archer, 2000). This underrepresentation of minorities among the ranks of teachers has tremendous ramifications for minority students. Research shows that minority educators can serve as role models, function as effective teachers, and offer distinct perspectives on the educational experience not only to students but to faculty, staff, and communities as well (Bruning, Schraw, & Ronning, 2004). The lack of minority educators in the public schools continues to be a major concern of the teaching profession today, as teacher preparation programs and school districts continue to pursue the recruitment of prospective minority teachers.

Being a teacher goes beyond providing instruction in your content-area or grade-level specialty.

From PRESERVICE to PRACTICE

Cows and a Career

Jan Miguel always wanted to be a teacher. She would soon be the first person in her Mexican American family to graduate from high school. Her parents were uncertain, however, about her college major and career choice. They were okay with the idea of her becoming an elementary school teacher after college. But Jan really wanted to major in secondary agriculture education. After all, her family ran a cattle ranch in Utah. As a youngster, Jan learned not only about Angus cows, but also how to run heavy-duty farm machinery used to plant and harvest hay. She also raised pygmy goats. Encouraged by her high school Ag teacher, Mrs. Johanssen, Jan was also active in the Future Farmers of America, where she showed and sold calves throughout her high school career. And riding horses and herding cattle in the summers were activities expected of all of her family members old enough to ride.

Nevertheless, Jan's father did not want her "majoring" in the business. He felt that ranching and agriculture were jobs for men. "Working with cows is not a career for women," he would grumble. Jan's mom, who also helped out on the ranch, disagreed. She felt that her daughter would be a great agricultural education teacher. In fact, she suggested to Jan, "Why not have Mrs. Johanssen over for dinner? Let's talk with her about what being an agriculture teacher is all about." Jan felt this was a great idea and was excited about having Mrs. Johanssen over to talk to her dad. She planned to invite her teacher the very next day.

Questions for Reflection

1. Given the traditional roles of women in education, what points do you think Mrs. Johanssen should share with Mr. Miguel?
2. In what ways could Jan, as a woman and a minority group member, contribute to an educational field historically dominated by male teachers?

The Process: Securing Licensure and Certification

The teaching profession is similar to a number of other professions, such as law and medicine, that require its practitioners to train and develop a specialized knowledge base. Historically, teaching standards have differed from state to state. To be eligible to practice, teacher must complete state and university requirements to secure a license or certification. As in such occupations as medicine, professional standards are established and must be met by those in the field. Professional teachers also collaborate, sharing ideas, decisions, and responsibility for others. Teachers are members of professional organizations that provide training, support, and opportunities for professional development, such as the National Council of Teachers of Mathematics. Other professional organizations, the American Federation of Teachers and the National Education Association, are unions that negotiate teacher salaries and health benefits, as well as lobby for the political interests of their members.

Teacher licensure and certification are based on standards established by a state government. Generally, teacher **licensure** is granted by a state agency in recognition of educators' meeting basic or minimal standards. **Certification** is granted when more rigorous teaching standards are met. Today, an increasing number of states look to the **Interstate New Teacher Assessment and Support Consortium** standards (INTASC) to formulate their teacher-licensing requirements. Superintendents of public instruction representing 17 states, as well as educational researchers, developed the INTASC standards. These standards introduce beginning teachers to essential concepts they need to be familiar with when entering the profession. These standards or principles are displayed in Figure 3.1.

Teachers are generally licensed when they complete a state-approved or accredited teacher education program and their transcripts are reviewed by the state education agency. Some states have reciprocity agreements, where teacher licenses are recognized and accepted by states other than the one where the student completed his or her teacher preparation program.

Alternative Routes to Licensure

Other forms of licensure include alternative or emergency plans. Currently, 45 out of 50 states offer alternative licensure programs wherein students may not have completed traditional teacher education programs but are required to complete teacher education courses while they teach. Generally, alternative or emergency licensure programs invite participants with other professional experiences or who have specialized skills to teach students in fields experiencing a high demand for teachers, such as math, science, and bilingual education, or in urban and rural settings. Such initiatives do not excuse participants from completing their teacher preparation coursework.

Critics of alternative licensure initiatives argue that they undermine traditional teacher preparation programs and that more teacher preparation is needed. Others contend, as did U.S. Secretary of Education Rod Paige in 2002, that teacher education programs are "broken" because of (1) inconsistencies between state licensing standards and testing and (2) questionable hiring practices (Glickman & Babyak, 2002). With 75,000 teachers receiving alternative licensure from 2000 to 2002 (Feistritzer, 2002), debate will continue about how educators will be prepared in the future while we seek ways to alleviate teacher shortages.

PRINCIPLE 1 *Concepts*

The teacher understands the central concepts, tools of inquiry, and structures of the discipline(s) he or she teaches and can create learning experiences that make these aspects of subject matter meaningful for students.

PRINCIPLE 2 *Student Learning*

The teacher understands how children learn and develop, and can provide learning opportunities that support their intellectual, social, and personal development.

PRINCIPLE 3 *Diverse Learners*

The teacher understands how students differ in their approaches to learning and creates instructional opportunities that are adapted to diverse learners.

PRINCIPLE 4 *Instructional Strategies*

The teacher understands and uses a variety of instructional strategies to encourage students' development of critical thinking, problem solving, and performance skills.

PRINCIPLE 5 *Learning Environment*

The teacher uses an understanding of individual and group motivation and behavior to create a learning environment that encourages positive social interaction, active engagement in learning, and self-motivation.

PRINCIPLE 6 *Communication*

The teacher uses knowledge of effective verbal, nonverbal, and media communication techniques to foster active inquiry, collaboration, and supportive interaction in the classroom.

PRINCIPLE 7 *Planning Instruction*

The teacher plans instruction based upon knowledge of subject matter, students, the community, and curriculum goals.

PRINCIPLE 8 *Assessment*

The teacher understands and uses formal and informal assessment strategies to evaluate and ensure the continuous intellectual, social, and physical development of the learner.

PRINCIPLE 9 *Reflection and Professional Development*

The teacher is a reflective practitioner who continually evaluates the effects of his or her instructional choices and actions on others (students, parents, and other professionals in the learning community) and who actively seeks out opportunities to grow professionally.

PRINCIPLE 10 *Partnerships*

The teacher fosters relationships with school colleagues, parents, and agencies in the larger community to support students' learning and well-being.

FIGURE **3.1**

Interstate New Teacher Assessment and Support Consortium Standards (INTASC)

Source: Interstate New Teacher Assessment and Support Consortium (INTASC) (1992), Model standards for beginning teacher licensing and development. Available at http://www.ccsso.org.

From PRESERVICE to PRACTICE

Alternative Licensure Program Model, San Juan Board of Cooperative Educational Services (BOCES), San Juan, Colorado

The Alternative Teacher Licensure Program (ATLP) is a state-approved non-traditional teacher licensure program offered by approved agencies within the state. San Juan BOCES has established a partnership with Centennial BOCES to offer this program in southwest Colorado for our member districts.

The program is a one-year on-the-job training program designed for teachers who have met the [following] program requirements.

Eligibility Requirements

You must hold a minimum of a bachelor's degree, have passed the PLACE or Praxis test for your subject area, and have a Statement of Eligibility from the Colorado Department of Education. Additionally, you must have been hired by one of our member districts in your area of eligibility.

Alternative Teacher Licensure Program Requirements

- Have full responsibility for a classroom for 1 year
- Attend a 4-day Orientation/Jump Start workshop at the San Juan BOCES
- Attend four to five evening seminars during the school year
- Complete a professional growth plan
- Show proficiency in all Performance-based Standards for Colorado Teachers
- Complete a proficient-level unit of instruction
- Receive support from a building administrator at the school site (10 hours), a building mentor (50 hours), a San Juan BOCES coach (12–14 hours), and a seminar instructor (45 hours)

Application Process

- *Step One:* Complete an application form with the Colorado Department of Education (CDE). Along with the application, and any necessary fees, you must submit an official college transcript from each college you attended.

- *Step Two:* After evaluating your transcripts, CDE will send you a letter telling you what you are qualified to teach, what additional coursework you might need, and information about the PLACE or Praxis tests that you will have to pass.
- *Step Three:* Take and pass the Praxis test for your CDE-approved content area.
- *Step Four:* CDE will issue you a document called the Statement of Eligibility.
- *Step Five:* Once approved by CDE, you must complete an application from the district to participate in the Alternative Teacher Licensure Program.
- *Step Six:* Now you are ready to apply to any participating school district for vacant positions in the approved level and subject area. Your teaching contract must be for a full-time position. According to CDE, full time is defined as at least 51 percent of the school day. More than half of your contracted time must be in your approved subject area.
- *Step Seven:* After securing a teaching position, but prior to the last working day of August, your hiring district must enroll you in Centennial BOCES Non-traditional Teacher Licensure Program. Then your support team will be established, and you will officially be on the roster for the Alternative Teacher Licensure Program.

Alternative Teacher Licensure Program

Candidates are paid a salary by the hiring district. Salary schedules vary by district. Fees for the program are the candidate's responsibility unless the hiring district has made other arrangements. Payroll deductions are available through most participating districts. District human resource offices will provide the details about the payroll deduction policy. Program fee for ATLP: $4000

Questions for Reflection

1. What are the strengths and weaknesses of this alternative teacher licensure program?
2. How do you feel it differs from earning licensure in a university program?
3. In what ways do you think such programs serve schools, students, and teachers?

Source: Adapted from San Juan Board of Cooperative Educational Services: http://www.sjbocs.org/programs_tlsalt.php.

From PRESERVICE to PRACTICE

To License or Not to License? That Is the Question

Pete was a college junior struggling to get through his teacher education program. He was a math major and looked forward to teaching middle school. He thought that teaching students at that grade level was important because so many students start to "turn off" to math at that age. He enjoyed his math methods classes at the university because there were so many new instructional strategies, technology, and hands-on manipulatives to use that could engage students better than when he was in seventh grade.

However, his student loan debt worried him. University tuition increased every semester. His folks tried to help out, but he could barely make a dent in the tuition costs. Pete was nervous about his upcoming semester of student teaching, not because of the new responsibilities and planning, but because of his university's requirement that students should not take on additional jobs beyond their student teaching assignments. He confided his

concerns to his brother James. James explained, "I have a friend, Tim, who graduated last semester with his bachelor's degree in mathematics. He didn't even take teacher education coursework at the university. After Tim graduated, he just applied for a teaching job at the local city school district. They hired him and he didn't even have a teaching license yet! He has to take education classes while he is working full-time with the district, but at least he receives a three-quarter salary and benefits. Why don't you quit your program and just apply for an alternative license?" Pete later wondered whether alternative licensure was something that he should pursue instead.

Questions for Reflection

1. With ever-changing public school needs and increasing college costs, alternative licensure is an attractive option for many recent graduates. Explain why.
2. What do you think are the positive and negative aspects of pursuing a license while maintaining a teaching position in a school?

Expectations of Teachers: Tenure and Evaluation

Securing Tenure

New teachers entering the field today may differ from those who entered the field 20 years ago. Unlike educators who entered the profession with the view that they would teach until retirement age, beginning teachers today acknowledge that they may choose to serve for a shorter period of time so that they can pursue other career interests. At the same time, teacher salaries, teacher shortages, and the rigors of the profession, with the drive toward teacher competency testing and standardized testing, add even more challenging expectations for new educators hoping to secure tenure. The term **tenure** refers to a permanent contract, generally offered after a probationary teaching period during which new teachers demonstrate their teaching skills and receive constructive evaluation. These ongoing, formative evaluations, conducted by school administrators, give new teachers feedback so that they can improve and refine their teaching techniques.

Competency Testing: The Certification Process

Moving beyond the standards established by teacher preparation programs in conjunction with state education agencies, a majority of states require new teachers to pass teacher competency tests. Before new teachers are awarded their license, they must pass competency tests, or national teacher examinations. The most common

From PRESERVICE to PRACTICE

Praxis Overview
Overview of Praxis I
What Are the Praxis I Tests? Praxis I: Pre-Professional Skills Assessments are designed to measure basic skills in reading, writing, and mathematics. The reading, writing, and mathematics assessments are available in two formats: paper-based or computer-based.

Who Takes the Tests and Why? Colleges and universities may use Praxis I: Pre-Professional Skills Assessments to evaluate individuals for entry into teacher education programs. The assessments are generally taken early in your college career.

Where Do People Take the Tests? Computer-based tests are offered by appointment through a national network of Prometric™ Testing Centers (many Prometric Testing Centers are located inside Sylvan Learning Centers) and select colleges and universities. Visit Computer-based Test Centers (http://etsis4.ets.org/tcenter/cbt_dm.cfm) for testing locations in your area.

Overview of Praxis II
What Are the Praxis II Tests? Praxis II: Subject Assessments measure knowledge of specific subjects that K–12 educators will teach, as well as general and subject-specific teaching skills and knowledge. There are Subject Assessments, Principles of Learning and Teaching (PLT) Tests, and Teaching Foundations Tests.

Who Takes the Tests and Why? Individuals entering the teaching profession take these tests as part of the teacher licensing and certification process required by many states. A number of professional associations and organizations require these tests as one criterion for professional licensing decisions.

Overview of Praxis III
What Is the Praxis III System? Praxis III: Classroom Performance Assessments make up a system for assessing the skills of beginning teachers in classroom settings. ETS developed Praxis III for use in teacher-licensing decisions made by states or local agencies empowered to license teachers. Under the guidelines that govern its use, Praxis III may not be used for the purpose of making employment decisions about teachers who are currently licensed.

This direct classroom assessment recognizes the importance of the teaching context, as well as the many diverse forms that excellent teaching can take. The Praxis III system utilizes a three-pronged method to assess the beginning teacher's performance: direct observation of classroom practice, a review of documentation prepared by the teacher, and semi-structured interviews.

Praxis III is an assessment system in that it consists of three separate, yet strongly interconnected, components. Individually, each component is designed to augment the value of the assessment. Collectively, the system is aimed at gaining a thorough understanding of the teaching skills of a beginning teacher. Overall, Praxis III provides insights into pedagogical areas in which a teacher may benefit from additional development.

- *Component 1:* Framework of knowledge and skills for a beginning teacher that assess the teaching performance across all grade levels and content areas.
- *Component 2:* Instruments used by trained assessors to collect data, analyze those data, and score the teaching performance.
- *Component 3:* Training of assessors to facilitate consistent, accurate, and fair assessments of a beginning teacher.

Who Takes the Test and Why? Beginning teachers residing and planning to teach in states that require Praxis III: Classroom Performance Assessments as part of the criteria for teacher licensing decisions have their teaching skills assessed in classroom settings, by trained assessors.

Where Do People Take It? The Praxis III Classroom Performance Assessments are completed within the classroom setting.

Testing Format: The Praxis III Classroom Performance Assessments consist of a framework of knowledge and skills for a beginning teacher that contains 19 assessment criteria in four interrelated domains.

These domains embrace the following teaching and learning experiences of the beginning teacher:
- Organizing content knowledge for student learning (planning to teach)
- Creating an environment for student learning (the classroom environment)
- Teaching for student learning (instruction)
- Teacher professionalism (professional responsibilities)

Source: Educational Testing Service: http://www.ets.org/portal/site/ets/menuitem.

tests are known as the **Praxis** series. These exams seek to measure a new teacher's professional education knowledge base and content-area knowledge. In general, the tests consist of three parts:

- The **Praxis I** test focuses on Academic Skills Assessments. This section measures teachers' basic literacy skills. The test is usually taken during the course of your teacher preparation program.

- The **Praxis II** test focuses on Subject Assessment. It examines teachers' content knowledge and is generally taken following the completion of your program. General Principles of Learning and Teaching (PLT) tests are also a part of Praxis II. These tests isolate specific grade levels of interest to beginning teachers, such as K–6, 5–9, and 7–12.

- The **Praxis III** test examines Classroom Performance Assessment. This test, fielded during the first year of teaching, uses classroom observation and instructional examples to evaluate new teachers' instructional planning, learner development, and cultural differences.

Thus INTASC teacher education standards and Praxis teacher competency tests seek to ensure a level of professionalism that emphasizes a specialized body of knowledge, specific teaching methods and skills, and performance standards for new teachers. Even so, these highly structured measures have detractors.

Critics contend that these initiatives limit the professional autonomy of teacher education programs and the teachers they train. In other words, teacher educators must also "teach to the test" by essentializing content to meet the generic criteria of a standardized test. How content is delivered to school-age children will vary depending on their needs. Meeting teacher education standards will not ensure that teacher education programs are producing effective teachers.

Teacher competency tests also have their critics. When beginning teachers pass competency exams, it does not necessarily mean that their students will achieve academically. Other factors affect learner outcomes, such as socioeconomic status, school resources, the educational attainment level of parents or guardians, and language, as well as a teacher's access to professional development. Nevertheless, standards-driven assessment of teacher preparation programs and the students they train reflects an educational reform movement that stresses accountability.

For Your CONSIDERATION

Visit the Educational Testing Service, Praxis Test website at **http://www.ets.org/portal/site/ets.** What kinds of review, test preparation, and study strategies are recommended? What suggestions are offered to reduce test anxiety?

Educational Reform's Impact on the Teaching Profession Today

The No Child Left Behind Act

In 2001, the No Child Left Behind Act (NCLB) was passed. The administration of President George W. Bush contends that greater teacher and student accountability are required to ensure that students graduate with the skills they need to enter the work force or college. This federal law also seeks to increase the quality of public school educators through educational reform. In addition to requiring annual progress on students' standardized test outcomes, states must ensure that their teachers are highly qualified (based on state-specified criteria), and paraprofessionals must pass a competency test or have completed 2 years of college.

With increased attention on teacher quality, educational reforms such as the NCLB Act also reflect an emphasis on improving teaching education programs. Thus, new teachers face more rigorous program admission standards and additional course requirements (which translate into longer teacher preparation programs), as well as competency testing. Standards for veteran teachers have also increased; as educators today must complete additional professional development coursework.

State accountability for student test outcomes means that individual states must set standards for student achievement, beginning with mathematics and reading scores. Children in grades 3–8 are now tested annually in math and reading. Students will be tested again in grades 10–12. Science testing will be field tested by 2007–2008. For states to continue to receive federal funding, states and schools are required to maintain test standards. They are to collect data that document student outcomes in terms of race, class, language, and gender classifications. When schools do not achieve their "adequate yearly progress" over the course of 2 years, students have the option to transfer to another school. After 3 years, students who attend an underperforming school can access tutoring at the expense of the district. If 4 years have passed and test outcomes have not improved, schools will face probation.

Connecting with the Cengage Learning Video Cases

Teacher Accountability: A Student Teacher's Perspective

1. Watch the Cengage Learning video case entitled "Teacher Accountability: A Student Teacher's Perspective."

2. What fears and concerns does student teacher Caitlin Hollister express about accountability? What insights from her colleagues can you take from this video and apply to your own teaching in the future? Mary Russo offers this advice as the best way to approach accountability: "Knowing the pedagogy, knowing the content, and knowing how to scaffold a lesson for students who are struggling" is the goal of a teacher. If you were to begin teaching tomorrow, would you apply Mary's advice? Why, or why not?

Student Website

NCLB and High Stakes Testing

Another reform that was initiated before the No Child Left Behind Act but whose adoption will be supported by NCLB is high stakes testing. **High stakes testing** consists of examinations that determine whether students will graduate from high school, will gain admission to specific courses of study, or will pass from one grade to another. States are now required to create and implement tests that meet NCLB standards. They must also report school performance on tests and rank them. States have the authority to take over, close, or restructure schools that are "failing."

The NCLB Act certainly has its detractors. First, critics contend that NCLB initiatives are unfunded federal mandates that are compromising state education budgets already stretched thin. Critics also argue that such educational reforms are not reforms at all. In essence, they provide only a snapshot of what students have learned, while bracketing what a teacher can and cannot deliver within the curriculum. In response to NCLB, educators must emphasize such fields as math, reading, and science. This raises concerns about neglect of content areas that reflect other cognitive domains, such as art, music, physical education, and the social sciences. Teachers also feel constrained by NCLB standards in that, in the rush to prepare students for their tests, best instructional practices and innovations may be abandoned.

The pressure associated with high stakes testing has negative effects on students and teachers alike. Teachers who are aware that they are working at underperforming schools have requested transfers, often from schools whose communities are poverty stricken and whose students are predominantly members of minority groups. There have even been cases of educators cheating and helping students with their tests (Viadero, 2000a). Teachers are very concerned about the "overidentification" of struggling schools, maintaining that adequate yearly progress standards should be decreased.

Many believe that such tests and test scores should not be the sole determinant of critical decisions about students' lives. Even though it can be argued that such educational reforms as NCLB and high stakes testing help to increase the accountability of teachers and the academic achievement of students, it can also be argued

From PRESERVICE to PRACTICE

Meeting the Challenges of NCLB

Teachers are eager to describe their experiences with the federal No Child Left Behind Act from a variety of perspectives. Sharie Stelzel of Wharton, Texas, noted how inadequate funding affects students who need bilingual/ESL (English as a second language) teachers, and Joanna Porreca, a music educator from Grove City, Ohio, reported that she and her colleagues believe the federal accountability requirements can be improved with more precision.

Ms. Stelzel, an ESL teacher and district ESL coordinator herself, said that adequate funding is needed for her district to attract and retain enough bilingual/ESL teachers to make sure "our students are not left behind." "Our district is not adequately funded to carry out all that is required," she wrote.

On the issue of accountability, Ms. Porreca, who teaches at the Westgate Alternative School in the Columbus school district, wrote, "Many of the teachers in my building feel that a more accurate picture of the improvement being made would be given with a value-added approach. The scores of each child should be tracked from one year to the next, rather than last year's fourth graders compared to this year's fourth graders."

She continued, "The children can change dramatically in their abilities from one year to the next. I personally would like to see a positive, supportive approach given to schools who are struggling to meet the expectations rather than the current punitive approach. While teacher competence is critical to success, there are many other variables involved, not the least being support from home."

Questions for Reflection

1. How do you think teachers can balance their instructional approaches to meet students' needs, while at the same time meeting NCLB standards?
2. How do you think NCLB will affect you?

Source: Members NCLB Stories: http://www.nea.org/esea/memberstories3.html.

that they serve only to discourage and disengage students, while leading to an increase in dropout rates (Amrein & Berliner, 2003). Some research results suggest that this is true of disadvantaged groups, such as African Americans and Latina/os, who historically score lower than white students on standardized tests. Specifically, educators believe that states should have autonomy when determining whether to administer tests in students' native language or in English. Special education students are also affected by NCLB testing, and their teachers argue that these students should be tested according to ability and not grade level.

Implications for Teachers

It stands to reason that educational reforms, such as NCLB and its testing measures, are important to measure teacher effectiveness and quality. However, questions remain. Do schools have the resources to implement NCLB initiatives? Are the outcomes of high stakes tests a true measure and predictor of student achievement, or are these tests merely sorting instruments to weed students out of the educational system? Are the tests fair or biased measures of student achievement, especially for those students living in poverty or learning English for the first time? It is not yet known whether these educational reforms will help close educational achievement gaps or entrench them further. Researchers and educational policymakers continue to pose these questions to the federal government.

The Function of Unions

Who represents the interests of educators as they confront these and other issues that affect their instructional effectiveness and professional satisfaction? The National Education Association (NEA), the American Federation of Teachers (AFT), and the many associations that represent specific disciplines offer conferences, committee activities, professional development and research journals to their members. However, the most recognizable are the NEA and AFT, teachers unions that negotiate or collectively bargain for the rights and interests of teachers specific to salary, health benefits, tenure, and other employment concerns.

At a school board meeting, teachers protest the lack of salary increases and the loss of health benefits.

National Education Association

The initial goal of the **National Education Association,** which was founded in 1857, was to elevate the status of the teaching profession. Today, membership comprises not only teachers but also counselors, librarians, school staff, bus drivers, and custodians. The union offers a number of services to its members, including salary negotiations, legal representation, teacher training, and research. With an estimated 2.6 million members, the NEA is a political lobby that also advocates for the professional interests of educators in Washington, DC, as well as at the state and local levels.

American Federation of Teachers

The **American Federation of Teachers** was founded in 1916. The result of a merger of 20 small teachers' unions, the AFT is currently affiliated with other labor unions, such as the American Federation of Labor–Congress of Industrial Organizations (AFL-CIO). The AFT has approximately 800,000 members and, together with the NEA, has fought hard for better working conditions, such as reductions in class size, salary increases, and health benefits for teachers and its other members. At times, the NEA and AFT positions on these issues have resulted in contentious work stoppages, walkouts, and strikes. And yet, these controversial actions have helped improve the quality of education, while at the same time serving to inform the public about the working conditions and professional concerns of the unions' members.

For Your CONSIDERATION

Visit the National Education Association website at **http://www.nea.org/index.html.** Also visit the American Federation of Teachers website at **http://www.aft.org.** Explore the resources available at both sites and the discussion of professional issues relevant to preservice and beginning teachers.

Teacher Salaries

Teacher salaries are a major concern for teachers and the unions that represent them. In fact, inadequate salaries are reported to be the main reason why teachers leave the profession (Ingersoll & Smith, 2003). The public often has a different view of teacher salaries and benefits. Some point out that teachers have excellent benefit packages that in a number of states include health, dental, and optical insurance, sick leave, and summer vacation, as well as retirement plans. Others note that teachers do not have to pursue intensive graduate studies, as do lawyers and doctors, and thus need not invest as much time and money in their professional preparation.

However, teacher salaries do not reflect the societal responsibilities that educators have, nor do they reflect the work teachers must complete after the last school bell rings. Many teachers also bear the costs for much of their professional development and continuing education.

In general, teachers' salaries have stayed relatively steady while teachers' health care costs have increased. This makes it difficult to attract and keep teachers in the profession. For example, in 2002–2003, the average teacher salary was $45,771, which represents a 3.3 percent increase from the previous year (AFT, 2003). The AFT estimates the 2003–2004 average beginning salary to be $31,704. According to the Bureau of Labor Statistics, however, while teacher salaries increased an average of 3.3 percent, the cost to teachers of their health insurance jumped, on average, a whopping 13 percent (U.S. Department of Labor, 2004). See Tables 3.1 and 3.2 for average salaries by state and by region.

In 2004–2005, District of Columbia had the country's highest average teacher salary, at $58,456. Other top-paying states included California, $57,876; Connecticut, $57,737; and Michigan, $56,973.In 2004–2005, South Dakota had the lowest average salary, at $34,040. Other low-paying states were Mississippi, $36,590; North Dakota, $36,695; and Oklahoma, $37,879.

For beginning teachers, Alaska had the highest average beginning salary in 2003–2004, at $40,027. Other high-paying states included New York, $36,400; and California, $35,135. In 2003–2004, Montana had the lowest average beginning salary, at $24,032. Maine followed at $25,901 and South Dakota at $25,504. The American Federation of Teachers and NEA maintain that beginning teacher salaries, in

TABLE 3.1 Average Salaries of U.S. Public School Teachers, Academic Year 2004–2005

Rank	State	Average Salary (in U.S. dollars)	Rank	State	Average Salary (in U.S. dollars)
1	District of Columbia	$58,456	27	Arizona	42,905
2	California	57,876	28	Virginia	42,768
3	Connecticut	57,737	29	South Carolina	42,189
4	Michigan	56,973	30	Idaho	42,122
5	New Jersey	56,682	31	Tennessee	42,076
6	New York	56,200	32	Florida	41,590
7	Illinois	55,421	33	Texas	41,011
8	Massachusetts	54,679	34	Kentucky	40,522
9	Rhode Island	53,473	35	Wyoming	40,497
10	Pennsylvania	53,258	36	Arkansas	40,495
11	Alaska	52,424	37	Maine	39,610
12	Maryland	52,331	38	Nebraska	39,456
13	Delaware	50,595	39	Utah	39,456
14	Ohio	48,692	40	New Mexico	39,391
15	Oregon	48,692	41	Kansas	39,345
16	Minnesota	46,906	42	Iowa	39,284
17	Indiana	46,583	43	Missouri	39,067
18	Georgia	46,526	44	Louisiana	39,022
19	Hawaii	46,149	45	Montana	38,485
20	Washington	45,718	46	West Virginia	38,360
21	Vermont	44,535	47	Alabama	38,186
22	Wisconsin	44,299	48	Oklahoma	37,879
23	Colorado	43,949	49	North Dakota	36,695
24	New Hampshire	43,941	50	Mississippi	36,590
25	Nevada	43,394	51	South Dakota	34,040
26	North Carolina	43,348			

Source: NEA Research, Estimates Database (2006).

general, are much lower than those earned by professionals in comparable fields, such as beginning accountants and engineers (2006).

What factors, then, influence where a new teacher will seek employment? Clearly, teacher salaries vary from region to region, based on a school district's property tax base, which is the main funding source for schools. Decisions regarding where to teach will be influenced by the school itself, the teaching assignment, and the colleagues a new teacher will work with. A region's cost of living will certainly have an impact on where teachers seek employment. Proximity to family and friends and opportunities for recreation can also influence the decision. Additional opportunities that increase an annual salary and can make an employment offer more attractive include teaching in a year-round school, coaching, serving as an advisor of student organizations, providing department service (such as working on curriculum development or assisting with accreditation reports), and mentoring student teachers.

TABLE 3.2 Beginning Teacher Salaries by Region, Academic Year 2003–2004

State	Average Beginning Salary (in U.S. dollars)	State	Average Beginning Salary (in U.S. dollars)
New England		**Southeast**	
Connecticut	$34,462	Georgia	35,116
Rhode Island	32,902	Virginia	32,437
Massachusetts	34,041	North Carolina	27,572
Vermont	25,819	South Carolina	27,883
New Hampshire	27,367	Florida	30,969
Maine	25,901	Tennessee	30,449
Mid-Atlantic		Kentucky	28,416
New York	36,400	Arkansas	26,129
New Jersey	37,061	West Virginia	26,692
Pennsylvania	34,140	Alabama	30,973
Delaware	34,566	Louisiana	29,655
Maryland	33,760	Mississippi	28,106
Great Lakes		**Rocky Mountains**	
Michigan	34,377	Colorado	31,296
Illinois	35,114	Idaho	25,908
Ohio	28,692	Wyoming	28,900
Indiana	29,784	Utah	26,130
Minnesota	30,772	Montana	24,032
Wisconsin	23,592	**Far West**	
Plains		California	35,135
Nebraska	28,527	Alaska	40,027
Kansas	28,530	Oregon	33,396
Iowa	26,967	Hawaii	37,615
Missouri	28,938	Washington	30,159
North Dakota	24,108	Nevada	27,942
South Dakota	25,504	U.S. average	31,704
Southwest			
Arizona	28,236		
Texas	32,741		
New Mexico	31,920		
Oklahoma	29,473		

Source: American Federation of Teachers, annual survey of state departments of education.

Some school districts offer merit pay or incentive pay for superior teaching or school performance (as demonstrated by students' test outcomes, administrator observation, or curriculum and portfolio development) or for providing instruction in underperforming schools or in high-need subjects such as math and science. On the other hand, incentive plans face criticism by educators. Some teachers find that determining who is an exemplary teacher and who is not is an extremely difficult process subject to many flaws. In essence, the competitive nature of merit pay tends to have a divisive effect among teachers. Nevertheless, such states as California continue to offer incentive pay to schools that bring about an increase in their students' standardized test scores.

PAUSE & REFLECT

Teacher salaries are often hotly debated in the public discourse. What can teachers do to better inform the public and elected officials about their needs to ensure that they can remain active and engaged members of the profession?

The Education Job Market: Projected Needs and Recruitment Strategies

Forty-five percent of federal employees are referred to today as baby boomers (born between 1946 and 1964). Baby boomers are eligible to retire in the next 5 to 10 years, and this will contribute to a marked increase in teacher turnover. The National Center for Educational Statistics (2001) estimates that 2.4 million new teachers will be needed over the next decade. Taking into account state goals for reducing class size boosts that estimate to 2.7 million teachers (NEA, 2001). Student population growth also affects the education market, and enrollment increases of 10.8 percent in elementary student populations (grades K–8) and 28.6 percent in secondary populations (grades 9–12) are projected to occur in the West through 2008 (NCES, 1998).

Fields with the most severe shortages include English as a second language (ESL), special education, math, science, and computer science. Bilingual teachers are also in demand, particularly in urban districts. Rural and urban districts often experience major teacher shortages. For example, the Los Angeles Unified School District annually faces 4,000 teacher vacancies, and New York City began the 2001 academic year with 1,000 jobs available (NEA, 2001).

Competition for licensed teachers in areas of high need has induced some districts to offer health insurance, signing bonuses, subsidized housing, and child care. Some states, such as California, Massachusetts, and South Carolina offer signing bonuses ranging from $5,000–$25,000 distributed over the course of 4 years.

The North Carolina legislature has extended to new teachers in communities experiencing high need fixed mortgage rates of 4.99 percent for 30 years and interest-free second mortgages of $5,000. Baltimore offers teachers low-cost housing and reimbursement of closing costs on the purchase of a home in the city, and Detroit offers signing bonuses, moving expenses, housing assistance, and graduate tuition to new educators. In sum, employment opportunities and incentives will continue to increase, especially for teachers committed to working in urban and rural areas and serving students and communities with the greatest needs.

Antidote to Early Burnout: New-Teacher Induction or Mentoring Programs

Retirement and increasing student populations have a major impact on teacher demand. The need for more teachers is especially critical: estimates are that 20 percent of all new teachers leave the profession within their first 3 years and as many as 50 percent resign within the first 5 years (NEA, 2001; Darling-Hammond, 1996). Beginning teachers leave the profession for many reasons, including better-paying career opportunities, dissatisfaction with the job, and district cutbacks. Subsequently, school administrators face challenges associated with teacher shortages, while, at the same time, they must maintain teacher quality (AFT, 2001).

One reason why new teachers experience professional dissatisfaction during their first year of instruction is lack of support and mentoring. Given the need for education majors to acquire thorough content-area knowledge, to develop instructional strategies, and to complete clinical experiences, student teachers have little time to develop the experience and techniques necessary for a successful first year of teaching. After all, the completion of a teacher preparation program should represent the beginning, not the end, of teacher training.

In response, both the AFT and NEA support the creation of teacher induction programs that are designed and implemented by state and local school

Math teacher Dan Mitchell transferred to a small charter school after serving for 10 years in a larger comprehensive high school. Class size was a major factor in his decision.

From PRESERVICE to PRACTICE

Why Do Teachers Leave the Profession?

There are numerous reasons why teachers leave the profession, but teachers report some reasons more frequently than others. When leavers were asked, in the 2000–2001 Teacher Follow-up Survey (NCES, 2005), to identify which of 17 factors were "very important" in their decision to leave teaching, they most commonly identified retirement (20 percent), followed by family reasons (16 percent), pregnancy/child rearing (14 percent), wanting a better salary and benefits (14 percent), and wanting to pursue a different kind of career (13 percent).

Among the factors *least* often reported as "very important" in their decision to leave were teachers' perceptions that the "school received little support from the community" and that there were too many policy changes at the school (both about 2 percent).

Besides asking teachers what factors influenced their decision to leave, the 2000–2001 Teacher Follow-up Survey asked them how satisfied they were with various features of the school they left. The five most commonly reported sources of dissatisfaction *among teachers who transferred to another school* were lack of planning time (65 percent), too heavy a workload (60 pecent), too low a salary (54 percent), problematic student behavior (53 percent), and a lack of influence over school policy (52 percent).

Among leavers, the five most commonly reported sources of dissatisfaction were a lack of planning time (60 percent), too heavy a workload (51 percent), too many students in a classroom (50 percent), too low a salary (48 percent), and problematic student behavior (44 percent). Examining the sources of dissatisfaction among out-of-field teachers (teachers teaching outside their area of expertise) who left teaching and highly qualified teachers who left teaching reveals that a greater percentage of out-of-field teachers than of highly qualified teachers reported dissatisfaction with salary (62 vs. 42 percent), whereas a greater percentage of highly qualified teachers than of out-of-field teachers reported dissatisfaction with lack of planning time (64 vs. 49 percent).

Source: National Center for Educational Statistics, Teacher Follow-up Survey, retrieved March 15, 2007, from http://nces.ed.gov/programs/coe/2005/analysis/sa09.asp.

districts. Although teacher **induction programs** differ from state to state, they generally include **mentoring,** professional development, evaluation, and opportunities for ongoing collaboration and remediation. These programs focus on meeting the unique needs and challenges new teachers face when beginning their careers.

PAUSE & REFLECT

With more states developing teacher induction or mentoring programs, what qualities and skills do you think "master teachers and mentors" require?

What are some features of successful teacher induction or mentoring programs? First, the AFT and NEA recommend that all beginning teachers participate in an induction program, including educators with emergency or alternative licensure. Second, to help promote successful early careers, a teacher induction program should run at least one to two years. Third, well-trained, carefully screened mentors should be matched with beginning teachers in both content area of instruction and grade level. For their service, mentors should receive a stipend. Fourth, participating beginning teachers and their mentors should receive release time or reduced teaching loads to collaborate and plan classroom strategies. Finally, the exchange of evaluation feedback and the reporting of related recommendations are important in every new-teacher induction program.

New-Teacher Induction Programs: Inconsistencies

The fact that less than 50 percent of the new teachers hired in the last decade participated in an induction or mentoring program may have contributed to low retention rates (AFT, 2001). However, even though teacher inductions programs hold great promise for the support and retention of new teachers, they also reflect a number of inconsistencies. Some states do not require all beginning teachers to participate. Of the 33 states that maintain induction programs, 20 exempt educators who hold emergency, alternative, or provisional licensure. This is troubling in that new teachers who have not completed a formal teacher preparation program and, in essence, are learning on the job, are not required to collaborate with more experienced mentors.

Programs also differ widely in funding, which impacts program policies, duration, and quality. Some districts may make a large financial commitment as part of their annual budgets, but some offer less costly, one- or two-week new-teacher induction workshops held at the beginning of an academic year. Such initiatives often do not have a long-term impact on beginning teachers' instructional practices. Other school districts do not provide release time or reduced loads for mentors and new teachers to collaborate, nor do they provide stipends for mentor teachers.

States also vary in their approaches to mentor selection and training. The criteria for becoming a mentor generally include three or more years of teaching experience, superior teaching evaluations, and participation in a mentor-training program. Such programs are provided by the school district; they often focus on observation strategies, peer feedback approaches, and evaluation measures.

Few states' teacher induction programs offer all five of these vital components (full participant inclusion, program length of at least one year, mentor training, release time for mentors and beginning teachers, and summative evaluation). But with increases in both student population and retirement rates, the education profession must focus on the retention of new teachers. By investing in teacher induction programs, school districts can improve teacher quality and enhance the long-term career satisfaction and commitment of its educators.

SUMMARY

Entering the teaching profession is a multilayered process that continues to evolve. The idealism and commitment that draw us into the profession are just one facet of what has become a rigorous program of preparation, field experience, competency testing, securing employment, and maintaining a satisfying career. The decisions we make about where we teach are influenced not only by our determination to serve students equitably but also by the resources and programs provided by states and school districts that help us perform our work more effectively. Teachers' interests are represented by professional organizations, such as the American Federation of Teachers and the National Education Association. With their support, collaborative teacher recruitment and induction efforts can help districts to increase the quality of their educators, while promoting the academic achievement of all students.

DISCUSSION QUESTIONS

1. In what ways do American public education and its teachers play a role in supporting the American democracy? Describe an example you have observed in a classroom.

2. What are the processes that lead to licensure and certification? What is alternative licensure and why is it necessary? Explain the pros and cons of such alternative licensure.

3. How does the No Child Left Behind Act affect teacher quality and morale? What are the possible ramifications of high stakes testing for low-performing schools?

4. What is the purpose of teachers' unions? What is the public perception of the unions as they confront such issues as low teacher salaries and shrinking medical benefits?

5. What is a teacher induction or mentoring program? Explain the goals of such incentives. Why are more and more state offices of education offering such programs for new teachers?

ACTIVITIES

1. Research the steps involved in teacher licensure in your state. Create a poster board that displays those steps. Include the features of any alternative licensure programs.

2. Interview a new teacher (one to five years in the field) and a veteran teacher. Pose the following questions: (a) What factors led you into the profession? (b) What was the process that you followed toward licensure? (c) What was your experience with new-teacher mentoring or induction programs? (d) How do accountability measures such as NCLB affect your school? (e) What is the role of the teachers' union in your school district? Compare and contrast their responses. How do these responses differ from or resemble one another?

3. Interview a teachers' union representative at a local school. Investigate the responsibilities the representative must fulfill. Why is it important for preservice and new teachers to be aware of the purpose and functions of teachers' unions? Present your findings to the class.

WEBSITES

American Federation of Teachers
http://www.aft.org
This website also addresses a number of issues that are relevant to the teaching profession and community.

Educational Testing Service, Praxis Test
http://www.ets.org/praxis
This website provides information about content-area and grade level testing for teacher licensure. The site also offers study tips and sample questions for test preparation.

National Education Association
http://www.nea.org/index.html
This website addresses a great many professional issues relevant to the teaching profession, including instructional, community, and political concerns of teachers, students, and their families.

The NEA Foundation for the Improvement of Education
http://www.neafoundation.org/publications/mentoring.htm#usefulness
This website provides information for beginning teachers about new-teacher mentoring and induction programs.

U.S. Department of Education, No Child Left Behind
http://www.ed.gov/nclb/landing.jhtml
This website provides an overview of the No Child Left Behind Act. State outcomes and program models are presented on this comprehensive site. Instructional strategies for increasing student outcomes are discussed.

REFERENCES

American Federation of Teachers. (2001, September). Beginning teacher induction: The essential bridge. *Educational Issues Policy Brief, 13*. Available online at http://www.aft.org/topics/teacher-quality/induction.htm

American Federation of Teachers. (2003). *Survey and analysis of teacher salary trends 2002*. Available online at http://www.aft.org/research/survey02/SalarySurvey02.pdf

Amrein, A., & Berliner, D. (2003). The effects of high stakes testing on student motivation and learning. *Educational Leadership, 60*(5), 32–38.

Archer, J. (2000). Competition fierce for minority teachers. *Education Week, 19*(18), 32–33.

Bradley, A. (2000a). Chicago makes deal with feds to hire foreign teachers. *Education Week, 19*(28), 3.

Bruning, R., Schraw, G., & Ronning, R. (2004). *Cognitive psychology and instruction* (3rd ed.). Upper Saddle River, NJ: Prentice-Hall.

Darling-Hammond, L., & Sclan, E. (1996). Who teachers are and why: Dilemmas of building a profession for twenty-first-century schools. In J. Sikula (Ed.), *Handbook for research on teacher education* (2nd ed., pp. 67–101). New York: Macmillan.

Feistritzer, E. (2002). Alternative routes for certifying teachers escalate to meet multiple demands. Available online at http://www.ncei.com/

Glickman, J., & Babyak, S. (2002, June 11). Paige releases report to Congress that calls for overhaul of state teacher certification systems. Available online at http://www.ed.gov/PressReleases/06-2002/06112002.html

Hussar, W., & Gerald, D. (2001). *Projections of educational statistics to 2011*. Washington, DC: U.S. Department of Education.

Ingersoll, R., & Smith, T. (2003). The wrong solution to the teacher shortage. *Educational Leadership, 60*(8), 30–33.

Interstate New Teacher Assessment and Support Consortium Standards. (1992). *Model standards for beginning teacher licensing and development*. Available online at http://www.ccsso.org

National Center for Educational Statistics. (1997). *America's teachers: Profile of a profession, 1993–1994*. Washington, DC: U.S. Department of Education.

National Center for Educational Statistics. (1998). *Digest of educational statistics*. Washington, DC: U.S. Department of Education.

National Center for Educational Statistics. (2005). *2000–2001 teacher follow-up survey*. Available online at http://nces.ed.gov/programs/coe/2005/analysis/sa09.asp

National Education Association. (2006). New teacher pay lags behind comparable professions. Available online at http://www.nea.org/pay/maps/teachermap.html

National Education Association. (2001). Fact sheet on teacher shortages. Available online at http://www.plsweb.com/resources/newsletters/hot_archives/95/teacher_shortage/

Viadero, D. (2000a). High stakes tests lead debate at researchers' gathering. *Education Week, 19*(34), 6.

CHAPTER 4

Equity and Educational Practice

FIRST PERSON

Minority Communities "Don't Care About Kids" and Other Myths

L ooking back on my own elementary educational experiences, my first memories are of Santa Barbara Avenue Elementary School and Transfiguration Catholic School in South Central Los Angeles, where I attended from kindergarten to grade 6. The playgrounds of this public school and this private school were unused sections of parking lots and concrete courtyards. My teachers were mostly white and very strict. Our classes focused on such skills as reading, writing, and mathematics and, in the case of my Catholic school, catechism. Textbooks never went home because there weren't enough, or they simply did not travel well with their frayed spines. Once we were at school, our teachers demanded that we stay quiet, listen, and read. When we weren't reading, we were told to write. Spankings happened.

These inner-city public and private schools did not have a music program or wonderful play gyms or green fields to enjoy at recess. We had tetherball poles and one chain-link backstop. Hopscotch and four-square lines were painted on gravel. At both schools, the auditorium served as lunchroom, library, nurse's office, and assembly hall.

The majority of the local community consisted of the urban, working poor. Our neighbors were African American and Latina/o families and kids. The neighborhood was neat, but the old rental houses and bungalows were accented with black security doors and windows. Everyone always seemed to be going to work or returning from work in run-down cars.

After school, we kids were expected to go home and finish our chores. I was lucky. My mom was there when I arrived, while my dad worked at the market, stacking produce. By the time I was in the fourth grade, my mom made sure we completed our homework first, chores second. My chores were to vacuum, help with the laundry, take out the trash, pick up dog poop, ride my bike to the market for groceries, or deliver cash payments to the gas and electric companies.

CHAPTER OBJECTIVES

- Readers will analyze the concept of equal opportunity and its relationship to schooling in the United States.

- Readers will consider the interrelationship among poverty, segregated communities, and segregated schools.

- Readers will understand how poverty affects public schools in regions across the United States.

- Readers will analyze the educational outcomes and graduation rates of students from low socioeconomic backgrounds and communities.

- By exploring a sociocultural approach to understanding family social networks and knowledge construction, readers will explore the funds-of-knowledge approach to parent outreach and curriculum development.

My parents did not have credit cards or a checking account because of their distrust of banks (both had experienced the Great Depression). Everything was paid for in cash—and sometimes in pennies. My best toy, my bike, was cheap, but the lock was expensive. Kids' bikes, including mine, were always getting stolen in the neighborhood. Nevertheless, we all had bikes to help out with jobs and errands (my mom did not drive, and my dad was often at work).

We had no parks or community center in our local neighborhood. We did have a free clinic, where I remember sitting for hours in the waiting room with my mom and brothers when we needed immunizations. A USC Mobile Dentist also came to our neighborhood once or twice a year. We would line up for hours to let the dental students have a crack at our mouths.

For fun, we played in the streets or in our neighbor's little backyard. The game of choice, our only choice, was kickball. There were no organized leagues of any sort, for boys or girls. We girls often had to fight for a chance to play kickball with the boys. When they wouldn't let us play, we'd find a yard with a garage to bounce a handball against, or we simply went home—to read.

Come nightfall, we stayed inside. We knew there were robberies because we'd hear our parents talking about them. Occasionally, we would see men hanging out in the alley behind our garage, drinking "tall boys" of Colt 45. Our parents instructed us to not talk to them, although they didn't explain why.

In the evenings, we did not attend social or community activities, scouts, or boys' or girls' clubs because there were none. Instead, we watched black-and-white TV shows such as *Father Knows Best* and *The Flintstones* or listened to the radio as the Dodgers played baseball. Once in a while, my mother watched a telenovella. We listened to Dad's jazz, Mom's Latin music, or my brothers' Smokey Robinson and the Doors albums. Mostly, I read books checked out from our small school library, sometimes the same ones over and over again. Or I would read the newspapers my dad brought home from work.

Some evenings were punctuated by the sounds of police helicopters and ambulances and what I thought were firecrackers, although one of my brothers would later correct me: "No, that's a gun shot." I heard them while reading my Scholastic paperback books.

But by the next morning, we were back on the streets, zooming off to school on our bikes. Our community embraced us during the day; at night, we respected the darkness. But I was not afraid, nor was I taught to be afraid, of our community.

As I reflect on growing up among our African American and Latina/o neighbors and classmates, I recall what we shared as a community. We did not have much, but everyone worked hard to have what we needed—rent money, food, clothing, and (most important) love and unity. I don't remember ever being on welfare or using food stamps.

In retrospect, I learned much from inner-city life. I learned responsibility. Among minority neighbors interconnected in a struggle, I observed people with a work ethic, people who were creative in making ends meet. Our community was proud and resilient. In fact, I did not know that people thought less of us until we left South Central L.A. and got a taste of "upward" mobility in a suburb just a few miles away.

Even though I spent my early years living in a ghetto or barrio or whatever label I would soon become familiar with, my South Central Los Angeles community gave me what it could give. Without romanticizing the struggles of living in a segregated place where there was some violence and many school resources were lacking, I would simply say that South Central L.A. life gave me a sense of community.

But today, given our increasingly competitive and technological society, is a sense of community enough? In this chapter, I explore the outcomes of poverty and segregation that communities and schools experience when cohesiveness simply cannot overcome the effects of long-term inequities. What are the ramifications of maintaining a segregated educational system that continues to sort and stratify the working poor from those who have access to a variety of educational and employment opportunities?

What Is Equal Opportunity?

What does the term **equal opportunity** mean exactly? In essence, it refers to the idea that all the people in a society have the chance to pursue any occupation or economic status they choose. This does not ensure that everyone who graduates from high school will make a million dollars as a company's chief executive officer. But it does mean that we all have an equal chance to pursue goals related to educational objectives and to compete for economic rewards—whatever our race, class, sex, language, and physical ability.

People often use the metaphor of "participating on a level playing field" when they discuss equal opportunity. To ensure that a level playing field is provided to all "players," we must extend the metaphor further. How do coaches and teachers determine which players and students step onto the field or into a college preparatory classroom? What prior training experiences do the participants bring to the field or classroom? Players and students with more refined skills are likely to have had extra training opportunities, equipment, and resources with which to prepare and practice. Other players and students who are just as potentially talented will not have had any prior training and therefore may not have developed the skills needed to play on the field or take college preparatory classes.

Who selects the coaches and teachers to make such judgments about players and students and determines what criteria or standards will be applied? What kind of training did the coaches and teachers receive, and what measures do they use to identify select players and students to advance onto the "field"? What resources were available to assist them in their own preparation?

In other words, although we may believe that the "playing field is level" and that all participants can compete, there will be players and students who are not equally prepared to compete. Inequality comes into play when families and communities do not have the economic status needed to access equal educational opportunities both in and outside of school settings. These players and students languish on the sidelines with limited access to training and sanctioned learning experiences, because they did not have the resources to hone their skills and thus fall further and further behind.

Factors that dramatically impede access to a level playing field include stereo-types about economic status and racial bias. Such assumptions suggest that certain groups have less motivation and intellectual capacity and thus are themselves solely responsible for their lack of educational achievement and economic re-sources. Often individuals are blamed or celebrated for their life's successes and failures, regardless of the quality of educational experiences they accessed. This notion of **meritocracy**—success based solely on one's own ability or on another metaphor, "pulling oneself up by the bootstraps"—ignores the fact that some schools are better funded, hire better-qualified teachers, secure more resources, and employ better leaders than other schools do.

What, then, is the responsibility of an education system that is charged with equally preparing students to pursue the educational paths and employment of their choice? Do schools actively pursue equal opportunities for their students, or do they simply reproduce the economic class distinctions evident in society today?

PAUSE & REFLECT

Americans often maintain that success is based exclusively on an individual's own merits. Do you agree or disagree with this position? How do a community and its institutions affect and contribute to the success of individuals in a society?

Poverty, Segregated Communities, and Segregated Schools

To live in poverty means different things to different people. The U.S. government has identified a poverty threshold, or baseline, that is the lowest annual income a family needs to meet its most basic needs. According to a 2002 U.S. Bureau of the Census report, the 2001 **poverty threshold** for a family of four was $18,267. The report adds that compared to other developed countries, the United States has the highest child pov-erty rates, with estimates ranging from 17 to 22 percent.

Poverty and Minority Students

Poverty is more evident among U.S. minority students (see Table 4.1) and among families with a single mother as head of the house-hold than it is among white students. African American students living in households headed by women increased from 38 percent to 54 percent from 1973 to 1994. During the same period, among Latinos, the percentage of single mothers who headed households nearly doubled from 20 percent to 39 percent (Hauser, Simmons, & Pager, 2004).

Equally important is the economic segre-gation of communities, which affects the ex-tent to which school systems can provide equal educational opportunities, particularly for black and Latina/o students whose schools

TABLE 4.1   Percent Poor in Schools Attended by K–12 Students, by Race and Year

	Percent Poor*				
	Whites	**Blacks**	**Latinos**	**Asians**	**Native Americans**
1996-1997	19	43	46	29	31
1998-1999	20	39	44	26	35
2000-2001	19	45	44	26	31
2002-2003	23	49	48	27	39

*These numbers include both students eligible for and students receiving free and reduced price lunch.

Source: NCES Common Care of Data.

reflect that segregation. Public school populations are now 41 percent minority students, and most of these minority students attend schools in which they are the *majority*. Because of high poverty levels, limited employment, inaccessible housing, as well as homelessness, the poor are excluded from living in middle-class communities and attending school with middle-class students. As a result, many poor, minority children live and attend schools isolated from middle-class, Euro-American communities (Orfield & Lee, 2005). Conversely, many whites have little, if any experience living in diverse, less affluent communities.

Poverty in Inner Cities

This is not to say that predominantly African American or Latina/o communities are inferior and maintain inferior schools. Nor are all-white communities and schools superior. After all, school segregation by race is only one form of separatism. Economic

From PRESERVICE to PRACTICE

Advocate for Educational Equity: Jonathan Kozol

In the passion of the civil rights campaigns of 1964 and 1965, activist, writer, and educator Jonathan Kozol moved from Harvard Square in Cambridge, Massachusetts, into a poor neighborhood of Boston and became a fourth-grade public school teacher. For over 30 years he has written about education and social justice in the United States.

Death at an Early Age, published in 1967, chronicles

Jonathan Kozol.

Kozol's first year as a teacher and received the 1968 National Book Award. His other works include *Rachel and Her Children*, which received the Robert F. Kennedy Book Award for 1989, and *Savage Inequalities* (1991), which won the New England Book Award.

In his 2000 work *Ordinary Resurrections*, Kozol remains a fierce defender of public schools, a critic of the school voucher movement, and a supporter of teachers. He challenges the educational inequalities that persist in the United States and critiques the apartheid that he feels prevails in New York, where African American and Latina/o children live in environmentally unhealthful communities and where the air is so poor that they experience the highest rate of pediatric asthma in America. These stories are presented in the children's words, not in the language of the Harvard-educated Kozol.

Kozol extends these arguments in his next book, *The Shame of the Nation: The Restoration of Apartheid Schooling in America*, where he continues to challenge the funding inequities that persist between inner-city and suburban schools (2005).

Questions for Reflection

1. Do you agree with Kozol's stance on education today? Why or why not?
2. Do you believe apartheid schooling is indeed evident in the United States, as Kozol suggests? How can communities respond to inequities present in today's public schools?
3. Why do you think that Kozol is opposed to school vouchers? Do you agree or disagree? Explain your position.

Source: International Creative Management. Available online at http://www.icmtalent.com/lect/jprofiles/50046.html.

class, as well as locale, segregates schools. However, since the 1970s and "white flight" (the shift of white families out of metropolitan centers and into suburbs), large populations of African American and Latina/o students remain in central cities.

These communities face a number of overwhelming challenges that are not easily overcome, such as dilapidated housing, inadequate social services and health care, and job shortages (Karnasiewicz, 2005; Rothstein, 2004). In addition to poverty, inner-city students must confront poor health care and nutrition, crime and gang violence, and defeatist beliefs that can demoralize anyone caught in the cycle of poverty. Low-income white families must also send their children to schools severely damaged by economically segregated communities, thus debunking the myth that segregation is only a racial issue.

Regional Diversity in Public Schools

Shifts in immigration have transformed U.S. schools beyond almost anyone's expectations. Since the 1970s, African American student populations have grown slowly, while Latina/o and Asian populations have increased rapidly, with Euro-American enrollments, in proportion to the total, having declined. As illustrated in Table 4.2, enrollment statistics for the 2002–2003 school year show the diverse nature of U.S. public schools; Latinos are the largest minority group at 18 percent, and African Americans follow at 17 percent. These two groups now represent one-third of the total public school population.

The country's the two most populous regions, the West and the South, teach a combined 54 percent of the nation's public school students. Thirty percent of African American and Latina/o students live in the western and southern states. Also, Asian/Pacific Islanders now outnumber African American students in the West. In the Northeast, African American students represent 16 percent of the student population,

TABLE 4.2   Racial Composition of U.S. Public Schools by Region, 2002–2003

Region	Total Enrollment	White	Black	Latina/o	Asian	Native American
West	11,086,700	48	7	35	8	2
Border	3,518,342	70	21	4	2	3
Midwest	9,850,818	75	15	7	3	1
South	13,880,097	51	27	19	2	0
Northeast	8,296,140	66	16	13	5	0
Alaska	134,364	59	5	4	6	26
Hawaii	183,829	20	2	5	72	1
Bureau of Indian Affairs	46,126	0	0	0	0	100
U.S. total	46,996,416	59	17	18	4	1

Note: Definition of the regions: **South:** Alabama, Arkansas, Florida, Georgia, Louisiana, Mississippi, North Carolina, South Carolina, Tennessee, Texas, and Virginia; **Border:** Delaware, Kentucky, Maryland, Missouri, Oklahoma, and West Virginia; **Northeast:** Connecticut, Maine, Massachusetts, New Hampshire, New Jersey, New York, Pennsylvania, Rhode Island, and Vermont; **Midwest:** Illinois, Indiana, Iowa, Kansas, Michigan, Minnesota, Nebraska, North Dakota, Ohio, South Dakota, and Wisconsin; **West:** Arizona, California, Colorado, Montana, Nevada, New Mexico, Oregon, Utah, Washington, and Wyoming. Note: Hawaii and Alaska, which have very distinctive populations are treated separately and the District of Columbia is treated as a city rather than a state.

Sources: NCES Common Core of Data (2002–2003); Orfield & Lee (2005).

although growth in the Latina/o student population, at 13 percent, continued to increase in 2002–2003.

In the West, South, and Northeast, public school students are more likely to attend culturally diverse, biracial schools than are students in midwestern states, where Euro-American, white students represent 70 percent of the public school population (Orfield & Lee, 2005). Given these ongoing trends, with concentrations of Latinos in the West and of African Americans in the South (and with Latina/o populations increasing in such states as Georgia and North Carolina), what remains constant is the need to provide equitable education and resources to our increasingly diverse, yet economically segregated, communities nationwide.

For Your CONSIDERATION

Visit the Harvard University, Civil Rights website at
http://www.civilrightsproject.harvard.edu/research/deseg/deseg05.php.
Read Gary Orfield and Chungmei Lee's argument that school segregation still matters in light of ongoing poverty, educational inequities, and the No Child Left Behind Act.

As noted in Table 4.3, African American and Latina/o students make up 80 percent of the student population in schools that serve neighborhoods where extreme poverty exists; 90 to 100 percent of the students in such schools were identified as poor in 2002–2003 (NCES, 2003). In the Midwest, Northeast, and South, African Americans represent 50 to over 60 percent of the students who attend the public schools affected by poverty. As for the West, Latina/o students account for 76 percent of the student population who attend extreme-poverty schools. This information helps explain why

TABLE 4.3 Racial Composition of Extreme-Poverty Schools by Region, 2002–2003 (percentage of students in schools with 90 to 100 percent poor students)

Region	White	Black	Latina/o	Asian	Native American	Total
West	7	9	76	6	2	100
Border	66	27	5	1	2.2	100
Midwest	13	54	30	2	2	100
South	7	62	31	1	0.2	100
Northeast	9	55	34	2	0.3	100
Racial composition of extreme-poverty schools	16	39	41	2	1	100

Note: Definition of the regions: **South:** Alabama, Arkansas, Florida, Georgia, Louisiana, Mississippi, North Carolina, South Carolina, Tennessee, Texas, and Virginia; **Border:** Delaware, Kentucky, Maryland, Missouri, Oklahoma, and West Virginia; **Northeast:** Connecticut, Maine, Massachusetts, New Hampshire, New Jersey, New York, Pennsylvania, Rhode Island, and Vermont; **Midwest:** Illinois, Indiana, Iowa, Kansas, Michigan, Minnesota, Nebraska, North Dakota, Ohio, South Dakota, and Wisconsin; **West:** Arizona, California, Colorado, Montana, Nevada, New Mexico, Oregon, Utah, Washington, and Wyoming. *Note:* Hawaii and Alaska, which have very distinctive populations, are treated separately, and the District of Columbia is treated as a city rather than as a state.

Sources: NCES Common Core of Data (2002–2003); Orfield & Lee (2005).

Middle-school students enjoy a quick lunch before their next class.

issues arising from poverty are often associated with minority populations as they experience numerous economic challenges related to the regions where they live and the schools they attend.

Low-Income Status and Free Lunch

Across the nation, another measure of a family's low-income status is the percentage of students eligible for **free or reduced-price lunch** at school. In 2003, 40 percent of U.S. fourth graders were eligible for the program, including 70 percent of African American students, 71 percent of Latina/o students, and 23 percent of white students (NCES, 2003).

In essence, as the proportion of minority students (African Americans and Latinos) increases, so does the proportion of

From PRESERVICE to PRACTICE

Where Should I Teach?

As soon as senior Devin McNabb finished his student teaching assignment and physical education degree, he was thrilled to be graduating from college. "Sure, college was fun, but I'm ready to get a job. I need to make some money. Plus, I want to be a football coach," he told his fellow classmates. But his friends also wanted to know where Devin would apply for a job.

"Well, I want to go back to Shoshoni, Wyoming, where I grew up. It's a small, rural town, but it's in the country, not far from national parks. There are a few schools there, a few businesses, and not much else. But most of my family still lives there," Devin explained.

Devin later found out that it would be tough to get a job back in his hometown. He wanted to coach football. In fact, his old high school coach was still there, and it did not look like he was planning to retire soon. To make matters worse, Devin found out from his uncle, who worked at the local school district, that there were no secondary physical education jobs openings for the fall semester. His uncle added, "You could move back anyway and substitute teach and do some ranch-hand work until something opens up in the school district."

Devin was devastated. No way did he want to substitute teach. He had his heart set on moving back to the country and coaching. He grew weary of listening to his education professors spewing data about poor, inner-city

schools with large minority populations. There were no minority students at his high school. There were only a handful of English language learners where he student taught. Devin felt uncomfortable with the idea of working in a big city with people he knew very little about, except from TV and a multicultural education class he had taken in college.

Devin's college would soon be offering a job fair for teachers. There would be representatives from a number of school districts across the nation. His friend Lindsay asked if he would like to attend the job fair with her. She was eager to meet district representatives from Las Vegas. She explained to Devin, "I got on the Internet and looked up school districts in Las Vegas. Did you know that some districts offer beginning teachers close to $40,000 in salary?"

"That beats the beginning salary back home by at least $10,000," Devin admitted, but he still had his heart set on Wyoming. Lindsay argued, "But the needs are in the big cities. The students need us there."

Questions for Reflection

1. What do you think Devin should do?
2. Given the diverse opportunities and challenges associated with the teaching profession, what factors should new teachers consider as they apply for their first teaching positions?

students eligible for free or reduced-price school lunch. According to a 2003 survey by the National Center for Educational Statistics, 47 percent of African American and 51 percent of Latina/o students attended high-poverty schools, with more than 75 percent of the students eligible for the lunch program. By contrast, only 5 percent of Euro-American students attended high-poverty schools.

School location also is a factor when identifying student poverty rates. In 2003, minority fourth graders were more likely than Euro-American fourth graders to be eligible for free or reduced-price lunch in schools located in urban, rural, and inner-city (or center-city) areas. Within these school settings, the NCES study also found that minority students were more likely than Euro-American students to be enrolled in high-poverty schools with large concentrations of other African American and Latina/o students. For example, 61 percent of African American and 64 percent of Latina/o students attended the highest-poverty urban schools, compared to 12 percent of Euro-American students. At the same time, 38 percent of African American and 39 percent of Latina/o fourth graders attended schools in which 90 percent of the students were members of minority groups (NCES, 2003).

Social and Educational Outcomes of Desegregation

The desegregation of the public schools during the 1960s was driven by law to enable minority students, particularly African American and Latina/o students, to attend middle-class schools with access to better resources, improved programming, and highly qualified teachers. Students were bused from their community schools in high-poverty areas in hopes that they would have equal educational opportunities to compete with their white peers.

Over time, research concerning desegregated schools has established that social and educational outcomes have been positive. Findings show that with increased ethnic and racial exposure, the cycle of lifelong segregation in communities and schools can be interrupted, if not broken. Such exposure empowers students' social, as well as cognitive, development as they become more familiar and comfortable living and working with diverse groups, and especially as they challenge the perpetuation of racism within insulated communities and schools (Orfield & Lee, 2005; Kurlaender & Yun, 2001; Wells & Crain, 1994).

Research highlighting the benefits of desegregated schools can also be found in the context of higher education, as illustrated in the study of affirmative action. For example, in *Grutter v. Bollinger*, 539 U.S. 306 (2003), the U.S. Supreme Court ruled in support of affirmative action, and the majority opinion expressed the conviction that all students benefit from the knowledge gained from cross-cultural interactions. According to expert testimony and reports presented in the trial, this evidence established that a diverse student population advances learning and helps prepare all students to take part in a diverse society and workforce (Chang, Witt, Jones, & Hakuta, 2003).

A 2004 review of the desegregation research by Willis Hawley of the University of Maryland (in Orfield & Lee, 2005, p. 42) also reported the following:

- African American and Hispanic students learn somewhat more in schools that are majority white than in schools that are predominantly nonwhite. This appears to be particularly the case for higher-ability African American students.

- The earlier students experience desegregated learning environments, the greater the positive impact on their achievement.

- The integration of schools that remain majority white appears to have no negative effect on white students. However, white students in predominantly nonwhite schools may achieve at lower levels than students from similar socioeconomic backgrounds who attend majority white schools.

What this and other research reveals is that given the economic inequities that affect communities and their schools, segregation will only continue to exacerbate the discrepancies between the educational access, opportunities, and the economic outcomes of students living in poverty and those of students who are middle-class.

PAUSE & REFLECT

In what way has desegregation helped close the achievement gap between minority and mainstream students? Given your own educational experiences, do you believe that desegregated schools can help improve cross-cultural relationships? How so?

Intersections Between Educational Practice and Socioeconomic Status

Ironically, some educational policies, practices, and programs that are useful and effective for teachers and for students preparing to go to college may simultaneously limit access to equal educational opportunities for disadvantaged students. For example, ability grouping, ineffective counseling, unwarranted teacher expectations, and tracking can have a negative effect on some students' academic achievement and on their graduation and college attendance rates. A continuing challenge for schools is to resolve this dilemma, which, like widely divergent funding for school expenditures in different communities, is an outgrowth of differences in socioeconomic status.

Ability Grouping and Tracking of Students

The term **ability grouping** refers to the practice of sorting elementary or secondary students on the basis of their skills into specific groups within a class. **Tracking** is the sorting of secondary students into specific academic curricula, such as vocational, college preparatory, and general education programs. Students are identified and assessed for such placements via standardized tests and teachers' informal assessments, such as ongoing observations and skill demonstrations.

Research shows that as early as the 1920s, there is a correlation or relationship between family income and the levels, or tracks, into which students are grouped in school (Oakes, 1985). In other words, students placed in high-ability groups or in a college preparatory track often have families with high incomes. Students whose families have low incomes are generally tracked in vocational or general education courses of study or in low-ability groups. Children are readily aware that their families' economic status may differ from that of their peers. Being from a different ethnic group, not having the best clothing or the "hottest" technology, or living in a section of the community that others try to avoid can all serve as identifiers of a student's economic status.

Ability grouping and tracking can have a profound effect on student self-perceptions, **teacher expectations**, and instructional design. That is, if poor students are identified as low achievers, teacher expectations regarding their performance may be lower than what they might expect from the other student populations they serve. Given these perceived deficits, how teachers design and deliver instruction to students from low socioeconomic backgrounds can affect students' academic performance and, ultimately, their life outcomes. For example, instruction may be limited to remedial work and rote learning. This kind of instruction often does not meet the goal of equal educational access and equal opportunity to achieve in school.

Placement in low-achieving groups or tracks leaves students vulnerable to the teacher perception that it is the students' *behaviors* that impede their learning, rather than the institutional and educational programming, teacher quality, and resources available to them in the school system. By contrast, college-bound students with high socioeconomic status are expected to excel in well-funded, computer-loaded schools with highly qualified teachers. Those with behavior problems are perceived as merely bored or perhaps even gifted.

Compounding this, students can be poorly counseled, on the basis of their sociocultural, economic status, into educational programs that limit equal educational opportunities and access to the curriculum. English-language learners are often tracked into ESL *and* remedial content-area classes because of their emergent English skills. However, they may possess literacy skills in their native language or in other content areas such as math and science that do not require remediation. In addition, counselors may assume that children from wealthy families should be counseled into a college-track program, whereas children from poor families must pursue vocational education programs.

Student responses to ability grouping and tracking may be life-altering. Consigned to a lower economic and educational standing than that of their peers, these students may fall victim to a **self-fulfilling prophecy;** that is, their teachers' low expectations for their educational success may convince them that they will never do well in school—and so they don't. Teachers may even subscribe to these beliefs, coming to assume that all students living in poverty have little or no interest in learning, have poor skills, and will ultimately fail in school. The curriculum and instruction that such teachers provide may reflect their low expectations. They may not advocate for these students, design rigorous and challenging lessons, or provide high-quality feedback, thus contributing to the students' sense that school is irrelevant to their lives.

Advantages of Students with a High Socioeconomic Background

Charter schools, magnet programs, and voucher-funded private schools provide additional outlets for students from high socioeconomic backgrounds to access specialized college preparatory programs. Wealthier families can help support their college-bound learners through summer school programs and workshops, tutoring, advance placement courses offered at local colleges, and college entrance exam preparation courses. Wealthier families can also purchase computers and other technologies that provide tremendous opportunities for students to develop skills critical to college and career advancement.

Economic status and educational opportunity are intertwined variables that have important ramifications for the maintenance of educational equity. Though well intended, such practices as ability grouping, tracking, and unenlightened counseling have served only to pigeonhole students and, along with unwarranted low expectations communicated by teachers, have predetermined the futures of many students before they even entered high school.

For Your CONSIDERATION

Explore the website of the Institute for Democracy, Education, and Access (IDEA) at the University of California at Los Angeles (UCLA) at **http://idea.gseis.ucla.edu.** The institute is a network of UCLA scholars and students, professionals in schools and public agencies, community advocates, and urban youth. IDEA's mission is to make high-quality public schooling and successful college participation a routine occurrence in low-income neighborhoods of color.

Dropout Rates and Their Relationship to Poverty, Segregation, and Race

Research continues to establish the interrelationships among academic outcomes, poverty, segregation, and race. Graduation rates differ among minority groups. In 2001, slightly over 50 percent of African American, Latina/o, and Native American students graduated from high school, and Asian students had the higher graduation rate at 77 percent. Euro-American students followed at 75 percent (Orfield et al., 2004).

Schools with high rates of poverty (as determined by the proportion of students receiving free and reduced-price lunches) generally have high minority student populations. And urban or central school districts with "minority majority" populations, limited economic resources, and large numbers of unqualified teachers often have the highest dropout rates. Urban high schools with high rates of poverty and large numbers of students who do not graduate have been described as "dropout factories" (Balfanz & Legters, 2004).

Despite the attention given to test-driven initiatives such as the No Child Left Behind Act, high dropout rates continue to plague both the poor and minority groups. This has tremendous ramifications for our society's future workforce and for its technological, global economy. And more important, we cannot begin to measure the trauma the dropout phenomenon inflicts on the lives of individual students and their families.

In the United States, there are 24 central or urban school districts whose responsibility is to teach more than 4.5 million students in predominantly (50 to 90 percent) minority schools (Balfanz & Legters, 2004). Many of these districts include high-poverty schools. For example, in such western cities as Dallas, El Paso, and Santa Ana, 100 percent of Latina/o students attend schools whose student population is a "minority majority." In 15 other school districts, 90 percent of Latina/o students go to schools where over 50 percent of their classmates are members of minority groups (NCES, 2003).

Within these large central and urban districts are segregated communities where more than three-quarters of minority students are enrolled in the public schools. Add to this the effects of poverty and inadequate school resources, and it comes as no surprise that schools in these districts have some of the highest dropout rates. These cities include Chicago, Los Angeles, and New York City.

In comparison, high graduation rates tend to be found in predominantly Euro-American, white suburban school districts with low rates of reduced-price or free-lunch participation. These large suburban school districts include Baltimore County

(Maryland), Ft. Bend (outside Houston, Texas), and Jordan (outside Salt Lake City, Utah). It is rare for large numbers of white students to attend predominantly minority schools, although there are a handful of exceptions, such as Dekalb County, Georgia; Long Beach, California; Northside, Texas; and Prince George's County, Maryland (NCES, 2003).

Conversely, minority students are concentrated in urban, central schools, segregated from middle- or upper-income white peers who attend suburban schools. Such communities generally have ample educational resources and can attract qualified teachers who foster a school climate that stresses academic achievement and college preparation.

From PRESERVICE to PRACTICE

Empowerment of a Dropout

Marilee Coles just completed her first year as a second-grade teacher. She and her husband Mark, also a teacher, were excited about having their first summer off. With their savings, they looked forward to turning their unfinished basement into a family room for their two small children before the next winter. Their funds for the project, however, were limited. They worried that they could not afford the bid a professional construction company submitted. With a growing family and a pressing need for more space in their two-bedroom bungalow, Marilee wondered how they could ever afford to get the job done before the next snow fell.

When Marilee mentioned her concerns to a friend at church, her friend Denise recommended that Marilee and her husband hire a young man by the name of Cesar to complete the job. But Cesar worked with a licensed contractor and could not tackle Marilee's basement until after the company's larger jobs were completed. This meant that he worked during the late afternoons and early evenings.

Cesar and his boss offered Marilee and Mark a bid that was within their budget. A contract was signed, and the work began. Cesar redesigned the basement framing, began measuring and cutting the drywall, and constructed the new walls and door frames. Marilee soon learned that Cesar was quick and accurate with his measurements and vision for design. He could multitask, and he made framing suggestions that offered the best use of space for the kids' play area and a small study. Cesar worked "clean" and efficient, never left a mess, and always explained and met the day's goals.

Marilee and Mark soon became friends with Cesar. They learned he was 19 years old and a high school dropout. They were shocked to learn this, because he was such a creative and fast thinker and was a true craftsman. They asked Cesar, "Why did you quit school?" He replied, "I was in the lower-track classes it seems like all of my life. All I remember about high school was doing worksheets and answering problems in my textbooks—and dressing and undressing for gym. We never had computers or small classes. A lot of my classes were taught by substitutes. Nobody talked to me about college. After a while, I just stopped caring about school. My folks didn't go to college either, so they were happy that I became a construction apprentice. That way, I could help them with the rent and my little brother's medical bills. What can I say? High school offered nothing to me, and I guess I had nothing to offer high school."

Marilee and Mark decided to investigate construction management classes offered at a local vocational school. And they wondered about the GED. They planned to talk with Cesar again and learn more about his aspirations. Maybe his company would help support further education for someone who was clearly one of their best employees.

Questions for Reflection

1. Why do you think Cesar lost interest in high school?
2. What stereotypes about dropouts does his experience challenge?
3. What kinds of interventions do you think teachers could utilize to better engage students like Cesar so that they wouldn't drop out?

The No Child Left Behind Act and Educational Equity

Even though it appears that the No Child Left Behind (NCLB) Act initiative seeks to improve low-achieving schools, it does not address the larger challenges facing segregated, poverty-strained communities and schools. The No Child Left Behind Act represents the current trend in the accountability movement (Orstein & Levine, 2006). Such schools are vulnerable to not meeting "adequate yearly progress" test standards and will be identified as failing. The NCLB law requires often segregated, poor, urban school districts to make greater annual progress than affluent suburban schools. Schools that do not make adequate progress must report this to the communities and face, after much scrutiny, the possible closure of the school.

In addition, although securing "highly qualified" teachers is another goal of this law, research reveals that most teachers who work in segregated, poor schools do not intend to remain in the districts for their entire careers. Consequently, NCLB may have a negative impact on the retention of teachers in districts that experience high teacher turnover (Rothstein, 2004). Federal, state, and local leaders need to explore together how best to assist segregated, low-income schools in ways that support equal opportunity and positive educational outcomes, such as examining school funding, program design, and instructional practices.

Implications for Educators

With the link firmly established between low-income communities and low-quality schools that affect the education and long-term income of students, what can educators do to break the cycle of "social reproduction"? School funding is discussed in Chapter 6, but let's examine factors that teachers should consider when making decisions about employment, school programming and practices relevant to equal opportunity, community development, and academic achievement for all learners.

Making Decisions About Employment

New teachers who research the areas where they believe they want to work are the most likely to remain committed to serving diverse communities if they decide to do so. They come prepared to seek ways to pursue academic excellence despite the obstacles of poverty and segregation (Kozol, 2005). Although such urban school districts as Los Angeles and New York City may offer relatively high salaries and incentives for new educators, without the awareness and commitment to the school and community that educational equity requires, your job effectiveness, satisfaction, and even attendance may fall short.

Dealing with Classroom Size

Class size remains an issue that has a major influence on the quality of instruction that a teacher provides. With large classes come less individual and small-group instruction, fewer opportunities to provide feedback to students, limited access to instructional materials and technology, and the need to devote much more time to instructional planning, professional development, and interaction with families. Class size is an important negotiating point for teachers and the unions that represent them.

New teachers are often invited by their administrators to admit additional students to their classrooms. Although accepting more students into a class may seem like an appropriate response, educators must reflect on the ramifications. With larger classes, are instructors able to ensure that all students will receive an equitable and effective educational experience, an experience that will not require the teacher to compromise on expectations, instructional design, and student feedback? No beginning teacher wants to challenge an administrator who seeks to balance the needs of the campuswide community, but new educators can collaborate with administrators, department chairs, and colleagues to keep class sizes from limiting the quality of education they deliver.

Strategies such as designing team-teaching programs, sharing jobs, employing paraprofessionals, and using university clinical teachers and mentoring programs can help minimize the problems associated with a high student-to-teacher ratio. After-school and summer tutoring programs (such as Upward Bound) and early intervention programs (such as Head Start) can offer educational support for students attending overcrowded, low-achieving schools.

Effects of Ability Grouping and Tracking

Instructional practices such as ability grouping and tracking often do not promote educational equity, as we noted earlier. In 1992, the NEA adopted a resolution that denounced the practice of tracking not simply because it groups students according to ability but also because it segregates students along the lines of race, class, and sex. Research shows that tracking and ability grouping have not improved the academic achievement of students with either advanced or low skills (Oakes, 1985).

Not all educators support the elimination of tracking and ability grouping. Supporters of programs for the gifted and talented argue that ability grouping makes it easier for teachers to design instruction for students who can progress quickly. Other proponents of grouping contend that because students possess different levels of academic potential and skills, instruction should be tailored to those different levels of skills and abilities. However, although educational researchers and teachers agree that students have different abilities and needs, the long-term effects of tracking and ability grouping tend to further entrench low teacher expectations and to distance many students from a rigorous, academic curriculum.

Students soon recognize when their school programs are not serving them equitably. They realize when the programs they are enrolled in are not preparing them for college or equipping them for careers of their choice. Thus, it comes as no surprise that students who are continually assigned to low-level classes develop feelings of resentment about schooling and express their defiance in unproductive ways. Or they simply stop attending school.

Bring Communities Together

It becomes imperative, then, that new teachers, who are often "saddled" with teaching low-level classes or groups, begin a dialogue with administrators, chairs, colleagues, and families about how all students can have access to the core curriculum as much as possible. Asking questions about what content objectives and teaching strategies can be used in the classroom can help better shape instructional practice. Asking the students themselves what content areas are relevant to their interests can also help teachers make the "instructional turns" needed to reexamine content integration and methods.

Working more closely with counselors, curriculum specialists, and administrators can help you begin the dialogue about closing the gaps between communities, educational opportunities, and access to resources. By exploring how school programs are delivered and to whom, educators can design policies that ensure that students will have access to a broad range of curriculum choices that introduce them to more learning and life opportunities. Even though confronting the systemic challenges inflicted by a legacy of poverty and segregation is primarily the responsibility of our political leadership, this does not absolve educators, as advocates for their students, from pursuing equal opportunity in the local community and in the classroom. Questioning longstanding practices that research shows perpetuate segregation and class stratification is one way to begin that advocacy.

PAUSE & REFLECT

What forms of tracking have you observed in the public schools? How is tracking useful for students and for classroom teachers? On the other hand, how does tracking promote unequal access to the curriculum and limit students' college and career opportunities?

Engaging Family and Community

How can teachers begin to work in a community that is segregated? Why is there a continual disconnect between educators and the families and students they serve? For that matter, why are new teachers resistant to teaching in communities that have the most needs?

One faulty assumption that troubles some educators is the idea that low-income students and their families have no intellectual interests or skills. These educators believe that low-income, minority students bring little or no knowledge to the classroom, at least not the kinds of knowledge sanctioned by the schools. This emphasis on deficits offers justification for educators to lower their expectations for students, while maintaining an uninformed and inaccurate view of low-income minority families and their children. Indeed, given these assumptions, who *would* want to teach in these communities?

Secondary students using their funds of knowledge by helping a teacher repair her car in the faculty parking lot.

Funds of Knowledge

One way to confront these damaging stereotypes is to develop an understanding of communities and families. To begin, educators can adopt an instructional philosophy that is focused on family knowledge as well as classroom knowledge. This student-centered approach can help educators understand the histories of families, which include culture, social networks, language, religion, labor, skills, and other interests and concerns.

By developing their knowledge about families, educators can arrive at a better understanding of what skills students bring to the classroom. These skills, also known as **funds of knowledge,** consist of those historically acquired and accumulated practices (skills and strategies) that are critical to a household's operation and happiness (Moll & González, 2004). Funds of knowledge can be appreciated by visiting the homes of students, interviewing family members, engaging with community members, and participating in community activities. It is critical for educators working in a segregated community to enter that community. Limiting interactions to those that take place in a classroom cannot help educators and the community to strategize how to interrupt poverty and segregation.

Ethnographic research shows us that funds of knowledge are abundant and diverse among low-income communities and families. For example, families often create social networks with other families, and as they develop social relationships, they exchange resources (Moll et al., 1992). A key characteristic of these exchanges is *reciprocity*. Vélez-Ibáñez (1988) explains that reciprocity represents an "attempt to establish a social relationship on an enduring basis. Whether symmetrical or asymmetrical, the exchange expresses and symbolizes human social interdependence" (p. 142). Each reciprocal exchange among a community of families and friends can reveal specific knowledge and skills in many arenas, including music, art, dance,

From PRESERVICE to PRACTICE

Excerpts from Martha Tenery's Home Visit: La Visita

As I got out of my Honda Accord holding a manila folder, I wanted nothing more than to be inconspicuous. Instead, I stuck out like a sore thumb: a tall, blonde-haired, blue-eyed Anglo teacher in the middle of a Mexican barrio. With permission from the school district, I had arranged an interview with the parents of one of my students.

I left school alone at 3:30 p.m., armed with an address and a map of the neighborhood for my first home visit. I had never before ventured outside the school into this neighborhood, and I was nervous. Making matters worse, I could not find my student's street and trailer, as spaces were out of numerical order. I stopped and asked, unsure which language to use in addressing community members. As I finally approached the address, a middle-aged Mexican woman in a sleeveless cotton dress pulled back a blue homemade curtain and looked out her window. Two children, my student and a younger child, took turns peeking out.

I wondered what the family would think of me and if they would be suspicious of my motives. I worried that I was imposing on their family time and wondered what to say. This meeting was simply about getting to know them better. I planned to follow up with more interviews later.

By the time I reached the house, the door was already swinging open, and the mother smiled as she invited me in. I introduced myself and consciously allowed the parents to start the conversation. Our talk flowed naturally and centered on background information, medical problems, salaries, and their personal lives. I was impressed with how openly and warmly they received me. Two men were seated in the living room, and they stood to greet me and shake my hand. We exchanged introductions, and I explained that I hoped to be a better teacher from what I learned from them.

María's father, after introducing himself, began telling me about a palace his brother had built in Cholula, just eight blocks from their house. He told María to find the *Selecciones (Reader's Digest)* magazine that featured her uncle. María went to the chest of drawers and rummaged through papers, notebooks, books from Mexico, a *Lengua Española* book, an English workbook, and all kinds of worksheets before coming across the magazine her father had requested. The feature in *Selecciones* told of a palace with fifteen rooms and several staircases built over a period of six years by a man of striking resemblance to María's father. Our conversation evolved into a discussion of other areas of interest in Puebla, tourist sites in Mexico, import and property taxes, and a description of his job. He purchases televisions, radios, stereos, appliances, and clothes—either on sale or used—in Tucson and sells them in Mexico. Consequently, he travels frequently between Mexico and Tucson [to maintain their lives together].

Questions for Reflection

1. In your preservice experiences, have you met with families of students? In what ways can you relate to Martha's experience?
2. Martha and María's father talk a lot about his life but don't talk about María as a student. Why is it important for Martha, as a teacher, to understand María's home life and family history?

language translation, culinary practices, fashion design, building renovation, automobile repair, agricultural practices, and business and finance.

Using Funds of Knowledge in the Classroom

According to Tenery (2005), several kinds of funds of knowledge lend themselves to instructional practice:

- *The strategizing household.* To maintain their own economic security, families may pool resources, divide household chores, and trade and exchange goods and services. Students therefore have responsibilities and have expectations placed on them by the community, which can also be mirrored in school leadership settings, such as in student government or classroom situations.

- *Domains of knowledge.* Low-income households often confront unstable work situations due to layoffs and unemployment. As a result, families must strategize within a community to find work or exchange labor for goods and services. Families' specific domains of knowledge, such as construction and home repair, can be developed into hands-on instructional lessons that incorporate mathematics and science.

- *Interactional patterns.* Large families, combined households, and temporary guests can result in adults cohabiting in a single residence to meet rental or mortgage expenses. Because families rely on social networks to adapt to such challenges as unemployment and child care, maintaining positive social relations is an important part of daily life. Thus, youth engage in cross-generational relationships with parents and relatives, while assisting with such household responsibilities as cooking, cleaning, child care, yard work, home repairs, and animal care. These skills can be used in instructional designs that emphasize cooperative learning, group projects and presentations, hands-on activities, and the development of leadership and peer mentoring skills informed by interactional patterns taking place at home.

- *Cultural practices.* Within the intimacy of family households, cultural traditions are evident in such forms as language, literacy practices (reading, writing, and media use), as well as cultural and religious customs. These practices affirm families' cultural identity and solidarity. Family traditions such as coming-of-age celebrations (quinceañeras) and family visits (visitas de respeto) offer a feeling of unity, tradition, and cultural maintenance (Tenery, 2005). Preserving native language, religion, and traditions helps families retain a connection to their homelands and to relatives who still reside there. Instructional strategies that integrate or introduce histories, language, and culturally relevant content to students can help engage them in learning that is pertinent to their knowledge base.

Teacher educators often highlight the importance of parent outreach and collaboration. Teachers have opportunities to work positively within communities because of their teacher preparation, knowledge, and ability to interact closely and consistently with students and their families. University researchers and community activists do not always have such long-term access.

Therefore, teachers must use these opportunities to collaborate within segregated communities by conducting home visits to explore families' funds of knowledge. As trust develops, teachers can plan instruction based on strengths found in the homes to better meet the needs of students and community.

Classroom instruction that is designed in ways that are relevant to the students' domains of knowledge, cultural practices, and interactional patterns is significant to the lives of students and can also be integrated within a school's core curriculum. By implementing a funds-of-knowledge approach to family outreach, teachers can become better informed about the many aspects of student and family life. For example, a student may be a caregiver, translator, dancer, and DJ. A parent may be a wife, mother, aunt, seamstress, Catholic, and household bookkeeper. Home and school interviews and observations can empower teachers to dispel previously held assumptions about low-income, segregated communities. By identifying students' funds of knowledge, educators can confront stereotypes regarding race, culture, and poverty within their own curriculum.

Connecting to the Cengage Learning Video Cases

Parental Involvement in the School Culture

Watch the Cengage Learning Video Case entitled "Parental Involvement in the School Culture." Elementary school parent Patricia speaks about the advantages of being involved in her child's education.

Video Case Study

According to literacy specialist Linda Schwertz, the Amigos School tries to entice parents to participate in a whole range of activities, some academic and some purely social, like a dance. Linda feels that it's the parents and students who create the culture of the school.

1. If you were to begin teaching tomorrow, how would you reach out to parents as allies in promoting their child's progress?
2. Do you agree or disagree with Linda Schwertz's approach? Explain your thinking.

Student Website

SUMMARY

This chapter discusses the challenges associated with providing equal educational opportunities for all learners. Although the ideal of equal opportunity is for all people to be able to pursue the education, occupation, or economic status that they choose, factors such as racism, poverty, and segregation have interfered with the realization of such goals. The interconnectedness of racism, poverty, and segregation also affect the educational access of minority students, many of whom live in low-income communities and attend school there. With severely limited educational resources, these schools struggle to deliver a college preparatory curriculum within programs that tend to track, or group, many students in low-level or vocational courses of study. Staffed by teachers who hold low expectations for students, these segregated schools do not offer them the benefits of programming and interactions that middle-class students experience in desegregated schools.

Strategies that new educators can consider when seeking employment in low-income, segregated school settings include researching and posing questions to administrators, department chairs, and colleagues about program design, class size, and resource access. Team teaching, job sharing, mentoring, and tutoring can help provide better instruction to students with the greatest needs. Interacting within the community using a funds-of-knowledge approach to family outreach can also help establish rapport with students, as well as inform teachers how to design instruction that capitalizes on student knowledge and affirms cultural practices.

DISCUSSION QUESTIONS

1. How has the United States responded to the need to provide equal educational opportunities to segregated communities? How do the educational experiences in low-income segregated communities differ from those available in more affluent, mainstream communities?

2. In what ways does poverty affect a community of learners? How does the No Child Left Behind Act support students' access to an equitable education? How does it constrain that access?

3. Compare and contrast regional differences in the percentage of minority students enrollment and in socioeconomic status. How do these differences affect diverse students' access to educational resources and master teachers?

4. How do educational practices such as tracking promote or detract from students' equal educational access to the curriculum and to career opportunities?

5. What are funds of knowledge? Describe an example of such "funds" that you have become aware of as a consequence of your own experiences in the community where you live. How can a funds-of-knowledge approach to parent and student outreach and curriculum development help close the achievement gap between minority and mainstream students?

ACTIVITIES

1. Read and explore the work on tracking done by Jeannie Oakes, a professor at the University of California at Los Angeles. Create a poster board that highlights her key findings and suggestions about multitracking and year-round schooling.

2. Interview two or three public school teachers. Describe their experiences with tracking. How do they differentiate the curriculum to ensure that all students have access to it? What do they see as the strengths and weaknesses of tracking?

3. Research and identify the most recent graduation rates of three states across the country. Consult the National Center for Educational Statistics website at http://nces.ed.gov. Compare and contrast your findings. Describe some of the factors that contribute to these differences.

4. With permission from a school principal and family members, conduct a funds-of-knowledge home visit with a student's family. Generate an interview and a two- or three-page report based on your findings.

WEBSITES

Harvard University Civil Rights Project
http://www.civilrightsproject.Harvard.edu
This website offers an overview of the history and legal precedents relevant to civil rights in America. The site also provides a thorough discussion and analysis of the effects of school segregation and inequities today.

National Center for Educational Statistics
http://nces.ed.gov
Readers can locate the most recent national and regional data on the socioeconomic status of minority and mainstream students. The site also provides NCLB data about poverty rates, parent and student interaction, and

language diversity and offers numerous other data sets that are relevant to education in the United States.

National Center for Research on Cultural Diversity and Second Language Learning
http://www.ncel.gwu.edu/pubs/ncrcds11/epr6.htm
This website provides an overview and strategies that are relevant to taking a funds-of-knowledge approach to family outreach, curriculum development, and instructional strategies.

Chang, M., Witt, D., Jones, J., & Hakuta, K. (2003). *Compelling interest: Examining the evidence on racial dynamics in colleges and universities.* Palo Alto: Stanford University Press.

Balfanz, R., & Legters, N. (2004). Locating the dropout crisis: Which high schools produce the nation's dropouts? In Gary Orfield (Ed.), *Dropouts in America: Confronting the graduation rate crisis.* Cambridge, MA: Harvard Education Press.

Hauser, R., Simmons, S., & Pager, D. (2004). High school dropout, race/ethnicity, and social background from the 1970s to the 1990s. In G. Orfield (Ed.), *Dropouts in America: Confronting the graduation rate crisis.* Cambridge, MA: Harvard Education Press.

Karnasiewicz, S. (2005, November). Apartheid American. *Salon.com.* Retrieved March 6, 2007, from http://dir.salon.com/story/mwt/feature/2005/09/22/kozol/index.html

Kozol, J. (2005). *The shame of the nation: The restoration of apartheid schooling in America.* New York: Crown

Kurlaender, M., & Yun, J. (2001). Is diversity a compelling educational interest? Evidence from Louisville. In Gary Orfield and Michal Kurlaender (Eds.), *Diversity challenged: Evidence on the impact of affirmative action.* Cambridge, MA: Harvard Education Publishing Group.

Moll, L., Amanti, C., Neff, D., & González, N. (1992). Funds of knowledge for teaching: A qualitative approach to connect households and classrooms. *Theory into Practice, 31*(2), 132–141.

Moll, L., & González, N. (2004). Engaging life: A funds-of-knowledge approach to multicultural education. In J. Banks & C. Banks (Eds.), *Handbook of research on multicultural education.* San Francisco: Jossey-Bass.

National Center for Educational Statistics. (2002–2003). *NCES common core of data* Washington, DC: U.S. Department of Education.

National Center for Educational Statistics. (2003). *The condition of education.* Washington, DC: U.S. Department of Education.

Oakes, J. (1985). *Keeping track: How schools structure inequality.* New Haven, CT: Yale University Press.

Orfield, G., & Lee, C. (2005). Why segregation matters: Poverty and educational inequality. Retrieved March 11, 2005, from http://www.civilrightsproject.Harvard.edu/research/deseg/deseg05.php

Orfield, G., Losen, D., Wald, J., & Swanson, C. (2004). *Losing our future: How minority youth are being left behind by the graduation rate crisis.* Cambridge, MA: Civil Rights Project at Harvard University.

Ornstein, A., & Levine, D. (2006). *Foundations of education* (9th ed.). Boston: Houghton Mifflin.

Rothstein, R. (2004). *Class and schools: Using social, economic, and educational reform to close the black-white achievement gap.* Washington, DC: Economic Policy Institute.

Tenery, M. F. (2005). La visita. In Moll, L., Amanti, C., & González, N. (Eds.), *Funds of knowledge: Theorizing practices in households and classrooms.* Mahwah, NJ: Lawrence Erlbaum.

U.S. Bureau of the Census. (2002). *Poverty in the United States.* Washington, DC: U.S. Government Printing Office.

Vélez-Ibáñez, C. G. (1988). Networks of exchange among Mexicans in the U.S. and Mexico: Local level mediating responses to national and international transformations. *Urban Anthropology, 17*(1), 27–51.

Wells, A. S., & Crain, R. L. (1994). Perpetuation theory and the long-term effects of school desegregation. *Review of Educational Research, 64,* 531–555.

3

School Structure, Finance, and Public School Law

CHAPTERS

5 School Governance and Community Ties

6 Paying the Bills: School Funding

CHAPTER 5

School Governance and Community Ties

FIRST PERSON

We Don't Care About the Politics!

As a first-year teacher, I quickly began to get into a rhythm of testing my own lessons while trying to encourage students to attend class consistently. I struggled to make core curriculum literary works, such as Dickens's *A Tale of Two Cities*, engaging to my diverse sophomore students. (It's a novel that I must admit I also found difficult to get excited about.) Nevertheless, when working with certain short stories, poetry, journalism, and music lyrics, the students and I were able to identify and share literature that was relevant to their lives, loves, culture, and other teenage concerns they wrestled with. And yes, there were the larger issues to write about that reflected their fears and feelings of uncertainty: gang membership, substance abuse, violence, and sexuality. Building student trust became a major goal of my teaching philosophy; after all, the classroom was our domain.

And yet I quickly became aware of other educational responsibilities that I previously had had no idea about. During late Friday afternoon faculty meetings, senior faculty members would debate and haggle about the latest of the edicts that I naïvely assumed originated in our principal's office. Suddenly, I would learn that the school accreditation data reports we were charged to compile and write emanated not from the principal's office but from the state office of education and national accreditation organizations. Where would I find the time to collect data and compose a report when I had 120 essays to grade each week?

Our department chair informed the faculty that our school needed to "pass" accreditation so that we would have our five-year license extended. Our board of education was concerned because another local high school had failed to meet accreditation standards during its last review period. This resulted in a probationary period, after which the accreditation process would take place again in three quick years. Our principal "warned" us that he did not

- Readers will identify the role of the federal, state, and local governments in educational policy, funding, assessment standards, and curriculum and instruction.

- Readers will understand how local control is negotiated among school boards, district offices of education, and superintendents.

- Readers will analyze the arguments that support and challenge school choice and voucher plans.

- Readers will examine the charter school movement and its relationship to desegregation of the public schools.

- By exploring a sociocultural approach to understanding family social networks and knowledge construction, readers will become familiar with the funds-of-knowledge approach to curriculum development and community outreach.

want that to happen to our school. Thus, we had to respond quickly and develop an accreditation plan to meet both regional and state standards.

"Rookie" teachers would assume the responsibility for collecting data and writing up findings relevant to their content-area and grade level accreditation standards. We would then forward our work to our co-chairs, who would synthesize the data. We would reconvene in a month to discuss revisions. Everyone was to begin work immediately, whether tenured or not.

With this initiation into the addition of unexpected responsibilities to an already overwhelming job, I began to understand that there was more to teaching than what was taking place in my own classroom. Faculty members could be heard grumbling in the faculty lounge. When would we find the time to complete these tasks? Why didn't we have more release time to work on them? What was the teachers' union doing to negotiate more release time? What were our union dues paying for anyway?

I would soon learn from my fellow faculty members about our union representatives and what their responsibilities were. I could associate the faces of our union representatives with the names printed on flyers announcing upcoming union meetings and agenda items. Upon receiving my first paycheck, I took notice of the union's automatic payroll deduction.

Although some faculty members were not always in agreement with union negotiation strategies, consensus was generally reached when class size, teaching loads, employee salary, benefits, and (surprisingly) political endorsements, were discussed. Political endorsements? I hadn't learned much about that in my teacher preparation program. It soon became apparent that candidates were eager to attend union meetings and speak about their educational agendas. We would hear what we wanted to hear as candidate after candidate were served up as guest speakers. They would promise more funding for teacher salaries, lower class sizes, and precious release time to complete school responsibilities beyond teaching our classes.

In less than two months of teaching, I found myself bombarded with union stewards lobbying for specific candidates while identifying and rejecting others for not having supported the interests of teachers and education in general. By November, contract negotiations for the upcoming academic year were at a standstill. A walkout was organized. Union members were informed of the date. Come December, there were union members in the teachers' parking lot passing out cardboard signs proclaiming, "Will teach for food!" In this, my first semester of teaching, I found myself pacing the sidewalk with many other faculty members, while my students entered the campus. I witnessed some of my veteran colleagues yelling "Scaaaaabs!" at the substitute teachers who crossed our line in order to get keys for the day's assignment. In the back of my mind, I worried about how long this strike would last and whether I would be able to afford next month's rent, car payment, and insurance.

I mentioned my fears to my department chair who walked alongside me. She argued, "Education is a business that must take care of the future of its employees. How can we best serve students if our basic needs are not met and our compensation improved? We are required to respond to national and state standards, but when we make that point, it falls on deaf ears. The only time the politicians listen to us is when we strike."

Luckily, that strike did not last long, about 10 days. Our union leaders worked the media hard, challenged political leaders to fulfill promises, and mobilized the most vocal of parents to support teachers' concerns. Perhaps it was a miracle, but I found myself back at work that December, with a small raise and a monthly release day in the next academic year.

Later in my career, I found myself teaching new educators, who would complain about reading a chapter on school governance, political issues, and union activism, "Why do we have to read this? We just want to teach our classes. We're not interested in the politics!" But that is a narrow-minded view. It's time to examine how government influences the teaching profession.

Federal Role: U.S. Department of Education and Political Contexts

Education represents a major component of American culture and also provides its labor force. The management of schools at the federal, state, and local levels is referred to as **school governance.** Historically, the federal government has played an important role in public education (see Table 5.1). Individual states, however, assume the majority of educational responsibilities. A broad interpretation of the Tenth Amendment to the U.S. Constitution allows for this state control, because educational programming is not specifically addressed in this document, and when the Constitution does not assign powers elsewhere, they are reserved to the states.

The U.S. Department of Education was established in 1867. Over time, it would also be known as the Office of Education and the Bureau of Education. In 1979, President Jimmy Carter and the U.S. Congress supported the division of what was once the Department of Health, Education and Welfare into the Department of Education and the Department of Health and Human Services. This followed education's 26 years under the auspices of the Department of Health, Education and Welfare.

The federal government's role in the development of public education is represented in a variety of forms—for example, its establishment and support of the Army, Navy and Air Force military academies. In 1862, Congress passed the Morrill Act, which set aside land for each state to fund land grant colleges of agriculture, mechanical arts, and industrial arts. The federal government also established the GI Bill, legislation that guaranteed college funding for veterans, following World War II.

In 1957, the federal government responded to the U.S. Supreme Court's 1954 *Brown v. Board of Topeka* decision by calling for the desegregation of the public

TABLE 5.1 Major Federal Educational Initiatives		
Morrill Act	1862	Land for each state to fund land grant colleges of agriculture, mechanical arts, and industrial arts
National Defense Education Act	1962	Funding for math, science, and foreign language instruction and for low-interest college loans
Elementary and Secondary Education Act	1965	Grants for K–12 school programs for children of low-income families
Education of the Handicapped Act	1975	Educational programming for students with special needs
Indian Self-Determination and Education Assistance Act	1975	Authorized the Bureau of Indian Affairs to contract out the operation of its own schools

schools. This included the funds for sending federal troops to Arkansas to ensure African American student access to Little Rock's Central High School.

Concerns about American's ability to compete with schools internationally spurred the federal government to pass the 1958 National Defense Education Act. With the passage of this act, the federal government provided funding for math, science, and foreign language instruction and established a low-interest, college student loan program. By 1965, the federal government authorized funding for the Elementary and Secondary Education Act that offers grants for K–12 school programs for children of low-income families.

In 1975, federal funds were made available for such initiatives as the Education of the Handicapped Act for the design of educational programming for students with special needs. Another initiative, the 1975 Indian Self-Determination and Education Assistance Act, supports the participation of American Indians in the development of their own educational programs. Today, the U.S. Bureau of Indian Affairs, Office of Indian Education programs, operates 195 schools in 23 states.

The federal government also supports and administers Department of Defense Schools for children in military families. In addition, the federal government finances schools in Puerto Rico and in such U.S. territories as the Virgin Islands, Guam, and Samoa.

Presently, the U.S. Department of Education continues to influence education by way of legislation, program initiatives, research, and professional development grants. For example, federal funding for education during the 2004 fiscal year reached $56 billion (U.S. Department of Education, 2004), with the largest grants supporting such initiatives as those described in Table 5.2.

TABLE 5.2   Programs Funded Through the 2004 No Child Left Behind Act

Program	Funding Amount	Description of Program
Improving Teacher Quality grants	$2.93 billion	This program is designed to improve teacher skills and increase their knowledge base to develop a highly qualified teacher workforce. Funds can be used to update teacher licensure or certification requirements, alternative certification, merit pay, tenure reform, and bonus-pay salary schedules for high-need subject areas. These grants can also support teacher mentoring programs.
Reading First state grants	$1.1 billion	These funds are intended for research-based reading instruction to meet the goal of every student having the ability to read by the end of the third grade. These grants are intended to provide professional development for teachers in the area of reading assessment, reading instruction, and reading curriculum development.
Educational technology state grants	$695.9 million	Technology training is available for states to provide instruction for teachers to help them integrate technology within the curriculum. These grants assist educators in developing technology skills to use in the classroom and in having access to technical support training. These grants also provide resources for technology software and online course development.
State assessments and enhanced assessment instruments	$390 million	Funds are available for the development of assessment instruments specific to the No Child Left Behind Act. This grant also supports the testing of students in grades 3–8. Professional development for state NCLB assessment and the development of reporting systems can also be supported with this grant.
Mathematics and science partnerships	$149.1 million	These grants promote the professional development of math and science teachers. The objective of this program is to increase the academic achievement of elementary and secondary learners in math and science.

Source: U.S. Department of Education, Grant Programs (2004), *Department of educational congressional action, fiscal year 2004.* Retrieved April 9, 2005, from http://www.ed.gov/about/overview/budget/states/index.html.

PAUSE & REFLECT

Consider how the federal government has influenced public education over the years. In what ways has education been utilized to meet the diverse, as well as the defense, needs of our increasingly complex society?

The Role of the State Board of Education and Office of Education

Society's political climate has a significant impact on education. Indeed, the agendas of the executive branch and of other political leaders shape educational policy. Politicians articulate their educational positions throughout their election campaigns. Constituents, and their votes, are won and lost on the basis of those positions. For example, President George W. Bush remains an advocate for his No Child Left Behind initiative, which focuses on high stakes testing, accountability, and school choice, despite some state resistance and criticism from the public.

How states interpret the Tenth Amendment and their perspectives on education vary. The social, political, economic, cultural, and religious climate of a state affects the educational priorities of communities within it. States may require new teachers to pass content-area exams before granting full licensure or require all educators to complete professional development coursework to renew their teaching licenses. Many states and school districts are requiring new teachers to have training to better serve English language learners.

Individual states may also mandate such initiatives as basic skills testing for secondary students prior to graduation, and they may even support a comprehensive sex education curriculum that is not limited to an abstinence-only approach. On the other hand, conservative states may have educational policies that differ considerably from those enacted in states whose community perspectives are reflected in their educational policies.

From PRESERVICE to PRACTICE

Do Medical Inaccuracies in Abstinence-Only Programs Put Youth at Risk?

In 2004, the National Education Association (NEA), the National Education Association's Health Information Network (NEA HIN), and the Sexuality Information and Education Council of the U.S. (SIECUS) released reviews of three abstinence-only-until-marriage curricula used in federally funded programs. Although the programs vary, the NEA and SIECUS reviewed curricula, they argued, that send messages of fear and shame, reinforce gender stereotypes, and spread medical misinformation regarding abstinence-only sex education to youth.

"These reviews provide an excellent portrait of the types of abstinence-only-until-marriage curricula used in programs funded by the federal government," said William Smith, vice president for public policy at SIECUS. "We hope this information will give educators, policymakers, community leaders, and parents the true picture of what our nation's young people are and, in many cases, are not learning with respect to their health," Smith continued.

SIECUS reviewed (1) WAIT (Why Am I Tempted?), (2) Why kNOw, and (3) Heritage Keepers. These curricula are taught in federally funded abstinence-only-until-marriage programs used in more than a dozen states across the nation, including Arizona, Colorado, Florida, Georgia, Maine, Missouri, Ohio, Pennsylvania, Rhode Island, South Carolina, and Tennessee. Since 2001, the programs that use these curricula have received more than $6 million. Examples of the curricula include the following:

- **Why kNOw:** "The condom has a 14% failure rate in preventing pregnancy . . . since the HIV virus is smaller than a sperm and can infect you any day of the month, the failure rate of the condom to prevent AIDS is logically much worse than its failure rate to prevent pregnancy." (*Why kNOw?*, eighth grade and high school, p. 96)

  The tradition of lifting the veil shows that "the groom [is] the only man allowed to 'uncover the bride,'" and demonstrates "her respect for him by illustrating that she [has] not allowed any other man to lay claim to her." (*Why kNOw?*, seventh grade, p. 60)

- **WAIT Training:** "Sexually speaking, it has been said that men are like microwaves and women are like crock pots. What does that mean? Generally, men get stimulated more easily than women, and women take longer to get stimulated. Men are visual responders and women respond when they feel connected and close to someone." (*WAIT Training*, p. 62)

  "While in 'theory' teen use of contraception every time sounds good, it isn't realistic to expect. Thus, a condom is actually setting a teen up for failure when we realize, as adults, that condoms won't be used 'consistently and correctly' every single time." (*WAIT Training*, p. 36)

- **Heritage Keepers:** "Males are more sight orientated whereas females are more touch orientated. This is why girls need to be careful with what they wear, because males are looking! The girl might be thinking fashion, while the boy is thinking sex. For this reason, girls have a responsibility to wear modest clothing that doesn't invite lustful thoughts." (*Heritage Keepers Student Manual*, p. 46)

New research published by the Economic and Social Research Council (ESRC) and reported in the *Washington Post* in August 2006, also reviewed studies of successful behavior change of the past 25 years. Its conclusion was that fear-based health messages are ineffective. This supports what public health experts have long known about abstinence-only-until-marriage programs; no sound study exists that shows these programs have any long-term beneficial impact on young people's sexual behavior.

In contrast, numerous studies and evaluations published in peer-reviewed literature suggest that comprehensive education about sexuality—that is, programs that teach teens about both abstinence and contraception—are an effective strategy to help young people delay their initiation of sexual intercourse. "SIECUS believes in time-tested and proven evidence that finds teaching abstinence alongside other issues, not in isolation from them, provides the best long-term outcomes for youth," said Smith.

"Curricula that instill fear and shame in young people, disparage condom use, [and] perpetuate gender stereotypes . . . have no place in any program for school-aged young people, let alone programs sanctioned by the federal government, and paid for with hard-earned tax dollars," Smith said. Since 2000, nearly $800 million federal dollars have been spent on abstinence-only-until-marriage programs, and President George W. Bush was seeking an additional $204 million in 2007 alone.

Questions for Reflection

Sexuality education is a process of acquiring information and forming attitudes, beliefs, and values about identity, relationships and intimacy. It encompasses sexual development, reproductive health, interpersonal relationships, affection, intimacy, body image, and gender roles.

1. Given the NEA and SIECUS findings, what do you think should be the federal government's role regarding sex education today?
2. What does a comprehensive school-based sexuality education curriculum include?
3. How can such a curriculum respect the diversity of values and beliefs represented in the community while augmenting the sexuality education children receive from their families?

Source: Sexuality Information and Education Council of the U.S. (2004). How medical inaccuracies, fear, and shame in federally funded abstinence-only-until-marriage programs put youth at risk. Retrieved October 16, 2006, from http://www.siecus.org/media/press/press0133.html

The **state board of education** is a governing body that oversees the operation of the state's schools and is responsible for managing its overall educational framework (see Figure 5.1). Members of a state board of education are generally lay persons who are elected or appointed by the governor. States may also have two governing educational bodies, one for grades pre-K–12 and another designated for higher education.

Essentially, the role of a state board of education is to (1) establish core curriculum standards, (2) set employee qualification and certification standards for administrators

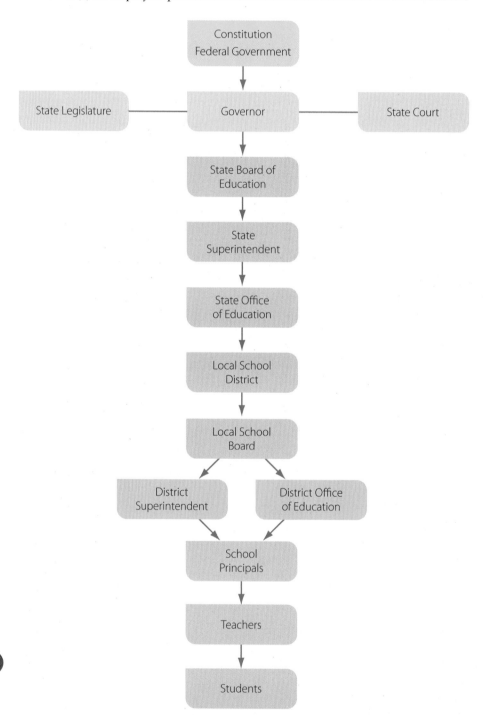

FIGURE 5.1

State Public Education Organizational Structure

and teachers, (3) issue recommendations for educational policy to such bodies as the state legislature, (4) implement federal programs and initiatives, (5) assist in the collection of school data for such purposes as accreditation, and (6) establish and maintain an equal protection and due process system for students and employees. Forty-nine states, excluding South Dakota, maintain state standards boards.

These boards also maintain an advisory committee that addresses such issues as employee dismissal. A state standards board may also conduct research, monitor compliance with federal programs, conduct hearings on state education law, develop teacher recruitment programs, and review school budgets and audit reports. A state superintendent or state board of education appoints members.

A **state office of education** is responsible for the implementation of educational policy set forth by the state board of education. Employees of the state office of education are generally professionals in the field of education. Roles within the office include a lead superintendent and assistant superintendent. These positions are also appointed by the state governor or state board of education.

Similar to the charge of the state board of education, the responsibilities of the state office of education include oversight of teacher licensing (where new teachers can apply for certification), curriculum design, textbook adoption, data collection, and general physical planning.

Local Control: School Districts, School Boards, and Departments of Education

School districts are geographic regions within a state and are charged with providing educational programming for students who reside within that region. These districts vary widely from state to state in number and size. The approximately 15,000 school districts in the United States are not equally distributed among individual states (Texas maintains at least 1,000 school districts, the state of Hawaii one).

District size also varies considerably. Consider, for example, the 2001 enrollment of the nation's largest school districts. The New York City School District and the Los Angeles Unified School District served over 1 million students each. At the same time, 48 percent of U.S. school districts enrolled fewer than 1,000 students per year. The most striking fact is that the largest school districts (those enrolling over 10,000 to 1 million students) are educating more than 50 percent of the students in the United States (NCES, 2002). These school districts represent only 4 percent of the total number of school districts in the country.

Debate continues about the relative effectiveness of large and smaller school districts. Proponents of large school districts maintain that more services can be offered. Program replication can be reduced, and unnecessary staff is not retained. On the other hand, critics argue that large districts are often bureaucratic and that access to services can be difficult and contacts impersonal as teachers and parents wade through various departments and committees for assistance. Supporters of smaller school districts contend that problems are solved more rapidly when personal and responsive support services are available.

School districts have the responsibility of interpreting and implementing curriculum content as established by the state board of education and the state office of education. They too must adhere to federal guidelines and standards, such as those noted in the No Child Left Behind Act. Individual districts also assume responsibility for the hiring and firing of their teachers.

The Role of the Local School Board

Each local school district includes a superintendent, a school board, and an administrative staff. Local **school boards** attend to such issues as school finance, district
program infrastructure, personnel decisions, curriculum content, and student issues. Local school board members are often lay persons elected to 3–4-year terms,
whose responsibility is to establish the educational policy to be implemented by the
local school district. Alternatively, the local mayors or city council may appoint
board members.

Historically, school board members have been upper-middle-class Euro-American
males at least 40 years old. In other words, they seldom represent the demographics
of their communities, particularly of low-income communities (Carr, 2003). Some
33 percent of U.S. students are members of minority groups, and this percentage will
increase in the next decade, but only 19 percent of local school board members are
minorities (U.S. Department of Education, 2003).

In its most essential role, the local school board provides oversight of school
funding. Financial matters such as proposing funding plans (such as bonds and tax
increases for school programming, busing, teacher salaries, and benefits) fall under
the auspices of the local school board. Local school boards must also address other
budget-related issues, including class size and financial resources for new technologies and textbooks. See Figure 5.2 for a sample blog from the National School Board
website.

The hiring and firing of district employees, such as support staff, custodians, and
bus drivers, as well as teachers and principals, is also a responsibility of the local
school board. Because so much of the local school board's work is associated with
district finance, employment issues are an important component of their work. The
local board is responsible for approving employment contracts offered to all personnel, including teachers.

Other duties of the local school board, together with the board of education, include defining and implementing curriculum standards. Board members may collaborate with curriculum committees made up of teachers to help refine what is
taught in the classroom and to ensure that curricula meet federal, state, and local
district standards.

The local school board also develops policies that affect students, such as standards
of conduct, attendance, and dress. Policies relevant to extracurricular activities or organizations, such as grade requirements for sports participation or the establishment
of a Gay, Lesbian, and Straight Student Alliance on school campuses are also under the
jurisdiction of the local school board.

Board**Buzz**

NSBA's daily weblog
100,000 visitors and climbing

Georgia approves bible courses statewide

A tip of the hat to our friends over at NSBA's Legal Clips, who report that the Georgia Board of Education has voted unanimously to add two courses to its list of approved courses: Literature and History of the Old Testament Era, and Literature and History of the New Testament Era. The Associated Press covers the story here.

The move follows the state legislature's passage of a bill approving the two courses. The new law allows, but does not require, the state's 180 school districts to decide whether to offer the courses. Included in AP's report is a comment by Charles Haynes of the First Amendment Center who says the Georgia policy is the nation's first to endorse and fund bible classes on a statewide level. Supporters insist the courses will steer clear of religious teaching, pointing to the legislative language that provides the courses will be taught in "an objective and nondevotional manner with no attempt made to indoctrinate students." Critics counter that while the language may pass constitutional muster, that could change in the classroom if instructors stray.

According to Maggie Garrett, legislative counsel for the Georgia chapter of the American Civil Liberties Union, the curriculum approved by the board, like the legislation itself, is vague. "They didn't put in any outlines describing what they can and can't do constitutionally," she says. "The same traps are there for teachers who decide to teach the class." She adds some teachers might seek to include their own beliefs or be pushed by students into conversations that include religious proselytizing.

More detail can be found at the Georgia Department of Education's Web site.

FIGURE 5.2

Board Buzz: The National School Board Association at Work

In what ways is the NSBA's weblog a useful tool for accessing information about a school district, especially for new teachers who are relocating and seeking employment in another state? How do you think Georgia's approval of statewide Bible courses might affect other school districts nationwide?

National School Board homepage, retrieved March 18, 2007, from http://www.nsba.org/site/index.asp.

Thus, the responsibilities of a local school board are quite broad and far-reaching. They range from replacing an aging school bus and reviewing the consequences of the student expulsion policy to hiring teachers and developing a financial plan to build a new school to meet increasing enrollments. School boards have a tremendous influence on the nation's public schools. And their job can subject them to considerable tension and pressure as they struggle to satisfy local needs, while simultaneously trying to help teachers and students meet today's accountability standards.

PAUSE & REFLECT

Local school boards have been known both to support and to resist progressive approaches to education. How have the local school boards in your community affected the educational experience of students? In what ways have they been responsive to the needs of students and teachers?

The Role of the Superintendent and Local District Office

Superintendents work closely with school board members as they develop educational policies. In essence, the **superintendent** is the chief executive officer of a school district, who is selected by the school board for an average six-year period of service. Traditionally, superintendents hold advanced practitioner degrees in education, although it is not uncommon for some states to employ superintendents whose expertise is not in education, but in such fields as business administration, management, political science, or law (Williams, 2002).

A superintendent must negotiate among a number of conflicting parties and issues. Whether representing the school board, negotiating with representatives of the teachers' union, or working with staff at the local office of education, a superintendent must address such issues as standardized testing, accountability, school finance, and school violence. Thus, it comes as no surprise that superintendents may or may not lay the groundwork for positive change within a school district and that their work is often politically charged and controversial.

Minorities are underrepresented in the superintendent ranks. Only 5 percent of superintendents represented minority groups in 2000, whereas 33 percent of the student population represented minority groups (Richard, 2000). Women are also underrepresented, making up only 13 percent of superintendents while representing 75 percent of the teacher workforce.

Supporting a superintendent as he or she implements policies established by the school board is the local or district office of education. The district office is responsible for school-wide program implementation. In addition to maintaining departments of curriculum and instruction, a district office of education helps administer standardized tests and provides evaluation services to teachers and administrators. District offices also provide support to teachers in the form of training workshops, mentoring programs, and collaborative opportunities for curriculum development.

Houston Superintendent Adriana Tamez and elementary principal Sue Ann Payne welcome an evacuee from Hurricane Katrina.

The Role of Principals

The overall operation of a school is the responsibility of the **principal**. The principal provides administrative and educational leadership to fellow administrators, faculty, staff, students, parents, and community members. It is not uncommon for schools to have more than one principal, known as assistant principals, who share responsibilities such as the oversight of curriculum and instruction, teacher selection and evaluation, organization of standardized testing procedures, student affairs, scheduling, special education, extracurricular activities, parent/community outreach, and professional development.

New principal Frank Summers previously taught secondary social studies and English as a second language.

Most important, principals help establish a positive campus climate that supports effective teaching and learning by working with teachers, students, and parents and by maintaining a presence both on campus and in the community. The principal is responsible for the day-to-day operations and maintenance of a school and its facilities. Establishing and maintaining the school budget is also a major responsibility of a principal. In addition, a principal must help coordinate the services of other educational specialists, such as nurses, school psychologists, and speech therapists.

As is true of school board members and superintendents, most principals are still male Euro-Americans, particularly in the secondary education ranks (U.S. Department of Education, 2001). Women principals outnumber their male counterparts in the elementary schools, as illustrated in Table 5.3. Over 80 percent of principals hold master's degrees, professional certificates/licenses, or doctorates.

A principal can help provide leadership to a school in ways that inspire educational excellence among students, faculty, and staff alike. Conversely, a principal may also be unresponsive to the needs of students and staff. When new teachers apply for a position in a school, it is imperative that, during the interview process, they ask questions of the principal to get a sense of her or his educational philosophy, role, and vision for the school. All teachers benefit from having principals who provide hands-on leadership relevant to classroom instruction, professional development, mentoring and feedback, rather than administrators who distance themselves from faculty, students, and the needs of a diverse community.

Finally, today's principals are assisted by a support staff. This staff can include curriculum and instructional specialists, such as bilingual educators, translators, paraprofessional teaching assistants, school counselors, psychologists, and nurses. Other staff members may include special educators, school/community liaisons, speech and hearing therapists, and office managers and clerical staff.

TABLE 5.3 Public School Principal Demographics (in percents)			
	Elementary Principals	Middle School and Junior High Principals	Secondary Principals
Gender			
Female	55.2	33.2	22.2
Male	48.8	66.8	78.8
Ethnicity			
Euro-American	80.8	83.0	85.9
African American	12.0	10.5	8.4
Latina/o	5.8	5.1	3.8
Asian American	0.7	0.7	0.9
American Indian	0.7	0.8	1.1
Other	0.6	—	0.7
Salary (over 12 months)	$73,114	$78,176	$83,944

Source: U.S. Department of Education (2001).

From PRESERVICE to PRACTICE

Principals in Transition

David Wheatly, a veteran principal, was recently asked by his district administrator to consider a transfer, in the upcoming year, to a "continuation" or "alternative" high school, Century High School, after 18 years of service at a local comprehensive high school. The continuation high school served students who either chose to attend a smaller campus or were transferred for some reason, such as truancy, fighting, substance abuse, or other challenges, such as teen pregnancy.

The current Century High principal, a former student of David's named John Saunders, was being pressured to resign by the district, after five years at the helm. But this pressure was not being exerted in response to complaints involving kids who attended the school. John was increasingly frustrated by the lack of support he received from his teaching staff. Although the teachers were good people, John was concerned by the absence of high expectations for the student body among these teachers. He was not satisfied by the basic skills curriculum the teachers dispensed to the students.

Faculty meeting after faculty meeting, John asked his staff to address how they were specifically preparing their students to attend at least a local community college. After a while, the teachers became resentful about the pressure placed on them by the principal. The teachers felt that John was out of touch with the skill and interest levels of the students. In fact, they felt they were doing a great job with this year's senior class, because the majority were indeed going to graduate from Century.

As tensions increased, the individual teachers began to complain to upper-level district administrators about John and his top-down style of leadership. Soon it became apparent that the district leadership had to respond to the situation. It was at this point that David Wheatly was approached about taking the job as Century High principal.

But David had no idea what decision to make. After all, John was not only a colleague but also a young friend whom he had mentored early in his administrative career. It was going to be a tough call.

Questions for Reflection

1. What would you do in David's situation?
2. What qualities do you think the Century High teaching staff is looking for in a principal?
3. What qualities do you think are needed for a teaching staff who works with special populations?
4. How could a compromise be reached between the priorities of the faculty and those of the administration?

School Structures, School Choices

Public school districts are arranged to meet the learning and socialization needs of children from various age groups and skill levels, ranging from prekindergarten (pre-K) to grade 12. School programs and services can be organized in a number of ways, depending on the size of the district and the needs of the students. School districts are commonly structured in a fairly conventional framework that includes pre-K, elementary schools (grades K–6), middle schools (grades 5–8) and secondary schools (junior high, grades 7 and 8 or 7–9), and high schools, grades 9–12 or 10–12), but other educational formats are available. These formats, both public and private, include alternative schools, charter schools, early childhood schools (such as Head Start), magnet schools, military academies, parochial schools, and vocational schools, as well as home schooling.

School choice programs offer parents the opportunity to select schools for their children other than those intended for students based on where they live. However, school choice in itself is often viewed as controversial because it entails the use of public funds, or, in some districts, vouchers, for private school tuition or for public school attendance outside of district boundaries.

Even though school choice programs empower some parents and students, conflicts arise when not all families have access to school choice programs for various reasons, such as a lack of information, schools with enrollment restrictions, or little or no transportation availability. In addition, teachers' unions question the financing of school choice programs (both private and public) and vouchers when public funds could instead be used to improve struggling schools and/or districts.

The 2001 No Child Left Behind Act (NCLB) also has tremendous ramifications for school choice programming. If students attending Title I public schools (those schools receiving federal funds to improve the academic achievement of low-income children) have not made adequate yearly progress (AYP) for two or more consecutive years, the NCLB Act requires these school districts to provide school choice to these low-income, low-achieving students and their families. These families can now participate in school choice interventions if they so choose.

The goal of this option is to mandate that low-achieving schools find ways to improve instruction and provide equal educational opportunities for all students. Thus, the competitive nature of school choice, supporters believe, will help improve U.S. schools overall. As a result, in addition to the NCLB Act, one-half of the states currently have laws that endorse school choice programs. Other programs have "spun off" the school choice movement, including charter and magnet schools. Whether the public endorses or opposes school choice, these programs are here to stay, giving new teachers more options in where and how they want to practice their profession.

For Your CONSIDERATION

Visit The School Tree website at **http://schooltree.org/**.
This comprehensive website offers parents and educators information about state and local school districts across the nation, including student demographics, standardized test scores, socioeconomic status, and class sizes.

Privatization of Public Schools: Charter Schools

A **charter school** is a school "custom designed" by groups or individuals contracted to do so by the school's organizers and a sponsor, such as the state or local board of education. It embodies a particular vision or field of study that reflects innovative education reforms, local control, and a less bureaucratic educational culture. The first approved charter school was established in Minnesota in 1991. States, school districts, private foundations, and individual donors fund charter schools. These independently operated schools are responsible for maintaining their own budgets and hiring their own staffs. Figure 5.3 shows the homepage of a Salt Lake City charter school, which includes information on admissions, curriculum features, and school standards and expectations.

As of 2004, charter schools exist in 40 states and are quite popular with the public, although their educational outcomes vary. Arizona maintains the most charter schools with 495, followed by California with 471 schools, Florida with 258, Texas

FIGURE **5.3**

A Sample Charter School Homepage

What educational priorities do you think are valued by parents who seek to enroll their children in the Dual Immersion Academy? What would be some of the strengths of such a charter school? What kinds of challenges might teachers face when teaching in such a school?

Dual Immersion Academy, Salt Lake City, Utah. Retrieved March 2007 at http://www.diacharter.org.

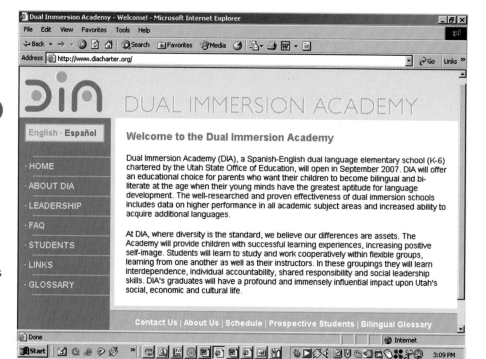

with 241, and Michigan with 210 (US Charter Schools, 2004). At the other end of the spectrum, charter schools are prohibited in the state of Kentucky.

Driven by special-interest groups, charter schools strive to offer education in a small-school setting. Unlike private schools, charter schools are subject to some state educational laws and regulations, but not all. Charter schools today focus on such fields as the arts, literacy development, technology, math and science, and classical literature, as well as on culturally relevant curricula (for example, African studies). They can also target special populations, such as exceptional learners or young mothers.

Charter schools remain attractive to some parents because of their smaller size and the subject areas in which they concentrate. Compared to public school teachers, charter school educators tend to have greater autonomy and to be more involved in curriculum development, selection of instructional materials, and decision making (Gresham, Hess, Maranto, & Millman, 2000). In addition, with smaller class sizes, charter school teachers are more willing to experiment with innovative instructional approaches.

This is not to say that all charter schools are successful. Some have been found to simply mirror traditional educational approaches while offering little, if any, innovative instruction or increase in academic achievement. Others have mismanaged their budgets and have been shut down by their contracting state and school board. Ironically, without much bureaucratic oversight, some charter schools in California and Texas have been found to employ unprepared and unlicensed teachers and have neglected to administer student achievement tests. For example, 43 percent of charter school teachers, compared to 9 percent of public school teachers, did not hold teaching credentials (Brown, 2003).

Finally, charter schools struggle to access instructional supplies and resources, despite some financial support provided by business and corporate sponsors. Thus, charter schools today cannot claim they are increasing student achievement more effectively than their public school counterparts, at least for the time being.

For Your CONSIDERATION

Visit the US Charter Schools website at **http://www.uscharterschools.org.** This website offers parents and educators information about the charter school movement across the nation. It also provides specific school and student outcome data relevant to programs across the country.

Charter, School Choice, and Voucher Initiatives: Controversial Implications

School choice initiatives, though attractive to many Americans because they offer families the opportunity to select the best educational settings for their children, also provoke much political controversy. For example, **vouchers** (based on a state's average per-pupil expenditure) utilize public funds for tuition not only in public schools but in parochial, or religious, schools as well. Raising the issue of separation between church and state, critics argue that parochial schools are the greatest beneficiaries of voucher programs, given that 80 percent of the nation's private schools are affiliated with a religion (Brimley & Garfield, 2002). Critics also argue that such plans result in segregated schools, where low-income districts do not benefit from vouchers. Instead, state funds make their way to private schools—schools whose students have already been attending private schools and whose vouchers now subsidize their tuition.

On the other hand, supporters of voucher plans contend that their tax dollars already finance public education, so why should they be expected to pay their own tuition to a private school? The U.S. Supreme Court appears to agree with supporters. The Court found, in 2002, that parents themselves receive vouchers, not the parochial school directly. Thus, by a narrow margin (5 to 4), the Court did not find the Cleveland, Ohio, voucher plan in violation of separation of church and state. Other supporters note that public schools are already segregated. They contend that when school choice and voucher plans are designed and financed carefully— for example, through public magnet schools that emphasize specific content areas, such as math and science/medicine, the arts, or bilingual education—the numbers of students being educated in segregated classrooms decrease (Greene, 2000).

Whether voucher plans or school choice programs increase the academic achievement of diverse learners remains uncertain. Programs that work for some populations are not necessarily generalizable to another population, which may experience smaller academic gains (NEA, 2002). The NCLB Act also has ramifications for school choice plans serving low-income, low-achieving schools, whose insufficient adequate yearly progress may result in thousands of minority students qualifying for school vouchers.

But where would these students attend school? School choice, charter schools, and voucher plans are not necessarily a panacea for low-income school districts. After all, students with "choices-in-hand" would probably have to compete for enrollment in higher-achieving schools. These schools, whether public or private, can limit enrollment and impose admission requirements that inhibit the access of low-achieving students from families with limited resources, to say nothing of transportation problems.

Consequently, it seems unlikely that the majority of low-income, low-achieving students could take full advantage of school choice programs, charter schools, or voucher plans. Furthermore, these initiatives can actually be responsible for ongoing school segregation, because low-achieving schools, with high minority student enrollment, may be unable to compete against richer, smaller, and more selective schools.

Charter schools can also foster school segregation on the basis of race and ethnicity. Depending on community demographics, religious and cultural ties, and rigorous admission standards or specific curriculum focus, it is not uncommon for charter schools to be predominantly Euro-American or Latina/o or African American. Nevertheless, in a 1997 poll called The Public's Attitude Toward Public Schools, it was reported that African Americans supported voucher plans because of their dissatisfaction with the funding of public schools.

School choice plans continue to elicit conflicting opinions from politicians, professional educators, and families. Inequities continue to emerge, as school choice plans often do not address special education students, whose educational expenses generally exceed the average per-pupil expenditure. It is unlikely that exceptional students would have equal opportunity to attend a charter school or private school simply by utilizing their state-issued voucher. Therefore, opinion on school choice and voucher plans varies from utter disdain on the part of teachers unions and voters in such states as California and Michigan to enthusiasm in some other states, such as Texas and Louisiana, which continue to introduce (through their legislatures) voucher plans intended for low-income students who attend low-achieving school districts.

PAUSE & REFLECT

Why is there resistance to school voucher plans among public school educators? Why are voucher plans attractive to some minority groups who feel they do not have equal educational access in public school settings? And yet, how do voucher plans widen the achievement gap among minority populations?

The Home School Movement

Families who choose to educate children in their homes are participating in an educational movement known as **home schooling.** In contemporary times, home schooling is often associated with fundamentalist Christian families who feel that their values, interests, and skills are presented more effectively by those who hold similar perspectives. However, some families choose to home-school their children for other than religious reasons.

Home schooling has existed throughout American's educational history. Its supporters are not limited to conservatives but include moderates, independents, and liberals as well. Some proponents of home schooling believe that both public and private schools are restrictive or unsafe, and others feel that schools are impersonal and unresponsive to students' needs. Home schooling affords parents the opportunity to address specific curricular, linguistic, and pedagogical concerns and even to design their own cross-cultural, bilingual, or experiential education program.

Today's home school proponents represent a variety of educational perspectives. Some advocates want to impart a value-laden curriculum to their children. Other proponents support a home school plan that emphasizes empowerment, social activism, and a progressive pedagogical approach to instruction. At the same time, there are supporters whose home school interests encompass a number of concerns, including access to equal educational opportunities, academic freedom, and individualized instruction. Thus, no single conservative or liberal position is typical among the parents who choose to home-school their children. Indeed, people's educational philosophies and priorities not only vary but also can change over time.

A family engaged in home schooling.

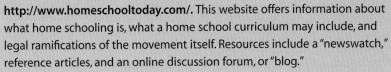

For Your CONSIDERATION

Visit the Homeschooling Today website at **http://www.homeschooltoday.com/.** This website offers information about what home schooling is, what a home school curriculum may include, and legal ramifications of the movement itself. Resources include a "newswatch," reference articles, and an online discussion forum, or "blog."

Educational outcomes of home schooling have been mixed. Although it is not uncommon to encounter reports in the national press that highlight some home-schooled student's academic success, such as high scores on standardized tests (Mathews, 1999), critics question the intent of such individualized instruction, which does not encourage diverse children to learn and work together. One goal of American education is to bring citizens together. The issue of socialization continues to challenge proponents of home schooling. Supporters contend that their children have numerous opportunities to socialize with their peers outside of the home school, and point out that socialization in schools can have negative consequences.

At the same time, families have forged alliances with school districts so that home schooled children can participate in team sports and other extracurricular activities. Today, school district policies on collaborations between school and home school vary from state to state.

Finally, the quality of home school teaching will also vary. Some parents may be better able than others to deliver instruction to their children.

SUMMARY

As noted earlier, the structure of education in the United States is built on the management of schools at the federal, state, and local levels. The governance of public education has been established at the federal level, with the funding of several initiatives such as the Morrill Act, the National Defense Act, the Elementary and Secondary Education Act, and the No Child Left Behind Act. Thus, the federal government plays an ongoing role in American public education. And yet, individual states assume the majority of educational responsibilities, including funding, administration, teacher licensure, and oversight of efforts to meet standards. A broad interpretation of the Tenth Amendment to the U.S. Constitution allows for this state control, because educational programming is not specifically addressed, and powers not explicitly delegated in the Constitution are reserved to the states. Today, school choice, voucher programs, and home schooling challenge the efficacy of federal- and state-sponsored public education, despite serious questions about the equity of such movements.

DISCUSSION QUESTIONS

1. Describe the distinct roles of the federal, state, and local governments in educational policy, teacher licensure, funding, and curriculum and assessment standards.

2. What are the functions of local school boards, district offices of education, and superintendents? How do the three entities work together?

3. Explain the arguments that support and challenge school choice and voucher plans. What do you see as the strengths and weaknesses of such programs in terms of their effects on the education of low-income and minority student populations?

4. What are charter schools? How has the charter school movement enhanced or hindered the desegregation of the public schools?

5. Describe the concept known as "funds of knowledge." In what ways can a funds-of-knowledge approach to understanding family and community social networks be used to improve cross-cultural understanding and curriculum development in the classroom?

ACTIVITIES

1. Compare and contrast three state education websites of your choice. Describe each district's structure of educational governance in terms of teacher licensure, funding, curriculum development, and the district's approaches to meeting No Child Left Behind standards.

2. Identify charter schools in your community. Visit a school site and interview a staff member. Learn about the features of the school and present them in your college foundations course.

3. Interview two school principals at different schools. Explore what they feel is the focus and mission of their role at their school. What do they feel are their strengths and the challenges that they face when serving students, families, and fellow educators?

4. With permission from a family, practice conducting a funds-of-knowledge home visit and interview. Describe what you learned during your visit, and explain how such knowledge can be used to enhance your rapport with students, as well as to inform your curriculum development.

Great Schools
http://www.greatschools.net
This site offers state and local school district data relevant to the socioeconomic status of students, demographics, and outcomes on standardized tests. In particular, this site provides discussion topics to better inform parents and families about school choice.

The School Tree
http://www.greatschools.net
This site also offers state and local school district data relevant to the socioeconomic status of students, demographics, and outcomes on standardized tests.

United States Department of Education
http://www.ed.gov/about/overview/budget
This site provides comprehensive information about the federal role in education. Fact sheets and links to other pertinent topics (such as school choice voucher plans and NCLB) and websites are useful sources to help you understand the relationship among the federal, state, and local education entities.

US Charter Schools
http://ww.uscharterschools.org
This site identifies nonsectarian, public charter schools of choice across the United States. The website provides examples of "charters," or performance contracts detailing a school's mission, program, goals, and students served.

Abstinence Education Inc. (n.d.). *Why kNOw public school curriculum.* Retrieved May 29, 2007, from https://whyknow.org/www/products/117.2, p. 96.

Brimley, V., & Garfield, R. (2002). *Financing education* (8th ed.). Boston. Allyn & Bacon.

Carr, N. (2003). The toughest job in America: Education's vital signs [Supplement.]. *American School Board Journal, 190*(2), 14–19.

Greene, J. (2000). Why school choice can promote integration. *Education Week, 19*(31), 52, 72.

Gresham, A., Hess, F., Maranto, R., & Millman, S. (2000). Desert bloom: Arizona's free market in education. *Phi Delta Kappan, 81,* 751–757.

Heritage Community Services. (n.d.). *Heritage keepers abstinence education.* Retrieved May 29, 2007, from http://www.heritageservices.org/ourprograms.html, p. 46.

Mathews, J. (1999, March 24). A home run for home schooling. *Washington Post,* p. A11.

National Education Association. (2002). *School vouchers: The emerging track record.* Washington, DC: Author.

National Center for Educational Statistics. (2002). *The condition of education: Past and projected elementary and secondary school enrollment* (pp. 44–45). Washington, DC: U.S. Department of Education, Institute for Educational Sciences.

Richard, A. (2000b). Studies cite lack of diversity in top position. *Education Week, 19*(25), 3.

United States Department of Education. (2001). *Schools and staffing survey, 1999–2000.* Washington, DC: National Center for Educational Statistics.

United States Department of Education. (2003). *Digest of educational statistics, 2002.* Washington, DC: U.S. Government Printing Office.

United States Department of Education, Grant Programs. (2004). *Department of Education congressional action, fiscal year 2004.* Retrieved April 9, 2005, from http://www.ed.gov/about/overview/budget/states/index.html

US Charter Schools. (n.d.). *History of the charter school movement.* Retrieved May 29, 2007, from http://www.uscharterschools.org/pub/uscs_docs/o/history.htm

Why Am I Tempted (WAIT) Training. (n.d.). *WAIT training manual.* Retrieved May 29, 2007, from http://www.waittraining.com/programs.asp, p. 62.

Williams, A. (2002). Principals' salaries, 2001–2002. *Principal, 81*(5), 66–70.

CHAPTER 6

Paying the Bills: School Funding

FIRST PERSON

Unequal Funding Equals Unequal Schools

Access to well-funded K–12 schooling, whether it is public or private, can determine the quality of the educational preparation students receive as they pursue such future goals as college admission, professional programs, and job-training opportunities. However, because school funding and resources are distributed unequally in the United States, students' educational outcomes remain disproportionate across racial and social class lines.

As a child, I attended Catholic and public elementary schools that struggled to make ends meet in low-income South Central Los Angeles. Working-class families made do with blue-collar jobs, had access to a free clinic, and shopped at a small local supermarket and a meat market. There were no parks nearby, let alone green space. My African American classmates and I would walk to school in the morning and take the public RTD (Rapid Transit District) bus home quickly before it got dark.

To help sustain enrollment, the Catholic school offered incentives for families to send their children to school. Families with three or more children enrolled were charged a reduced tuition for each additional child. This served our family well, as my father would work six days a week at the local market to help cover tuition costs. My parents liked the fact that we had to wear uniforms at Catholic school. Girls and boys could wear the same salt-and-pepper skirt or pants, white shirts and blouses, sweaters, shoes, and socks two or three times a week, which ultimately meant less expense. Nor did our parents have to listen to their kids complaining about not having the coolest or the latest clothes.

The school had few resources, however. We bought our own equipment, such as paper, crayons, scissors, and glue, and there were times when our teachers purchased these items for us. As for recess, the parking lot was our

CHAPTER OBJECTIVES

- Readers will develop an understanding of the history of American educational finance by exploring how a new country established new schools.

- Readers will identify and describe the role of the federal government in the financing of public education.

- Readers will identify and describe the role of state and local governments in the financing of public education.

- With the implementation of the 2002 No Child Left Behind Act, readers will examine the impact of standards-based accountability on educational funding.

- Given regional differences, readers will recognize how state and community values influence school funding decisions and priorities.

- Readers will reflect on the pursuit of equitable educational funding in the United States as our country seeks to respond to the needs of diverse learners.

playground. The cars of faculty members represented either a field goal or an automatic ground-rule double.

In the classroom, the nuns and lay teachers were tough on students. Discipline and rigor were strong elements of our curriculum. Books were torn and tattered, but we read them anyway. Our yellow "Pee-chee" folders held notebook paper for our writing assignments or there would be a call home. As children, we thought life was hard at Catholic school—learning was more of a punishment than a joy. It was not until we moved into a white suburb on the edge of East L.A. that we discovered that schools could offer students more.

When our family left the inner city for the lower-middle-class suburb, the contrast was profound. There were a grass field, several basketball courts (with nets!), and a new asphalt field. Each classroom had a small library of its own, with new lightweight plastic desks and a beanbag or two. Windows that opened, counter space, individual student cubbie holes, and a sink with a drinking fountain were also distinct classroom features. Sometimes there was a pet hamster. Teachers had aides in the classroom who helped individual students with their reading, writing, and math. In fact, I remember one sixth-grade teacher inviting a few students to participate in a reading research project she was conducting. I wondered, "What is research? I never heard teachers talk about that at my other school."

We had plenty of materials for art and equipment for sports. There was a music teacher, and students could even take lessons and borrow an instrument. Occasionally we would have field trips to the L.A. library, city hall, art museums, and the La Brea Tar Pits. Suddenly I was excited about school! After-school sports and crafts kept me on the school grounds much longer than I could even imagine sticking around my Catholic school. In fact, I could ride my bike home safely right before the sun went down. On weekends, I could play sports at the local gym and park. School and community life suddenly was much better than inner-city life. However, it was not until later that I would learn that school funding was a direct reflection of my new community's wealth.

Education Funding: A Historical Overview

Today, funding plans for school districts rely on three sources: the federal government, state funds, and local taxes. The majority of the funding is derived from local taxes. Thus, communities with more assets will have additional sources of taxable wealth, such as property tax, that can be used to support educational programming, staffing, and instructional resources. Over time, shifts in educational funding have taken place. During the colonial period of U.S. history, local communities held primary responsibility for the financing of schools. The federal government had no role in funding schools.

Then, in the twentieth century, school finance emerged as an agenda item for political leadership, and many people argued that our society needed to prepare an educated, competitive workforce. As a result, the federal government's role has increased, with an emphasis on equalizing funding among states (Biddle & Berliner, 2002). Nevertheless, there remains much debate about which entities, federal or state, should carry the most responsibility for funding the nation's schools.

School Finance: A Reflection of Early American Values

Early educational efforts in America, as far back as the 1600s, reveal a new society's concerns about the preparation of a citizenry both literate and empowered to make an economic contribution to the state. **The Massachusetts Act of 1642** sought to ensure that parents attended to the values, as well as education, of their sons. Boys not only learned to read Biblical scriptures but also were taught "labor skills," while girls were trained in household tasks (Cubberly, 1920). In addition, community leaders were charged with monitoring families' adherence to the Massachusetts Act of 1642.

However, the Act of 1642 was eventually replaced by "Ye Olde Deluder Act," which required children to specifically develop reading skills to independently study the Bible and ward off the influence of Satan (the "old deluder"). With the passage of this act, settlements of 50 households or more were required to employ and pay for one male reading and writing teacher. In communities of 100 or more families, property owners were required to pay taxes to support grammar schools. Property owners who did not pay their taxes for education were often fined and, in some cases, locked in the public stocks.

What these responses reflect is the fundamental belief held by early American government leaders that education not only was important to a developing society but also was linked to the future prosperity of its economy. In turn, prosperity was measured by the value of property held by its citizens. Hence it became, and remains, the responsibility of the citizenry to fund the public schools thorough the taxation of property.

Establishing New Schools in a New Country

Educational historian Ellwood Cubberly (1947) explains that an American public school system was established because of the groundwork set forth by the Massachusetts Act of 1642 and the 1647 Ye Olde Deluder Act. States were now required to fund both elementary and secondary schools in rural or larger communities that had a tax base. Soon other colonies across New England began to implement similar property tax laws to fund public schools. Thus, a tradition was established in the United States that continues today: the financing of public schools primarily through the taxation of property owners. Funding differed among regions; some colonies could meet only their most basic educational needs, whereas others could afford to finance large school buildings and extensive curricula.

With the passage of the Declaration of Independence, the new country maintained its commitment to a democratic republic. And yet, with a fledgling economy, its citizenry had to be educated in order to sustain it. The debate concerning who would take responsibility for education, the federal government or state governments, remained in question. Not addressed in the U.S. Constitution's initial ten amendments, education was left in the hands of the states. This decision had tremendous ramifications and still affects schools today, as educational finance and policy remain under the auspices of states, whose policies and financial resources still vary widely across the country.

PAUSE & REFLECT

Education in the United States has its historical roots embedded in both a secular and a Christian foundation. How has contemporary society balanced the issues of equity and religious freedom relevant to education?

Federal Educational Initiatives: New Responsibilities

The country's founding fathers recognized the importance of a literate and educated population to both national security and economic viability. With the passage of the Land Ordinance of 1785, townships 36 miles square in the western territories would be divided into 36 one-square-mile lots, with four of the lots identified for sale. The proceeds from the sale of lot number 16 could be reserved for the financing of public schools, and that lot soon became known as the "sixteenth section" of the 1785 Land Ordinance. With this ordinance, the federal government's role in educational finance became clearly established from a policy perspective.

A second law, known as the Northwest Ordinance, was passed in 1787. Similar to the 1785 land grant policy, this ordinance also maintained that new territories, which envisioned the establishment of state status, must include an education provision as part of their state laws. Other ordinances soon followed, and a third land grant ordinance set aside nearly 5 million acres for development.

In 1802, a fourth federal ordinance was passed that required the sale and proceeds from a township's "sixteenth section" to be used to fund public schools in the new state of Ohio. Debate would later emerge about the extent to which states could tax federal land holdings located within them. A compromise was reached, with the states agreeing that federal lands would not be taxed. In turn, the U.S. government would provide the states 5 percent of the proceeds from the sale of public lands, to be used to finance the public schools. As a result of these ordinances and negotiations, the relationship between the federal and state government and educational financing was established.

In 1836, the decentralization of the federal government resulted in the collection of what Congress then considered excess dollars. With the states still in need of additional support, the 1836 Surplus Revenue Deposit Act, or **Surplus Act,** released 28 million dollars of federal funding, which was used to help establish public schools across the country.

Other federal educational funding initiatives followed this Surplus Act. They included the federal government's commitment to the country's national security interests. This commitment resulted in Congress's establishment of the U.S. Military Academy in 1802. Congress supported the creation of the Naval Academy in 1845 and that of the Coast Guard Academy in 1876. Sixty years later, in 1936, the Merchant Marine Academy was founded, followed by the U.S. Air Force Academy in 1954. Thus, the role of the federal government and its educational interests were clearly established, as Congress financed both public schooling and national security initiatives through passage of land grant ordinances and the formation of military academies.

Land grant initiatives, such as the 1862 Morrill Act, continued to be extended and implemented during the Civil War. The Morrill Act enabled states to establish agricultural and technical colleges on public lands. A second Morrill Act was passed in 1890, which provided support for instruction in the colleges financed and founded as a result of the initial Morrill Act. Following the end of the Civil War, Congress financed the 1867 creation of the U.S. Department of Education. Again, this initiative provided a federal infrastructure for educational policy development and leadership. This infrastructure would soon be called to respond to difficult events in American history: World War I, the Great Depression, and World War II. Postwar educational, vocational and rehabilitation programs, free lunch programs, and resources for higher education were new initiatives now supported by the federal government (see Table 6.1).

TABLE 6.1   Federal Government Educational Initiatives in the Twentieth Century

Year Congress Approved Funding	Name of Act	Program Funded
1917 to post-WWI	Smith-Hughes Act	Vocational education
1918 to post-WWI	Vocational Rehabilitation Act	Veterans workforce training
1919 to post-WWI	Act to Provide Further Educational Facilities	Vocational program equipment
1920 to post-WWI	Smith-Bankhead Act	Vocational rehabilitation
1935 to post-Depression	Agricultural Adjustment Act	Foodstuffs for schools
1943 to post-WWI	Vocational Rehabilitation Act, Public Law 78-16	Veterans workforce training
1944 to post-WWII	Servicemen's Readjustment Act, Public Law 78-346	GI Bill (education and housing benefits)
1949	Federal and Administrative Services Act, Public Law 81-152	Resources for colleges and schools to meet increased fiscal needs
1958	National Defense Education Act, Public Law 85-864	Math and science education
1958	Education of Mentally Retarded Children Act, Public Law 85-926	Teacher training for educators to work with disabled students
1965	Elementary and Secondary Education Act, Public Law 98-10	Titles I–V: programming for low-income students, special education, bilingual education, gender equity initiatives, materials, research laboratories, and state education agencies
1975	Education for All Handicapped Children Act, Public Law 101-46	A percentage of special education services to the states

Contemporary Finance Systems

Following the post–World War II prosperity that middle-class Americans began to experience, it soon became clear, with the Russian launching of Sputnik in 1957, that this upswing would not last. The GI Bill had resulted in an increase in college attendance and the emergence of the suburbs, but nothing could eclipse the fact that the United States had not been first to launch a satellite into space. Apparently, American public education was not as competitive as had been assumed.

In response, the United States embarked on new educational initiatives to help strengthen its national defense and to confront educational inequities (see Table 6.1). With the 1958 National Defense Education Act (NDEA), Public Law 85-864, Congress emphasized the importance, nationwide, of math and science education and foreign language instruction, while providing financial support for testing, data collection, and counseling. In addition, the NDEA offered support for technical training, fellowships, and student loans.

Education of Mentally Retarded Children Act

In the same year, 1958, Congress passed the **Education of Mentally Retarded Children Act,** Public Law 85-926. This was the first law enacted to provide teacher training for educators to work with students with disabilities. Prior to this act, the only legislation addressing the needs of the disabled was intended to help injured World War I and II veterans. With little if any state funding available, families were left to find their own resources and services to meet the needs of disabled children.

The EMRC Act was a first step in providing assistance to families. But it was not until the 1971 *Pennsylvania Association of Retarded Citizens v. Commonwealth* (of Pennsylvania) federal district case and the 1972 case *Mills v. Board of Education in Washington, D.C.* that the lack of educational services for exceptional learners was challenged in court. These cases paved the way for passage of the 1975 Education for All Handicapped Children Act, Public Law 101-46. Initially, this act included a commitment by the federal government to fund 40 percent of special education services, with the states and local school districts paying the difference. Since 1975, however, federal support for special education has fallen far short of this commitment, with the federal government funding only 17 percent of special education services (NEA, 2004).

Breaking Ground: The Elementary and Secondary Education Act

The **Elementary and Secondary Education Act**, Public Law 89-10, is considered one of the most sweeping educational funding initiatives set forth by the federal government for its time. This act, passed by Congress in 1965, includes Titles I to V:

- *Title I* funding provides instructional support for low-income students. Through the distribution of basic grants, state education agencies can provide funds to local school districts on the basis of such factors as the number of eligible students attending a school and the state's average per-pupil expenditure. Concentration grants are intended for school districts where eligible, low-income students make up more than 15 percent of the school population. And yet Title I funding varies annually because of political considerations and resource allocation. Inflation adjustment also plays a role in the "buying power" of such grants. For example, while inflation rates were increasing in the early 1990s, districts received not less than 85 percent of the funds they were allocated the previous year. This Title I provision, however, does not take into account the increased number of students eligible for the program during a period of increased inflation, when dollars purchase less and less.

- *Title II* funds are appropriated for a variety of educational initiatives, as well as for instructional materials. In addition, Title II funds also support programs for the gifted and talented, women's educational equity initiatives, bilingual education, substance abuse prevention, and magnet school funding.

- *Title III* provides additional support to special education programs.

- *Title IV* finances educational research laboratories across the United States.

- *Title V* funds support State Education Agencies (SEAs). These SEAs provide an infrastructure for states to offer support and guidance to local school districts, offer assistance in the development of core curricula, establish and monitor teacher licensure, and collect data for the federal government.

Other contemporary federal education initiatives include the 1967 Public Broadcasting Act, which established the Corporation for Public Broadcasting educational television programming, such as "Mister Rogers' Neighborhood," "Sesame Street," and "The Electric Company."

Social Needs and Federal Policy Responses

As social movements in American history continued to gain momentum, the federal government also had to respond in kind. For example, in 1970, with the passage of *Brown v. Board of Education II,* the Office of Education Appropriation Act made funds available to assist with expenses incurred in desegregation of the public schools. By 1977, educational initiatives that focused on vocational and career education were funded, including the Career Education Implementation Incentive Act. In addition, states could compete for federal categorical grants that offered support for educational needs such as teacher training, preschool programs for low-income children, and student loans for college. By 1980, the federal government also awarded **block grants**, or specific amounts of dollars, to states for use at their discretion.

Administrative policy changes occurred in 1979, as Congress voted to support the separation of the U.S. Office of Education from the Department of Health, Education and Welfare. The newly established Department of Education, with a cabinet post filled via nomination by President Jimmy Carter, symbolized the elevated status now enjoyed by education in competition for resources and "the ear" of the executive branch.

However, this status was short lived. With passage of the 1981 Education Consolidation and Improvement Act, 42 different programs were collapsed into seven. As a result of this consolidation, federal educational funding decreased more than 20 percent between 1980 and 1985. Interest was redirected to elementary and secondary math and science educational funding with passage of the 1984 Education for Economic Security Act. This initiative provided support for magnet schools and math/science outreach programs.

The Hawkins-Stafford Elementary and Secondary School Improvement Amendment and its reauthorization (1988 and 1993) also provided major support of a number of educational initiatives, including programs that assist learners achieving below grade level (these are also known as Chapter 1 and Chapter 2). Other programs financed by the Hawkins-Stafford Amendment include math and science education and magnet schools.

In 1990, Congress approved the Americans with Disabilities Act (ADA) that finally barred discrimination against persons with disabilities. In contrast to the 1973 Rehabilitation Act, the ADA addressed settings specific to transportation and accommodations that are especially relevant to the needs of special education students in the public schools. It would not be until 1997 that the **Individuals with Disabilities Education Act** (IDEA), formerly known as the 1990 Education for All Handicapped Children Act, would be reauthorized for funding for the support of special education students and their families.

From PRESERVICE to PRACTICE

Grant Writing and Salvaging Savage Inequalities

Many teachers continue their education while maintaining their jobs in public school teaching. After nine years of teaching secondary English, journalism, and transitional English in Los Angeles County, I decided to pursue a doctoral degree in education. While attending a graduate course called Economics of Education, I was required to read a book entitled *Savage Inequalities,* by Jonathan Kozol. In this acclaimed work, Kozol (1992) examines the inequalities in the U.S. public school system by interviewing teachers, students, coaches, and administrators in six of the nation's poorest urban areas: San Antonio, East St. Louis, Chicago's South Side, New York's South Bronx, Washington, DC, and Camden, NJ. Kozol compares the day-to-day experience of students in well-funded, predominantly white, suburban schools to the experience of students living in predominantly African American and Latina/o urban communities.

Kozol notes that many problems facing urban schools (deteriorated facilities, high dropout rates, large class sizes, and poorly paid teachers) are the result of funding inequalities. After reading Kozol's book, I promised myself I would return to the public schools one day with a grant in hand and help low-income students and teachers whose classrooms were like those described in *Savage.* After five years of receiving grant rejection letters, I finally was awarded a U.S. Department of Education, Training for All Teachers federal grant for ESL/bilingual teachers and students. An important element of the grant engaged university preservice teachers and secondary ESL students in college outreach activities. This collaboration included student and preservice teacher attendance at a higher-education fair held at a local community college.

Standards-Based Accountability and Federal Funding

The 1990s also saw the emergence of federal educational funding driven by assessment initiatives, or **standards-based accountability**. In 1993, the National Assessment of Educational Progress (NAEP) Assessment Authorization implemented the use of the "Nation's Report Card," in which state comparisons of students' standardized test outcomes were collected, analyzed, and reported. The Goals 2000—Educate America Act initiative of 1994 sought to establish partnerships between the federal government and the states by providing grants to reform schools and authorize the voluntary national certification of state standards and assessment models.

Title I was also reauthorized in 1994. This far-reaching funding initiative, designed to meet the needs of low-income students, was an original feature of the Elementary and Secondary Education Act. The reauthorization, however, also included resources for the professional development of teachers, for drug-free school programs, and for efforts to achieve educational equity.

The Impact of the No Child Left Behind Act on School Funding

School accountability is the emphasis of the 2002 federal initiative the **No Child Left Behind Act.** Also known as the reauthorization of the Elementary and Secondary Education Act (ESEA), this act was set forth by President George W. Bush. Federal funding for state education programming and local school districts was henceforth to be determined by the assessment of annual testing outcomes in such content areas as reading, math, and science. Based on state-adopted criteria for adequate yearly progress (AYP), the progress of students in these subjects is monitored and reported to federal and state educational agencies. Under specific review are the educational outcomes and AYP of low-income students, minority populations, English language learners, and special education students.

For those schools not achieving AYP in any two consecutive years (also known as "Schools in Need of Improvement"), punitive actions are implemented in stages. Parents may choose to have their children transfer to another public school, transfer to a public charter school, or receive supplementary tutoring at their current school. All schools must employ "highly qualified teachers," those who hold college degrees and are state-certified in their content areas (U.S. Dept. of Education, 2006). Therefore, recruiting, training, and retaining teachers during this era of NCLB is costly for school districts that already have limited resources and are facing teacher shortages, particularly in low-income school districts.

The No Child Left Behind Act remains highly controversial. In general, this underfunded mandate has been met with much criticism by educators and state officials. The National Education Association (NEA), for example, continues to challenge the efficacy of the NCLB Act. This professional teachers' organization argues that NCLB creates bureaucratic barriers that impede the learning process and the interaction between teachers and students. The NEA maintains that the NCLB Act punishes schools rather than providing them with assistance (NEA, 2006).

Initiatives such as NCLB are especially vulnerable to the political climate. Numerous educators continue to be convinced that a "one-size-fits-all" accountability policy, without teacher input and flexibility, cannot possibly address the specific and diverse learning needs of students across the United States. In addition, the organization contends that the NCLB Act disregards research that supports best practices. This initiative, the NEA maintains, creates another standardized testing bureaucracy that constrains individual teachers and students as they engage in curriculum-focused problem solving and skill development (NEA, 2006).

Schools already struggling with inadequate resources are challenged when the federal government cuts educational funding while they try to comply with underfunded mandates such as the No Child Left Behind Act. Providing teacher training so that teachers meet the "highly qualified" standard is extremely difficult when teacher quality grants continue to be cut. According to the NEA, "The cuts come at a time when there is broad agreement that teacher quality is the main factor in improving student achievement and closing achievement gaps between student populations" (2006).

State Funding of the Public Schools: Taxation

The History of Taxation

The taxing of individuals though property ownership is a time-honored practice that was present even among early Greek and Roman societies. In America, the financing of education based on a community's property tax base is a funding approach that has essentially been in place since the establishment of the New England colonies in the 1600s. Of course, in early history, various kinds of property were taxed at different rates, such as cultivated acreage and uncleared land. Equipment and livestock were also subject to taxation. Thus, the production of a farm led to questions regarding the worth of that property beyond its mere acreage. What emerged was a system of local government tax assessment rates based on the economic, or market, value of the property.

Taxation represents a revenue source for governments to sustain, protect, and educate their citizenry. Educational funding represents a society's investment in itself, in its economic viability, its technology, its health care, its security, and its support of disadvantaged and disempowered citizens.

From PRESERVICE to PRACTICE

Limited Funds and the Competition for Resources

The preservice teachers attending my Diversity in Education course would be missing class on Tuesday. They told me they would be attending a job fair in Salt Lake City

Preservice university students attend a college fair for secondary students.

and were extremely excited about their prospects. After all, the local newspaper, the *Salt Lake Tribune*, had recently reported that one of the larger school districts in the region, Jordan, recorded 260 teacher retirements in the 2005–2006 school year. This was in sharp contrast to the 2004–2005 school year, when 84 teachers retired. Why the dramatic difference? According to district and union officials, drastic cuts in retirement benefits and the competition for funding were major factors. No longer available would be health insurance after retirement, payouts for

unused sick leave, and cash incentives for early retirement. The school board argued that these benefits were simply too expensive to maintain. New teachers would now be covered only through a state retirement plan.

These savings would not come without cost to the students attending Jordan District. As the veteran teachers retired to take advantage of the old benefits, years of experience would be lost. Superintendent Barry Newbold said, "There could be a downside if we're not able to replace those who are leaving with quality candidates. Really, time will tell if that proves to be a disadvantage or not." In anticipating this concern, the district responded by seeking new teachers from a wider geographic area than usual. Jordan District spokesperson Melinda Colton added, "We're not just filling them to get a warm body in there."

However, for early retiree John Day, choosing to leave the profession was not only about collecting retirement benefits. He explained, "Sure, the old benefits were great. But there are so many pressures that a teacher faces today, with the expectations that come with a poorly funded mandate like NCLB, and few dollars to keep our class sizes down. I just figured it was time for some new teachers, new blood, and new energy, to help our students." Thus, the loss of veteran teachers due to declining resources and the pressures associated with standardized testing may foreshadow what is ahead for other U.S. school districts as they scramble to fill teaching vacancies. As for my own preservice education students, I canceled class that day and wished them well in their interviews.

The use of property taxes to fund education goes as far back in American history as the Massachusetts Law of 1647, which provided for the financing of one teacher per town of 100 or more citizens. Today, federal, state, and local governments assess property tax and production taxes, such as the personal income tax and retail sales tax, which together provide funding for social services. Personal property taxes on such items as cars, machinery, and equipment represent revenue for public schools. As competing interests vie for scarce state dollars, educational funding relies exclusively on these tax dollars to support itself, unlike a for-profit company. The federal government does not finance competing educational interests equally. Subsequently, states must balance the need for equal educational funding of its programs with the fact that running an education system is extremely expensive.

Tax equalization remains the "Holy Grail" of American society. In a perfect world, taxes would be distributed equally over the society for whom services were provided.

What we see today, however, is unequal tax distribution and, as a result, an unequal school funding structure. **Proportional taxes** reflect this inequality, where the tax takes the same percentage of income from all groups. For example, a person with an income of $100,000 may pay $10,000 or 10 percent, in income tax. A person with an income of $10,000 would also pay 10 percent, in this case $1,000, in income tax. This system places an unequal burden on the poor, who (unlike the wealthy) are left with very little money to pay for essentials. Others argue that the wealthy purchase more and for this reason pay more taxes. Thus, some states choose not to tax, or to tax at a lower rate, purchases of food and prescription drugs.

According to the U.S. Internal Revenue Service, **regressive taxes** take a larger percentage of income from low-income groups than from high-income groups. For example, an individual earning $10,000 and facing a 5 percent income tax rate would pay $500. In contrast, an individual earning $100,000 could pay 3 percent income tax, or $3,000. **Progressive tax** rates take a larger percentage of income from high-income groups than from low-income groups. Federal income tax formulas are generally progressive and are often viewed favorably by the public, whereas regressive tax formulas are perceived negatively.

PAUSE & REFLECT

> How do progressive, regressive, and proportional tax formulas affect educational funding? Compare and contrast how these tax formulas impact school funding in school districts located in your state.

Types of Taxes That Generate School Funding

Property taxes remain the foundation of educational funding. Taxes are determined by the assessed value of a home or property and the amount of tax revenue that a community must raise to provide services. Assessing fair market property values remains an imperfect practice that depends on a somewhat subjective analysis of the real estate market. But assessed value may bear little relation to the price paid for the home. As property values increase, so do taxes, thus creating a climate of resentment among property owners and those living on fixed incomes, such as many senior citizens. Because property taxes primarily fund schools, it is no wonder that property owners challenge the efficacy of the public school system. Upper-class communities, with high property values, can afford to support a variety of school programs, small classes, and highly qualified teachers. Communities with a modest or low tax base simply do not have the resources to support an extensive education infrastructure.

Maintaining a property tax and assessment program is also a costly and labor-intensive endeavor. Keeping a record of property assessments, noting any upgrades, and overseeing an appeals process for challenging assessment decisions are important elements of an already complicated program that must also maintain accounts, collect taxes, and pursue delinquent taxpayers.

Once utilized to pay debts following the Civil War, **income taxes** have been a source of federal revenue for over 100 years. In 1894, shortly after this initial tax plan expired, Congress implemented a flat 2 percent income tax. However, in 1895 this tax was deemed unconstitutional by the U.S. Supreme Court, at least until the Constitution could be amended. With the 1913 ratification of the

Sixteenth Amendment, the federal government again began collecting income tax. And yet federal income taxes provide only an estimated 7 percent of state school funding, while state taxes finance the majority of educational programming (Hovey & Hovey, 2002).

State **sales taxes** serve as sources of revenue for local schools. Some states may not have a direct sales tax for food and other purchases, but states do generate revenue with gasoline taxes, utility taxes, cable television taxes, and telephone taxes. Another state funding source is **bonds**. Bonds are presented before a state and local vote to finance the construction and renovation of school facilities. Bonds guarantee payment of debts and interest by a government at a specific time (the bond's maturity date) in the future.

State lotteries and gambling also provide funding for schools. When a state sponsors a lottery, or, say, horse racing, winners must pay both federal and state taxes on the prize. Opinions differ on the ethical or moral dimensions of legal gambling, but there is no doubt that it represents a major revenue source for education in 47 out of 50 states (excluding Hawaii, Tennessee, and Utah), with a combined gross of over $50 billion dollars in 2000 (Hovey & Hovey, 2002). See Table 6.2 for the revenues generated by legal gambling in the ten states where it provides the most funding to support education, as well as other services.

TABLE 6.2 Revenue Generated by Legal Gambling in 10 States, 2000

State Rank (by revenue in millions)	Gross Revenue	Per-Capita Revenue
1. Nevada	9,632	4,820
2. New Jersey	5,451	648
3. New York	2,739	144
4. Mississippi	2,685	944
5. Illinois	2,680	216
6. California	2,629	78
7. Louisiana	2,194	491
8. Indiana	2,049	337
9. Michigan	1,706	172
10. Florida	1,618	101

Source: Hovey and Hovey (2002).

In addition, **sumptuary, excise, or "sin" taxes** on alcohol and tobacco purchases both give states a way to regulate activities not perceived as benefiting "the common good" of its citizenry and offer states yet another source of tax revenue. Also, federal court settlements against the tobacco industry provide states with revenue for social services and programs, including education.

Another tax revenue source is **severance taxes**. These taxes are based on the value and quantity of natural products (fish, gas, minerals, oil, timber, and the like) available within a state. For some states, such as Alaska, Wyoming, and New Mexico, this is a very lucrative tax revenue source, whereas 15 other states, including Missouri, Illinois, and Indiana, have no severance taxes (U.S. Department of Commerce, 1992). In general, severance taxes account for less than 1 percent of all state revenues.

In 1909, Congress imposed a **corporate income tax** on companies for the opportunity to conduct business. This tax is based on the sales revenue a company generates after production, facility, equipment, and other costs, as well as state taxes, are accounted for. Although there is resistance to the imposition of this tax from corporations who could use such revenue to bolster stock values and pension plan investments, the corporate income tax provides less than 10 percent of federal revenue (King, Swanson & Sweetland, 2003).

For Your CONSIDERATION

Visit the Third World Traveler website at **http:www.thirdworldtraveler. com/Third_Wiorld_USJonathanKozol_page.html.** This site includes excerpts from the writings of Jonathan Kozol, as he addresses inequitable school funding, challenges the efficacy of NCLB, and argues that the emergence of urban charter schools further establishes the persistence of segregation in America.

Other Views of Educational Finance and Taxes

From 1995 to 2002, the proportion of total revenue for public elementary and secondary education from local sources increased slightly (see Table 6.3). This increase reflects limited increases in both property tax revenue and other local revenue. Conversely, the proportion of total revenue from both federal and state sources increased between these years. The Midwest experienced slight increases in the proportion of total revenue from local sources—from 38.3 percent in 1995–1996 to 44 percent in 2001–2002. The Northeast also experienced increases in the proportion of revenue from local sources, from 44.1 billion dollars to 47.3 billion dollars. In both regions, there were increases in the proportion of total revenue from federal and state sources.

Small increases were seen in the South and West from 1995 to 2002. And yet, the proportion of funding from property tax revenue in the South increased from 27 percent in 1989–1990 to 31 percent in 2001–2002. In contrast, funding from property taxes increased in the West, from 18.3 billion dollars to 23.1. In 2001–2002, the Northeast used property tax revenue (rather than local sources) to fund education.

What do these data suggest? A state's fiscal capacity to pay for goods and services, including education, varies greatly depending on the wealth, or tax base, of a region. Fiscal capacity depends on a state's ability to generate revenue, be it from property taxes, personal income taxes, sales taxes, corporate income taxes, lottery and gambling taxes, or severance and sumptuary taxes. Whether a state has the fiscal capacity to fund its schools also depends on a number of other variables, such as the region's history or attitudes about taxation, the state's tax structure, the number of students attending schools, demographics, the education level of communities in the state, perceptions about local schools, and the numbers of students attending private, charter, and home schools. All of these factors ultimately affect the commitment and effort that states make to fund education, and their impact can be as significant as a state's fiscal capacity to do so.

Funding Schools Equitably

Can states fund schools equally? This question can be misleading, given the diverse needs of communities, families, and students across the country. To fund schools equally does not necessarily reflect an equitable response for low-income districts whose property tax base and other tax resources cannot support additional teachers,

TABLE 6.3 Changes in School Revenue, 1995 to 2002 (in billions of constant 2001–2002 dollars)

| | Year of Revenue Sources | | | |
	1995–1996	1997–1998	1999–2000	2001–2002
Northeast				
Federal	3.9	4.1	4.9	5.6
State	30.3	31.7	38.1	42.3
Local:	44.1	45.7	46.1	47.3
From property taxes	39.0	40.5	40.4	41.8
From other sources	5.1	5.1	5.6	5.6
Total	78.3	81.5	89.1	95.2
Midwest				
Federal	4.5	5.2	5.9	6.8
State	37.5	41.0	44.6	48.2
Local:	38.3	40.8	42.4	44.0
From property taxes	31.0	32.5	33.4	35.1
From other sources	7.2	8.3	8.9	8.9
Total	80.4	87.0	92.9	99.0
South				
Federal	8.0	9.1	10.5	12.2
State	51.4	56.2	62.6	62.6
Local:	45.6	48.6	52.5	57.5
From property taxes	29.1	30.5	36.6	41.2
From other sources	16.4	18.1	15.9	16.3
Total	105.0	113.8	125.6	132.3
West				
Federal	5.5	6.1	7.3	8.6
State	38.4	44.8	49.0	53.7
Local:	24.3	25.9	28.7	31.0
From property taxes	18.3	19.0	20.8	23.1
From other sources	6.0	6.9	7.9	7.9
Total	68.1	76.8	85.0	93.3
United States				
Federal	22.0	24.5	28.5	33.2
State	157.6	173.7	194.3	206.8
Local:	152.2	160.9	169.7	179.8
From property taxes	117.4	122.5	131.3	141.1
From other sources	34.8	38.4	38.4	38.79
Total	331.8	359.1	392.5	419.8

Source: U.S. Department of Education (2005a).
Note: Details may not sum to totals because of rounding. Revenues are in constant 2001–2002 dollars.

staff, facilities, curriculum materials, equipment, and supplementary educational services for such students as those eligible for free or reduced-cost lunch, special education students, and English language learners. Thus, it comes as no surprise that low-income schools require more resources than other schools if they are to meet federal and state standards such as those set forth by No Child Left Behind legislation.

Equity, then, remains a critical concept as schools strive to offer students equal educational opportunities. To provide students with such opportunities, schools with the greatest needs require additional funding. In other words, because schools and students have different needs, unequal treatment is essential in any effort to achieve equity. This concept is referred to as **vertical equity** (Berne & Stiefel, 1984). Approaches to achieving vertical equity differ from state to state and district to district. How resources are allocated differs according to local community values and recommendations made by school boards, district- and site-based administrators, and educational personnel.

Another approach, **fiscal neutrality,** reflects a commitment to respond to the desires and wants of the public regarding educational funding priorities (Berne & Stiefel, 1984). This concept does not focus on the amount of capital available for education on the basis of property taxes and other tax sources. Instead, if the public wants a school district to focus on teacher training in preparation for NCLB standardized testing, then this preference will "trump" the financing of other educational needs. Whether or not a district has the capacity to pay for such priorities and services is secondary to the taxpayers' preferences, which come first. Balancing fiscal neutrality with equity concerns has resulted in an educational funding approach known as fiscal equalization.

Fiscal equalization consists of the formulas and methods states utilize in their pursuit of equitable school funding. According to Alexander and Salmon (1995), the extent to which states and districts aspire to *absolute* or, more realistically speaking, *approximate* fiscal equalization depends on the following factors:

- To what extent the differences between local school districts' fiscal *status* are minimized

- To what extent the differences in fiscal initiatives or efforts between local school districts are eliminated

- To what extent the educational needs of diverse learners have been accommodated

Thus absolute fiscal equalization may be appropriate when school districts have similar financial resources available to them and when they can demonstrate an identical level of effort as they seek equal school funding and finance programs to support the needs of diverse learners. However, this is a very high standard that few states and districts ever meet.

Approximate fiscal equalization, according to Alexander and Salmon, is a more attainable approach to school finance and equity goals. With approximate fiscal equalization, there exists flexibility of fiscal efforts between local schools, as each can determine how funds will be spent.

Other approaches to school funding include the distribution of grants and foundation programs. Each state seeks equalization through the distribution of school funds based on legislative measures and constitutional guidelines. Out of state revenues, grants are distributed to school districts in accordance with their specific needs. Equity may or may not be a factor, because state legislation often mandates how funds will be dispersed. Foundation programs, on the other hand, set a legal baseline (or minimum) per-pupil allotment based on a combination of available local and state school funds, which may or may not be adequate for poor schools. Low-income districts are provided with state funds, however minimal, to meet this baseline, whereas affluent districts have enough local resources to easily exceed the per-pupil funding baseline.

For Your CONSIDERATION

Visit the Digest of Educational Statistics website at **http://nces.ed.gov/programs/digest/** to find the federal government's contributions to public school funding from 1995 to 2005. This site also offers data related to government finance and economic trends.

Charter and Private School Funding: School Choice

As we noted in Chapter 5, **charter schools** are state-funded public schools first established in Minnesota in 1991. Small and autonomous, charter schools are attractive to communities because they are not subject to many of the regulations that restrict larger public schools. Parents, teachers, and other interested parties, such as sponsoring universities or local school boards, establish a contract (or charter) to create an innovative school setting that focuses on a specific curriculum (such as math and science), philosophy, or population (for example, youth in custody).

Because charter schools are free from many public school regulations, charter school administrators can employ and terminate faculty without the constraints of tenure. In turn, the sponsor of the charter school guarantees to parents and students specific educational reforms and achievement outcomes that exceed those of the local public schools. Together, parents and educators in charter schools have more input into curriculum development and instructional practices. In 2005, there were nearly 3,500 charter schools operating in 40 states and the District of Columbia and Puerto Rico, and they enrolled approximately one million students (U.S. Charter Schools, 2006). At present, the states of California, with 574 schools and Arizona with 499, maintain the largest numbers of charter schools in the country.

Today, funding of charter schools remains dependent on public funding. Questions remain about the quality of charter schools. That is, do they really deliver what they promise, given that they are not required to employ licensed teachers?

Private schools, on the other hand, are independent, special-interest schools that are financed through private funds, grants, and endowments. Private schools are regulated by state law, regardless of their secular, religious, or military orientation. As a result, private schools vary in size, grade level, focus, curriculum, academic standards, and religious orientation. Private schools can either be residential in nature (i.e., boarding schools) or function as day schools. Eighty percent of private schools are religious institutions (Brimley & Garfield, 2002), which raises the issue of the separation of church and state.

In 2003, the National Center for Educational Statistics found that there were 28,384 private schools in the United States and that they enrolled 5,122,772 students and employed 425,238 full-time teachers (NCES, 2006). Private school students represented an estimated 10 percent of the total K–12 enrollment in the United States in 2003–2004.

Should Public Funds Be Used to Finance Private Schools?

A major point of contention regarding private school funding is the use of publicly funded vouchers. A **voucher** is a check or document issued to parents by a state to fund the purchase of private or public educational services. Supporters argue that parents are the best judges of what kind of education their children need. They also argue that the public schools are essentially a monopoly, so the use of vouchers results in a competitive and improved educational market. With a voucher in hand, parents can spend their dollars in competing schools; thus the best schools would attract the best students, and inferior schools would ultimately be closed.

Public school administrators and teachers alike argue that the use of private school vouchers drains funds away from low-income districts that cannot compete with affluent school districts. Teachers' unions such as the NEA and the American Federation of Teachers maintain that voucher plans serve only to resegregate the public schools and steal funds from already strapped urban schools.

The U.S. Supreme Court ruled in 2002 that a Cleveland voucher program did not violate the separation between church and state. The Court argued that the parents themselves received the vouchers and not the religious schools, at least not directly. Since 1990, only three states have implemented voucher plans: Florida, Ohio, and Wisconsin (NCES, 2006). Questions still remain about the impact of voucher programs on academic achievement, particularly among minority students who, thus far, have had little academic achievement gains (Gewertz, 2003). Who pays for the vouchers remains uncertain.

PAUSE & *REFLECT*

Why do school voucher plans receive both resistance and support? Why do such plans raise such volatile concerns regarding equal access to educational opportunity, school funding, and accountability? For further discussion of these issues, visit Rethinking School Online at http://www.rethinkingschools.org/special_reports/voucher_report/index.shtml.

The Impact of Changing Demographics on School Finance

As communities continue to grow across the United States, demographic changes have a tremendous impact on educational finance and planning. With population growth, schools must not only respond to increasing student enrollment but also address community diversity, instructional programming (such as bilingual education and special education services) and teacher, as well as administrative, training to ensure that all students have equal access to the best education possible.

As communities transform, so must the schools. Schools with enrollment increases may have more low-income students (indicated by the percentage of students participating in free or reduced-cost lunch programs) whose families work one or more jobs. Thus, families and children today require preschool, day care, health services, after-school programming, and migrant education. Professional development, in turn, is a must for administrators and teachers who are inexperienced with developing such programs for populations different from their own. Although such proactive planning is initially costly, it is an important investment in the academic achievement of students.

How can educators address changing demographics in a school? Responsiveness to a growing community requires the research and design of educational programs that assess and meet student needs. A financial strategy must be developed to compete for, secure, and disperse funding. Budgets must be monitored as program goals are identified, implemented, and evaluated for effectiveness. Thus, it is not uncommon for the role of administrators and teachers today to include that of grant writer.

Changing teacher demographics and turnover also impact educational finance, as educators retire, teacher shortages emerge in specific content areas, and student enrollments increase. The U.S. Department of Education contends that in the next 10 years, over 2 million teachers will have to be replaced (Howard, 2003). Teachers leave the profession for a number of reasons, including retirement, lack of job satisfaction, and the need for career changes. Nearly 40 percent of beginning

Middle-school ESL students with their teacher. Changing demographics in many U.S. schools contribute to the need for such programming.

teachers leave the field within their first 5 years, the major reasons being dissatisfaction with salary and the lack of support (Ingersoll, 2001).

What efforts have been made to help recruit and retain new teachers? New-teacher **mentoring programs** can be implemented to provide veteran mentors who support, train, and help retain new teachers. However, such programs represent a costly expenditure for school districts.

Without teacher retention programs and other investments (such as teacher incentive pay), low-income schools are particularly vulnerable to teacher shortages and turnover. High-quality teachers are particularly in demand in low-income schools. This impacts student achievement and increases school district costs when teachers leave the profession or a school. **Alternative licensure programs** (for teaching candidates with bachelor's degrees in fields other than education) can help relieve some of the pressure that school districts face as they try to meet the needs of schools.

However, these programs vary in quality and may not be cost-effective if teachers with alternative licensure are poorly trained and leave the profession, as well. Therefore, careful investment in quality alternative licensure programs is critical for teacher recruitment and retention.

SUMMARY

Over the course of American educational history, school funding has emerged as a vital component of U.S. democracy in action. A tension persists today regarding the pursuit of equal educational opportunity and an equitable way to fund teachers, administrators, and professional development and retention initiatives. In addition, school programming, instructional materials, school facilities, and staff must be supported. The use of property taxes to fund schools, with supplemental financing from sales and utility taxes, lottery taxes, and corporate taxes, reflects the educational investment Americans must make. This commitment, however, has its limitations. Americans expect a "bang for their buck," or a measurable outcome that represents a positive return on their investment. Thus school districts must strike a balance among equity, student achievement, standardized test scores, and increased graduation rates for all learners as they attempt to allocate the investment that communities make in the education of their students.

DISCUSSION QUESTIONS

1. Describe what historical factors or antecedents impact the structure of U.S. public education funding today.

2. In what ways have such events as World War I, World War II, and the Great Depression affected federal educational funding?

3. Compare and contrast state approaches to funding local school districts. Explain why such funding schemes remain unequal.

4. What are the differences between the funding of charter schools and that of private schools? Why are voucher plans so controversial today?

5. What factors influence how tax dollars are distributed to the public schools? What suggestions would you have for local politicians to ensure that funding plans are more equitable?

ACTIVITIES

1. Conduct a debate in your educational foundations course in which two teams present the pros and cons of school voucher plans to the rest of the group.

2. Interview school administrators from two different districts. How do they differ in access to school funding? What do the districts do to ensure fiscal equalization? How do the districts reconcile funding inequities? What are their funding priorities?

3. Some states rely more than others on sumptuary, or "sin," taxes to fund the public schools. Compare and contrast the states of Nevada and Utah. How do these states differ in their access to sumptuary funds? How do states without such funding plans compensate for this lack of revenue?

4. Visit your local school district's webpage. Identify budget links that note district funding allocations. What are the district's largest expenditures? How do such categories as salaries, health benefits, and building and transportation support and maintenance compare? Compare this information with that for another school district. How do they differ? Which allocations take precedence? What do you think the communities' role is in contributing to these differences?

WEBSITES

National Center for Education Statistics
http://nces.ed.gov
This site provides national and state data on schooling funding, teacher salaries, and socioeconomic status of public school students in regions across the country.

National Education Association
http://www.nea.org
This site presents an ongoing discussion of topics related to educational finance. Topics include voucher plans, teacher salaries, and school funding.

United States Census Bureau, Federal, State, and Local Governments Public Elementary-Secondary Education Finance Data
http://www.census.gov/govs/www/school.html
Education finance data include revenues, expenditures, debt, and assets (cash and security holdings) of elementary and secondary public school systems. Statistics cover all states, including the District of Columbia, and are available on an annual basis.

Alexander, K., & Salmon, R. (1995). *Public school finance*. Boston: Allyn and Bacon.

Berne, R., & Stiefel, L. (1984). *The measurement of equity in school finance*. Baltimore: Johns Hopkins University Press.

Biddle, B., & Berliner, D. (2002). Unequal schools: Funding in the United States. *Education Leadership, 59*(8), 48–59.

Brimley, V., & Garfield, R. (2002). *Financing education* (8th ed.). Boston: Allyn & Bacon.

Bureau of the Census. (1992, November). *State government tax collections*. Washington, DC: U.S. Department of Commerce.

Cubberly, E. (1920). *The history of education*. Boston: Houghton Mifflin.

Cubberly, E, (1947). *Public education in the United States: A study and interpretation of American educational history*. Boston: Houghton Mifflin.

Gewertz, C. (2003). Study: No academic gains from vouchers for black students. *Education Week, 19*(31), 10.

Hovey, K., & Hovey, H. (2002). *Rankings across America: Congressional Quarterly's state fact finder*. Washington, DC: Congressional Quarterly Press.

Howard, T. (2003, Winter). Who receives the short end of the shortage? Implications of the U.S. teacher shortage on urban schools. *Journal of Curriculum and Supervision 18*(2), 142–160.

Ingersoll, R. (2001, Fall). Teacher turnover and teacher shortages: An organizational analysis. *American Educational Research Journal, 38*(3), 449–534.

King, R., Swanson, A., & Sweetland, S. (2003). *School finance: Achieving high standards with equity and efficiency*. Boston: Allyn and Bacon.

Kozol, J. (1992). *Savage inequalities: Children in America's schools*. London: Harper Perennial.

National Center for Educational Statistics. (2006). Private School Survey. Retrieved July 5, 2006, from http://nces.ed.gov/pubsearch/pubsinfo.asp?pubid=2006319

National Education Association. (2004). Special education funding. Retrieved from http:///www.nex.org/specialed/index.html

National Education Association. (2006). *No Child Left Behind Act/ESEA*. Retrieved July 3, 2006, from http://www.nea.org/esea/more.html

U.S. Charter Schools. (2006). *National statistics overview*. Retrieved July 5, 2006, from http://www.uscharterschools.org/pub/uscs_docs/o/index.htm#national

United States Department of Education. (2006). *No Child Left Behind Act*. Retrieved July 4, 2006, from http://www.ed.gov

United States Department of Education, National Center for Education Statistics. (2005). *The condition of education 2005, NCES 2005–094*. Washington, DC: U.S. Government Printing Office.

CHAPTER 7

Public School Law

FIRST PERSON

Following the Law: Did I Do My Job?

Over the course of my high school teaching career in Los Angeles, I soon realized that there were a number of issues my education professors were reluctant to discuss extensively with preservice teachers, including myself, as we prepared to begin our first high school teaching assignment. This lack of preparation was exposed during my first year of employment when one of my best journalism students, Dana, not only wanted to talk about dating but specifically asked me, "How far should I go?" on a date! In an immediate retreat from the topic, all I could mumble in response was "I can't talk about that with you. You'd better discuss that with your parents." I can still see the instant disappointment on her face as her expression and spirit sank. At the time, I thought this was the best response I could give. After all, it fit nicely with state education law, and, well, that was what I was taught in my own college education coursework.

I felt extremely disappointed and frustrated with this response as the weeks passed. Dana and I had grown close during my first year of teaching. She was a very articulate writer in my general English class, a soft-spoken Chicana student who had a very hip, easy-going style. Her fellow students readily welcomed Dana's occasional role as an unassuming leader and peer writing tutor. Nevertheless, she often rushed home to help take care of younger siblings, and as a result, Dana did not participate in extracurricular activities at school.

Meanwhile, I struggled with my own extracurricular teaching assignment as adviser of the student newspaper staff. I quickly learned that many of the journalism students were not very interested in reporting. What did fuel their interests were the previous teacher's low expectations and the easy elective credits they could earn. Recruiting students from my general English classes became my way to involve and affirm diverse writers who did not participate

CHAPTER OBJECTIVES

- Readers will become familiar with the process of securing a teaching contract for employment, as well as with the factors contributing to a breach of contract.

- Readers will understand what the purpose of the tenure process is, how it is achieved, and what constitutes termination when tenure is secured.

- Readers will examine educators' rights and responsibilities relevant to such topics as liability, child abuse, academic freedom, and teacher privacy concerns.

- Readers will analyze curriculum issues related to such controversial topics as sex education, religion and education, and AIDS education.

- Readers will identify students' legal rights both on campus and in the classroom.

in on-campus activities. Dana was one of those writers who would soon enjoy writing movie and music reviews. Over the course of time, she was able to rearrange her schedule to report on after-school events. Because of Dana's role modeling, I was able to recruit new journalism students from our general English class.

Admittedly, I was thrilled that Dana and I were able to develop a rapport around writing, poetry, music (we were both early U2 fans), and, most important, culture. She had her Spanish and maintained familial ties to Mexico. As the year progressed, so did her self-esteem and her attractiveness to boys. I began to notice that she would attend class sporting an occasional hickey or two. I blew it off as "teens being teens," even though her classroom work ethic began to slip. That was when she posed her question, which was really about premarital sex. But state law instructed me that I could not go there. Our relationship soon turned from close to remote.

A month passed. Dana stopped coming to class regularly. We no longer talked and no longer seemed to get along. Instead, I nagged her about attendance and missed deadlines. I called home, no answer. I contacted her counselor, who informed me that Dana would soon be enrolling in our teen mother program. And just like that, she was gone.

I tried not to feel so self-important as to believe that if I had really addressed Dana's initial question, perhaps we could have talked about relationships and intimacy in ways she might have felt comfortable about. After all, information was communicated through the appropriate counseling channels, and her education went on. But I cannot help but feel that maybe, just maybe, I could have been a sounding board for her— that I could have encouraged her to focus her energies on school, on planning for college, and on leadership to our community. Instead, I followed the law and did my job.

Or did I?

Teachers and the Law: An Introduction

Becoming a teacher for many of us entails completing an education program, student teaching, securing job interviews, and signing a contract. We look forward to the day when we receive the first set of keys to a classroom where we will teach our favorite subjects and guide extracurricular activities. But we don't want to think about such things as violence in schools, or teachers who become intimately involved with students, or educators who tamper with the standardized tests scores of students, and the loop after loop of news bites that play such stories numerous times on television.

Nor do we generally think about the topics that are addressed in this chapter, such as the terms of our employment contract, tenure guidelines, the role of unions, potential job liabilities, due process, freedom of expression and association, sex education, discrimination, teacher privacy, and religious freedom, not to mention libel, slander, and copyright law. This list, however, does not suggest that new teachers should enter a school building escorted by an attorney, even in today's litigious times. What it does suggest is that teachers need to become well informed about school law.

TABLE 7.1   Categories of School Law Information Provided by the National School Board Association

Visit the National School Board Association webpage, and select one of the categories listed below. What are some of the general legal issues relevant to students and teachers that affect the category you selected? What are some examples of recent cases and arguments specific to that category?

Topic	Description
Athletics	The Athletics page provides a broad range of information on topics such as Title IX, gender equity, student-athlete drug testing and codes of conduct, school district liability for sports-related injuries, and disabled students' participation in interscholastic sports.
Curriculum	Issues involving state and federal standards, teacher and student classroom speech, religious rights, and controversies over instruction, textbooks, and classroom and library materials.
Employment and Labor	Included is information about the major employment laws affecting schools: Title VII (discrimination and sexual harassment), the Americans with Disabilities Act (ADA), the Age Discrimination in Employment Act (ADEA), the Family Medical Leave Act (FMLA), and the Fair Labor Standards Act (FLSA). Also, find out more about other employment topics, including collective bargaining, fringe benefits, teacher free speech rights, discipline and discharge of employees, and the No Child Left Behind Act's requirements regarding teacher and paraprofessional qualifications.
Equity and Discrimation	Issues involving age, disability, race, ethnic origin, gender, and homeless status, including Titles VI, VI, and IX, and desegregation.
Facilities, Property, and School Business	School property includes public land, facilities, and equipment. Issues often arise over control of property, purchasing procedure, eminent domain, and buildings and construction. This category also includes legal information on issues arising from school business operations, such as vendor contracts
Finance	State constitutional provisions empower or require state legislatures to provide a system of public education. The state legislature has the authority to tax and distribute funds for public schools. Litigation that arises usually involves the methods used to collect taxes and distribute revenue to districts. Many cases question the legal authority of school districts to issue bonds, hold bond elections, or impose fees and charges.
Health and Nutrition	Resources and cases pertaining to nutrition and student and employee health issues such as insurance, confidentiality of health records, health-related services, drugs, contagious diseases, and accommodations for health conditions.
Liability and Legal System	Public schools function in a complex legal environment. They must comply with constitutional, statutory, regulatory, and judicial legal requirements at the federal, state, and local levels. They may encounter liability claims from any part of this system. This section contains information on the American legal system generally and on general issues of the liability and immunity of public school systems, including insurance.
Local Governance	Read about legal and practical issues related to local school board control and how school boards operate, including school board ethics, open meetings laws, conflicts of interest, board roles and responsibilities, parliamentary procedure, policy and decision making, strategic planning, budgeting, complaint procedures, elections, committees, board minutes, board self-evaluation, and hearing procedure.
No Child Left Behind Act	The No Child Left Behind Act was signed into law on January 8, 2002. It is a massive law that has revamped the Elementary and Secondary Education Act and imposed staggering obligations on public schools. Chief among these are new testing requirements and accountability standards intended to reduce achievement gaps among student subgroups. But there are many other provisions to which schools will be required to adhere.
Privatization and Choice	Legal issues involving various reform measures, including public school choice, charter schools, privatization, vouchers, and alternative schools.
Religion	The religion page is devoted to First Amendment, Establishment, Free Exercise, and Free Speech clause issues related to the role of religion in public schools. Topics covered include prayer, religious instruction, religious garb, religious observations, and religious displays. This page also looks at claims raised under the federal Equal Access Act.

TABLE 7.1   Categories of School Law Information Provided by the National School Board Association (cont.)

Topic	Description
School Safety	Issues concerning student safety, school violence, and student rights, including issues of harassment and bullying.
Special Education and Disabilities	Serving students with disabilities raises many complex legal issues for schools. These issues often involve understanding and complying with federal laws such as the Individuals with Disabilities Education Act, § 504 of the Rehabilitation Act, and the Americans with Disabilities Act.
Student Achievement	Find legal information on standardized tests, high stakes testing, and academic honors.
Student Rights and Discipline	The student rights and discipline page provides information regarding the challenges school districts face in balancing students' First, Fourth, and Fifth Amendment rights with their educational mission to maintain a safe, nondisruptive learning environment. Topics covered will include due process, equal protection, search and seizure, freedom of speech, free exercise of religion, and privacy issues related to the Family Educational Rights and Privacy Act.
Technology	The technology page deals with legal issues related to Internet, e-mail, video, and other emerging technology. This section will provide information on E-rate, software filters, social networking, and other off-campus student websites and free speech, Internet acceptable use policies, and privacy.

Source: National School Board Association. Retrieved March 25, 2007, from http://www.nsba.org/site/page.asp?TRACKID5&CID5381&DID58622.

This chapter explores those legal concepts and information that teachers need to be familiar with student and teacher rights, as well as the systems in place to protect them both. With this knowledge, teachers are better prepared to discharge their responsibilities regarding lawful and unlawful school practices in ways that are preemptive and mindful of proper legal procedures.

Administrators and teachers alike need to be aware of the possibility of lawsuits in a number of specific legal categories (see Table 7.1). However, the law should not be viewed as a minefield that must be circumvented by educators. Instead, school law must be approached in the same way as the constitution is approached, with respect and understanding of complex interpretations and ongoing changes in the law, due process, and legislative processes. Thus, public school law is a very difficult and broad topic to address during the course of one's teacher preparation coursework.

In essence, this chapter discusses topics most central to the professional experiences of teachers, so that they can view the law as a source of information, assistance, and protection that serves students as well as educators. Readers need to be mindful that state school laws differ from one state to another and that they may change. The issues addressed here reflect a general understanding of federal and state legal systems relevant to educational policy.

Securing Employment, Securing a Contract

Upon completion of a teacher education program and state certification, preservice teachers can pursue employment contracts in a school district. In addition to holding a teaching certificate (or a provisional certificate), new teachers must meet other criteria, such as U.S. citizenship (or having filed a declaration to become a citizen), and pass state teacher examinations. School boards have the responsibility of accepting, or ratifying, a teacher contract at their discretion. Thus, a contract is not binding until a school board has approved it.

Terms of a Contract

The terms of a contract differ from state to state and district to district. Who decides on the terms of a teacher contract? They generally are based on negotiations, also known as **collective bargaining**, between the district administration and a teachers' union. The content of a contract varies, but it generally includes information about a teacher's salary and the conditions of employment, which may include the following:

• Teacher salary schedules or rates based on years of service and university credits or degrees earned

• Tenure, provisional contract, and dismissal terms

• Teaching assignments, rules and regulations relevant to state law

• Length or time period of the contract

• Health insurance, disability plans, and sick pay requirements

• State retirement term

The duration of a contract is also described in a nontenured employee agreement, which usually applies for one year or less. Teachers can also work without a contract, in provisional assignments, internships, or long-term substitute positions. However, working without a contract can result in little or no access to health benefits and in difficulties recouping salary if a school district does not honor an employment agreement. Also, a school has no obligation to employ a nontenured teacher for the following year, with or without a contract.

Not all information regarding a teacher's employment is included in a contract. Class size, extracurricular activity assignments, and all rules, regulations, and provisions specific to this contract (including those rules adopted after the contract was ratified) may not be part of the language in the original contract. It is especially important for employees to review a teacher handbook to better understand the specific

From PRESERVICE to PRACTICE

Missouri Supreme Court Hears Oral Arguments in Case About Public-Sector Collective-Bargaining Rights

The Missouri Supreme Court has heard oral arguments in a case between a school district and unions over whether the Missouri Constitution's guarantee of collective-bargaining rights extends to public-sector employees. The court has long said that the answer to that question is no. At issue is an April 2002 decision by the school board that altered the way it negotiated salaries and working conditions for teachers and other employees. In their legal briefs, the unions said Missouri Supreme Court precedents

that gave the employees little power to fight the policy change are "at odds ... with the modern recognition that meaningful public-sector labor relations promote the goal of labor peace." The school district argued that the court's stance is good public policy, especially in this case, because the possible disruption in schools is at odds with the "paramount importance" of education.

Question for Reflection

1. Why would a school district be reluctant to participate in the collective bargaining process with teachers unions?

Source: National School Board Association. Retrieved March 25, 2007, from http://www.nsba.org/site/doc_cosa.asp?TRACKID=&VID=50&CID=445&DID=40227.

content and terms of a contract. Teacher handbooks are distributed to faculty members upon employment, with addenda or revisions provided annually.

Contracts can also be disputed, on the basis of challenges to the interpretation of contract language, the contexts of the dispute, and state law. School districts often retain a full-time attorney whose expertise is educational law, as do many teachers' unions. Members of a teachers' union can retain the counsel of the union lawyer or employ their own personal representation.

For Your CONSIDERATION

Visit state offices of education and teachers' union websites to review employee contracts and teachers' rights. For example, you can visit the Idaho State Department of Education site at **http://www.sde.state.id.us/ admin/teacher_contracts.asp** or the Texas Classroom Teachers Association site at **http://www.tcta.org/legal/contracts/sgcon.htm** to see sample contracts and policies.

Breach of Contract

Breaking, or **breaching**, a contract occurs when a teacher or school district does not meet the commitment set forth in a contract. Either party can breach a contract; for example, breach of contract occurs if a teacher does not complete a teaching assignment based on the terms of the contract, or if a school district refuses to pay a teacher compensation for services such as extracurricular activity coaching and/or advisement.

If the terms of a contract are changed by a school district after the contract is in effect, this is also a breach of contract. Teachers also breach a contract if they seek changes midway through the contract period. Of course, the interpretation of contract language definitely comes into play, because the courts must determine the intentions of the contract given the context of the situation.

There are certainly legal consequences when a contract is breached. When terms are broken, monetary compensation or damages must be paid to the party who has been aggrieved. The specific amount of money to be paid is based on the court's findings. For example, amount of salary owed to a teacher, minus the effect of teacher demand and surplus (where a teacher can be easily replaced), can limit the amount of damages a court will award. Other damages collected under state or federal law may include attorney fees and expenses incurred while a teacher seeks new employment.

Conversely, a school district can seek damages from a teacher when he or she breaks a contract. For instance, when a teacher leaves school in the middle of an academic year, the district can pursue damages to cover the expenses it incurred while seeking a replacement. Districts can also request additional compensation if the replacement teacher requires a higher salary. Or a district can include, in its contract terms, liquidated damages clauses, which are predetermined damages to be paid by a teacher who breaks a contract.

In sum, contracts are used by school districts to identify the employment responsibilities of the teacher workforce. Contracts also reflect a general overview of school district policies and employee expectations that are often negotiated between districts and teachers' unions. The terms of a contract go into effect once a school board has ratified the contract.

A contract is breached if a district or teacher violates the terms of the contract. Districts that do not meet their contractual obligations are required to pay damages to a teacher for lost salary while he or she seeks another teaching position. A court may also require a school district to meet its contractual obligations and reinstate a teacher. By the same token, a teacher who does not fulfill contractual terms is subject to paying damages to the school district, such as fees for securing a replacement. School district contract policies vary from state to state and should be reviewed carefully, but in general, teacher contracts reflect these kinds of general principles.

PAUSE & REFLECT

When a school district does not retain a teacher for an entire academic year, despite the fact that he or she and the district had signed a contract, what rights does an educator have to reclaim lost wages? Whom do you think the teacher can consult with, given such a situation?

The Importance of Being Tenured

Two different kinds of employment contracts are offered to teachers. They are term contracts, which are valid and renewable at the discretion of a school district for a specific length of time, and **tenure** contracts, which historically have been created through states' legislative actions and ensure that teachers will be terminated only for just cause and through due process. Tenure statutes, also known as "teacher tenure acts" in many states, were established as early as the 1890s. These statutes vary from state to state, and their specific tenure requirements and procedures for dismissing a tenured teacher serve both to protect the rights of teachers and to safeguard school districts' rights to make personnel decisions.

Earning tenure is a critical process in a teacher's career. Following the completion of a probationary period whose duration is generally two to three years, tenure represents the permanent, contractual employment of a teacher until retirement. Tenure helps maintain a stable and professional teaching staff within a school district. Tenure also protects the faculty from arbitrary employment decisions by the district administration. It does not, however, guarantee tenured teachers a specific teaching assignment or offer complete protect from termination.

States maintain school codes or laws that outline causes for termination and due process. Before a teacher is released from instructional duties, a school district must establish a legal cause for dismissal. When a district, through the local school board, seeks to terminate a tenured teacher, it refers to these laws, which differ from state to state. In turn, teachers must be notified of the charges against them. Teachers, tenured and nontenured, are also protected by the notification and hearing rights under the due process clause of the Fourteenth Amendment to the U.S. Constitution.

How Teachers Achieve Tenure

State law, and the interpretation of that law, establish the specific terms and requirements that determine the awarding of tenure. The two- to three-year probationary period means that teachers work in the same school or district under the terms of a yearly contract. The probationary contract may not be renewed following the completion of service described in the contract terms.

In some states, tenure may be granted automatically after a certified teacher completes the probationary period, whereas other states may require administrative recommendations and school board ratification. Annual contracts can also be

From PRESERVICE to PRACTICE

Earning Tenure

Mary Macias was excited about having earned tenure following her third year of teaching sixth graders at Evergreen Elementary School in Los Angeles. She had worked diligently to redesign a literacy curriculum to better meet the needs of her English language learners. Mary had also welcomed the suggestions provided by her administrators to improve her classroom management skills and instructional strategies. In addition, she had established a number of contacts with local families in order to tap into their community interests, understand their concerns, and generate more school involvement.

With her teaching position now secure, Mary was eager to begin her fourth year at Evergreen. But then she learned that her husband Reynoldo's accounting firm was relocating to Chicago and was offering him a new position and a pay increase. For Mary, securing a new teaching position in Chicago could be aided by enthusiastic letters of recommendation from her principal, mentor teachers, and parent association chairperson. Nevertheless, Mary was reluctant to leave.

She explained to Reynoldo, "I don't know if we should move. While I want to support *us* in our future, at the same time I don't want us to leave our families. I don't want us to leave our community. Plus, I'd have to start the tenure process all over again. I'm not sure if I want to do that. And we also need to start thinking about starting our own family." Reynoldo agreed with Mary's concerns, but at the same time, he thought, "That's a sweet job offer in Chicago, too. I'd hate to pass it up."

Questions for Reflection

1. What would you do if you were in Mary and Reynoldo's situation?
2. What factors would you weigh as you consider these choices?
3. Given the tenure process that Mary has just completed, why would she be reluctant to seek tenure in another state and school district?

renewed automatically on a continual basis, until the school board determines that the teacher's services are no longer needed in the upcoming academic year.

The protection that tenure offers is usually limited to the teacher workforce. School administrators may hold long-term positions or may have their contracts renewed continually. However, because many educational administrators have served as teachers in the same district, they often already hold tenure.

Unlike nontenured teachers, those holding tenure maintain a number of rights. They have the right of continual employment that can be terminated only for a specific cause established by state law. A school board does have the right to make teacher reassignments and transfers in order to meet district needs. And yet tenured teachers *cannot* be transferred if the transfer would do the following:

- Follow a termination without a hearing,
- Require a teacher to take an assignment where he or she has no content-area background,
- Require the teacher to pursue supplementary training at his or her expense in preparation for the reassignment, or
- Result in a salary cut.

Tenured teachers *can* be transferred in response to court-ordered desegregation plans. In an effort to achieve more racially balanced schools, courts have found that tenure laws are not in effect under these circumstances, particularly in districts that resist transferring teachers.

PAUSE & REFLECT

Much debate has emerged in the public dialogue about the repeal of teacher tenure laws. Some would argue that tenure serves only to protect ineffective teachers from dismissal. Others argue that tenure is necessary to protect the rights of teachers who fall out of political or social favor with the administration, community members, and students when they present controversial content in the curriculum. In your view, should tenure be maintained?

Termination of Tenured and of Nontenured Teachers

Specific state codes and laws list the causes that school districts feel warrant the dismissal of tenured and nontenured teachers. These causes are related to the performance of contractual duties. For example, legal language can include "incompetence," "immorality," "negligence," "cruelty," and the failure of a teacher to satisfactorily complete a performance plan. A performance plan generally consists of a set of guidelines that a teacher must follow to be awarded tenure. Teachers can also lose tenure by resigning or by accepting a position in another school district.

Before a tenured teacher is terminated, written notification of charges must be made and a hearing held according to state or district codes. In many states, tenured teachers have an opportunity to "correct" their performance and avoid termination by following a remediation plan before they are dismissed. Correctable charges include classroom management difficulties, ineffective instruction, and excessive absences. If corrections are not successfully completed within a predetermined period of time, the termination process can move forward. Of course, there are causes for termination that cannot be corrected. These include sexual relations with a student and criminal activity that impedes teaching performance.

As notification of charges, school boards must provide, in writing, specific statements regarding the grounds for termination. These statements must be clear and detailed so that the educator under review is aware of the charges and can prepare a defense. This information must include the dates of the charges, as well as the details surrounding them. Other factors that can contribute to termination include ineffective instructional practices; unsatisfactory relationships with students, parents, teachers, administration, and/or staff; insubordination; disruptive campus behavior and influence; and disregard for the school's educational philosophy or mission.

School boards must be careful when classifying correctable and uncorrectable reasons for termination. According to due process, teachers must first receive notice of the charges against them. If these charges are deemed correctable or there is a lack of evidence to substantiate the charge, then the employee has an opportunity to seek remediation and *possibly* reinstatement.

As part of the educational code, states may include a hearing in which a teacher can meet before an impartial hearing officer prior to a dismissal decision. This officer is frequently appointed by the board of education. Depending on the state code, either a teacher or the board itself can request that the hearing be made public. Under oath, witnesses can be called to attend the hearing and "testify" regarding the teacher and the charges at hand. Teachers do have the right to attend the hearing accompanied by an attorney, who can call witnesses to refute the charges.

However, unlike tenured teachers, nontenured teachers generally do not have the right to a hearing. This can vary from state to state, as second-year nontenured teachers may be given school board notice of, or may request in writing, the causes of contract nonrenewal.

Losing a Job: Contributing Factors Regarding Dismissal

A number of institutional bodies inform the laws that constitute grounds for teacher termination. State legislatures, local school boards, and teachers' unions participate in the determination of which violations are cause for termination. According to Fischer, Schimmel, and Kelly (2003), the major reasons for termination most often noted in state law include incompetency, immorality, unprofessional conduct, and insubordination. Of course, school boards must prove that these charges are true and violate state law before a teacher can be terminated.

What Does It Mean to Be Incompetent?

To be identified as an incompetent teacher reflects an educator's inability to meet the educational responsibilities described in the teacher's contract. Generally, incompetency lies in the educator's lack of instructional and content-area knowledge and preparation. For example, a teacher may not have a grasp of the subject matter he or she is employed to teach, such as English grammar, mathematical concepts, or geography content. A deficit in classroom management can also contribute to incompetency. An unremittingly boisterous classroom can undermine an effective instructional environment for all students.

Incompetency should *not* be assumed, however, when a teacher makes an occasional error in content-area instruction or is having a challenging day with a challenging group of students. Incompetency generally manifests itself over the course of time and over multiple incidents.

Other Causes for Termination

Termination can be the end result of a number of contributing factors known as unprofessional conduct, taking place while children are in the custody of a teacher. However broad the interpretation of "unprofessional conduct" may be, violations against state code can include lying, cheating, the use of obscene language or sexually explicit materials in the classroom, substance abuse, and sexual misconduct. Nor can teachers use cruel or sarcastic language in the classroom or excessive force and restraint against students.

Teachers can also be terminated for what many states broadly refer to as "good and just cause." This broad term provides school boards with great latitude beyond specific state law when seeking the dismissal of a teacher. For example, good and just cause can be employed when charges of teacher insubordination arise or when teachers use the classroom for purposes other than instruction, such as political organizing or lobbying. Teachers who do not follow departmental policy and programming can also be subject to termination.

Tenured and nontenured teachers can be dismissed as a consequence of school district budget constraints. The most common such causes are (1) a projected decline in student enrollment, (2) curtailment of a program, (c) the consolidation of schools, and (4) district reorganization. A school board can eliminate departments, programs, and teaching positions if the districts can no longer afford to support certain operations. The school board can also reallocate school resources and reorganize programs, as well as the curriculum.

From PRESERVICE to PRACTICE

New Jersey Teacher Tenure Laws Make Removal of a Teacher Complicated and Costly

Instituted almost a century ago to prevent political interference in New Jersey school employment, state teacher tenure laws require districts to negotiate a complicated and expensive process to prove that a teacher does not belong in a classroom. As a result, not one of the more than 10,000 teachers in Bergen County, New Jersey, has been fired via the state's tenure-hearing process in at least a decade. In the past nine years, only about 50 of the state's 100,000 teachers were removed from the classroom.

The high cost incurred by school districts when they attempt to remove a teacher makes it unrealistic to bring tenure charges, according to former state Commissioner of Education William Librera. School districts often try the "express route" of brokering deals that entice teachers to walk away with payouts and even clean records. As more boards contend with state-mandated budget caps, there has been a push toward settlements over tenure charges, says school boards attorney Joseph Morano. "Boards are forced to pick and choose their battles," he says. "If you know you're going to spend $15,000 on a case, you want to know that you'll win. With all the spending cuts and the lack of money available, everything a board does is scrutinized."

The New Jersey Education Association places the blame on administrators who fail to give bad evaluations. Mr. Morano agrees that administrators often couch negative evaluations in positive terms, and districts require a documented record to fire a tenured teacher.

But North Bergen principal Patrick J. Capotorto says that districts face procedures that make it hard to write up a teacher in the first place. Contracts regularly allow teachers to challenge parts of their evaluation, and teachers must be given an appropriate length of time to improve if they are accused of inefficiency.

Tenure probably won't be eliminated any time soon. "Tenure is one issue that the teachers' unions will fight for tooth and nail," says New Jersey School Boards Association spokesman Michael Yaple. "Legislators that think of themselves as the most staunch education reformers will stop short when it comes to tenure."

Questions for Reflection

1. As illustrated in this case, what are the positive and negative aspects of the tenure system?
2. How are students impacted by ineffective teachers and by state education systems that do not have policies in place to challenge their tenure?

Source: National School Board Association. Retrieved March 25, 2007, from http://www.nsba.org/site/doc_cosa.asp?TRAICKID=&VID=50&CID=445&DID=38965.

In some states, such as Alabama, if a reduction in the educator workforce is needed, even tenured teachers can be terminated because of a loss of school funding. However, when budget limitations arise in such states as Illinois, nontenured teachers are subject to termination before tenured teachers. And seniority counts; teachers who have had tenure for the shortest time are dismissed first.

This does not suggest that a school board has complete jurisdiction over the contract renewal and termination of its tenured workforce. Teachers' unions do negotiate agreements that guarantee some rights for their members. Such an agreement may indicate which teachers will be selected for dismissal when workforce reductions go into effect. Terminations, or "layoffs," must still follow **due process**, which includes the identification of administrators who take part in such a decision, the criteria and evaluation data used for dismissal, employee notification, and a hearing. In addition, school districts cannot use workforce reductions or economic shortfalls to avoid granting tenure or to discriminate against teachers.

For Your CONSIDERATION

Visit the National Staff Development Council (NSDC) webpage for information on teacher quality and school improvement. For example, you can visit the NSDC site and access articles from the *Journal of Staff Development* library at **http://www.nsdc.org/index.cfm** for information regarding professional development.

Teachers' Rights and Liability Issues

Preservice teachers often are concerned about the extent to which they are liable for injuries sustained by students under their supervision. In the United States, which many consider the most litigious of societies, this concern comes as no surprise. What exactly are teachers' responsibilities when working with students? What are their rights? This section provides a brief overview and response to these questions.

Teachers in general hold the primary responsibility to supervise students under their immediate control. Students can hold teachers liable for damages if all of the following conditions prevail:

- The teacher had the responsibility to protect a student from injury.
- The teacher did not use care in protecting the student.
- Because of the teacher's carelessness, the student sustained an injury.
- Thus, the student experienced damages that can be proved.

And yet, it is often necessary to ask, what exactly caused a student to be injured? Did the teacher truly neglect his or her duties, and if so, how much in monetary damages should be awarded?

A teacher helps guide a visually impaired student jump rope.

When Are Teachers Negligent?

A teacher is considered to have been negligent when he or she injures a student or does not exercise reasonable care to protect students from injury. The term *reasonable care* refers to the level of care a teacher would be expected to use given such circumstances as the age, experience, and maturity of the students and the dangers at hand. Reasonable care can also vary. For example, a high school industrial arts teacher must demonstrate greater care when supervising students who are using electrical tools than an elementary teacher on playground duty. Even so, accidents *do* occur on the playground, and elementary teachers must also demonstrate reasonable care by explaining and enforcing the rules of play and by providing protective equipment (such as a backstop or plastic, padded playground equipment).

"Duty of care" extends not only to teachers on campus, but to teachers and counselors both on and off campus, especially if instructional assignments (such as science experiments) are dangerous. Also, teachers and counselors have the responsibility to notify parents if students are engaged in self-injurious, suicidal, or violent behaviors and if they make threats against themselves or others. As part of their professional duties, educators must take reasonable care to prevent such tragedies. If they do not do so, they can be held liable for negligence.

This is not to suggest that an educator is always responsible for his or her students' every movement at all times. Under certain circumstances, teachers may not be able to anticipate a dangerous event, given the context of a particular situation. In the Illinois case of *Mancha v. Field Museum of Natural History* (1972), the family of student Robert Mancha, 12, sued teachers for negligence following his participation in a museum field trip. Boys not associated with his school attacked Robert at the museum. Because the teachers did not protect Robert from injury, his family sued the teachers for negligence. However, the court found that the teachers, given such a heavy burden of supervision, did not have the "duty of care" at a location not associated with known danger and risks. Teachers could not anticipate such an event occurring. Note, however, that even though the court supported the teachers in this case, the judge did add that constant supervision *would* be necessary during field trips where certain risks might be expected to occur (such as in outdoor recreational or industrial settings).

By the same token, if school administrators are aware of a student's violent tendencies or of patterns of aggressive behavior toward other students, self, or school staff, then those officials are responsible for informing teachers about such a student. An educator who has this knowledge has a duty to exercise care to prevent such actions or injury from occurring. If teachers do not have access to this knowledge, a school itself can be found to be negligent (Cambron et al., 2003).

If a teacher is careless about his or her duties, however, it does not automatically result in damages being awarded to the plaintiff. Carelessness must be established in court, and it must be shown that because of this neglect of duty, an injury was inflicted on a student. A student could be injured on the playground with or without supervision, and, depending on the injury, it could have occurred regardless of the presence of supervision. A student at baseball practice could be hit on the head by a foul ball, but such an injury does not constitute negligence. Whether a coach was in the vicinity of the accident or not, supervision would not have changed the direction of a flying baseball, which is a natural consequence of the game. Thus, not all teachers who are charged with neglect are automatically liable for the injury to students under their supervision.

Liability and Child Abuse

New teachers often pose another important question: "Am I responsible for reporting an incident of child abuse to authorities?" A law that is consistent across the United States requires that *all teachers, counselors, and administrators report suspected cases of child abuse and neglect to senior administrators,* who in turn must communicate this information to local educational and social service authorities. Educators who report these charges to their superiors are immune from liability, assuming that the charges have been made without malicious intent.

What exactly constitutes child abuse? Again, because individual state laws differ, we must turn to the 1974 federal law, the National Child Abuse Prevention and Treatment Act, to arrive at a working definition. Under this law, neglect and child abuse include "physical or mental injury, sexual abuse or exploitation, negligent treatment, or maltreatment of a child under the age of 18 or the age specified by the child protection law of the state in question, by a person who is responsible for the child's welfare, under circumstances which indicate that the child's health or welfare is harmed or threatened" (in Fischer et al., 2003).

From PRESERVICE to PRACTICE

Breaking Up a Fight

Let's consider two scenarios.

Scenario 1: Let's say teacher Mary heard a fight starting outside her classroom. Two students who were engaged in an argument began to push and shove each other. She told the students to break it up and report to their next class. One agreed, but the other threw a punch at his classmate. Mary then grabbed the student who was continuing the confrontation and led him away. The student snarled at her, "Get your hands off me. I have my rights." Did Mary violate his rights?

A very similar situation was described in *Wallace v. Batavia* (1995). In this case, the school board and an individual teacher were sued by the parent of a student who had been involved in a fight. The teacher had to take one of the students by the wrist and escort her out of the classroom. The parents sued under a federal statute rather than a state tort law, but the case sheds light on what courts would do in a similar situation in which a state tort law was used. The court recognized that immediate, effective action was sometimes needed to deal with disruptive behavior. Furthermore, the court held that in seeking to maintain order and discipline, a teacher is constrained only by the need to take reasonable actions to achieve those goals. Depending on the circumstances, the court found, such reasonable action may include the physical seizure of a student in the face of provocative or disruptive behavior.

Scenario 2: One of your students attends a general education classroom for art and music. Because of the aggressive nature of the student, goals have been included on his individualized education program (IEP) that address his frequent outbursts of anger. The IEP team determines that he will be mainstreamed in a few classes; however, the principal believes that, because of confidentiality requirements, the general education teacher should not be told of the student's aggressive tendencies. One day the student attacks and injures a student in your art class. Can you be sued for the incident?

When a student with a history of violent behavior is placed in a situation in which other students may be put at risk, appropriate preventive actions must be taken. If they are not, and a student is injured, a lawsuit and liability are a real possibility. The IEP team is the proper forum in which to address such situations. Additionally, all personnel involved with the student should be informed of any hazardous situations. It is not true that confidentiality requirements prevent a person working with students from being informed about their behavioral history.

Source: Yell (1999).

Because child abuse is a state crime and not a federal one, definitions do vary. Nevertheless, they have similar elements that include emotional or mental injury, physical injury, sexual molestation, and exploitation.

The federal government provides funding to the states to help them develop child abuse policies and guidelines that establish standards for reporting abuse cases. This funding also offers support for community-based agencies to develop emergency assistance and prevention programs, and it supplies assistance for criminal investigations.

Another difficult question that educators confront is "How can I be certain that abuse or neglect has taken place?" Because abuse generally occurs without witnesses present, teachers are not required to be certain when reporting abuse, but they must have "reasonable cause" when such abuse is alleged. Indicators of various forms of abuse and neglect are presented in Table 7.2.

As educators develop experience in observing and working with youth, they can begin to recognize those behaviors and signs that may indicate abuse. This list is not

TABLE 7.2 Sample Indicators of Child Abuse and Neglect

Abuse	Indicators
Physical abuse	Unexplained abrasions, bruises, burns, fractures, lacerations, and welts
	Student behavior indicators: withdrawn, fear of adults, afraid to go home, emotional extremes, frightened by parents, little interest in school
Physical neglect	Poor hygiene, inappropriate attire, hunger, unattended medical needs, lack of supervision/abandonment
	Student behavior indicators: long stays at school (early arrival and late departures), delinquency, fatigue or sleeping in class, stealing or begging for food, substance abuse, disinterest in school, learning delays
Sexual abuse	Bloody or stained undergarments, difficulty walking and sitting, injuries or bruises in genital areas, sexually transmitted disease
	Student behavior indicators: reluctance to participate in physical activities or gym, withdrawal from others, sophisticated knowledge of sexual behavior, delinquency or runaway behaviors, disinterest in school, learning delays.

exhaustive. It does not reflect all of the possible indicators of abuse and neglect. Conversely, these indicators *do not necessarily mean* that abuse has taken place. This list can help teachers to become aware of and sensitive to emotional and behavioral changes that can affect their students' health, well-being, and academic achievement.

Allegations of child abuse are not taken lightly. Being charged with child abuse and neglect has serious consequences and may damage a reputation and even destroy a career. Due process also should be followed, and an investigation by the appropriate authorities must take place before any charges are formally filed.

Educators can be held liable for the failure to report child abuse or neglect, depending on state law. This misdemeanor is difficult to prosecute, because it is hard to determine whether the witness knowingly chose not to report the abuse. The criteria for proving civil liability (where guilt is measured in fines or monetary damages) also differ from state to state. Today, federal policy and state laws are in place to ensure that educators and counselors report child abuse and neglect so that interventions and support services can be provided.

Teachers' Private Lives

Teachers lead public lives in communities where they may be expected to have exemplary lifestyles. In other words, they may be held to a higher standard than other people. The role of a schoolteacher often extends outside of the classroom, with participation in extracurricular activities and attendance at school-related events both commonplace and expected. This visible presence in the community leaves educators vulnerable to scrutiny of their personal lives.

Can teachers be fired for what they do in their private lives? Teachers are not only content-area instructors; they are also viewed as role models for students. Depending on the values of a community, conflicts can arise when teachers don't meet the expectations of parents. After all, the moral standards of a rural community may differ completely from those of an urban community. For example, in a city environment, teachers can blend into the society without much scrutiny, whereas in a small town, notoriety on the part of a teacher can be much more glaring.

The concept of notoriety is often used by the courts to determine whether a teacher's private activities jeopardize his or her effectiveness as an instructor and status as a role model. Notoriety, then, is the extent to which teachers are well known for undesirable and controversial acts.

There remains no definitive legal standard for what is considered immoral and unprofessional behavior, which may range from cohabitation without marriage, to unpopular political activism, to drinking beer at a sports bar. A teacher who lives with a partner instead of getting married may be received differently in a small town than in a large city. However, community disapproval of that lifestyle does not establish valid grounds for termination, as long as the behavior does not affect the teacher's job performance.

Gay teachers, historically speaking, have been especially vulnerable to termination regardless of whether they have been found to be negligent of their teaching duties. Depending on state law, gay teachers cannot be terminated unless their behavior is criminal. Community discourse regarding homosexuality comes into play, because some individuals believe that homosexuality is morally wrong, whereas others believe it is a biological attribute. In any case, it has been ruled that homosexual conduct has no impact on the professionalism and effectiveness of teachers (*Morrison v. State Board of Education*, 1969).

Certain other private behaviors decisively and rightly threaten the employment of teachers. Teachers, given their status and authority as trusted role models second only to parents, cannot have sexual relations with students. This certainly violates professional standards. Nor can teachers have felony convictions on their records; the existence of any such conviction renders them subject to dismissal.

Teachers' Rights

Academic Freedom

In general, teachers in the United States enjoy privileges protected by the First Amendment. Academic freedom and freedom of speech enable teachers to express themselves freely in the classroom about their content-area subject matter, their interpretation and evaluation of that subject matter, and appropriate instructional strategies and relevant materials. This freedom reflects our democratic society in action, as teachers are encouraged to introduce new ideas and content with students as together they seek to solve problems and examine issues. Of course, this does not suggest that teachers' pedagogical decisions are free from debate or controversy when their ideas and practices conflict with certain societal values.

Controversy is known to arise in a number of educational contexts. Because of state curriculum codes and laws, textbooks and literature are often under the scrutiny of school boards who reserve the right to ban texts from the curriculum. Teachers and school board members can disagree about the readings in question, but the school board has the power to decide which texts will remain part of the curriculum and which will be removed.

School boards cannot remove books arbitrarily, however. For example, advocating a particular religion or political ideology by eliminating other readings from the curriculum is unconstitutional. In other words, certain ideas cannot be imposed on students by the removal of other ideas from the curriculum. The First Amendment affirms that controversial issues that are inherent in and relevant to a content area can be presented by a teacher who is exercising freedom of speech, if the presentation is objective, fair, and free from indoctrination.

Religion and Education

Historically, the presence of religion in the public schools has stimulated both passion and dissonance in the United States. Certain issues still provoke lively debate in the educational arena: Should prayer be allowed in the public schools? Can creationism and "intelligent design" be taught along with evolution? Why is religion excluded from the curriculum? The First Amendment, which ensures that there will be no establishment of a national religion, does not ensure that these questions will not continue to be raised.

In keeping with the separation between church and state, the U.S. Supreme Court found, in the case of Pennsylvania's *Abington School District v. Schemp* (1963), that public school districts cannot require prayer or readings of the Bible when they become part of a state-sponsored curriculum. Study *about* religion, however, remains acceptable; it includes such topics as the role of religion in art, history, and music, as well as comparative religious studies. Furthermore, students can pray in private, but not before an audience.

Students enjoy Chanukah latkes near a poster board decorated with foil menorahs.

A number of lower-court cases have focused on whether prayers are appropriate at high school graduations and athletic events. These lower-court decisions have had conflicting results. In the U.S. Supreme Court case of *Lee v. Weisman* (1992), the Court found, in a 5-to-4 decision, that a state-sponsored benediction, even though nondenominational and delivered at a voluntary student event, was unconstitutional. The benediction was organized by the principal, who also selected the presiding clergyman. In addition, the principal provided suggestions for the content of the prayer delivered at the benediction. Subsequently, the Court found the principal, as a representative of the government, to be in violation of the First Amendment's call for separation between church and state. Religious symbols and prayer are not allowed in the public schools.

The practice of religious traditions, rituals, and events is in violation of the law, whether or not students and teachers participate voluntarily. And yet, Christmas celebrations often challenge this position, as the public schools tend to be focal points for the use of symbols and music of the holiday. The Supreme Court has weighed in on the constitutionality of the issue, and here again, interpretation of the law hinges on the teaching about religion—in this case, the secular ideals of peace, universal acceptance, and pluralism that encompass, but are not limited to, celebration of the Christmas holiday.

Extracurricular religious clubs can meet on a public school campus, before or after school hours, although organized prayer in school remains illegal. In *Board of Education of the Westside Community School v. Mergens* (1990), the Supreme Court found that political, philosophical, and religious groups must have access to the use of school facilities, just like any other extracurricular group on campus. This ruling also applies to gay-straight alliances on high school campuses. The goals of these alliances are to (1) create safe environments in schools for students to support each other and learn about homophobia; (2) educate the school community about homophobia, gender identity, and sexual orientation issues; and (3) fight discrimination, harassment, and violence in schools (Gay-Straight Alliance Network, 2006).

Students can also receive religious instruction during school hours, as long as this instruction occurs off campus and is provided by teachers not associated with and paid by the public school district. This type of instructional release time is common, for example, in the state of Utah, where secondary student members of the Church of Jesus Christ of Latter Day Saints attend daily seminary classes in off-campus facilities located adjacent to the public high schools and middle schools.

In Utah, the criteria for enrollment in release-time religious instruction is defined by state code. The code specifies that LDS seminaries are private schools and distinct from public schools. Students must provide the public school with written permission from their parents to participate. In addition, seminary classes must not conflict with required school classes. Utah high schools also maintain similar release time for student employment, as well as for programs and classes such as vocational education and advanced placement courses.

From PRESERVICE to PRACTICE

Florida Student Sues Principal and School Board for Not Allowing Gay-Straight Alliance Club to Meet

A Florida high school senior and the club she helped form to promote tolerance of lesbians and gay men have sued her school principal and the Okeechobee County School Board, claiming they wrongfully prohibited the club from meeting on school grounds. Yasmin Gonzalez, who is being represented by the American Civil Liberties Union (ACLU-FL), argues that the school's failure to recognize the Gay-Straight Alliance of Okeechobee High School and allow it to meet at the school violates the federal Equal Access Act.

According to her complaint filed in U.S. district court, the federal law mandates that if a school allows one non-curricular group to meet on campus, it must allow all other noncurricular groups to meet there. Robert Rosenwald, ACLU-FL's lead counsel on the case, says the ACLU has litigated similar suits successfully before. "There's nothing very new in this case," he says. "The school is taking a legally indefensible stance, simply out of anti-gay bigotry." Assistant Superintendent Ken Kenworthy says little about the case: "We're very guarded in what we do say, simply in that we don't want anything to be misinterpreted." OCSB Chairman David Williams says he was aware of the controversy at the high school but that the board never discussed it as a group.

Board member Gay Carlton adds, "I guess I just didn't realize it was that big a problem." Yasmin charges that the school often has been intolerant of gay students. She and the other students retained a faculty adviser and sought Principal Toni Wiersma's approval of the GSA, as required by school district policy. But the principal kept brushing them off, she says. He first said the school didn't allow any noncurricular clubs on campus, according to Rosenwald, but when Yasmin pointed out there were several others, he told her the school had too many. According to the OHS handbook, the school recognizes several noncurricular clubs, including the Art Club, Poetry Club, and Future Business Leaders of America. In addition, Superintendent Patricia Cooper was quoted in a local newspaper as saying, "We are an abstinence-only district and we do not condone or promote any type of sexual activity." In the article, she also argued that the GSA club was rejected because of unrest on campus after fights broke out several weeks ago. Yasmin acknowledges that there have been fights at OHS but insists that they were not related to the GSA.

Questions for Reflection

1. Given the goals of the Gay-Straight Alliance Network, what are the perceptions of school officials regarding the establishment of a gay-straight alliance on campus?
2. How can school districts develop an extracurricular club policy that is equitable for all student organizations?

Source: National School Board Association. Retrieved March 25, 2007, from http://www.nsba.org/site/doc_cosa.asp?TRACKID=&VID=50&CID=448&DID=39760.

Utah's religious release programs differ from public education programs in the following ways:

- Registration for seminary classes is separate from public school registration. Seminary credits do not count toward graduation. Seminary grades are not included on school transcripts.

- Seminary classes are not held in public school facilities. Seminary teachers are not members of the public school faculty.

- Public funds or equipment may not be used for religious instruction or for the support of seminary events. This includes the use of facilities, computers, audio-visual equipment, telephones, and other resources.

- Participation in seminary classes is voluntary. In Utah, public schools cannot require students to attend seminary. Conversely, students who do not enroll in seminary classes cannot be punished for this choice.

Nevertheless, it is not uncommon for public schools across the country to acknowledge and educate students about a number of religious and cultural traditions, such as Hanukkah and Kwanzaa, in order to present a more balanced curriculum. It is also not uncommon for schools and school districts to continue to introduce religion in classrooms, as prayers are spoken at assemblies, sporting events, and in daily bulletins. School boards, school administrators, and community members have been known to challenge the interpretation of the First Amendment, "Congress shall make no law respecting the establishment of religion, or prohibiting the free exercise thereof." What is the bottom line? Public schools must be neutral and balanced—yet free from advocacy—when addressing religion within the curriculum (U.S. Department of Education, 1999).

What Can and What Cannot Be Taught?

Approved curriculum content varies from state to state as well. Each state will have different perspectives about what is acceptable content and what is not, based on the community's religious, social, political, and cultural perspectives. The most volatile community concerns are those associated with the teaching of evolution and sex education, in addition to the introduction of certain kinds of literature and R-rated films in the classroom. Nationwide, school districts allow parents to choose whether to permit their children to participate during the instruction of such content.

Teaching Evolution

Creationism is a theory that contends the universe was created by God. **Evolution** is a theory based on a scientific record that shows that all living things have responded to environmental change through a process known as natural selection. Evolution remains a controversial topic, particularly in science education. In the Scopes "Monkey Trial" of 1925, high school teacher John Scopes was charged by the state of Tennessee with breaking a law that made it illegal to teach "any theory which denies the story of the Divine Creation of man as taught in the Bible and to teach instead that man descended from a lower order of animals." Scopes countered this belief by arguing that evolution was substantiated by scientific research and that his academic freedom was being compromised. Although Scopes maintained that evolution was important content to impart to his biology students, he was found guilty and fined $100. Because of a technicality, this decision was later reversed.

The removal of evolution from the curriculum has been pursued by other states, such as Arkansas in 1960. States have also fought to include creationism, along with evolution, in the curriculum. In 1982, the state of Louisiana passed a "Balanced Treatment Act" whereby both positions would be presented in the schools equally. This law was tested before the Supreme Court, which found it unconstitutional due to the religious nature of creationism.

In 1999 the Kansas State Board of Education approved the removal of references to evolution from its state standards (Keller & Coles, 1999). As a result, local school districts could determine the nature and extent to which they would now include evolution within the curriculum, especially because students would no longer be tested on it. A public outcry ensued across the nation, but no legal statutes were violated. The decision now stands.

Sex and AIDS/HIV Education in the Public Schools

The inclusion of sex education in the public schools remains controversial. Although some community members feel that such content does not belong in the schools and should be addressed at home, others argue that because the United States has the highest teen pregnancy rate in the Western industrialized world, public education must bear more responsibility (National Campaign to Prevent Teen Pregnancy, 2003). With 35 percent of women, or 850,000 annually, becoming pregnant before the age of 20, health educators contend that families and religious organizations are not providing effective sex education to the youth of today. As a result, the courts have supported school districts' right to offer sex education in the public schools with parental permission (Fischer et al., 2003).

A 1999 study conducted by Landry, Kaeser, and Richards found that 69 percent of the nation's public school districts maintain sex education policies. However, 35 percent of these school policies focus on *abstinence-only* curricula as the primary approach to contraception, with little or no positive discussion of other contraception or measures to prevent sexually transmitted diseases. An *abstinence-plus* sex education curriculum policy was employed by 51 percent of the school districts. This approach emphasizes abstinence but also leaves room for discussion about contraception. Fourteen percent of the districts utilized a more *comprehensive sex education* approach by addressing abstinence as only one of several contraception methods.

Even though recent surveys of Americans have found that as many as 93 percent of Americans support sex education in the public schools (Sexuality Information and Education Council of the United States and Advocates for Youth, 1999), contradictions from the public and from the federal government continue to circulate. Congress now funds abstinence-only programs, while committing no dollars to comprehensive sex education approaches.

AIDS/HIV education remains a controversial topic, despite the fact that AIDS-related diseases were the sixth leading cause of death among Americans 13 to 24 years old in 1999 and accounted for 13 percent of all AIDS cases in 2004 (Centers for Disease Control and Prevention, 2004). See Table 7.3 for AIDS diagnosis rates among various adolescent and young-adult ethnic groups.

This 2005 cover of the magazine *Science* illustrates a model DNA molecule.

TABLE 7.3　AIDS/HIV in Adolescents and Young Adults, 2000 to 2004

All Adolescents and Young Adults (ages 13–24)

Of the estimated 944,306 AIDS cases diagnosed in the United States since the beginning of the epidemic through 2004, 40,059 were among persons 13–24 years of age.

Adolescents and young adults account for 2,174 new AIDS diagnoses in 2004, including 60 among 13–14-year-olds and 2,114 among 15–24-year-olds.

Account for an estimated 13 percent of HIV/AIDS cases newly diagnosed in 2004.

An estimated total of 5,895 adolescents 13–19 years of age have been diagnosed with AIDS through 2004.

Female Adolescents and Young Adults

Represent an estimated 38 percent of HIV/AIDS cases newly diagnosed in this age group in 2004.

African American Adolescents and Young Adults

Account for 46 percent of total AIDS cases diagnosed in people 13–24 years old through 2002.

Account for 61 percent of AIDS cases newly diagnosed in 2002 among 13–24-year-olds.

Represent an estimated 62 percent of all persons newly diagnosed with HIV for ages 20–24 in 2002.

Males ages 13–24 account for 39 percent of total AIDS cases diagnosed through 2002 for that age group among males.

Females ages 13–24 account for 60 percent of total AIDS cases diagnosed through 2002 for that age group among females.

Females between 13 and 19 years of age represent an estimated 74 percent of all young women newly diagnosed with HIV in that age group in 2002.

Latina/o Adolescents and Young Adults

Account for 22 percent of AIDS cases newly diagnosed in 2002 among 13–24-year-olds. Represent an estimated 11 percent of all persons ages 20–24 who were newly diagnosed with HIV in 2002.

Account for 21 percent of total AIDS cases diagnosed in people 13–24 years old through 2002.

White Adolescents and Young Adults

Represent an estimated 25 percent of all persons ages 20–24 who were newly diagnosed with HIV in 2002.

Source: Centers for Disease Control and Prevention, *HIV/AIDS Surveillance Report 2004*, vol. 16, retrieved October 6, 2006, from http://www.cdc.gov/hiv/stats/2004surveilancereport.pdf.

It is often assumed that AIDS/HIV is spread mainly among male homosexuals and intravenous drug users, but it is also transmitted between heterosexuals. With the incidence of sexually transmitted diseases such AIDS/HIV on the rise, this calls into question the efficacy of abstinence-only approaches to sex education, even though states and communities may differ in their responses to comprehensive sex education in the public schools.

McNergney and McNergney (2004) suggest these approaches to AIDS/HIV education in the pubic schools:

- Identification of risk-taking behaviors that contribute to HIV/AIDS
- Identifying and practicing refusal skills, including avoidance of "high-risk" partners and the use of drugs and alcohol
- Identifying and critiquing media influences on sexual behaviors
- Promoting abstinence, condom use, and "safe sex" practices
- Inviting respected speakers who can share responsible views about preventing HIV/AIDS

Students' Rights

Free Speech

Law dictates the rights of students. The free speech of students, like that of adults, is protected by the First Amendment. The Supreme Court has found that students can express their opinions, as long as they are not disruptive to the school environment and the learning process and their expressions are not lewd, indecent, or offensive (*Tinker v. Des Moines Community School District*, 1969; *Bethel School District No. 403 v. Fraser*, 1986).

School newspapers also are limited in the content of their articles. In 1988, the Supreme Court found that articles could be censored if they in any way raised "legitimate pedagogical concerns" for the privacy of those interviewed in the student-generated stories (*Hazelwood School District v. Kuhlmeier*, 1988). With freedom of speech, the Court found, students must also be taught that there can be limitations if the writings impinge on the rights of others.

Student Records

Since Congress's passage of the 1974 **Family Educational Rights and Privacy Act (FERPA),** also known as the Buckley Amendment, students' records (such as grades, test scores, teacher and counselor reports, and letters of recommendations) must be made accessible to students and their guardians. This access includes procedures that families can follow in order to change or amend content in the records that they feel is inaccurate. The Buckley Amendment also establishes protections that limit access to the students' records by third parties.

A high school journalism teacher and a student editor meet with school newspaper staff.

There are limitations to the kind of school information that parents and students have access to. The personal notes of teachers cannot be released without their consent. Letters of recommendation written by teachers may not become public if students choose to waive their right to access such a letter. In addition, homework and classroom work are not considered to be representative of an educational record and thus are not subject to the provisions of FERPA, according to the Supreme Court. Students can grade other students' papers and are not violating privacy laws.

Search and Seizure

Although the Fourth Amendment guards citizens from illegal searches and seizures without warrants, public school students face different circumstances. Public schools are not jails, and students have a right to privacy. But with campus violence taking place across the country, as well as increases in substance abuse, school administrators may freely conduct searches of students and lockers with the use of metal detectors and police dogs if they have probable cause.

The Supreme Court has upheld a 1985 *New Jersey v. T.L.O.* decision that school officials had a reasonable suspicion or probable cause when they conducted a search of a student's purse and found marijuana in it while she was in the high school restroom.

The nature of a search can influence its legality. School lockers are considered to be school property and can be searched, but other searches may be regarded as more intrusive. For example, the Supreme Court found random drug testing of athletes to be legal when the safety of a student and the school environment is in jeopardy (Zirkel, 1999). Strip-searches of students, however, can seriously intrude on a student's privacy. School officials can be held liable if they do not establish probable cause in such a case.

From PRESERVICE to PRACTICE

Illinois High School Association Considers Random Steroid Testing

The Illinois High School Association (IHSA) is considering random testing for steroids and growth hormones in state finals for football, basketball, track, and other selected sports. Athletes testing positive would be banned from competition for one year and would have to pass a follow-up test before returning. Those refusing the test would be barred from competing. Because testing would not be completed until the championships concluded, athletes in individual sports who failed would forfeit their medals, but school teams in which a team member tested positive would not have to surrender their trophy.

Currently, only New Jersey has implemented random drug testing for high school athletes that includes scanning for steroids. Beginning this fall, the New Jersey program will test 500 athletes for approximately 80 banned substances from amphetamines to steroids, at a cost of $90,000. The Illinois High School Association assistant executive director, Kurt Gibson, believes testing will deter high school athletes from using the harmful drugs and will maintain competitive balance among the association's 750 member schools. Some school officials are skeptical that the program is worth the estimated cost of $175 per test. Others, who support testing, argue that it will dissuade high school athletes from entering college athletics dependent on performance-enhancing drugs. Gibson agrees that steroid use often begins in high school because of the lure of college athletic scholarships.

The American Medical Association reports that youth steroid use increased from 2.1 percent of high school seniors in 1991 to 4 percent in 2002. AMA officials agree that steroid use is best stopped early, but they wonder whether the money might be better spent on educational approaches. They also point out that a false positive can label an athlete. "We're not endorsing testing programs, though we're not opposing them either," says AMA president-elect Dr. Ron Davis. "We just think there are concerns that need to be addressed."

Gibson notes that IHSA has beefed up its educational programs, but he insists that testing still needs to be considered. Acknowledging that cost is a primary concern for school officials, he says IHSA is looking into private grants and other sources and will not pass the cost on to member schools. Meanwhile, IHSA and other state associations will be monitoring the New Jersey program. Although Bob Baly, assistant director of the New Jersey State Interscholastic Athletic Association (NJSIAA), cautions that it may be years before the program's success can be gauged, he believes the threat of tests will have an immediate impact on steroid use and will raise people's consciousness.

Questions for Reflection

1. Given the cost of drug testing, how can school districts address the use of steroids among their student athletes?
2. Do you believe that random drug testing is an invasion of students' right to privacy? Why or why not?

Source: National School Board Association, retrieved March 25, 2007, from http://www.nsba.org/site/doc_cosa.asp?TRACKID=&VID=50&CID=436&DID=39286.

Pending Issues

Today, technology imposes new challenges on every state and local district. For example, policies on the use of wireless laptop computers and cell phones vary from district to district. On the one hand, teachers find laptops useful at the middle and secondary levels. On the other hand, students can use such technology, including cell phones, to engage in off-task behaviors.

However, families may feel that student access to cell phones is critical to student safety, given the ongoing threats of violence in our society. Districts are now charged with developing policies that reflect the use of new technologies in the classroom for the purposes of teaching, for learning, and as communication tools. At the same, teachers and families must balance the use of these tools with the maintenance of environments that are conducive to learning.

SUMMARY

Becoming a teacher has ramifications that extend beyond the completion of a degree and licensure. Teachers must adhere to state laws and codes that serve as guides to understanding what it means to be a professional teacher. Knowledge of these laws is important to all educators. It remains the teacher's professional responsibility to follow them.

The curriculum is not free from legal constraints. Religion and the separation between church and state influence what citizens feel are appropriate activities and curricula in the public schools. Advocacy of a particular religion is not acceptable in public school settings. Organized prayer is banned from the schools, but individual students can pray privately. Religious clubs can also meet on campus, as can all other approved clubs, including gay-straight student alliances.

Finally, students do enjoy a number of rights on campus. Freedom of speech is a premier right that students possess, although teachers must inform them that with this right comes responsibility for the rights of others. Searches and seizures can occur on campus, but school officials must have reasonable cause before they conduct them. Student records are protected by FERPA, also known as the Buckley Amendment. Families can have access to student records and can even challenge and amend inaccurate information. Confidentiality is a critical feature of this act, because it is critical to parents, students, and teachers as they make important educational decisions.

DISCUSSION QUESTIONS

1. What factors must a teacher consider when seeking a teaching contract? What incidents contribute to a breach of contract?

2. Explain the purpose of tenure. How does one achieve tenure? Does tenure guarantee lifelong employment? Explain.

3. Explain teachers' legal rights and responsibilities regarding general liability issues, the reporting of suspected child abuse cases, and academic freedom.

4. What limitations do teachers face when introducing controversial curriculum topics such as evolution and sex education? How can teachers protect themselves from litigation while introducing vital curriculum content?

5. What rights do students attending school have? Discuss drug testing, search and seizure, and freedom of speech in the context of school settings.

ACTIVITIES

1. Interview a school district attorney. Explore some of the general responsibilities required of him or her. What kinds of challenges does he or she face? Explore how he or she balances the responsibilities of representing the interests of the district, community, teachers, and students.

2. Conduct a review of local newspaper articles addressing legal issues that have arisen in area schools. What issues have emerged? How have they been addressed in the media? How have the district administration, school boards, teachers, students, and community members responded?

3. Research two or three states' policy approaches to sex education. Compare and contrast the comprehensive health education curriculum and abstinence-only approaches. In what ways do states measure their sex education program's efficacy?

4. Interview school district security personnel. What are some of the challenges they face in ensuring school safely while upholding students' rights? Under what circumstances must they search lockers or book bags? What is the school's policy on drug testing? Under what circumstances must school personnel defer to the legal authority of local police?

WEBSITES

American Federation of Teachers
http://www.aft.org
National Educators Association
http://www.nea.org/index.html
These sites provide feature articles on teacher rights, salaries, and regional union contacts across the country.

Department of Education: Just for Teachers
http://www.ed.gov/teachers/landing.jhtml?src=pn
Here you will find links to identify specific state and local contracts, laws, and initiatives relevant to employment, and teacher quality across the country.

First Amendment Center Online
http://ww.firstamendmentcenter.org
This is a comprehensive website that addresses freedom of speech and religious liberty; it also offers lesson plans for teachers.

Gay-Straight Alliance Legal Rights
http://www.gsanetwork.org/resources/legal.html
This site presents ongoing discussion of topics relevant to gay youth in the public schools. Topics include discrimination, antidiscrimination efforts, activities, and college scholarship fund raising.

REFERENCES

Abington School District v. Schemp, 374 U.S. 203 (1963).

Bethel School District No. 403 v. Fraser, 755 F.2d 1356 (1986).

Board of Education of the Westside Community School v. Mergens, 496 U.S. 226 (1990).

Cambron-McCabe, N., McCarthy, M., & Thomas, S. (2003). *Public school law: Teachers' and students' rights* (5th ed.). New York: Allyn & Bacon.

Centers for Disease Control and Prevention. (2004). *HIV/AIDS surveillance report 2004*. Vol. 16. Retrieved from www.cdc.gov/hiv/stats/2004surveillancereport.pdf

Fischer, L., Schimmel, D., & Kelly, C. (2003). *Teachers and the law* (6th ed.). New York: Longman.

Gay-Straight Alliance Network. (2006). *Gay students' rights*. Retrieved from http://www.gsanetwork.org

Hazelwood School District v. Kuhlmeier, 484 U.S. 260 (1988).

Keller, B., & Coles, A. (1999). Kansas evolution controversy gives rise to national debate. *Education Week*, 19(1), 1, 24–25.

Landry, D., Kaeser, L., & Richards, C. (1999). Abstinence promotion and the provision of information about public school district sexuality education policies. *Family Planning Perspectives*, 31, 280–286.

Lee v. Weisman, 505 U.S. 577 (1992).

Mancha v. Field Museum of Natural History, 283 N.E.2d 899, Ill. App. Ct. (1972).

McNergney, R., & McNergney, J. (2004). *Foundations of education: The challenge of professional practice*. Boston: Pearson Education.

Morrison v. State Board of Education, 461 P.2d 375 (Cal. 1969).

National Campaign to Prevent Teen Pregnancy. (2003). *Teen pregnancy: So what?* Retrieved from http://www.teenpregnancy.org/whycare/sowhat.asp

New Jersey v. T.L.O., 469 U.S. 325 (1985).

Sexuality Information and Education Council of the United States and Advocates for Youth. (1999). *SIECUS Advocates for Youth survey of Americans' views on sexuality education*. Washington, DC: Author.

Tinker v. Des Moines Community School District, 393 U.S. 503 (1969).

U.S. Department of Education. (1999). *Teachers' guide to religion in the public schools*. Washington, DC: Author.

Wallace v. Batavia School District, 68 F.3d 1010 (7th Cir. 1995).

Yell, M. (1999). *Teacher liability for student injury and misconduct*. Retrieved June 7, 2007, from http://cecp.air.org/interact/author.asp

Zirkel, P. (1999). Urinalysis? *Phi Delta Kappan*, 80, 409–410.

PART 4

Educators in Action: The Local Classroom, the Global Classroom

CHAPTERS

8 Teacher Practice: Understanding the Work

9 Understanding Assessment

10 Exploring the Relationship Between American Culture and Education

11 Teaching English Language Learners: Bilingual and English as a Second Language Efforts

12 Globalization and Schooling

CHAPTER 8

Teacher Practice: Understanding the Work

CHAPTER OBJECTIVES

- Readers will develop an understanding of the kinds of instructional planning decisions teachers make to increase the academic achievement of all learners.

- Readers will identify and describe the characteristics and classroom management strategies used by effective teachers.

- Readers will identify and describe the distinctions between Eurocentric and multicultural curricula.

- Readers will examine how schools sort and track learners and consider the possible outcomes of these practices.

- Readers will understand that on-task behaviors and engagement in learning activities are learned responses.

- Readers will develop a systematic approach to handle students' off-task behaviors and create a plan for establishing and enforcing standards of conduct.

- Readers will consider the role of family participation in the learning process.

FIRST PERSON

Minority Parents "Don't Care About Their Kids"

My tenth-grade English class was certainly a "motley crew" of student diversity and language skills. Two students remain in my memory. Carlos, from El Salvador, was a baseball nut whose favorite in-class reading was the sports page of the *L.A. Times*. His writing skills were developing through his journal writing, although he wasn't interested in poetry. Jessie was his first girlfriend. Her Vietnamese name was Trien, the name that appeared on my role sheet. She was a gentle yet serious student who was caught between the traditional world of her family and the lure of her first crush. Both students came from immigrant families who struggled to leave their homelands due to the lingering hostilities of war, poverty, and an uncertain future.

The two students talked energetically in class, but their conversations were not constantly off-task and annoying. They discussed their assignments for that day, their plans for lunch, their after-school care of younger siblings, and whether they could rearrange their schedules to participate in extracurricular activities. I admit that I had a vested interest in these conversations. I felt minority students were not always encouraged to participate in these after-school activities, and as the school newspaper adviser, I was always looking for new reporters. Because of Carlos's interest in sports, I recruited him to be a sports writer. Jessie was interested in student government, had an unassuming confidence, and cared for both her classmates and her school, so I encouraged her to run for sophomore class president and write out a campaign plan and speech. Much to Jessie's surprise, as the underdog candidate, she was elected that semester.

This chapter was coauthored with my colleagues at Utah State University: Barbara Cangelosi, Department of Secondary Education, and Jim Cangelosi, Department of Mathematics and Statistics.

I was eager to meet Jessie's and Carlos's parents. With parent-teacher conferences pending, I shamelessly offered extra credit points to students in my classes who brought their parents or guardians to the conference meetings. Why? Parents' schedules were busy. After all, supporting and maintaining a household is both expensive and complex. Parents too needed incentives to participate in what I came to refer to as an "educational exchange." I wanted to learn about the parents; I wanted to them to learn about my goals and strategies in the classroom with their students; I wanted to discuss what we could do together to help their daughter or son achieve to the best of her or his ability. I didn't want parents to miss conferences because these meetings had historically offered so little to engage them.

My parent participation numbers increased that year. Carlos's and Jessie's parents attended open house and did not speak English fluently. Nevertheless, other openings for relationship building occurred during our initial meeting. I showed the parents samples of their teenagers' work—sports writing, the campaign speech, and English essays they had written and printed out in our computer lab. The students were also in attendance, and I asked them to read from their writing. They translated excerpts for their folks, whose smiles demonstrated a humble pride.

With my own English, Spanish, and ESL communication skills, I could explain that Carlos and Jessie were attending class consistently, honing their writing skills, and collaborating well with their peers. I also added that I was happy they were participating in extracurricular activities. I offered to help the families meet with a school counselor who could explain college requirements to them. Carlos's dad worked with a landscaping company, and Jessie's father cooked in a Vietnamese restaurant. Both mothers worked part-time in local restaurants as well. I didn't inquire about the families' immigration status.

But the parents were thrilled about the possibility of their children attending college someday. Carlos and Jessie smiled too, while looking down shyly at their feet. Their brothers and sisters, who also attended the meeting, giggled. The conference ended with commitments by Carlos and Jessie and myself to schedule meetings with their counselors during a time when both parents could again attend. Privately, I promised myself that I would identify translators to attend those meetings as well. Following these counselor meetings, I was visited by Carlos's and Jessie's parents even when their children were no longer in my English class.

The next two years were bumpy for Carlos and Jessie, as they juggled home and school responsibilities. Graduation day arrived, and, balloons and mortar boards in hand, Carlos and Jessie said their goodbyes. Their parents each hugged me. Their children were bound for East Los Angeles College. And I also knew they were bound for something great.

Effective Teaching: Characteristics, Theory, and Strategies

As we review both the history and the contemporary challenges facing schools over the course of time, it is apparent that numerous issues impact the effectiveness of teachers today. Every day educators must make decisions that require quick action, as well as careful reflection. But what exactly makes some teachers' instructional strategies more effective than those of others? What personality features of effective teachers stand out? How do these educators efficiently manage their classrooms? And how do teachers reach out to families as they too participate in the educational process with their children? According to the research of Good and Brophy (2003), answers to these questions have revealed critical differences between effective and ineffective teachers. Consider the following variables that influence the effectiveness of teachers' decision making:

- The personal characteristics and traits of a teacher
- The nature and extent of instructional planning
- The implementation of teaching strategies
- Efficient, businesslike classroom management
- Variable approaches to student assessment

Personal Traits

Let's first examine personal traits of effective teachers. Personal teaching efficacy is a term coined by Roger Bruning and colleagues (2004). Bruning maintains that a student-centered teacher can promote student learning regardless of his or her background and skill level. For example, in the case study described above, the narrator articulated her belief that Carlos and Jessie not only could succeed in the classroom but also could experience success as active participants in the larger school and community. According to Bruning et al. (2000), this kind of belief has been found to be an indicator of personal teaching efficacy.

What is intriguing about personal teaching efficacy is that it leaves little room for teachers who are quick to blame ineffective instruction on the students, citing such factors as family upbringing, home and community environments, or the lack of intelligence. Instead, a teacher's belief that any student can learn and excel helps to establish a positive, well-managed classroom environment where a motivating and affirming instructional climate thrives (Stipek, 2002).

On the other hand, low-efficacy teachers are less student centered and tend to disregard low-achieving learners. Such teachers have been found to be less likely to use technology to support instruction, and they are reluctant to implement new instructional strategies with students who are "turned off" by paper-and-pencil class work (Roblyer, 2003). Thus, students taught by high-efficacy educators have been found to be more effective learners than students whose low-efficacy instructors doubt the capability of the children they are employed to teach.

For Your CONSIDERATION

Visit the Arizona State University, Education Policy Studies webpage at **http://www.asu.edu/educ/epsl/EPRU/documents/ EPRU%202002-101/Chapter%2008-Glass-Final.htm** for school reform proposals by Dr. Gene V. Glass to learn more about teacher characteristics.

Characteristics of Caring Teachers

As students ourselves, we can all relate a story or two about a teacher in our lives who "went the extra mile" to help us in the classroom and out. That teacher may have extended an invitation for after-school tutoring or offered extra help and access to resources to better prepare for that next exam. Another teacher may have listened to you and provided some much-needed understanding when things were not going well at home or with your best friend. This ability to demonstrate empathy with young people as they learn and develop is known as *caring* (Noddings, 1999).

Researcher Nel Noddings has found that the development of caring professionals is a critical component of teacher preparation. After all, it is the caring teacher with whom parents and guardians want their children to be associated; it is the caring teacher whose class all students know about and want to take. The impact of caring on student motivation and academic achievement continues to be reported by educational researchers (Noddings, 1999; Stipek, 2002). But what does it mean to be a caring and effective teacher?

An elementary teacher reading poetry to young students.

Caring teachers possess *enthusiasm*. When teachers model a high level of energy and passion for what they are teaching, this zeal demonstrates to students that the instructor is excited about the subject and finds it meaningful (Good & Brophy, 2003). By expressing enthusiasm for the content, teachers are *modeling behaviors that can influence students' motivation for learning* and interest level. For example, students will observe their instructor coming to class on time, being well prepared, and showing respect for students' feelings and views. When teachers arrive late to class, are unprepared, or exhibit a lack of interest in the subject matter or a lack of respect for their students, student achievement and confidence about learning the material plummet (Kauchak & Eggan, 2005).

Maintaining *high expectations* for student academic achievement is another quality that caring and effective teachers possess (Lee, 2000). What does it mean to have high expectations? Teachers who have high expectations for students tend to treat students differently. Such teachers provide more *emotional support* for students by engaging in positive interactions with them on a regular basis. Teachers who maintain high expectations for learners expend more instructional effort to students by patiently supplying directions, providing explanations, and offering high-level questions and probes. These teachers also offer thorough feedback for students by giving more praise as well as constructive criticism.

Students as young as those in first grade have been found to be well aware of differential treatment by teachers (Stipek, 2002). This finding holds tremendous ramifications for teachers. If students detect that teachers do not provide them with the same encouragement and support, it becomes clear why the self-fulfilling prophecy affects the self-assurance and motivation levels of students at a very early age. Teachers may be unaware that they hold different expectations for learners, but these assumptions ultimately impact student confidence and, equally important, their access to the core curriculum.

Understanding Ability Differences: Multiple Intelligences

New teachers are often surprised when they discover the vast ability differences their students present in the classroom. Not only do the students reflect gender,

From PRESERVICE to PRACTICE

Is Loving Kids Enough to Be an Effective Teacher?

As a former elementary teacher and, at present, a children's librarian in Los Angeles, California, Regina Powers writes that she is concerned with the simplistic image of teachers who believe that caring and love for children are enough to guarantee their effectiveness. However, she agrees that a caring teacher is one who exercises specific professional qualities in the classroom:

Seasoned instructors know that "loving" a classroom is not enough and won't get the job done. In fact, candidates for credential programs or teaching jobs who claim their reason for teaching is because they "love kids" should be eliminated from the running.

The job of a teacher is to present the curriculum using methods that have been found to be the most effective. Teachers also must be able to identify and articulate their enthusiasm for reasoning, learning, thinking, and reading. They must possess a passion for the material they present for their students. They must adapt lessons to fit each student's needs, language skills, and cognitive development.

They should, as many already do, lie awake at night redesigning lesson plans or figuring out the best way to reach the seemingly unteachable child. They should spend "summers off" reading new research, analyzing perpetually changing textbooks, and attending conferences.... They need to admit the truth to themselves, to their employers, to their peers, and to the parents that trust them. The truth is that "loving kids" has very little to do with teaching. Ultimately, students come to school to learn—not to be loved.

Questions for Reflection

1. What are your perceptions of Regina Powers's argument about what it means to be an effective teacher?
2. Does her position reflect an emotional distancing from students or embrace a level of professionalism reflective of personal teaching efficacy?

cultural, language, and physical differences, they also possess a variety of reading, writing, and computation skills. As you can imagine, teachers meet students who have an immediate grasp of the content and skills introduced in the class. At the same time, they also encounter students for whom their class will be a continuing struggle. How have teachers confronted these instructional challenges?

First, we must consider the notion of intelligence. We traditionally have believed that those we deem "intelligent" are those who can demonstrate specific forms of knowledge quickly and easily and who can demonstrate that ability when given standardized tests. At the same time, educational researchers and teachers alike agree that we cannot define intelligence solely on the basis of outcomes on standardized tests . Intelligence encompasses qualities that include the ability to process knowledge in different kinds of ways, to reason and think in the abstract, and to solve problems. Thus, intelligence reflects our lived experiences and background knowledge as we engage in these activities.

In the past, intelligence was perceived as a single quality that individuals either did or did not possess. Today, however, cognitive psychologists and educational researchers contend that intelligence consists of several different characteristics that emerge in a variety of combinations, depending on the individual. Harvard psychologist Howard Gardner has offered a theory of **multiple intelligences** that proposes eight independent

Middle-school science students touch sting rays in a tank at the Aquarium of the Pacific, Long Beach, California.

dimensions of overall intelligence. According to Gardner (in Checkley, 1997), these intelligences include linguistic, logical-mathematical, spatial, bodily kinesthetic, musical, interpersonal, intrapersonal, and naturalist intelligences (see Table 8.1).

Ironically, even though Gardner's theory is readily accepted by the educational community, it remains disconnected from such initiatives as No Child Left Behind and standardized testing. Such domains as the logical-mathematical intelligence are heavily emphasized in the classroom, but the others are less prominent within the curriculum. Nevertheless, the theory of multiple intelligences challenges the assumption that intelligence is something we are simply born with. Because of the complexity of schools and schooling, Gardner argues that his theory is not to be confused with learning styles. He believes that students' individual differences should guide instructional design and assessment. He feels that the link between instruction and the recognition of multiple intelligences is important to curriculum development and pedagogy. See Table 8.2, a sample history lesson plan incorporating multiple intelligences, and Table 8.3, an inventory to gauge your own learning styles.

TABLE 8.1 Gardner's Multiple Intelligences

Intelligence	Qualities
Linguistic	The capacity to use language (your native language and perhaps other languages) to express what's on your mind and to understand other people. Writers specialize in linguistic intelligence.
Logical-mathematical	The ability to understand the underlying principles of kind of a causal system (as scientists and logicians do) or to manipulate numbers, quantities, and operations (as mathematicians do).
Spatial	The ability to represent the spatial world internally in your mind. Sailors and airplane pilots navigate using spatial intelligence, and chess players and sculptors also do so.
Bodily kinesthetic	The capacity to use your whole body or parts of your body (hands, fingers, arms, feet) to solve a problem, make something, or put on some kind of a production. Athletes and performing artists specialize in bodily kinesthetic intelligence.
Musical	The capacity to think in music by hearing, recognizing, remembering, and manipulating sound patterns. People who have a strong musical intelligence can't get music out of their minds.
Interpersonal	The understanding of other people. It is an ability that we all need but is at a premium if you are a teacher, clinician, salesperson, or politician.
Intrapersonal	The understanding of yourself, of knowing who you are, what you can do, what you want to do, how you react to things, which things to avoid, and which things to gravitate toward.
Naturalist	The ability to discriminate among living things (plants, animals) as well as sensitivity to other features of the natural world (clouds, rock configurations). This ability was of value in our evolutionary past as hunters and gatherers and continues to be central in such roles as farmer, botanist, and chef.

Source: Gardner in Checkley (1997).

TABLE 8.2	**Sample Lesson Plan for U.S. History Reflecting Multiple Intelligences**

Title: Pearl Harbor

Time: 90 minutes

Materials: VCR, videotape, posters, pictures

Objectives:

1. The student will summarize reasons for the entry of the United States into World War II.

2. The student will evaluate the pros and cons of these reasons.

Setting the stage: Show pictures of the attack on Pearl Harbor. (visual/spatial)

Discuss: Background from homework reading. (verbal/linguistics; interpersonal)

Construct: Timeline of WWII events. (visual/spatial; logical, mathematics)

Groups: Present some reasons for a country to go to war. Refer to textbook and previous class notes. (verbal/linguistics; interpersonal)

Show: Anti-Japan and anti-German posters and newsclips/video. (visual/spatial; musical, bodily kinesthetic; role plays)

Journal: What role did emotions play in the U.S. entry into WWII? Defend or critique the decision to go to war. (verbal/linguistics; interpersonal)

Source: Stephen Holtrip Webpage, Writing Lesson Plans. Retrieved March 27, 2007, from http://www .Huntington.edu/education/lessonplanning/Gardner.html

TABLE 8.3	**Multiple Intelligences Inventory**

Place a check in all boxes that best describe you, and tally your multiple intelligence scores.

Linguistic

___	I really enjoy books.
✓	I hear words in my head before I write, read, or speak them.
✓	I remember more when I listen to the radio or a CD than from television or films.
✓	I enjoy word games such as crossword puzzles, Scrabble, anagrams, or Password.
___	I like puns, tongue twisters, nonsense rhymes, and double meanings.
✓	English, social studies, and history were easier subjects for me than science and math.
___	When I'm driving, I like to read the billboards and signs and notice them more than the scenery along the road.
✓	I often refer to things I have read or heard in conversations.
___	People often ask me the meaning of words.
✓	I have written something recently that I was proud of or that was published or recognized.
5	Total linguistic boxes checked

Logical

___	I can quickly and easily compute numbers in my head. (Example: I can double or triple a cooking recipe or carpentry measurement without having to write it on paper.)
___	I enjoy math and science in school.
___	I like solving brainteasers, logical games, and other strategy games such as chess or checkers.
___	I like to set up "what if" experiments. (Example: "What if I fertilized my plants twice as often?")
✓	I look for structure, patterns, sequences, or logical order.
___	I wonder about how some things work and keep up-to-date on new scientific developments and discoveries.

TABLE 8.3 Multiple Intelligences Inventory (cont.)

_____ I believe that there is a rational explanation for almost everything.

_____ I can think in abstract, clear, imageless concepts.

_____ I can find logical flows in things people say and do at work or home.

_____ I feel more comfortable when things have been quantified, measured, categorized, or analyzed in some way.

__1__ Total logical boxes checked

Spatial

_____ When I close my eyes, I can see clear visual images.

✓ I'm responsive to color.

_____ I often use a camcorder or camera to record my surroundings.

✓ I enjoy visual puzzles such as mazes, jigsaw puzzles, or 3-D images.

✓ I have vivid dreams at night.

✓ I navigate well in unfamiliar places.

✓ I often draw or doodle.

✓ Geometry was easier than algebra.

_____ I can imagine what something would look like from a bird's eye view.

✓ I prefer reading books, newspaper, and magazines that have many illustrations.

__7__ Total spatial boxes checked

Bodily Kinesthetic

_____ I take part in at least one sport or physical activity regularly.

_____ I find it difficult to sit still for long periods of time.

✓ I like working with my hands (for example, sewing, weaving, carving, carpentry, model-building).

_____ I frequently get insights or ideas when I am involved in physical activities, such as walking, swimming, or jogging.

✓ I enjoy spending my free time outside.

✓ I tend to use gestures and other body language when engaged in conversations.

✓ I need to touch or hold objects to learn more about them.

✓ I enjoy dare-devil activities such as parachuting, bungee jumping, and thrilling amusement rides.

✓ I am well coordinated.

✓ To learn new skills, I need to practice them rather than simply read about them or watch them being performed.

__8__ Total bodily kinesthetic boxes checked

Musical

✓ I have a nice singing voice.

✓ I know when musical notes are off-key.

✓ I often listen to musical selections on radio, records, tapes, and CDs.

_____ I play an instrument.

✓ My life would be less dynamic without music.

✓ I often have a tune running through my mind during the day.

Continues

TABLE 8.3 Multiple Intelligences Inventory (cont.)

✓	I can keep time to a piece of music.
✓	I know the melodies of many songs or musical pieces.
✓	If I hear a musical piece once or twice, I can easily repeat it.
✓	I often tap, whistle, hum, or sing when engaged in a task.
8	
	Total musical boxes checked

Interpersonal

✓	People often come to me to seek advice or counsel.
✓	I prefer team and group sports to individual sports.
✓	When I have problems, I prefer to seek help from other people rather than work it out alone.
✓	I have at least three close friends.
✓	I enjoy social pastimes like board games and charades more than individual ones such as video games and solitare.
✓	I like the challenge of teaching other people what I know how to do.
✓	I have been called a leader and consider myself one.
✓	I am comfortable in a crowd of people.
✓	I am involved in local school, neighborhood, church, and community activities.
✓	I would rather spend a Saturday night at a party than spend it at home alone.
10	
	Total interpersonal boxes checked

Intrapersonal

___	I regularly spend time reflecting, meditating or thinking about important life questions.
___	I have attended classes, seminars, and workshops to gain insight about myself and experience personal growth.
___	My opinions and views distinguish me from others.
___	I have a hobby, pastime, or special activity that I do alone.
✓	I have specific goals in life that I think about regularly.
✓	I have a realistic view of my own strengths and weaknesses backed up by accurate feedback from others.
___	I would rather spend a weekend in a cabin or hide-away than at a large resort with lots of people.
___	I am independent-minded and strong willed.
___	I keep a journal or diary to record the events of my inner life.
___	I am self-employed or have seriously considered starting my own business.
2	
	Total intrapersonal boxes checked

Questions for Reflection

1. In which of the multiple intelligences categories did you score the highest? *Interpersonal*
2. Given your survey results, what content areas and instructional strategies do you think are the most relevant and effective for you as a learner?
3. How would such an inventory help inform teachers when they design their own curriculum and instructional strategies?

Source: Multiple Intelligences Inventory, retrieved March 26, 2007, from http://jeffcoweb.jeffco.k12.co.us/high/wotc/confli3.htm.

PAUSE & REFLECT

In what ways can understanding Gardner's theory of multiple intelligences better inform teachers as they strive to engage and motivate their students? How can this theory challenge the assumptions associated with standardized test outcomes?

Understanding Sorting and Tracking

As teachers seek understanding of how students learn, schools are also engaged in the practice of assessing, evaluating, and sorting students in terms of what are perceived as their academic abilities and skill levels. Sorting is used not only to compare students against their own progress, but also to compare school performance across districts, states, and countries.

Students are grouped by ability, or **tracked**, into different curricula—for example, advanced placement (AP), English language learner, gifted and talented, learning disabled, and remedial learner. Ability grouping or sorting begins in the public schools as early as kindergarten and extends through high school. On the basis of English, reading, mathematics, or other content-area test scores, past grades, or teacher recommendations, elementary and secondary students may be ability-grouped for part of a day or week or for a semester within a self-contained class. Alternatively, they may be "pulled out" into another classroom setting.

Ideally, the establishment of these categories can help educators identify and develop programs and instructional strategies to better serve diverse learners. At the same time, however, limitations associated with the assignment of a label and the "locking in" of students within these categories (and others like them) continues to be hotly debated by educators and families alike. Why?

Test results have often been used to predict whether students have the ability and skills to be admitted into advanced placement classes or programs for the gifted and talented. And yet, the accuracy of these predictions and designations has been called into question by educational researchers (Oakes & Lipton, 2007). After all, student identification, labeling, and grouping policies differ from district to district. Thus, teacher observations and their recommendations can be arbitrary and imprecise. In addition, past student performance may not always reveal a student's potential for academic achievement.

Researchers have also found that labels tend to stick. Students are often assigned to class schedules or blocks that reflect assumptions about their achievement across the curriculum. For example, it is not uncommon to find students who are placed in remedial reading classes to be assigned to remedial math courses as well. By the same token, AP math students have been found to be enrolled in AP English classes (Oakes & Lipton, 2007). Because the concepts introduced in such content areas build upon one another or are sequenced, it then becomes difficult for students to break from the low-level tracks. Students are designated within these tracks as early as elementary and middle school and may remain there well into high school. This can be positive for those students identified as high achievers, but if not interrupted, it can be disastrous for those mistakenly designated as low achievers. The ramifications for these students are tremendous, given that their prospects for attending college are, by then, nil.

PAUSE & REFLECT

What is the original intent of tracking and sorting students? Why does the practice of tracking trouble many educators today? Why is the practice of sorting or ability grouping imperfect?

The Impact of Tracking on Diverse Learners

As is often reported in the popular press, the achievement gap between minority students and mainstream learners continues to increase. One indicator, in addition to low standardized test scores, is the overrepresentation of minority students and those labeled disabled in remedial and special education classes. Schools that serve predominantly minority populations also tend to have more vocational, remedial, and "resource" (special education) programming. Researchers have also found that low achievers are stigmatized by being continually placed in low-level tracks. Thus, these students are plagued by poor self-esteem and often remain unengaged and unmotivated by the curricula presented to them.

It comes as no surprise, then, that students placed in low-level tracks also have high rates of absenteeism. Finally, a lasting negative outcome of the tracking of minority students is the ongoing segregation of the public schools. Racially and culturally diverse students continually tracked in low-level classes are denied the opportunity to attend classes with mainstream peers, let alone have equal access to an engaging, high-level curriculum taught by exemplary teachers (Good & Brophy, 2003).

How can equity be maintained while supporting the instructional practices of teachers? Detracking, or the heterogeneous grouping of students, has been found to be a useful strategy to reduce a school's reliance on ability grouping. The introduction of mixed-ability classes, combined with the reduction of low-level class offerings, is one way to offset the challenges associated with tracking.

In a more purposeful, heterogeneous classroom community, teachers can offer honors-level coursework and credit. Administrators can reexamine class scheduling to offer more time for difficult content-area instruction. Other supplementary program reconfigurations can include after-school homework centers, intensive summer classes, and peer tutoring initiatives. The introduction of culturally relevant content has also been found to be useful to engage students who were previously unmotivated by a curriculum of little interest to them.

Other strategies that schools employ to reduce segregation in tracked schools include the implementation of open-access advanced placement or honors courses and the introduction of specialized college outreach and preparation programs. In essence, this approach guarantees access to "high tracking" for all learners. Here are some other useful detracking strategies:

- Inform and increase parent knowledge about school tracking practices.
- Introduce difficult content in segments (scaffolding).
- Utilize peer tutoring and cooperative grouping.
- Offer a variety of options when designing course assignments and assessment strategies.

Challenges to the Implementation of Detracking

Many school administrators are reluctant to detrack their classrooms. Many do not have the experience to do so, and they may even fear a backlash from community members and parents whose children are enrolled in programs for the gifted and talented. Supporters of ability grouping argue that with detracking, gifted students will lose access to challenging content, quality instruction, and resources. On the other hand, advocates of detracking maintain that all students should have access to an equally challenging curriculum, master teachers, and cutting-edge instructional materials.

Underlying the position of those who support ability grouping is the belief that American students thrive when introduced to competition and meritocracy. They view tracking as a means by which individuals make their own way in the public schools. In other words, students alone are responsible for their level of academic achievement. Those who are most successful academically deserve to have access to high-level programming and classes. As a result of this belief, resistance to detracking persists.

We see the ramifications of this resistance in the political support of home schooling, school vouchers, and charter and magnet school initiatives. These initiatives represent the establishment of homogeneous schooling whose target populations are uninterested in heterogeneous public schooling. Supporters of detracking must then continue to lobby and inform the community of the benefits of heterogeneous classrooms where all students, regardless of race, class, language, gender, and physical ability have access to high-quality curricula and instruction.

For Your CONSIDERATION

The Rand Corporation website offers free downloads of research studies by Dr. Jeannie Oakes on tracking practices in the United States, as well as in math and science courses specifically. Visit the site at **http://www. rand.org/pubs/authors/o/oakes_jeannie.html**.

Linking Theory and Practice

Early in the twentieth century, how teachers taught was heavily driven by behavioral theory, a theory based on the assumption that when students are subject to a repeated stimulus and reward, they learn to respond to teachers in a particular way. Knowledge and skills are transmitted to students in segments, and along the way, rewards (reinforcement) are shared once that specific knowledge is tested, observed, and perceived as "learned." According to B. F. Skinner (1904–1990), behaviorism is a learning theory that focuses on observable, desired behaviors and responses and on what stimulates those responses to take place. Today, behavioral theory is not the only driving force behind instructional design. It does, however, represent a major influence in the way some teachers design learning activities when the desired student outcomes are observable.

The research contributions of cultural and educational anthropologists, linguists, psychologists, and neurologists have established that there is much more to learning

From PRESERVICE to PRACTICE

Theory to Practice

Ann Jones is a seventh-grade social studies teacher. She uses behavioral approaches to instruction when preparing her students for a multiple-choice quiz on the causes of the Civil War. She begins by reviewing the content knowledge that students must demonstrate on their first quiz. She explains her approach as follows:

We play a Jeopardy-like game with the students working in cooperative groups or teams. I prepare the questions in advance on note cards. Student groups then quiz one another. The team that scores the most points by providing the correct "fact" responses, receives positive reinforcement that I hope will serve to model test preparation behavior, in this case memorization, to the other students in the class. We reinforce content and play the game two or three times while I introduce more content segments. This is one use of behaviorism that I apply to the unit.

But the memorization of facts is not the only way to observe whether learning is taking place. It's just one step. I begin there and then move on to higher level–critical thinking probes and other instructional strategies, such as role plays, poster board presentations, computer-lab-based structured activities, that supplement traditional approaches to assessing content comprehension, such as written responses on a test exam.

By using a variety of teaching approaches, I can generate a deeper understanding of social studies content. We can explore the impact of the Buffalo soldiers on the Civil War after viewing the film *Glory*, read primary documents and view images of the soldiers on the Internet, and discuss the role of minority groups and women in the military today. This way, our discussions and responses are more open-ended, more interpretive, and not tied to the memorization of facts. That's where I start, though. That's where I first observe their knowledge base when we play Jeopardy.

Questions for Reflection

1. What are the strengths and weaknesses of instruction that focuses on the memorization of facts?
2. What other instructional methods can teachers use to introduce content-area knowledge?

than responding to a stimulus and observing behaviors. They have shown that the learning process is also based on human interactions, social contexts, and cognitive and linguistic development. Such legendary scholars as Swiss psychologist and sociologist Jean Piaget (1896–1980) and Russian developmental psychologist Lev Vygotsky (1896–1934) were interested in these kinds of intellectual development that are dependent on one's curiosity and on the nature of our relationships within communities.

Piaget argued that, given their natural curiosity within their own environment, children think in ways that are distinct from those typical of adults. He maintained that children's understanding of the world develops as they continue to gain more experience with it. Piaget observed these stages in his research and documented the different ways in which children make meaning of their world as independent learners.

Piaget's view of **constructivism** contends that learners construct their own understanding of the world around them. Thus, teachers access students' background or prior knowledge and then design their instructional strategies, activities, and questions in ways that guide the learners to the next level of content-area knowledge or skills.

Vygotsky, on the other hand, felt that learning is the result of an exchange between adults and children. Learning is not solely the result of social interaction. Rather, it acts in concert with one's own thinking to help generate cognitive development and meaning-making. Vygotsky also described what he called the zone of proximal development (ZPD), a construct used to gauge a child's ability and potential in terms of two levels. On one boundary of the zone is the *actual development level,* where a student possesses enough knowledge to problem-solve on his or her own. This sets a baseline for the child's knowledge and is generally what is assessed and valued in schools.

On the zone's other boundary is the *potential development level,* which consists of knowledge a student can acquire when developmentally ready and when working with a knowledgeable peer or teacher. The difference between these two levels of ability constitutes the ZPD. The idea of an adult guiding a student through the ZPD is known as scaffolding. This concept has been further developed by American psychologist Jerome Bruner (b. 1915) and influenced his related concept of *instructional scaffolding.*

Both Piaget's and Vygotsky's perspectives on learning—such as the understanding of learner readiness, the impact of interactions with others on student learning, the use of cooperative and peer group instruction, and scaffolding—are significant to teachers and affect their approach to instructional design.

What Is Scaffolding?

Wood, Bruner, and Ross (1976) coined the term **scaffolding**. This metaphor describes an instructional approach presented by a teacher or peer to guide and support learning when the student cannot do it alone. Through this process, the instructor *collaborates* with the student and *supports and models* only when those skills are beyond the learner's ability. However, the teacher must first encourage the student to complete as much of the work as possible as independently as possible to establish *ownership* of his or her skills. Then the teacher offers encouragement and feedback to the learner as he or she demonstrates and *internalizes* the knowledge and skills that were introduced.

Once the learner demonstrates an understanding of the new knowledge or skills, the teacher begins gradually to remove the scaffolding (a process also referred to as fading), which enables the student to work independently. "Scaffolding is actually a bridge used to build upon what students already know to arrive at something they do not know. If scaffolding is properly administered, it will act as an enabler, not as a disabler" (Benson, 1997). See Table 8.4 for a sample lesson plan that incorporates scaffolding.

Points to Consider When Implementing Instructional Scaffolding

Larkin (2002) suggests that teachers can follow a few effective techniques of scaffolding:

- Begin by boosting confidence. Introduce students first to tasks they can perform with little or no assistance. This will improve self-efficacy.
- Provide enough assistance to allow students to achieve success quickly. This will help lower frustration levels and ensure that students remain motivated as they advance to the next stage. It will also help guard against students giving up as a consequence of repeated failures.
- Help students "fit in." Students may actually work harder if they feel they resemble their peers.
- Gauge the students' level of motivation. Don't overwork skills or content once they are learned.
- Look for clues that the learner is mastering the task. Scaffolding should be removed gradually and then removed completely when mastery of the task is demonstrated.

TABLE 8.4 Sample U.S. History Plan Reflecting Scaffolding

Title: Pearl Harbor

Time: 90 minutes

Materials: VCR, videotape, posters, pictures

Objectives:

1. The student will summarize reasons for the entry of the United States into World War II. (appropriateness, ownership)

2. The student will evaluate the pros and cons of these reasons. (appropriateness)

Setting the stage: Show pictures of the attack on Pearl Harbor (appropriateness, support, ownership)

Discuss: Background from homework reading. (appropriateness, support, ownership)

Construct: Timeline of WWII events. (appropriateness, support, ownership)

Groups: Present some reasons for a country to go to war. Refer to textbook and previous class notes. (appropriateness, support, internalization, collaboration/modeling)

Show: Anti-Japan and anti-German posters and newsclips/video. (appropriateness, collaboration/modeling)

Journal: What role did emotions play in the U.S. entry into WWII? Defend or critique the decision to go to war (appropriateness, internalization, ownership).

Source: Adapted from Stephen Holtrip webpage, Writing Lesson Plans, retrieved March 27, 2007, from http://www.Huntington.edu/education/lessonplanning/Gardner.html.

Teachers can implement scaffolding at any grade level. However, effective scaffolding requires that teachers be acutely aware of the students' skill levels and prior knowledge, so that learners are not frustrated by content that is beyond their reach and readiness. The teacher must determine what students already know so that they can be motivated, or "hooked," by the new knowledge. Scaffolding strategies can include

- The introduction of content or skills in smaller, manageable segments,
- The demonstration of "think-alouds," or discussion of learning stages with students as they complete a skill or a content-area unit,
- The assignment of cooperative group-learning activities, which encourage teamwork and peer mentoring, and
- The use of discussions, questions, and role playing for critical thinking.

The Eurocentric and Inclusive Curricula

Since its inception, the curriculum of American public schools has focused primarily on the knowledge bases and contributions of males in European and Western societies. This kind of class content is commonly referred to as a **Eurocentric curriculum**. At the center of a Eurocentric curriculum are representations of history and knowledge presented as absolute truths driven by a single Western perspective. However, beginning with the emergence of the civil rights movement in the 1960s, the call for inclusion of curriculum content that reflects the diversity and contributions of all Americans has "decentered" the Eurocentric curriculum and charged educators to introduce a reformed curriculum that represents the pluralistic nature of the world.

Today, given our increasingly diverse society, the growth of a global economy, and the use of technology to increase awareness of our international neighbors, the reexamination of what we teach in the public schools remains an important facet of an educator's professional practice. However, the means of implementing an inclusive curriculum vary considerably. With little training and few resources available, well-intentioned educators have infused diverse or multicultural content that may only serve to trivialize and stereotype minority contributions to society.

For example, a "holidays and heroes" approaches to content integration, such as the single-day recognition of Martin Luther King, Jr. or of Cinco de Mayo, robs students of an opportunity to study other contributors (such as W. E. B. Du Bois) and historical movements (for example, the 1968 Chicana/o student protests or "blowouts"). Hence, such complex and critical subject matter remains absent from the curriculum.

This is a major concern for educational policymakers as they consider curriculum decisions that affect diverse students for whom the Eurocentric curriculum has not helped close the achievement gap. As a result, several inner-city elementary schools in Baltimore, Detroit, and Washington, DC, have implemented Afrocentric curriculum programs that emphasize the knowledge bases and contributions of Africans throughout history. This approach reflects educator and community attempts to better engage students in the learning process by developing a curriculum that is culturally relevant to them.

Students follow the "call to the village" for the morning Harambe ceremony at an Afrocentric elementary school in Akron.

To some educators, the dominance of a Eurocentric history curriculum supports the subordination of underrepresented groups. It renders invisible the identity of other cultures that have a major presence in society, including significant civilizations in Africa, China, and Latin America. And yet, the contributions of diverse groups in schools are often limited to marginalized, cultural symbols (such as steel drums, panda bears, and piñatas) presented at schoolyard food festivals. Minority students, then, become the "cultural educators" for their peers, while their histories, languages, and contributions are seldom presented within the valued, mainstream curriculum.

Thus, an inclusive, or **culturally relevant,** curriculum is one that introduces multiple ways of knowing and recenters different kinds of knowledge. *An inclusive curriculum does not supplant previously dominant European contributions.* Instead, it holds a shared position at the center of the curriculum so that other forms of knowledge can be introduced, analyzed, and affirmed.

The implementation of an inclusive curriculum does not necessarily require that teachers do *more* in the classroom. An inclusive curriculum requires teachers to do things *differently.* Teachers can, for example,

- Utilize a variety of literature that represents multiple perspectives.
- Compare and contrast various global events, movements, and events that occurred simultaneously in history.
- Introduce content-area subject matter from a global perspective, such as the arts, critical literacy, environmental studies, ethnomathematics (the study of mathematical concepts across cultures), and science.
- Examine the relevance of gender to historical contributions, as well as its contemporary impact.

From PRESERVICE to PRACTICE

Chicano Students Challenge Inequities and the Curriculum: The 1968 East Los Angeles Blowouts

Student protests in East Los Angeles helped transform Lincoln High into a comprehensive secondary school that offers Advanced Placement exams and an on-site math and science magnet program.

Having grown increasingly unhappy with educational inequities and a Eurocentric curriculum, Chicano students from five East Los Angeles high schools made history in March 1968 in what would come to be known as the East LA blowouts. For nearly two weeks, students organized and participated in picketing, sit-ins, walkouts, speeches, and, in some cases, vandalism to express their dissatisfaction with administrators and public schooling. Their struggle for a culturally sensitive, challenging education became a cornerstone of the Chicano movement, and the blowouts themselves are among the most effective expressions of student activism in Los Angeles history.

Leading up to the blowouts, Chicano students at Lincoln High School in East Los Angeles participated in a student-exchange program at an affluent, predominantly white high school in Los Angeles. The students became alarmingly aware of the inferiority of their education and told a teacher, Sal Castro, that they wanted to protest their inferior schools. Castro validated the students'

frustrations and made them aware of the importance of developing clear demands, planning speeches and peaceful protests, and establishing coalitions with other schools—while consistently emphasizing their right to a quality education.

Soon students at the five predominantly Chicano high schools in East Los Angeles (Lincoln, Wilson, Garfield, Belmont, and Roosevelt) were organized into a network to call for better education. The students wanted Mexican and Mexican American history and literature to be incorporated into the curriculum, the school district to hire more Mexican American teachers and administrators, instructional equipment and facilities to be improved to more closely resemble those in affluent high schools, and the opportunity to participate in a challenging education that emphasized college preparation instead of industrial trades.

When administrators at Wilson High School unexpectedly canceled a school play, Wilson High School students protested and soon were joined by other students throughout East Los Angeles. Students made speeches, and their marches and demonstrations were attended by 10,000 students and supporters. The police beat and arrested several student activists. Sal Castro emerged as the teacher spokesperson for the students and was arrested with twelve student organizers and charged with conspiracy to commit various crimes. The charges were soon dropped.

After several days of sit-ins and demonstrations, tensions began to ease, and students slowly returned to school. After days of protest, the students had succeeded in persuading school administrators to address some of their concerns. Mexican American studies and literature were implemented in the curriculum, and a careful longitudinal evaluation of the quality of education received by Mexican American students in the public schools ensued. What began with awareness and organized discontent on the part of Chicano students eventually contributed to significant educational reforms in bilingual and multicultural education in California.

Sources: Acuna (1988); Jimenez. Prepared by Alison Kreider (University of California, Los Angeles).

- Conduct media analysis/technology activities with students in ways that encourage critical thinking about how diversity is portrayed across race, class, gender, and exceptionality.

- Analyze community issues and strategize problem-solving activities with families and community members.

The use of critical thinking or critical analysis is an important dimension of an inclusive curriculum. Encouraging students to ask questions about what they are being taught, and why, reflects an instructional approach that addresses issues relevant to diversity, equality, and the role of society's institutions in the pursuit of social justice. This instructional approach is also known as critical pedagogy. **Critical pedagogy** encourages teachers to pose questions to students and present curriculum in ways that challenge their assumptions, biases, and beliefs about the knowledge they are constructing (Banks & Banks, 2004).

By posing such questions as "Who discovered America?" and "What is manifest destiny and who was impacted by it?" and "What role did Susan Butcher have in competitive outdoor sports and in environmental science?" teachers can not only help students reflect on and generate new knowledge but also enable them to analyze and construct knowledge that is not always accurately depicted in textbooks. Ultimately, an inclusive curriculum encompasses praxis. **Praxis** consists of the action students and teachers can generate as they extend their new knowledge to problem solving and community service.

Resistance to an inclusive or multicultural curriculum emerged in the 1980s. Political conservatives continue to challenge curriculum changes—changes, they argue, that threaten what they feel are indisputable content and values presented in the public schools. They contend that educators should teach what they feel is essential subject matter. In turn, students must demonstrate basic skills, or standards, and the content that E. D. Hirsch, Jr. describes in his book *Cultural Literacy* (1988) as the core knowledge students must memorize. Hirsch's emphasis on an essentialist curriculum has garnered so much support from conservatives that some educators argue that it set the stage for passage of the federal No Child Left Behind Act in 2002.

Today, however, teachers are at a crossroads as they confront mounting societal inequities that impact their students. Many seek to balance an inclusive curriculum with problem-solving strategies they co-construct with their students. At the same time, teachers cope with the pressures of teaching an essentialized, Eurocentric curriculum in preparation for a standardized test. Key questions remain: How is such a curriculum relevant to an inclusive education and to diverse learners? And are students being prepared to problem-solve as social inequities and segregated communities continue to increase in number?

PAUSE & REFLECT

In what ways can all learners benefit from being introduced to a diverse or multicultural curriculum? Why do you think there is resistance to a more inclusive curriculum in the public schools? How can teachers provide students with content-area instruction that includes multiple perspectives?

Who Is Responsible for Students' Classroom Behavior?

What causes students to be off-task, either disruptively or nondisruptively, when they should be engaged in lessons? Some teachers with whom we raised this question emphasized factors over which they had no control. Here are some of their responses:

- Two of my students were so high in class today that they couldn't think straight. This happens because there are drug dealers all over this town.

- Jim talked incessantly during a silent-reading session today because the classes at our school are too large for anyone to maintain order.

- Arlette failed to do her homework assignment because her parents let her watch television all night instead of encouraging her to do schoolwork.

- Charlene and Marion are more interested in each other than they are in history, so they talked to each other instead of listening to my history lecture.

Any undesirable, off-task behavior that a student exhibits while under the direction of a teacher can be "blamed" on the student or on causes outside the teacher's domain. But both the student and the teacher are responsible for the student's engagement or lack of engagement in a lesson. It is tempting to focus the "blame" for off-task behaviors on society, television, parents, or other factors. Too-large classes, excessive paperwork required by administrators, unexpected interruptions (such as band members being called out of the classroom during a lesson), uncooperative parents, time-consuming school regulations, student access to debilitating drugs, lack of suitable equipment—these are only a few of the obstacles that may make it difficult for teachers to keep students engaged in their lessons. Teachers must focus on what they can do to keep students engaged and on-task even in the face of these constraints.

In many situations, off-task behavior is more "normal" for students than engaged behavior. For example, in the last response cited, Marion and Charlene's greater interest in each other than in history is not only expected but can be considered healthy. In fact, off-task behavior such as relaxing is sometimes more natural for students than absorption in taking lecture notes. Thus, "What causes students to become engaged in lessons?" may be a more useful question for teachers to ask than "What causes students to be off-task?" Listed and discussed below are some strategies to help maintain student engagement in the classroom.

Twelve Classroom Management Strategies to Keep in Mind

Here are 12 strategies to consider when you are confronted with students who are off-task.

1. Deal with Off-Task Behavior as You Would Any Other Student Need. Suppose that you are trying to teach your students about something other than how to read (e.g., principles of nutrition). However, your lesson plan depends on the students' comprehending what they read from a textbook assignment. One of your students appears to lack the reading skill to comprehend the necessary information from the reading assignment. Visualize yourself dealing with this all-too-familiar situation. Are you angry with this student for not knowing how to read as well as you would like?

Rather than reacting in anger to the student's lack of reading proficiency, you would take steps either to help the student improve in reading skills or to work around the difficulty (e.g., by finding a means to communicate the information that doesn't depend on reading skill).

Most of us are more likely to react in anger to students' lack of cooperative, on-task behaviors than to their lack of some prerequisite academic skill. Students learn to supplant off-task behaviors with requisite on-task behaviors when we respond to their displays of off-task behaviors with sound, systematic pedagogical techniques, not when we respond out of anger. Research-based methods for teaching off-task students to be on task are reported in the professional literature (see, e.g., Cameron & Pierce, 1994; Cangelosi, 2006; Charles, 2005; Evertson, 2006; and Levin, Shanken-Kaye, & Shanken-Kaye, 2003). For each incident of off-task behavior, these methods generally require you to take the following steps.

- Determine whether the off-task behavior is disruptive to other students in the class. For a nondisruptive off-task behavior (e.g., a student daydreaming), you may not feel compelled to respond as quickly as you would for a disruptive off-task behavior (e.g., a student talking loudly during a planned quiet-reading period). Thus, for cases of nondisruptive off-task behaviors, you have more flexibility in when you intervene.

- Determine whether the off-task behavior is part of a habitual pattern or only an isolated incident. Your initial response to an incident of off-task behavior is to take action that will get the students back on-task. Off-task behavior patterns are more difficult to terminate than isolated incidents. However, you usually have the luxury of taking time to plan strategies for intervening in patterns, whereas isolated off-task behaviors typically need to be dealt with as they occur. Principles of behavior modification (Martin et al., 2002) are applicable in the design of methods for (1) helping students break off-task behavior patterns and (2) preventing students' isolated displays of off-task behaviors from becoming habitual.

- Decide on objectives. Just as you establish objectives for academic lessons, so should your strategy for responding to an off-task behavior systematically target one or more specific objectives.

- Plan a course of action for achieving the objectives.

- Implement the plan.

- Assess how well the objectives are being achieved.

2. Deal Decisively with an Off-Task Behavior, or Don't Deal with It at All. It is a waste of time and energy to use half-hearted attempts that do more harm than good. Jones and Jones (2006) have found that teachers handle discipline problems far more effectively when they speak face-to-face, directly to students, than when they speak "over-the-shoulder" in a "matter-of-fact" tone.

3. Control the Time and Place for Dealing with Disruptions. Some teachers feel obliged to demonstrate their authority by dealing in front of the class with a student who has been disruptive. Such tactics should be reconsidered. Usually, it is more efficient first to get everyone back on task and then, at a time and place that you can effectively control, to deal with preventing future occurrences. Don't worry that students will think that the disrupter "got off easy." Word will get back to them that you handled the situation decisively.

4. Always Leave Students a Face-Saving Way to Terminate an Incident. Teachers are asking for trouble whenever they do anything that leads students to feel embarrassed in front of their peers. Given that the student is a child and the teacher an adult, it is not surprising that the student is vulnerable to a witty put-down by a teacher reacting to a student's misbehavior. But playing such verbal games detracts from the dignity of a businesslike learning environment and fuels conflicts.

5. Utilize the Help of Colleagues, Parents, and Supervisors; Don't be Fooled by the "Myth of the Good Teacher." Some teachers are afraid to seek help from other adults because they are deluded by what Canter and Canter (2001) refer to as the "myth of the good teacher." According to the myth, teachers who are really "good" can handle all their own discipline problems without outside help. Teachers suffering under this myth feel guilty for bothering others with problems they think of themselves as too weak to handle. In reality, consulting with colleagues is more a sign of professional behavior than a sign of weakness (Abernathy, Manera, & Wright, 1985). Furthermore, your supervisors are legally and ethically responsible for supporting your instructional efforts (Oliva & Pawlas, 2004), and parents typically have greater influence over their children's behaviors than you do (Canter & Canter, 2001).

6. Maintain Professional Confidences. Clearly distinguish between (a) the professional practice of conferring with trusted colleague teachers, authorized supervisors, and students' own parents and (b) the unprofessional practice of gossiping about students or sharing "discipline problem" anecdotes with unauthorized persons.

Trust between a teacher and students is an important ingredient in establishing a classroom climate that is conducive to cooperation and on-task behaviors. Teachers who violate that trust by gossiping about students jeopardize the professional-client relationship that facilitates the efficient handling of discipline problems (Cangelosi, 2006).

7. Have Alternative Lesson Plans Available for Times When Students Do Not Cooperate as Planned. When conducting a planned lesson, you should expect students to cooperate with you and choose to be engaged in the learning activities. Your confident expectation increases the chances that they will cooperate. However, by being prepared, in case some students refuse to cooperate, you guard against operating under the stress of the lesson getting "out of control." A well-designed learning activity should not be aborted simply because it is not going as smoothly as you would like. However, there is an advantage to having alternative and less enjoyable activities ready for times when students' off-task behaviors render your original plan unworkable. These alternative activities should target the same learning objectives as the original activities.

8. Work as Diligently to Decrease the Incidence of Nondisruptive Off-Task Behaviors as to Decrease the Incidence of Disruptions. Nondisruptive off-task behaviors (e.g., mind-wandering, failing to attempt assignments, being under the influence of drugs during lessons, sleeping in class, and even cheating on tests) are sometimes disregarded because they do not necessarily interfere with the activities of the class as a whole.

9. Allow Students to Recognize for Themselves the Natural Consequences of Not Attempting Assignments or Failing to Participate in Lessons. It is not unusual for some teachers to punish students or to artificially manipulate their grades because the students fail to attempt assignments or to participate in class activities. However, assignments that are really meaningful to students make such punishment or grade manipulation unnecessary.

10. Never Lose Sight of the Fact that Each Person Controls Her or His Own Actions. Factors such as drug abuse, boredom, poor parenting, hyperactive personalities, and lack of confidence help explain why students misbehave in school. Understanding these factors helps us to systematically devise ways to teach students to cooperate, behave, and be on-task. However, our awareness of contributing factors should not be confused with excusing or tolerating misbehaviors.

Much of the research on classroom discipline emphasizes that each and every individual is responsible for her or his own behaviors and should be held accountable for them (Canter & Canter, 2001; Cangelosi, 2006; Charles, 2005; Evertson, 2006). Except for the relatively unusual cases where one person physically accosts another, one person cannot make another do something. Once students realize this, they are disarmed of virtually all of their excuses for misconduct. To lead students to understand that only they are in control of their own conduct, you should consistently use language that is free of suggestions that one person can control another. In other words, purge your language of statements such as these: "Be careful of what you say or you'll make Mia feel bad." "You made Allen cry." "Fred, don't get Tommy into trouble."

Such language should be replaced with: "Be careful of what you say or Mia may think you don't enjoy her company." "Allen was so unhappy with what you said that he cried." "Fred, don't encourage Tommy to do something he shouldn't."

11. Maintain Your Options; Avoid "Playing Your Last Card." Understand the extent and limits of your authority as a teacher. Never threaten a student with something if you cannot follow through. For example, if you tell a student, "Either sit down and start your work, or I'll make sure you never see the inside of this classroom again!" what are you going to do if the student refuses? You have extended your authority as far as it can reach. You have exhausted your options. Obtain the help of supervisors before you run out of ways to deal with undesirable situations.

12. Know Yourself and Know Your Students. Continually examine your own motives for dealing with students. Be receptive to individual differences. Measures that are effective with one may be disastrous with another. Be conservative in trying out new ideas with an entire group until you know the students and have found the ideas to be workable with the individuals you know best. On the other hand, don't give up on an idea because it won't work for all students all the time. This suggestion is perhaps the most important of all. The better you understand yourself and your students, the better you will be able to elicit your students' cooperation and respond sensitively, flexibly, and effectively to discipline problems whenever they do occur.

Connecting to the Cengage Learning Video Cases

Classroom Management: Basic Strategies
Watch the Cengage Learning video case entitled "Classroom Management: Basic Strategies." Consider viewing questions 2 and 3.

Video Case Study
High school history teacher Henry Turner stresses the need for consistency in managing a classroom.

1. Can you recall teachers of your own for whom consistency was a hallmark of their practice?
2. What did you learn from these teachers?
3. What's your response to the comments made by Robert, a student in Henry's class?

Student Website

Parental Involvement in the Learning Process

One very effective way to bridge curriculum concerns and teacher practice is to invite the participation of families and community members in the educational process. Not only do teachers influence students, their families, friends, coaches, clergy, and youth leaders; these individuals also influence *them*. Not to draw on the experiences of these adults is to ignore resources that can help students realize their full potential both in and out of the classroom.

A father helps his daughter with her homework.

Unfortunately, however, teacher frustrations tend to spill over when it comes to family involvement in the public schools. Educators are quick to blame parents for their lack of participation or to lament that the parents are "too poor to care." They often complain that families do not attend back-to-school events or help students with their schoolwork, and many are quick to assume that minority parents, in particular, take no responsibility for their children. Some educators maintain that parents do not want to speak English with the school staff. Teachers cite research that if families participated more in the schooling of their children, then attendance, motivation, and academic achievement would improve, regardless of their ethnicity and economic status.

And yet there is substantial evidence that low-income and/or culturally diverse families are very concerned about the education of their children (Valdez, 1996; Valenzuela, 1999; Stanton-Salazar, 2001). Their concerns stem from the hope that an education will help their children access opportunities that the families themselves have not yet experienced in America or in their homelands.

Ironically, it is also not uncommon for teachers to complain that some upper- and middle-income families participate too much in the schooling of their children. These parents, often college-educated, are well versed in accessing the school bureaucracy and are empowered to monitor their children's grades and performance. They feel comfortable challenging professional educators' decisions about grades, instructional approaches, and program design when they feel their children's needs are being compromised. Administrators are quick to respond to such parents because they do not want to be perceived in the local community as dismissive of their concerns.

It is no wonder, then, that communication can be strained among educators, members of students' families, and the community at large. When their positions collide, it is very difficult for teachers to respond. Teachers do not have the resources or the time to reach out to parents who do not understand or trust the schools and, as a result, distance themselves from it. Teachers then assume, mistakenly, that families do not care about education.

Framing Parent Involvement

How can teachers better respond to families without dismissing their questions, needs, and concerns? Maintaining a professional approach with a team of administrators and teachers who are united in the communication and promotion of equal educational programming for all students is one way to begin collaborative discussion and problem solving with parents. Such an approach may not eliminate the efforts of some parents to seek educational advantages for their children, but educators who strive to involve as many families as possible in discussion groups may serve as a catalyst for shared decision making and power-sharing.

Connecting to the Cengage Learning Video Cases

Communication with Parents: Tips and Strategies for Future Teachers

Watch the Cengage Learning video case entitled "Communication with Parents: Tips and Strategies for Future Teachers." Consider viewing questions 1, 3, and 5.

Video Case Study

1. In what ways can teachers communicate with parents?
2. What strategies can teachers use to involve parents more actively in their children's learning processes?
3. Should teachers respond to parents' concerns within a 24-hour time frame, as Principal Flynn suggests? Explain why and why not.

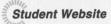
Student Website

Parent involvement isn't a "given," and student success depends on it. This involvement, however, has been expressed in rather broad terms. Research literature reviewed by the National Parent-Teacher Association (2000) on effective parent involvement programs suggests several conclusions:

- When families participate in their children's education, the students excel more, regardless of socioeconomic status, cultural background, or the parents' own educational opportunities or achievement.
- When families are involved, students display more positive attitudes.
- Parent involvement activities must be carefully planned. In particular, they must be inclusive for all families, including English language learners, blended families, single-parent families, and families headed by gay partners.
- Children from diverse backgrounds do better in school when educators and parents collaborate.
- Teacher morale improves when schools develop a careful, long-term family outreach plan.
- Schools with well-designed family outreach plans tend to foster greater academic achievement than programs that lack such comprehensive plans.
- Strong and effective programs are the result of a well-financed, collaborative approach that includes families, teachers, and administrators.
- Families must be included in the process and are provided with program information consistently. Research reveals that when families are comfortable and have input into program design and activities, they are more likely to implement those strategies in the home.
- Family collaboration with the schools is critical to the academic achievement of students, but it is not the only requirement for effective teaching and improved education programming.

Researcher Joyce Epstein cautions that although schools traditionally solicit the participation of parents through PTA meetings, parent-teacher conferences, back-to-school nights, and fund-raising events, educators must rethink how to involve families in much more specific and collaborative ways (Epstein et al., 1997). Epstein acknowledges that such planning extends administrators' and

A student works with his mother on a writing assignment.

From PRESERVICE to PRACTICE

Ten Ways for Parents to Help Elementary Teachers by Mimi Doe

Many teachers have written to me over the years, frustrated with how unprepared their students are—and they don't mean academically. Chris, a kindergarten teacher, wrote what many teachers have expressed: "I would love it if you could write a list of ten tips for parents to help us teachers do our increasingly demanding job. Many parents of children I teach have left the job of spiritual, character, and social/emotional education to me. I can't do it all in addition to teaching academic skills. I'm getting burned out and pretty soon won't have the energy left to nourish one child let alone 25."

So here goes. My ten tips:

1. Create a smooth takeoff each day. Give your child a hug before she ventures out the door and you head to work. Look her in the eye, and tell her how proud you are of her. Your child's self-confidence and security will help her do well both in school and in life.

2. Prepare for a happy landing at the end of the day when you reconvene. Create a predictable ritual such as 10 to 20 minutes listening to your child talk about his day—before you check phone messages, read the mail, or begin dinner. That way you are fully present to listen, and your child has a touchstone he can count on between school and home.

3. Fill your child's lunchbox with healthy snacks and lunches. Have dinner at a reasonable hour and a healthy breakfast. A well-balanced diet maximizes your child's learning potential.

4. Include calm, peaceful times in your children's afternoons and evenings. Maintain a schedule that allows them to go to school rested, and if they are sick, have a system in place so they are able to stay home.

5. Remember that it's your children's homework, not yours. Create a specific homework space that's clutter-free and quiet. Encourage editing and double-checking work, but allow your kids to make mistakes, as it's the only way teachers can gauge if they understand the material. It's also how children learn responsibility for the quality of their work.

6. Fill your child's life with a love for learning by showing him your own curiosity, respecting his questions, and encouraging his efforts.

7. Fill your home with books to read, books simply to look at, and books that provide answers to life's many questions. The public or school library is an excellent resource.

8. Be a partner with your child's teacher. When you need to speak to him or her in reference to a specific issue with your child, do it privately, not in front of your child. Make a point never to criticize your child's teacher in front of your child.

9. Set up a system where routine items are easily located—such as backpacks, shoes, signed notices. Create a central calendar for upcoming events to avoid the unexpected.

10. Tuck a "love note" in your child's lunch bag to let her know how special she is. Knowing they are loved makes it easier for children to be kind to others.

Questions for Reflection

1. In what ways are children's physical and emotional needs important as they enter the classroom environment?

2. Why is it important for children to have a "homework" or "school" station established in the home?

Source: Parent Teacher Association Homepage, retrieved March 26, 2007, from http://www.pta.org/archive_article_details_1118086988656.html.

teachers' already demanding schedules. Instead, she proposes a parent involvement typology consisting of specific areas to consider when planning for family involvement. These areas include parenting, communicating, volunteering, learning together at home, shared school decision making, and collaboration with community resources and services.

To better support the participation of families in the public schools, the National Parent-Teacher Association has endorsed putting Epstein's parent involvement typology into action. However, the implementation of this typology remains elusive when power is not equally shared among the stakeholders, including underrepresented family members, community members, and teachers.

The No Child Left Behind Act also mandates that schools have policies in place to solicit parent involvement and inform them about testing standards. But educators still struggle to find the time and resources to teach families about the mission, goals, and practices of a school. Epstein's parent involvement typology provides a framework for schools to follow, and by embracing parent involvement as an important component of a school's mission, educators can draw on the insights of parents *and* the professional perspectives of working teachers.

Engaging Families with the Curriculum Through Funds of Knowledge

Another way to engage families with the schools is to examine their funds of knowledge—that is, the kinds of accumulated knowledge, history, skills, and social networks they possess that are essential to a household's functioning and well-being. By conducting home and community visits and interviewing families about their histories, languages, traditions, interests, professions, customs, and skills, teachers become informed about the cultural capital that families possess. Then, in turn, they can design curricula, instruction, and parent outreach activities around those "funds."

Influenced by the work of educational researchers Norma Gonzalez and Luis Moll, a funds-of-knowledge approach to classroom instruction incorporates the knowledge generated in our students' homes and lives. A curriculum based on community knowledge is quite different from the curricula created by educators and curriculum specialists unfamiliar with local cultures and classrooms.

Proponents of a funds-of-knowledge approach to instruction maintain that local community knowledge has a rightful place in schools. Whatever the cultural background of the students and their families, there is knowledge in their homes that can be explored and incorporated within the curriculum and school activities (Gonzalez, Moll, & Amanti, 2005). This idea challenges the cultural deficit theory, which focuses on the knowledge that students and their families lack (knowledge that is often defined and sanctioned by educational institutions) rather than on the knowledge that students bring to the classroom.

Gonzalez, Moll, and Amanti assert that funds of knowledge are "abundant and diverse; they may include information about, for example, farming and animal husbandry, associated with households' rural origins, or knowledge about construction and building, related to urban occupations; or knowledge about many other matters, such as [international] trade, business, and finance" (2005, p. 5).

Following a visit (one of three) to a student's home, teacher Martha Floyd Tenery (2005) identified categories of "family funds" of knowledge to consider for curriculum development, as well as for parenting, communicating, and learning at home (as noted in Epstein's parent involvement typology). Examples of these categories include the *strategizing household,* where families and students help maintain the household culturally and economically through skills and activities such as pooling resources, the division of labor, exchanging goods and services with other families, and developing community support and business networks. Curriculum designs that build on these activities include such content areas as mathematics, business, and social studies.

Domains of knowledge are skills and talents that commonly exist in these households. According to Tenery, they can range from cross-cultural knowledge of international commerce, specialized skills and trades, language, and cultural traditions (2005). These "funds" can serve as a foundation for thematic units or lesson plans where teachers combine objectives and instructional strategies with community knowledge. Lessons then become culturally relevant, include familiar material, and build on diverse learners' prior knowledge (scaffolding).

Student domains of knowledge observed in the home (such as art, dance, music, bilingualism, technology uses, animal and plant care, sewing, cooking, and sports) can be elaborated on and shared with peers. *Family domains of knowledge*, Tenery notes, such as "knowledge of household repairs, construction, tile work, auto mechanics, and international trade can be developed into hands-on school activities on measurement, money, mathematics, and electricity" (Tenery, 2005, p. 129). Families can also be invited to the schools to demonstrate these skills and talents. In this way, funds of knowledge are incorporated within the curriculum to better engage students, while validating and increasing family participation on campus.

Connecting to the Cengage Learning Video Cases

Parent Involvement in School Culture

Watch the Cengage Learning video case entitled "Parent Involvement in School Culture: A Literacy Project." Consider viewing question 1.

Video Case Study

1. How do the perspectives of the parent, Patricia, reflect her family's funds of knowledge?
2. What strategies does she believe teachers should employ to better ensure parent involvement in the schools?
3. In this video case, what assumptions about minority parent participation does Patricia challenge?

Student Website

SUMMARY

To be a working teacher requires a license and a signed contract. Although these are necessary for employment, they are not sufficient for success. They do not in themselves make an effective teacher. Effective teachers possess specific qualities. They care for their students and maintain high expectations. Teachers are well prepared—in fact, they overprepare—in an effort to engage students, minimize classroom management issues, and maintain on-task time. They express enthusiasm for the content they teach, and they model behaviors that influence students' motivation for learning and interest level. Such teachers also offer emotional support for the students under their care.

Effective teachers are also mindful that there are different ways to understand intelligence. They acknowledge that there are many ways of knowing. Gardner's theory of multiple intelligences enables educators to recognize such

ability differences in the arts, sciences, kinesthetics, and interpersonal skills, to name only a few. This awareness opens up our understanding of what it means to be knowledgeable. Furthermore, the curriculum is not limited to the Western world but, rather, includes global perspectives.

Effective teachers utilize instructional strategies that build on prior knowledge, such as scaffolding. They are less tied to tracking. They implement a variety of programs and classroom management techniques, such as cooperative learning, the delivery of curriculum segments, and peer tutoring. They support after-school mentoring programs to help provide all levels of learners with equal access to the curriculum.

Finally, effective teachers and administrators methodically design strategies to keep parents informed and invite them to participate in the learning process. Epstein's parent involvement typology establishes a framework in which educators and families explore communication, decision making, and collaboration within the community. By utilizing a funds-of-knowledge approach, effective educators come to understand that they themselves have much to learn from parents. In essence, what teachers learn can go a long way in engaging students and welcoming families into their classrooms.

DISCUSSION QUESTIONS

1. Teachers must make numerous decisions during the course of their day in the classroom. Which decisions do you feel have the greatest impact on the academic achievement of a teacher's students? Explain why.

2. What characteristics do excellent teachers possess? How do these teachers differ from those who are mediocre or poor? Describe an educator you have had who possessed exemplary teaching characteristics, as discussed in this chapter.

3. Explain the differences between Eurocentric and multicultural curricula. In what ways can learners benefit from an understanding of a variety of curriculum perspectives? Give two or three examples relevant to your content areas of interest.

4. What is tracking? Why do schools continue to implement sorting policies, even though studies have found that tracking leads to educational inequities? What instructional strategies can teachers use to reduce the negative effects of tracking?

5. In what ways does a funds-of-knowledge approach to interacting with families differ from simple visits to students' homes? How can a teacher's understanding of families' social networking, literacy, and specialized knowledge bases and skills help enrich that teacher's curriculum and instruction?

ACTIVITIES

1. Interview three fellow college students. Have them describe their favorite teachers and instructors. Identify what characteristics these educators possessed.

2. Reflect on the curriculum you have been exposed to throughout your school and college career. What features of a Eurocentric curriculum and what features of a diverse curriculum have been introduced to you? How has a multiple-curriculum perspective informed your knowledge base, in terms of teacher education?

3. Research tracking practices in your state and local schools. Discuss tracking with a teacher or school administrator, and inquire about that individual's views regarding the sorting of students. How do her or his views compare to your own experiences?

4. Conduct a funds-of-knowledge home visit to a family you are familiar with, ideally one who represents lived experiences and/or perspectives different from your own. Describe that family's life in terms of languages, cultural traditions, religion, political perspectives, arts and literature, employment, health, diet, and other special skills or interests. Describe how you feel such "funds" can affect your educational philosophy and practice.

WEBSITES

American Anthropological Association
*http://www.aaanet.org/committees/commissions/aec/
fok.htm*
Here you will find a Funds of Knowledge for Teaching Project paper that provides a model and strategies for conducting, with families and students, your own "Funds" project relevant to curriculum development and classroom instruction.

Arizona State University, Education Policy Studies Laboratory
*http://www.asu.edu/educ/epsl/EPRU/documents/
EPRU%202002-101/Chapter%2008-Glass-Final.htm*
This webpage provides a number of full-text education studies and policy briefs. See School Reform Proposals by Dr. Gene V. Glass regarding teacher characteristics.

National Center for Cultural Diversity and Second Language Teaching
http://www.ncela.gwu.edu/pubs/ncrcdsll/epr6.htm
This site includes a full-text study entitled "Teacher Research on Funds of Knowledge: Learning from Households" by Norma Gonzalez, Luis Moll, Martha Floyd-Tenery, Anna Rivera, Patricia Rendon, Raquel Gonzales, and Cathy Amanti from the University of Arizona.

The Rand Corporation
http://www.rand.org/pubs/authors/o/oakes_jeanne.html
This website offers free downloads of research studies by Dr. Jeanne Oakes regarding tracking practices in the United States and especially in math and science courses.

REFERENCES

Abernathy, S., Manera, E., & Wright, R. (1985). What stresses student teachers most? *Clearing House, 58*, 361–362.

Acuña, R. (2007). *Occupied America: A history of Chicanos* (6th ed.). New York: Pearson Longman.

Banks, J., & Banks, C. (2004). *Handbook of research on multicultural education.* New York: Macmillan.

Benson, B. (1997). *Scaffolding.* In M. Orey (Ed.), *Emerging perspectives on learning, teaching, and technology.* Retrieved July 26, 2006, from http://www.coe.uga.edu/epltt/scaffolding.htm

Bruning, R., Schaw, G., Norby, M., & Ronning, R. (2004). *Cognitive psychology and instruction.* Upper Saddle River, NJ: Merrill/Prentice-Hall.

Cameron, J., & Pierce, W. D. (1994). Reinforcement, reward, and intrinsic motivation: A meta-analysis. *Review of Educational Research, 64*, 363–423.

Cangelosi, J. S. (2006). *Classroom management practices and schoolwide discipline policies.* Unpublished study, Utah State University, Logan.

Canter, L., & Canter, M. (2001). *Assertive discipline: Positive behavior management for today's schools* (3rd ed.). Santa Monica: Canter.

Charles, C. M. (2005). *Building classroom discipline* (8th ed.). Boston: Pearson/Allyn and Bacon.

Checkley, K. (1997). The first seven … and the eighth: A conversation with Howard Gardner. *Educational Researcher, 55*(1), 8–13.

Epstein, J., Coates, L., Salinas, K., Sanders, M., & Simon, B. (1997). *School, family and community partnerships: Your handbook for action.* Thousand Oaks, CA: Corwin Press.

Gonzalez, N., Moll, L., & Amanti, C. (2005). *Funds of knowledge: Theorizing practices in households and classrooms.* Mahwah, NJ: Erlbaum.

Good, T., & Brophy, J. (2003). *Looking in classrooms.* New York: HarperCollins.

Hirsch, E.D. (1988). *Cultural literacy: What every American needs to know.* New York: Vintage.

Jimenez, C. M. (1994). *The Mexican American Heritage.* Berkeley: TCS.

Jones, V., & Jones, L. (2006). *Comprehensive classroom management: Creating communities of support and solving problems* (8th ed.). Boston: Pearson/Allyn and Bacon.

Kauchak, D., & Eggan, P. (2005). *Introduction to teaching: Becoming a professional.* Upper Saddle River, NJ: Pearson/Merrill/Prentice-Hall.

Larkin, M. (2002). *Using scaffolded instruction to optimize learning.* Retrieved July 26, 2006, from http://ericec.org/digests/e639.html

Lee, V. (2000). Using hierarchical linear modeling to study social contexts: The case of school effects. *Educational Psychologist, 35*, 125–141.

Levin, J., & Shanken-Kaye, J. M., & Shanken-Kaye, J. (2003). *The self-control classroom.* Dubuque, Iowa: Kendall-Hunt.

Noddings, N. (1999, April). *Competence and caring as central in teacher education.* Paper presented at the annual meeting of the American Educational Research Association, Montreal, Canada.

Oakes, J., & Lipton, M. (2007). *Teaching to change the world.* Boston: McGraw-Hill.

Oliva, P. F., & Pawlas, G. E. (2004). *Supervision for today's schools* (7th ed.). New York: Wiley.

Roblyer, M. (2003). *Integrating educational technology into teaching.* Upper Saddle River, NJ: Merrill/Prentice-Hall.

Stanton-Salazar, R. (2001). *Manufacturing hope and despair: The school and kin support networks of U.S. Mexican youth.* New York: Teachers College Press.

Stipek, D. (2002). *Motivation to learn: Integrating theory and practice.* Boston: Allyn & Bacon.

Tenery, M. (2005). *La visita.* In N. Gonzalez, L. Moll, & C. Amanti (Eds.), *Funds of knowledge: Theorizing practices in households and classrooms.* Mahwah, NJ: Erlbaum.

Valdez, G. (1996). *Con respeto: Bridging the distances between culturally diverse families and schools.* New York: Teachers College Press.

Valenzuela, A. (1999). *Subtractive schooling: U.S. Mexican youth and the politics of caring.* Albany: SUNY Press.

Wood, D., Bruner, J. S., & Ross, G. (1976). The role of tutoring in problem solving. *Journal of Psychology and Psychiatry, 17*, 35–51.

CHAPTER 9

Understanding Assessment

FIRST PERSON

Teaching to the Test

As a first-year high school teacher, I enjoyed the challenge of finally having my own classroom and the freedom to teach students as I wanted to. My colleagues, however, were concerned about the ways that standardized testing could infringe on their approach to classroom instruction. I felt I was already teaching to the state standards, and yet I grew nervous as my colleagues' comments about how we must maintain certain test scores grew more heated. My students will do well, I thought. Hadn't I been "teaching to the tests" since the beginning of the school year anyway? Hadn't the others? As I began to ask around, my fellow teachers just looked at me and shook their heads. Finally, one said, "You don't get it, do you? It doesn't matter what you teach all year long. It's only how well your students do on state standardized tests that counts!"

I still doggedly believed that my students would do just fine on standardized tests. After all, during my undergraduate teacher education coursework, I was required to take a class on assessment. My classmates and I thought it would be a "snooze" class. It wasn't! We learned that you never teach to the test because teachers need to find out what students know or don't know. I came to understand that teaching, learning, and assessment are like pieces of a jigsaw puzzle. If a piece of the puzzle is missing, you can't see the whole picture and you never have a completed puzzle.

Once we created our instructional objectives based on the state core curriculum, we planned learning and assessment activities that focused on this content. By applying what we learned in the assessment course, I discovered various teaching methods to better assess student learning. We were also

This chapter was coauthored with my colleague in the Department of Secondary Education at Utah State University, L. Ruth Struyk.

CHAPTER OBJECTIVES

- Readers will explore the history and impact of student assessment on educational practice today.

- Readers will analyze how the political climate can influence national and state positions on student assessment.

- Readers will identify approaches and instruments commonly used to assess student knowledge.

- Readers will examine the effects of standardized testing on diverse learners, as well as on teachers.

- Readers will become familiar with various alternative assessment strategies and why they are useful to students and teachers alike.

introduced to other important information, such as what teaching strategies worked well to determine whether and when we needed to reteach before introducing new material.

Because I was taught to design my instructional objectives based on the state core curriculum and to create assessments to measure students' learning in relation to those objectives, I felt confident that I was not only teaching to the standardized tests—I was teaching beyond them.

This is not to suggest that my first year of teaching and testing went well. Five days before this exam was to be administered, my principal stopped by with an open box of the state standardized core tests my students would be taking. He told me I was to make sure my students passed the test. He explained that it was "okay" for me to look through one of the booklets to be sure the students could handle the questions. If I wanted, he added, I could use a couple of the items as practice questions to be certain my students did their very best. This made me very uncomfortable. I didn't want to worry about staff members thinking my students did well on the test because I had the exam in advance. In addition, I had nowhere to store the tests. I talked to other teachers, and they said it was common practice to "help" students on the test by having them practice with items from the actual exam. It didn't matter as long as the students' scores were high!

The next morning I took the box of tests back to the principal. I told him I could not have the tests in my room until the morning of the exam because I didn't have a place to keep them locked up. I explained that I didn't want to worry that students might get their hands on a test booklet before the exam. I added that I was sure my students would do fine on the test. He gave me a funny look, shook his head, and took the box of tests away. Did I do the right thing? Yes. My students did well on the standardized tests because we had explored the state core curriculum all year long. I taught and assessed the objectives that were covered by the state curriculum. But I did not teach the items that were specifically on the standardized test (even though I inadvertently had access to the exam). The difference was that I sought to teach the content that the test covered, thus "teaching to the test."

History of Student Assessment Strategies

Over the years, there has been much debate about whether teachers should teach to the test or not. But the history of assessment shows that we have always done so. As the human race was evolving, young men and women emulated their elders, practicing the skills that were necessary for survival. How were they assessed? When a young man went hunting the first time, he was assessed on whether he killed his prey and could provide for his family. If his kill was not clean, he learned from his mistakes so that he became an expert in the skill. Women became experts in their skills, through such gender role expectations as cooking the foods and by also providing for the children. How were they assessed? By how successful they were at performing these given tasks for the survival of their families. Notice that grades were not given.

The main purpose of assessing students is to improve their understanding of skills so that they will be successful in future career paths. Historically, the "school" curriculum was based on the knowledge and vocational skills that individuals needed to survive. The curriculum evolved to cover the information and skills that were deemed necessary for the times. When one-room schools were the norm, students at the same reading skill level were tested by a teacher using oral or essay questions (Haladyna, 2002). As classroom sizes increased, especially in the cities, and with the introduction of the Stanford Achievement Test Series (SAT) in 1926 (the test is now in its tenth series—SAT 10), teachers moved to multiple-choice and true-false tests because of the ease of scoring such tests.

Currently there are two approaches to schooling that influence student assessment strategies. The traditional approach, which is associated with B. F. Skinner and Edward L. Thorndike, is based on the idea that students need to be reinforced for their learning (Kohn, 1999). Schools that follow this model tend to teach academic fields separately (e.g., math, English, science, history), breaking down the content into small chunks of information that are taught in sequence. This particular model focuses on tests, quizzes, and homework that measure declarative knowledge and skills and uses traditional grades as a measure of student achievement (Haladyna, 2002).

In the progressive approach to learning, however, they learn by doing—in a manner very similar to the hunting example used earlier. Students are encouraged to ask questions, work cooperatively, and learn in mentor-apprenticeship relationships (Kohn, 1999). Students in this learning situation are more likely to be assessed via performance assessments and authentic assessments. **Performance assessments** measure how well a particular skill is completed, be it rebuilding a car engine or writing a formal letter. **Authentic assessments** imitate real-world experiences (Mertler, 2003; Tombari & Borich, 1999).

A student stands next to her science fair project about tornados.

PAUSE & REFLECT

As you recall your own schooling, how have performance and authentic assessments affected your educational experience? In what ways have these approaches accurately or inaccurately assessed your content-area knowledge bases and skill levels?

The Identification of Goals and Objectives

As teachers, we are charged with teaching and assessing the content area in which we specialized in college. For some of us it was history, for others English, and so on. No matter what content area we specialized in, we still must determine what, within that content area, we will teach to students. Many states have core curricula that reflect the State Office of Education's expectations of what will be taught at each grade level. But even with state curricula, teachers have a great deal of flexibility in what is taught. Teachers organize their teaching ideas into units and learning goals based on the state and district curriculum standards and the textbooks they are using. Teachers then develop their curriculum to meet these standards.

Because we all teach differently and have a variety of interests, not everyone spends the same amount of time on individual learning goals. Nor do teachers teach learning goals in the same order. Once teachers have determined what learning goals they will cover during the semester or school year, they divide each learning goal into instructional objectives. Instructional objectives help clarify what must be taught—what skills and knowledge students must know to successfully complete the learning goal. Most educators think of objectives in terms of student outcomes: what students will be able to do when they have learned the objective.

This also guides the assessment. If the learning goal is understanding the geometric and algebraic properties of linear equations, then one of the objectives will be "Students will be able to discriminate the differences in the slope of a linear equation." To assess how well students achieve this objective, students would have to look at a series of mathematical statements and determine that the slope of the line is based on the values of the x and y coordinates. Will all students be successful 100 percent of the time? Of course not. However, the assessment does measure the objective and provides the teacher and the students with feedback on one aspect of the learning goal of understanding the geometric and algebraic properties of linear equations.

From PRESERVICE to PRACTICE

An Authentic Assessment Toolbox

Review the following list to help clarify your understanding of key terms associated with student assessment.

analytic rubric: An analytic rubric articulates levels of performance for each criterion so that the teacher can assess student performance on each criterion.

authentic assessment: A form of assessment in which students are asked to perform real-world tasks that demonstrate meaningful application of essential knowledge and skills. Student performance on a task is typically scored on a rubric to determine how successfully the student has met specific standards. Some educators choose to distinguish between *authentic assessment* and *performance assessment*. For these educators, performance assessment meets the above definition except that the tasks do not reflect real-world (authentic) challenges. If we are going to ask students to construct knowledge on assessments, then virtually all such tasks should be authentic in

nature; otherwise, they lose some relevance to the students. Thus, for me, this distinction between performance and authentic assessments becomes insignificant, and I use the terms *authentic assessment* and *performance assessment* synonymously.

authentic task: An assignment designed to assess students' ability to apply standards-driven knowledge and skills to real-world challenges. A task is considered authentic when (1) students are asked to construct their own responses rather than to select from ones presented and (2) the task replicates challenges faced in the real world. Good performance on the task should demonstrate, or partly demonstrate, successful completion of one or more standards. The term *task* is often used synonymously with the term *assessment* in the field of authentic assessment.

content standards: Statements that describe what students should know or be able to do within the content of a specific discipline or at the intersection of two or more disciplines (for example, "Students will describe the effects of physical activity on the body"). Contrast with the terms *process standards* and *value standards*.

criteria: Characteristics of good performance on a particular task. For example, criteria for a persuasive essay might include "well organized," "clearly stated," and "sufficient support for arguments." (The singular of *criteria* is *criterion*.)

descriptors: Statements of expected performance at each level of performance for a particular criterion in a rubric—typically found in *analytic rubrics*.

distractors: The incorrect alternatives or choices in a selected-response item.

goal: In the field of student assessment, a goal is a very broad statement of what students should know or be able to do. Unlike a standard or an objective, a goal is often not written in language that is amenable to assessment. Rather, the purpose for crafting a set of goals typically is to give a brief and broad picture of what a school, district, state, or the like expects its students will know and be able to do upon graduation.

holistic rubric: In contrast to an *analytic rubric*, a holistic rubric does not list separate levels of performance for each criterion. Instead, a holistic rubric assigns a level of performance by assessing performance across multiple criteria as a whole.

objective: Much like a goal or standard, an objective is a statement of what students should know and be able to do. Typically, an objective is the most narrow of these statements, usually describing what a student should know or be able to do at the end of a specific lesson plan. Like a standard, an objective is amenable to assessment; that is, it is observable and measurable.

outcome: See *standard*. Preceding the current standards-based movement was a drive for outcome-based education. The term *standard* has replaced the term *outcome* and has much the same meaning.

performance assessment: See *authentic assessment*. I use these terms synonymously.

portfolio: A collection of a student's work specifically selected to tell a particular story about the student.

process standards: Statements that describe skills that students should develop to enhance the process of learning. Process standards are not specific to a particular discipline; rather, they are generic skills applicable to any discipline (for example, "Students will find and evaluate relevant information"). Contrast with *content standards* and *value standards*.

reliability: The degree to which a measure yields consistent results.

rubric: A scoring scale used to evaluate student work. A rubric is composed of at least two criteria by which student work is to be judged on a particular task and at least two levels of performance for each criterion.

standard: Much like a goal or objective, a standard is a statement of what students should know or be able to do. I distinguish between a standard and these other goal statements by indicating that a standard is broader than an objective but more narrow than a goal. Like an objective, and unlike a goal, a standard is amenable to assessment; that is, it is observable and measurable.

stem: A question or statement followed by a number of choices or alternatives that answer or complete the question or statement. (Stems are most commonly found in multiple-choice questions.

validity: "The degree to which a certain inference from a test is appropriate and meaningful" (AERA, APA, & NCME, 1985). For example, if I measure the circumference of your head to determine your level of intelligence, my measurement might be accurate. However, it would be inappropriate for me to draw a conclusion about your level of intelligence. Such an inference would be invalid.

value standards: Statements that describe attitudes that teachers would like students to develop toward learning (for example, "Students will value diversity of opinions or perspectives").

Questions for Reflection

1. Which terms are you familiar with, and which are unfamiliar to you? How have you observed teachers implement these concepts in the classroom?

2. Of the concepts listed above, which do you think would be the most difficult to apply to your content areas of interest? Explain why.

Source: Adapted from J. Mueller (2006), Authentic Assessment Toolbox. Retrieved April 1, 2007 from http://jonathan.mueller.faculty.noctrl.edu/toolbox/whatisit.htm.

How many objectives will be used to define the learning goal depends on how thoroughly the teacher wants to cover the learning goal. In a high school mathematics class, the learning goal of understanding geometric and algebraic properties of linear equations might be achieved with seven objectives; for a college mathematics course, the learning goal might be broken down into 10 objectives, for a master's mathematics course, the learning goal might require 30 or more objectives. The instructional objectives define the amount of understanding required, in terms of concepts, skills, relationships, applications, and facts teachers are going to cover. Whether the learning goal is playing volleyball or understanding algebra, history, or English, all content areas can be subdivided into smaller units with instructional objectives guiding the teaching.

Connecting to the Cengage Learning Video Cases

Assessment in the Middle Grades: Measurement of Student Learning
Watch the Cengage Learning video case entitled "Assessment in the Middle Grades: Measurement of Student Learning." Consider viewing question 4.

Video Case Study
1. What did you notice about how the teacher, Martin Somers, helps students during the actual testing period?
2. How did his responses reflect his learning goals for his students who were initially tentative about learning new and challenging mathematics objectives?

Student Website

The Politicization of National and State Assessment Standards

The push for the national and state assessment standards began in 1965 when one of the most significant pieces of legislation was passed through the U.S. Congress and signed into law by President Lyndon Johnson: Title I of the Elementary and Secondary Education Act of 1965. The spirit of this act was to help those communities with limited financial resources and had a high percentage of poor children enrolled in the public schools. Title I funding continues to be one of the largest sources of federal funding to the schools. As with all federal funding, lawmakers wanted to ensure that the funds were having a measurable impact on the students who were receiving them. The measures for determining the success of the use of Title I funds were "norm-referenced" standardized tests such as the Iowa Test of Basic Skills. This test enables students and schools who receive Title 1 funding to be compared to the "national norm."

By requiring schools that received Title I funding to be measured by objective measures (i.e., a standardized test), the law basically requires states to use standardized tests to evaluate any school that receives Title 1 funding (Haladyna, 2002). Although this law was passed in 1965, Congress and presidents have rewritten the law when reappropriating funds based on the political climate at the time. Beginning in 1988, to obtain and continue to receive Title 1 funding, schools where students failed to make adequate test scores were required to submit improvement plans to federal authorities. Schools were told they must develop outcomes for their federal dollars, outcomes that were to be measured by standardized tests (Kohn, 1999). An unfortunate side effect of the Title 1 testing was that schools extended the mandated testing to all of their students. This trend continues to be reinforced with the George W. Bush administration's implementation of the No Child Left Behind Act (NCLB).

Precursors to NCLB include President Ronald Reagan's initiative published in "A Nation a Risk: The Imperative for Educational Reform." This 1983 report became the most widely known report on school accountability and continued the push for educational accountability through standardized testing. During 1997, with President Bill Clinton in office, a public opinion poll indicated that more than half of individuals interviewed favored a national exam (Rose, Gallup, & Elam, 1997). As a result, President Clinton's Goals 2000 began the states' push toward state standards. Since that time, states have implemented state curriculum standards that are measured through core curriculum tests or such tests as the California Achievement Tests and the Iowa Tests of Basic Skills. President George W. Bush's No Child Left Behind has pushed all schools to have their achievement measured by some standardized achievement tests. Failure to do so results in the loss of Title I funding.

Currently, Title I law mandates that all students in schools must have passing scores on standardized tests, regardless of language barriers, national background, or learning disabilities. Continued funding with Title I monies depends on schools having a passing score from all of its students within a 2-year period. All schools must have passing scores by 2007 or they lose Title I funding—funding that was designed to help the very students who tend to do poorly on standardized tests.

For Your CONSIDERATION

The U.S. Department of Education maintains a webpage that provides an overview of Title I—Improving the Academic Achievement of the Disadvantaged. Information available includes the annual funding, for such programs as Reading First, prevention and intervention programs for "at-risk" youth, and priorities for school improvement. Visit the site at **http://www.ed.gov/policy/elsec/leg/esea02/pgl.html.**

National Organizations Generating Content-Area Standards

As a result of federal and state regulations, professional education organizations began developing and publishing standards that reflect what a well-educated individual will know about a specific educational domain. These standards are a result of reviews of professional literature and goals established by professional organizations themselves. The first organization to develop a set of standards was the National Council of Teachers of Mathematics (1989). With the release of the "Principles and Standards for School Mathematics," the National Council of Teachers of Mathematics was at the forefront of efforts to improve mathematics education in the United States (NCTM, 2006).

Since then, other professional educational organizations have followed with standards for content guidelines in their curriculum areas. The National Council of Teachers of English, the Teachers of English to Speakers of Other Languages (TESOL), the National Council of Social Studies, and the National Science Teachers Association are but a few of the professional organizations whose professional standards guide curriculum within K–12 schools and the content-area preparation of teachers. Professional organizations review and revise their standards based on current professional literature and best practices. In 1990, a committee made up of representatives from the American Federation of Teachers (AFT), the National Education Association (NEA), and the National Council on Measurement in Education (NCME) created the national Standards for Teacher Competence in Educational Assessment of Students. These standards address seven skills that preservice and in-service educators need in educational assessment:

- Selecting assessment methods
- Developing assessment methods
- Administering, scoring, and interpreting results of both standardized and teacher-developed assessment methods
- Using assessment results for decision making
- Developing grading procedures
- Communicating assessment results
- Recognizing unethical, illegal, and other inappropriate methods

These reflect basic areas of competence that teachers exhibit in their daily teaching activities.

What Knowledge Is Measured and How

In 1956, Benjamin Bloom created a taxonomy, or hierarchy, of classifications of specific categories of learning behaviors; these were later revised by Bloom and his associates (1984). The three main categories of learning in the taxonomy are known as the cognitive, psychomotor, and affective domains. These three are then subdivided into more specific behaviors. The cognitive domain comprises those learning activities that involve thinking skills. It is divided into two major subdivisions: knowledge (lower-level) and intellectual (higher-level) thinking skills. When students use thinking skills at the knowledge level, they are using memory-level skills. They are remembering, recalling, and recognizing facts. At this level, students could also be remembering a series of steps in a sequence such as mounting an onion cell on a slide in a biology class. This thinking skill still involves only remembering, but students must now remember a list or series of steps in sequence to be successful. The intellectual level within the cognitive domain requires the students to use reasoning, or rational thinking skills. The intellectual level is broken down into five levels:

- **Comprehension:** The ability to interpret the meaning of language or symbols.
- **Application:** The ability to use a learned rule in new situations.
- **Analysis:** The ability to break apart the whole so that individual components are understood.
- **Synthesis:** The ability to use prior knowledge to put together individual components to create a whole.
- **Evaluation:** The ability to make a judgment about the value of something.

Bloom divides the psychomotor domain into two levels. *Voluntary muscle ability* includes those skills that increase such overall performance as cardiovascular performance, flexibility, strength, and endurance. *The ability to perform a specific skill* is related to teaching students how to complete a specific physical skill. For a three- or four-year-old, such a skill might be how to tie a shoe; for a freshman in high school, it might be how to execute a slice serve in tennis. The affective domain is involved when students are taught to develop a particular appreciation of or attitude toward something. Examples of learning within the affective domain include a student coming to value the benefits of a well-balanced diet and to realize that drug use is illegal and dangerous to one's health.

Bloom developed his taxonomy not just to guide teachers in their instruction but also to guide them in their assessment activities. Teachers teach and measure knowledge-level learning activities differently than they do higher-level thinking activities. Say a teacher were teaching to the following knowledge-level objective: "Students will be able to recall the 50 states and their capitals." The assessment activities could look something like this:

What is the capital of South Dakota? Answer: Pierre
Which of the following is the capital of South Dakota?
a. Pierre (+1)
b. Sioux Falls
c. Aberdeen
d. Rapid City

Both of those questions required only that the students remember or memorize basic facts: the capitals and their states. For teachers to assess students on a higher-level thinking skill such as application, the students would have to choose to use a particular rule correctly. For example, if a teacher were assessing students' knowledge of first aid procedures, the objective might be "Given an injury, students will be able to determine the correct first aid procedure to use." The question to assess such an objective could look like the following:

While playing basketball, Nancy turns her right ankle to the inside. There are pain and swelling. Immediate first aid procedures should include
a. A bandage putting pressure on the outside of her right ankle. (+5)
b. A bandage putting pressure on the inside of her right ankle.
c. Heat applied to the outside of her right ankle.
d. Heat applied to the inside of her right ankle.

To answer the question, students must determine which side of the foot is swelling given the direction of sprain, so that they can apply pressure to contain the swelling.

Teachers who use Bloom's taxonomy, or other taxonomies that are revisions or refinements of Bloom's original taxonomy, have a guideline they can use to structure their students' learning activities. And as they are structuring their learning activities, teachers can structure their assessment activities as well. Remember that assessment activities are not just end-of-unit tests but also quizzes, homework, worksheets, crosswords—whatever activities teachers choose to use to find out what students know in relation to the learning objectives.

PAUSE & REFLECT

In what ways is Bloom's taxonomy useful for the design of learning goals and objectives? How can his five classifications for cognitive development be applied to any content area and grade level? Give examples.

Assessment Instruments Commonly Used: Strengths and Weaknesses

Paper and Pencil Tests

Whether teachers use more traditional assessment instruments or more authentic assessment instruments or techniques, they will find that every instrument has its strengths and their weaknesses. Let's start with paper and pencil tests. The use of paper and pencil tests for quizzes, end-of-unit tests, midterms, and finals is a perfectly acceptable practice. The key to using paper and pencil tests is to ensure that the test measures the instructional objectives both in terms of content and in terms of cognitive behavior. Unfortunately, many paper and pencil tests drop to memory-level items because it is harder to develop higher-level thinking questions in easy-to-score multiple-choice and true-false formats. It can be done, but designing those items takes more time and skill. Paper and pencil tests that consist mostly of multiple-choice, true-false, and matching items are much faster to score, which is why teachers prefer them.

Given that some teachers have six classes of 35 to 40 students each, that adds up to 240 tests that must be corrected. Even if every test contains only one 15-point essay, that is still 240 essay questions that must be read, corrected, and scored. It is easy to see why teachers prefer paper and pencil tests that students can answer using a computerized scantron sheet and have the tests corrected by machine. One serious disadvantage of this system is that the teacher sees only the end score, not the items that were missed. If the purpose of assessment is to find out what students know and what they don't know in relation to the instructional objectives, scantron scoring is not suitable, because it does not let teachers see error patterns.

Another weakness of paper and pencil tests is that they tend to be timed tests—not in the same sense as standardized tests, but in the sense of the school class time frame. Think back to the number of tests you never finished, or finished only because you rushed through the test. What a student can produce within a given time frame does not necessarily reflect what the student actually knows about the material. Power tests are tests that find out what the student knows. Time is not a factor. Many times a time limit is set to give the student a time frame in which to work. Many college comprehensive exams are set up in this manner. Students have five questions to answer, and they have a five-day period in which to write the answers to the questions. The time frame gives students time to research answers, to write answers, and to edit and proofread answers. Think about how many essays you answered on tests where you wished you had an extra 10 minutes to proofread your answers.

Rubrics

A **rubric** is an assessment instrument that has blended information that is assessed holistically (i.e., in a range of points that cannot be broken down or associated with specific information) and information that is assessed analytically (i.e., points can be clearly associated with specific information) (Struyk & Mehlig, 2004). Rubrics are designed by teachers who have a clear understanding of their instructional objectives and of the behaviors that students must demonstrate to successfully achieve instructional objectives. Rubrics most often measure several objectives at once, usually at four or more levels of proficiency. Rubrics provide both students and teachers with the criteria necessary for successfully completing the learning or assessment activity.

In many cases, when students have rubrics in advance, they begin to learn to be more critical of their work and become self-reflective learners as a result. With rubrics, students can also conduct peer evaluation and provide feedback to each other before the teacher receives the final paper. One of the weaknesses of rubrics is that they require teachers to differentiate very clearly between the different levels of success. Thus, if a teacher is using a rubric with four levels of proficiency, each level within the rubric must clearly indicate how that level is different from the one above it. Rubrics are created to help teachers grade essays, projects, and portfolios consistently and to speed up and ease the scoring or grading process. A poorly designed rubric, however, will actually increase the scoring time for teachers and decrease the consistency of scoring.

Portfolios

There are two types of **portfolios:** instructional portfolios and evaluation portfolios (Batzle, 1992; Struyk & Mehlig, 2004). There are several reasons for teachers to use *instructional portfolios* as part of the instructional and assessment processes for students. Instructional portfolios let students see the progress they are making. The

From PRESERVICE to PRACTICE

A Sample Book Review Rubric

We all have opinions about the novels we read, and the opportunity for you to voice your opinion is there. Often, you will recommend a good book to your friends or family members. Now, you will have the chance to reach a much larger audience. There are many websites that allow you to write up your review of the novels you have read and let the world know your opinion.

Your task is to write a review of a novel you have read and post it on the school's website. You also will have the opportunity to post it on another book review website of your choice.

In your review, you must

1. Include the title and author of the novel.
2. Include the story elements noted on the rubric.
3. Work the elements into your review in such a way so that you are not simply stating the elements but, rather, are incorporating them meaningfully throughout your analysis of the novel. (Be sure to look at the examples of good reviews to get a better understanding.)

The rubric on which you will be graded is shown below. Good luck!

	3	2	1
Conventions	Few or no grammatical or mechanical errors	Several grammatical or mechanical errors	Several grammatical or mechanical errors; obviously not proofread
	6	4	2
Elements	All elements contained in book review (setting, characters, theme, conflict)	Missing one element in review	Missing more than one element
Integration	Elements integrated throughout the review	Elements somewhat integrated throughout the review	Elements not integrated throughout the review

Source: J. Thill (2006), *Independent reading program*, retrieved April 1, 2007, from http://jonathan.muerller.faculty .noctrl.edu/toolbox/examples/tasks_middle_languagearts.htm.

Questions for Reflection

1. Which elements of this rubric are scored the highest? Why do you think this teacher weighted, or valued, these particular skills as most important for students to master?

2. This rubric is intended for upper or middle grades. How would you modify this rubric to meet the needs of younger readers?

A seven-year-old displays the fall section of his school portfolio.

students can see work they did at the beginning of the school year. They can also see how they have improved, or advanced, throughout the school year. This makes portfolios a great motivator for students. They can also help students recognize their strengths and weaknesses in any areas.

One of the best things about portfolios is that students can see how their understanding of even their weakest area is improving. With most grading systems, students who start out with a "C" tend to stay in the "C" range, especially those who do not speak English as their first language (Batzle, 1992). This can be extremely frustrating for students who know they are understanding more, but, because of the limitations of current grading systems (e.g., A, B, C), their grade does not reflect that increase in understanding. Portfolios are also great for parents. A portfolio shows parents not only the student's "best" work but also where their child is struggling.

A major disadvantage of instructional portfolios is how much storage space they require. Picture how much work is done in one subject area for one student, and then multiply that by 30 elementary students or anywhere from 180 to 240 middle school and high school students in one content area. Now think of the container or filing system that would be needed to store all of the work the students have done for the entire semester or year.

Evaluation portfolios don't raise the storage problems that instructional portfolios do. Usually only the students' best work is kept in the evaluation portfolio. As new work comes in, it replaces the old. Evaluation portfolios, however, must be evaluated at the end of the year. This is usually done by using an evaluation rubric that has been designed around the objectives of the portfolio. The portfolio can be designed around a content area such as language arts or can be designed around an entire grade (i.e., final papers, projects, and test of a ninth grader in all his or her classes). Although evaluation portfolios don't pose the storage problems that instructional portfolios do, the fact that they show only the students' best work can be a drawback. So it is easy for students and parents to forget where the students started. Sometimes, too, parents misinterpret an evaluation portfolio of best works as meriting an "A" rather than a "C" because all they see is the very best work the student has done, not the combination of work that has led to the grade or how the student compares to other students in the class.

Connecting to the Cengage Learning Video Cases

Portfolio Assessment in the Elementary Classroom: Measurement of Student Learning

Watch the Cengage Learning video case entitled "Portfolio Assessment in the Elementary Classroom: Measurement of Student Learning." Consider viewing questions 1 and 2.

Video Case Study

1. What is your response to high stakes standardized testing?
2. How does the teacher Fred Parks organize his portfolio assessment?
3. What do you think the most difficult part of the process will be for you in your content area and target grade level?

Student Website

Student Portfolio Night

Both instructional portfolios and evaluation portfolios can be used in a special way that helps students "own" their learning. Many times, teachers who have students doing portfolio work have a portfolio night. This can be conducted during parent-teacher conferences or can be another night that is dedicated to having the students show their work to parents, grandparents, friends, and members of the community.

In preparing for portfolio night, students are the ones who select the materials to place in the portfolio. They are also the ones who explain why they chose the work they did and why it is important to them. As visitors to portfolio night move around the room, students talk to the different visitors who stop to look at their portfolios. This experience gives students a chance to reflect on their work, see the value of their work, develop communication skills, and gain self-confidence (Kish, Sheehan, Cole, Struyk, & Kinder, 1997).

From PRESERVICE to PRACTICE

Blackstone Valley Tech High School Electronic Portfolio Guidelines

What is a portfolio? A portfolio is
- Selective
- Reflective
- Collaborative
- Information that shows development

A portfolio is not a project. It is an ongoing process.
- From the beginning of freshman year until graduation, students will develop their portfolios by selecting entries that show development of academic and vocational skills.
- Many academic and vocational schools have already been doing this to encourage students to demonstrate and showcase their academic growth.
- Through the creation of a formalized process that can be replicated in all vocational and academic areas, student work can be consolidated and presented in a total package.

Why should a student create a portfolio?
- Documenting content area and/or vocational competencies
- Building self-esteem
- Creating a way to show progress
- Allowing students to see their accomplishments
- Preserving a memory of achievements
- Building a feeling of pride
- Providing a measurement of growth

How can a portfolio be used?
- Open house
- Parents' night
- Recruitment
- Parent conferences
- Employers
- Mentors
- Job interviews
- Career days
- Promote vocational programs
- Co-op jobs
- School-to-work
- Postsecondary education

What items go into a portfolio?
- Student's résumé
- Career goals
- Student biography
- Research projects
- Extracurricular activities
- Vocational experience
- Reflective entries
- Vocational competencies
- Pictures of projects
- Outstanding tests
- Letters of recommendation
- Awards

What will the portfolio look like?

- At Blackstone Valley Tech High School, students are given three-ring binders, sheet protectors, and other materials to present paper portfolios.
- Students have also developed portfolios using web-pages. Students are provided with webpage templates that can be personalized using a program such as Microsoft FrontPage. These Electronic Portfolios can be distributed using CD-ROM or via the World Wide Web.

Why electronic portfolios?

- Electronic documents occupy less physical space.
- They can be transmitted long distances quickly via the Internet.
- Sound and video may be included.
- Technology integration is facilitated.

Do I need special computer hardware or software to create an electronic portfolio?

- Computer hardware
  - Computer: Use the best available, but even an i486 PC with a floppy drive can be used with limited success.
  - Digital camera: Take pictures of projects.
  - CD-RW drive: Will allow you to save up to 650MB on one disk.
  - Scanner: To turn paper assignments into electronic form.
  - Color printer: To print out portfolio pages for binder or distribution.
  - Modem or Web server: To distribute portfolios using the Internet.
- Computer software
  - Any presentation software (such as Powerpoint or Hyperstudio) could be used to author the portfolio, but the same software is needed to view the presentation.
  - Students at Blackstone Valley Tech use an HTML editor such as Microsoft FrontPage to create webpages, but even Microsoft Windows Notepad could be used with a little knowledge of HTML. These web-pages can be viewed by anyone with a computer and a Web browser such as Netscape Navigator or Microsoft Internet Explorer. This makes distribution much easier.
  - Image-editing software, such as Adobe Photoshop, is useful for editing and manipulating digital pictures.

Questions for Reflection

1. In what ways can a portfolio such as this be assessed by teachers? What kinds of indicators could be included in a rubric to evaluate this portfolio?

2. How can a portfolio model be modified for elementary school students? What kinds of artifacts could be included for a hard-copy version?

Source: Adapted from Blackstone Valley Tech High School, Upton, Massachusetts, retrieved April 1, 2007, from http://www.valleytech.k12.ma.us/portfolio/FAQ.htm#what%20is.

Planning and Evaluation of Portfolios

Whether teachers choose to use an instructional portfolio or an evaluation portfolio, they must remember that portfolio design and evaluation have structure. Using portfolios does not replace assigning grades; rather, portfolios are a different method of assessing work to determine the grade. A good rule of thumb for designing either type of portfolio for use in the classroom is the **R-ICE** method (Cole, Struyk, Kinder, Sheehan, & Kish, 1997).

Every portfolio should have a **Rationale (R)** or reason for developing the portfolio. Once the rationale is determined, then the goals of the portfolio must be **Identified (I)**. What specific standards or objectives are you working with that you wish to measure with the portfolio? Once the goals have been identified, you must determine what **Content (C)** should be included in the portfolio. A clear indication of goals and objectives will help to clarify what content should be included in the portfolio. The final step is to determine how the portfolio will be **Evaluated (E)**. What criteria are you using to link and judge the materials in the portfolio to the goals and objectives of the portfolio? Who will evaluate the portfolio? The four steps of the **R-ICE** method should be specified before students begin working on their portfolios.

Without a clear concept of what the intent of the portfolio is, it can easily become a file of student papers without meaningful purpose. Consider the student portfolio model guidelines from Blackstone Valley Tech High School in Upton, Massachusetts.

The Impact of Standardized Test Outcomes on Teachers

When talking about standardized tests, most individuals focus on the effects the tests have on students and on the school. However, the tests also affect the teachers. Many school districts choose to reward teachers whose students score high on the test and to "punish" teachers whose students score low on the tests. Teacher rewards usually are in the form of incentive pay or bonus pay or may include the promise of a better teaching assignment. Those districts that reward teachers monetarily (i.e., $1,000) for passing test scores are creating a competitive pressure within the school community. Those teachers whose students do not score well on the test receive nothing and may be assigned a less inviting teaching assignment. Unfortunately for teachers, however, the test results alone do not show who did a better job of teaching.

Students' Test Scores and Changes in Curriculum

When students do poorly on a standardized test that measures goals and objectives covered by the state and classroom curricula, one contributing factor may be when part of the curriculum was taught in relation to when the test was given. A fifth-grade teacher commented that the state core test was given in March and covered components of geometry that were not taught by the fifth-grade teachers until April. As a result, students' test scores were below average. The teachers knew why their students scored low but believed that the order in which they presented the math curriculum was the best for the students. The administration told them to move the teaching of geometry to the end of February so that students would learn the information just before the test in March. The students' scores did increase.

Two years later, the state moved the testing dates to the beginning of February. Students' scores dropped, because geometry once again was covered on the test but not taught until after the test. No Child Left Behind has caused many school districts to focus on changing the curriculum to better match the tests that the district uses. Curriculum packages are sold to schools based on what the test measures, not necessarily on what is best for students. Many educators have concerns that by focusing only on preparing for the test and using drill and practice, the tests result in the "dumbing down" of instruction (Kohn, 1999; Popham, 2006).

The No Child Left Behind Act and Its Effect on Teacher Certification

The No Child Left Behind Act has also had a tremendous impact on the state certification of teachers. Many states now require college graduates to take the Praxis Level II content test in the area in which the graduate wishes to teach. Preservice teachers who take the test look at it as another "hoop to jump through" to meet certification criteria. Some students taking the tests indicate that the test does a poor job of measuring what they know about their content area.

From PRESERVICE to PRACTICE

A Teachers' Union's Position on Assessment

Meeting the national No Child Left Behind Act's criteria for adequate yearly progress (AYP) and meeting the state's Utah Performance Assessment Systems for Students (U-PASS) standards are often at the top of educators' concerns. Several teachers I have met speak freely about "teaching to the test," or delivering language arts and math instruction that reflects specific content relevant to the national and state standardized tests. In fact, the testing issue is such a concern that the state's teachers union, the Utah Education Association (UEA), issued the following position statement (2006):

> Most teachers have resistance and some resentment to the increasing importance and pressure around test scores. One of the down sides of high stakes testing is that it puts more pressure to demonstrate academic achievement in a narrow manner. Most teachers resent the focus on testing because in their experience, there are many more ways to know if the student is learning than just a single test score. For example, teachers observe students' daily participation and work. Teachers observe the effort that is made. Teachers also see samples of students' work and can monitor their progress. Some students don't do well on tests but can do well when demonstrating in the classroom that they know the material. Other students can create products or processes that show they do know the material.
>
> In states where high stakes testing has been implemented, the phenomenon called "teaching to the test" has surfaced. This term suggests that teachers are only focused on making sure that students are drilled and prepared to take that test. The impact on judgment of the student, the teacher, and the school is just too high. In Utah, we say teaching to the test would be teaching

the CORE curriculum. Utah has established a CORE curriculum in language arts, math, science, and social studies. For each grade level, this CORE curriculum spells out the minimum concepts that students should be learning for that grade level. The end-of-level tests, called the CRTs, are the tests that test for knowledge of the CORE curriculum. So if a teacher is teaching the CORE, [she or he is] in fact teaching to the test.

> It is frustrating for most educators because there seems to be a growing assumption that just testing kids will improve education. Educators feel passionate about teaching children the broad range of what students need to know. There is frustration and concern that the curriculum will be narrowed when the focus is only on the CORE subjects. Many children respond and learn and grow through creative processes and programs such as band, orchestra, music, arts, speech, and debate. Therefore, it is important to protect the rights of students to learn and grow as a whole, well-rounded person. It is important that every student have a quality teacher who is doing quality work with students. However, the UEA is concerned when the approach is to focus solely on test scores as an indication of the quality of instruction and student learning. Just putting more pressure on students and teachers will not get the kind of results that we want. (UEA, 2006).

Questions for Reflection

1. Here we see this union position statement trying to reconcile the learning needs of the students, teacher accountability, and the testing pressures facing its workforce. Is high stakes testing as simple as presenting the state's core curriculum?
2. Or do a "drill 'til you drop" curriculum and instructional approach undermine the cognitive development of students and the professional creativity of teachers?

Source: Utah Education Association (2006), *Teaching to the Test*, retrieved November 7, 2006, from http://www.utea.org/index.htm.

On the other hand, for some teachers who are currently certified, the implementation of No Child Left Behind has seriously undermined their positions and status among colleagues and parents. The law indicates that for those teachers who are teaching in a content area that was not their major (as designated on their college transcript) or who have not passed a standardized test in that content area, the school must send a letter to the homes of the teacher's students indicating that the teacher is not highly qualified. Think of the impact it would have if you were teaching in your minor and

From PRESERVICE to PRACTICE

Highly Qualified or Stigmatized?

A well-respected first-grade teacher, Jamie Ritchie, who had been teaching for 15 years was asked to teach in the newly established kindergarten in her school. She was selected because she was so well respected by the parents of her students and her administrators. Jamie was also working toward a master's degree in early childhood education that would certify her to teach preschool through kindergarten. Her teaching certificate was in elementary education grades 1–8. The parents of Jamie's future students were sent a letter saying that she was *not* highly qualified to teach the kindergarten students.

Many parents, who understandably did not want their child taught by what they perceived to be a poor teacher, chose not to enroll their children in the new kindergarten program but, instead, to wait until the students started first grade. The kindergarten program was

canceled. The next year, the parents who would not enroll their child in the kindergarten with the "poor" teacher were demanding that the child be put in the classroom of the experienced, well-respected teacher because she did such a great job of teaching the young students. But both of these teachers were the same teacher, Jamie, who had been labeled and stigmatized the previous year! NCLB and its emphasis on standardized tests as a measure of a teacher's qualifications, whether accurate or not, have far-reaching effects on the professional lives of teachers.

Questions for Reflection
1. What would you have done if you had been Jamie?
2. How could she have worked with her administrators and parents to ensure that the students would have access to the best instruction possible?

the parents of your students received a letter stating that you were not highly qualified. What do you think the parents' reaction would be? They would probably want to remove their children from your classroom because they may assume that you are an inferior teacher. That is *not* what the letter said, but that is how most laypersons would interpret it.

The Impact of Standardized Test Outcomes on Diverse Learners

Standardized tests have a tremendous impact on students as more and more states use them to measure school success rates based on students' scores on standardized achievement tests. The Stanford-Binet Intelligence Test is one test used by school districts to assess the intelligence or cognitive development of young children to determine what students will be admitted to preschools and specialized programs. Using the results of the Stanford-Binet Intelligence test or other intelligence tests to track students has raised questions about the applicability of such tests to all children.

As with all standardized tests, the problem is that the test makers determine the correct answer. For example, when students are asked to select a picture of a mansion from among four home designs, test makers assume that all children will select the largest and most elaborately decorated picture as a mansion. But for a student who lives in a city housing project or a student who lives in a mobile home in a rural area, a mansion might be something as simple as a two-story home. To those same students, the test makers' idea of a "mansion" might appear to be a government building or office complex. And for a student who lives in Lake Forest, Illinois, there may be no house on the test grand enough to appear to be a "mansion."

Culture-biased items (items that favor one group over another) occur in all tests. When one considers that standardized tests are designed for use by many regions of the country, it becomes almost impossible for items not to be biased. Take, for example, what seems like a simple, straightforward question: "What is the definition of an elevator?" For students who live in cities and ride in a compartment that carries people between floors, an elevator is "a box or room that carries people up and down tall buildings." For a student who lives in a small rural community in Iowa, an elevator is "the piece of farm equipment that moves grain from the wagon to the silo." And for a student who lives in North Dakota, an elevator is "the large cooperative grain storage system where farms haul their harvest before it is loaded into rail cars." The item and the test makers mistakenly assumed that we all have the same cultural experiences.

Although test makers try to remove items that are biased in terms of culture or living experiences, it is challenging to do so accurately. For example, if you ask a person living in the Midwest, "Where is the nearest steak house?" that person will direct you to a restaurant that features steak. But if you pose the same question in Utah, you will be asked, "Which stake house do you mean?" In Utah, the predominant religion, the Church of Jesus Christ of Latter-Day Saints, uses the term *stake houses* to refer to church buildings where larger, biannual meetings of the congregation take place. When the question is asked orally, it must be asked in context. Even on a written test, a student might not notice the spelling difference or might assume it was a misprint on the test.

English Language Learners (ELLs)

Students who are learning English as a second (or third) language face challenges when taking standardized tests because of their developing English language skills. It does not matter whether the test is the Stanford-Binet Intelligence Test, the Iowa Test of Basic Skills, or any state core curriculum test. Standardized tests do not take into account the level of English that students speak or their proficiency in their native language. Early in life, students learn syntax patterns based on their first language.

If you have ever listened to anyone learning English as their second language, you will hear and see them search for correct words, and when they speak, they often do not use the same word order that a native speaker does. It also takes more time for them to formulate a sentence. Some test makers do recognize this difference and allow ELLs more time to take the test. Others do not. Under the No Child Left Behind law, ESL students have two years before they must make passing scores on tests written in English, even though research on language acquisition reveals that it takes five to seven years to acquire proficiency in academic English (Valdes, 2001).

Researchers suggest that ESL students take the test in their own language. The assumption is that students maintain multiple forms of literacy in their native language (Gonzalez, 2001). There are many students in our schools who speak Spanish at home but do not read Spanish. There are cities, such as Chicago, where high schools can have more than 20 different languages spoken in one school, with English being the language spoken by the smallest percentage. Those schools having a high population of ESL students usually have much lower test scores than schools made up largely of native language speakers. One would assume that bilingual students would perform better on standardized tests, but that is not true. Many times, knowing a second language causes young children to miss words on tests that are used for admission to the "right" preschools and elementary schools.

After the administration of the Stanford-Binet Intelligence Test to one four-year-old, the test supervisor asked the students' parents whether the student spoke another language at home because the student had trouble with some of the words on the test. The parents indicated that the student spoke Spanish at home. The difficulty he had with those few words caused the student to receive a low score on the test, and thus he was not admitted to the private school where his parents had hoped to enroll him (Mertler, 2003). Students who are learning two languages at once are bound to switch words from one language to another as they search for words to use in sentences or pronounce words. In the example above, the person who administered the test was quite sure what was causing the student to miss words. It wasn't his lack of knowledge but his wealth of knowledge instead.

Students with Special Needs

Under the Individuals with Disabilities Education Act (IDEA), students with disabilities are entitled to accommodations when taking standardized tests. The type of accommodation depends on the student's individualized education program (IEP), which should include what accommodations are necessary when this student is taking tests. Many times, teachers believe that by giving a student more time, they have accommodated the needs of the student. This does not always solve the problem, however. Picture a college student who has recently lost his sight. He is learning to read Braille, so the school arranges for him to take the test in Braille. Is he ready for a timed test using Braille? The answer is probably no. It might be better to have the test read to him. But during the testing, he kept getting mixed up about which of the four choices on each multiple-choice question was correct by the time the reader finished reading the question.

When students with disabilities take any test, let alone a standardized test, the individual student should really be considered. One accommodation (extra time) does not necessary fit all. For the young blind student, it would be better to have each multiple-choice question read with each answer choice as though the question consisted of four true-false questions. Doing so, would make the information provided by the test a better indicator of what the young man knew. Each state has guidelines for testing accommodations for students. These should be used in conjunction with recommendations from the students' school-based instructional team.

Students of Poverty

One of the biggest influences on students' performance on standardized tests is the socioeconomic status of the community from which the student comes. Many preservice teachers have asked why socioeconomic status makes such a difference.

Let's look at two different families living in two different school districts 20 miles apart in a large city. Both families consist of a single mother and two preschool-age children:

- Family A has an annual income of $19,000. Family A's parent works in an area where the cost of a one-bedroom apartment averages $1,000 monthly.

- Family B has an annual income of $1,000,000. Family B's parent spends $20,000 a month on a mortgage.

After housing, how much does each family have left for food, clothing, gas, utilities, and day care?

- Family A has $7,000.

- Family B has $750,000.

After food, gas, utilities, and clothing have been deducted, how much does each family have left for day care for two children? Even with subsidized day care, the children of family A will probably be taken care of by a neighbor or family member, who may or may not invest the time to read and play educational games with the children. Will family B be able to afford cay care? You get the picture.

Children of poverty perform below average in education and on standardized tests not only because of lack of early childhood educational experiences such as day care or other educational enrichment experiences, but also because many of these children lack sufficient and proper nutrition (Kohn, 1999). For many of our poor students, school is the only place where they receive both breakfast and lunch regularly. These are factors that affect how children develop. Anyone who has not eaten for a day will notice the resulting effect on his or her physical and mental energy and ability. Imagine the suffering of children whose only regular meals are provided when they are in school and who spend the rest of the week hungry (Kohn, 1999).

Alternative Assessment Strategies

When the No Child Left Behind Act of 2001 was passed, it mandated that all school children participate in accountability testing. This included English language learners (ELLs) and students with significant cognitive disabilities. Although one might expect that students with English as a second language would move forward and be able to make a passing score or what is considered adequate yearly progress (AYP), educators have serious concerns for those students who have significant cognitive disabilities. Passed in 2003, the final regulation, Title 1: Improving the Academic Achievement of the Disadvantaged, enables schools to use alternative assessments for these students. This regulation provides for students to be exempt from the grade-level standards set for typically developing students. A school is allowed to use alternative assessment standards to assess the accountability of no more than 1 percent of its student population. As with the regular accountability assessments, alternative assessments must measure skills in language arts and mathematics, with science to be added by the year 2007 (Hager & Slocum, 2005).

Alternative assessment may take the form of checklists, portfolios, analyzed IEPs, or performance assessment. Portfolios may be used because goals and objectives are defined and the assessment process developed before the student begins developing or contributing work to the portfolio. For ESL students, this method of alternative assessment would show whether students were making adequate yearly progress mastering concepts taught in mathematics and language arts without the test results being contaminated by limitations in the student's current understanding of the English language.

In other words, a student may have a very good understanding of mathematical concepts but still perform poorly on that section of the test because his or her language skills are at a lower level than that at which the test is written. This assessment method also works well for students with significant cognitive disabilities. Because the goals and objectives can be written around the student's IEP, the level of yearly progress can be determine on the basis of whether the student could perform the goals and objectives indicated.

However, for students with significant cognitive disabilities, checklists may be more appropriate, depending on the task and the level of cognitive disability. Skills that are not assessed under No Child Left Behind are those skills that are considered life skills. For students who have a significant cognitive disability, adequate yearly progress may be defined in their IEP as being able to perform basic life functions that would not be measured in the regular classroom. What is important in the accountability process is not the passing score on a test but successful learning on the part of the student.

Performance assessments are used as alternative assessments even though they may be included on paper and pencil tests (i.e., multiply two-digit integers by two-digit integers with regrouping). Performance assessment can be (1) included in portfolio assessments, (2) a checklist, or (3) a rubric. Performance assessment can be used for assessing the actual *doing* of a skill, such as observing how a student cooks oatmeal, or for assessing a final *product*, such as noting whether the oatmeal was runny, clumpy, crunchy, or mushy—and perhaps even tasting its flavor. In other words, how well did the student actually do at making a final product, oatmeal, of high quality?

SUMMARY

Whether alternative assessments are used for accountability, standardized tests, or teacher-made tests, the purpose of the assessment instruments should always be the same. Does the accountability assessment provide the decision makers with information about how well students understand the instructional goals and objectives of the curriculum as defined by the district or the state? No accountability measure, whether it is a standardized test or an alternative assessment measure, should be used if it does not provide information about how well the students are learning the defined curriculum.

DISCUSSION QUESTIONS

1. What historical factors contribute to how we view the goals of assessment today? How has the field evolved, and how does it affect teachers today?

2. In what ways does the nation's political climate influence the federal government's role in educational assessment policy? How is state educational policy also influenced by politics?

3. Identify and describe approaches and instruments commonly used to assess student knowledge. What are the strengths and weaknesses of these approaches?

4. What is Bloom's taxonomy? Describe how your own learning process reflects the classifications that Bloom identified.

5. What are some of the effects of standardized testing on both diverse learners and students from low socioeconomic backgrounds?

6. Describe portfolio assessment. Identify the learning goals and instructional design features of this alternative assessment approach.

ACTIVITIES

1. Interview two or three public school teachers. Ask them to describe their approaches to preparing students for standardized tests. How do they balance high stakes test preparation with alternative assessment approaches and meeting the needs of diverse learners?

2. What assessment strategies do you recall that best measured your cognitive development, content-area knowledge, and the skills you had learned? Which strategies worked best? Which failed?

3. Research the annual yearly progress (AYP) test outcomes in your state and local schools. Discuss with a teacher or school administrator their views about these test scores. What are states and schools doing to better meet AYP standards?

4. Collect two or three examples of alternative assessment strategies from professional teacher organization websites (for example, those of the National Council of the Social Studies and the National Council of Teachers of English). Identify their learning goals, instructional and assessment strategies, and rubrics.

WEBSITES

Institute for Educational Sciences, National Center for Educational Statistics
http://nces.ed.gov/nationsreportcard
This website is the home of the National Assessment of Educational Progress (NAEP), also known as "the nation's report card." It is the only nationally representative and continuing assessment of what America's students know and can do in various subject areas. At this site you will find assessment data on specific content areas, such as reading, mathematics, science, writing, U.S. history, civics, geography, and the arts.

U.S. Department of Education, No Child Left Behind
http://www.ed.gov/nclb/landing.jhtml
This webpage offers a comprehensive examination of the NCLB Act for parents, students, teachers, and administrators. The site includes links to information on highly qualified teachers, student assessment, and state and local initiatives relevant to annual yearly progress.

U.S. Department of Education, Special Education and Rehabilitation Services
http://www.ed.gov/offices/OSERS/IDEA
This webpage provides a number of technical assistance tools and topic briefs relevant to special education, standardized testing, and NCLB.

U.S. Department of Education, Title I: Improving the Academic Achievement of the Disadvantaged
http://www.ed.gov/policy/elsec/leg/esea02/pg1.html
Information available includes information on annual funding for Reading First, prevention and intervention programs for "at-risk" youth, and priorities for school improvement.

REFERENCES

American Educational Research Association, American Psychological Association, and National Council on Measurement in Education. (1985). *Standards for educational and psychological testing.* Washington, DC: APA.

Batzle, J. (1992). *Portfolio assessment and evaluation: Developing and using portfolios in the classroom.* Cypress, CA: Creative Teaching Press.

Bloom, B. S. (1956). *Taxonomy of educational objectives: The classification of education goals, Handbook I: Cognitive domain.* New York: McKay.

Bloom, B., Engelhart, M., Furst, E., Hill, W., & Krathwahl, D. (1984). *Taxonomy of educational objectives. Handbook I: Cognitive domain.* New York: Longman.

Cole, K. B., Struyk, L. R., Kinder, D., Sheehan, J. K., & Kish, C. K. (1997). Portfolio assessment: Challenges in secondary education. *High School Journal, 80*(4), 261–272.

González, N. (2001). *I am my language: Discourses of women and children in the borderlands.* Tucson: University of Arizona Press.

Hager, K. D., & Slocum, T. A. (2005). Using alternative assessment to improve educational outcomes. *Rural Special Education Quarterly, 24*(1), 54–59.

Haladyna, T. H. (2002). *Essentials of standardized achievement testing: Validity and accountability.* Boston: Allyn & Bacon.

Kish, C. K., Sheehan, J. K., Cole, K. B., Struyk, L. R., & Kinder, D. (1997). Portfolios in the classroom: A vehicle for developing reflective thinking. *High School Journal, 80*(4), 254–260.

Kohn, A. (1999). *The schools our children deserve: Moving beyond the traditional classrooms and "tougher standards."* Boston: Houghton Mifflin.

Mertler, C. (2003). *Classroom assessment: A practical guide for educators.* Los Angeles: Pyrczak.

National Council of Teachers of Mathematics. (n.d.). Principle and Standards for School Mathematics. Retrieved June 7, 2007 from http://www.nctm.org/standards/overview.htm

Popham, J. W. (2006). Assessment for learning: An endangered species? *Educational Leadership, 63*(5), 82–83.

Rose, L. C., Gallup, A. M., & Elam, S. M. (1997). The twenty-ninth annual Phi Delta Kappa / Gallup Poll of the public's attitude towards the public schools. *Phi Delta Kappan, 79*, 41–56.

Struyk, L. R., & Mehlig, L. M. (2004). Classroom assessment in social studies. In P. J. Farris, (Ed.), *Elementary and middle school social studies: An interdisciplinary, multicultural approach.* Boston: McGraw-Hill.

Tombari, M., & Borich, G. (1999). *Authentic assessment in the classroom: Applications and practice.* Upper Saddle River, NJ: Merrill.

Utah Educational Association. (2006). Teaching to the test. Retrieved June 7, 2007 from http://www.utea.org/index.htm.

Valdes, Guadalupe. (2001). *Learning and not learning English.* New York: Teachers College Press.

CHAPTER 10

Exploring the Relationship Between American Culture and Education

FIRST PERSON

Is a Culturally Relevant Curriculum Just About Celebrating Holidays?

Jenny, a seventh- and eighth-grade history teacher, aspired to be Teacher of the Year in my local school district. Professional realities closed in on that vision, however. After four years of teaching, challenges increased. Facing large class sizes, a lack of textbooks, little technology access, and the day-to-day grind of keeping students on task, Jenny fought the urge to succumb to worksheet-driven instruction.

Meanwhile, parent-teacher conferences loomed. With her 150 grade reports completed, Jenny strived to conduct the evening conferences with a positive, upbeat attitude. That night only a handful of parents arrived, representative of the predominantly middle-class, Euro-American suburban community. Surprising to Jenny was the attendance of Rosa, a Mexican American single parent. Her daughter Maria was a bright eighth grader, who enjoys an interest typical of many teenage girls—boys. Nevertheless, Jenny also knew that Maria was a productive student. This was just how Maria was at Marshall Junior High: steady, unassuming, blending in, and getting things done. These thoughts summed up Jenny's meeting with Rosa, as she reported Maria's "above average" progress. And yet, Rosa posed two questions that Jenny could not readily answer: "By the way, what are you teaching my daughter about Mexican American history? And, are you teaching her about different cultures?"

Jenny struggled to respond to Rosa's questions. She fumbled as she described to Rosa her social studies unit on the history of the American West. Only one textbook sidebar feature addressed Spanish colonization and the Treaty of Guadalupe. That was the extent to which Mexican American history was represented in the book. Later, Jenny wondered, "How can I seriously answer Rosa's question, or any other parent's for that matter? What do I know about that part of American history and the cultures that contributed to it?

CHAPTER OBJECTIVES

- Readers will describe factors that contribute to the shifting nature of culture.

- Readers will identify the concepts of enculturation and acculturation and their relationship to schooling.

- In the context of education, readers will contrast the features of American cultural viewpoints and distinguish them from other cultural perspectives and discourses.

- Readers will analyze the impact of language diversity and culture on the public schools.

- Readers will explore how educators can foster cross-cultural educational practices and understanding, while affirming multiple student identities.

Jenny remained disturbed by Rosa's questions. She reflected on her own instructional practices. Jenny arrived at the conclusion that her teaching strategies were rather lock-step, as if the students were sleep-walking through their day—and she was leading the march. Jenny thought, "What constitutes American culture? What do we really know and share together? What kinds of knowledge do we invite?" She came upon the idea that if she invited the students to explore their own histories, the issues of culture and identity might inspire a renewed sense of engagement, of affirmation, for all students and for what they share.

Jenny earnestly began to design an oral-history project for her classes. She wanted to give her students, such as Maria, an opportunity to interview family members and explore their cultures, authentically. The project itself did not supplant the core curriculum or the text, because Jenny recognized the importance of presenting facts and understanding specific events, particularly in these times of No Child Left Behind. And yet, she felt that one quality her American history text lacked was the human element. Jenny hoped that by guiding the students' own research, she could banish such comments and questions as "This book is so boring!" and "Why do we always have to read about dead people?" and perhaps even "What are you teaching about Mexican American history?"

As the oral-history interview data started to trickle in, Jenny discovered that her students had much more to learn about their families. Maria's interview with her mother, Rosa, was particularly interesting. The project enabled Maria to better understand the struggles her family confronted when they first moved to Utah from Mexico.

Maria presented the oral history of her mom to the class. She began:

"There were six kids in my mom's familia, three girls and three boys. She had a real good upbringing. Her dad was the provider. He worked for the Santa Fe railroad. And her mom stayed home until they got older. When they first moved to Utah, my mom was snubbed because she spoke Spanish. She didn't try to offend anyone; it was just the way people thought back then. The fact that she spoke Spanish meant that she was Mexican. If my mom was a Mexican, that meant she was going to be a maid. The [community] pocket where they lived was very, very uneducated and narrow-minded. I learned that to be narrow-minded means a person refuses to accept someone else's views or someone who is different.

"There were very few Mexicans in Utah when my mom grew up. Her parents and grandparents spoke Spanish at home. The girls were expected to help cook and clean. My mom's family was Catholic and they lived in a Mormon community. My mom said her parents never brought her up to be prejudiced against any religion. It wasn't talked about a lot, but it was there. My mom said, 'You just knew it.'"

Maria continued to relate her mom's life story to her classmates. Jenny was struck by the honest and pointed nature of the issues Maria had selected to present, such as her mom's childhood memories. Maria explained:

"My mom was actually blonde when she was young. [She pointed to the photo of her mom and uncles on a poster board.] We must have that gene because look how blonde my uncles are. People here are surprised that my uncles have light hair and I don't. They would say to my mom, 'Oh, these are your relatives?' 'Yep, these are my brothers,' she'd say. My mom said that people in the community would have social events, parties, and good times but because we were different, we weren't invited. Sometimes we were treated so cold. And people were surprised that we didn't have Spanish accents. They were amazed. They would say to my mom, 'You don't have an accent, Rosa!' And my mom would say, 'That's because I'm bilingual.'"

Maria added:

"My mom said she puts up with prejudice in Utah more than in any other place because she said, 'I know I drink the same water as whites.'"

Jenny's students were engrossed in Maria's oral-history presentation. Many of Jenny's students had had no long-term interactions with Mexican American people and, as a result, knew little about their experiences and concerns. As for Maria, it appeared to Jenny that Maria enjoyed reporting what she had learned. Maria talked about her mom's childhood, family, education, and goals. As Maria generated her own historical knowledge using Jenny's step-by-step oral-history model, Jenny felt she could actually guide her students to their own cross-cultural understanding.

As Maria summed up her presentation, Jenny knew that the other students listened well. There was none of the whispering and paper shuffling that she often had to manage during presentations. Nor was there any passing of notes. Jenny also realized that she had found a new starting point to address social studies topics relevant to the core curriculum *and* the democratic classroom. Indeed, Rosa's story inspired Jenny as well, as she began to organize additional ideas about her new multicultural history unit.

Maria concluded her presentation to the class as follows:

"Right now my mom works for AT&T. She works with corporate accounts. She also goes to conferences, where she sees the next generation of business leaders getting more involved in the community. So now she wants to start a scholarship fund at work. She wants to make a difference. My mom also wants me to set goals in life and be more involved in the community. All I can say is my mom believes that we kids must continue our education and make a difference. I think that's important to all cultures."

What Is Culture?

Anthropologists argue that the educational process is designed to transmit cultural traits to future generations (Spindler, 1973). The structure of the education system, the practices of the schools, and teacher-student relationships mirror societal organization and the cultural norms of that society. How the young are educated has also been perceived as a response to societal and cultural needs. For a culturally diverse population to have any effect on a school system requires that the system address the issues and challenges emerging from the differences that exist between the minority and dominant cultures. Educators today must recognize that students' learning styles are influenced by the beliefs, values, and cognitive and linguistic patterns that make up their particular culture. As a result, schools can no longer rely on strict adherence to culturally neutral teaching strategies.

It might seem that the relationship between education and culture is obvious, but the connections that bind the two elements have not been fully examined. Historically, the study of education has stressed psychology and measurement, rather than the cultural dimensions of the teaching and learning process (Spindler, 1973). Although the analysis of the cultural foundations of education receives some attention in educational psychology and philosophy of education, educators and caregivers themselves need to examine how cultural variables influence the learning styles of all students.

Culture, as a system of behavior patterns, values, and expectations, does not consist only of random personality traits. Rather, it represents concepts rooted in the unique and fundamental ideals and beliefs that educators must address through their instructional practices. This chapter explores the various dimensions of culture and shows how understanding these dimensions can assist educators as they design teaching strategies that address cultural sensitivity in the school and community.

According to Pai & Adler (1997), **culture** is generally viewed as a pattern of knowledge, skills, behaviors, attitudes, and beliefs, as well as material artifacts, produced by human society and transmitted from one generation to another. Culture is the whole of humanity's intellectual, social, technological, political, economic, religious, moral, and aesthetic accomplishments. Spindler (1993, p. 132) argues that central to the concept of culture is the fact that any culture is goal oriented:

> These goals are expressed, patterned, lived out by people in their behaviors and aspirations in the form of value—objects or possessions, conditions of existence, features of personality or characters and states of mind that are conceived desirable, and act as motivating determinants of behaviors.

Culture is more than a collection of unconnected events and views. Instead, it should be seen as an integrated set of norms or standards, human behaviors, and beliefs. The American anthropologist Clifford Geertz (1973, p. 44) explains,

> Culture is best seen not as complexes or concrete behavior patterns—customs, usages, traditions, habit clusters—as has been the case up to now, but as a set of control mechanisms—plans, recipes, rules, instructions—for governing of behavior.

Kathryn Au, an educational researcher who studies literacy development of students of diverse cultural and linguistic backgrounds, finds that culture is a process in which people make sense of their lives. She explains that culture is learned, shared, and continually evolving. Children are not born with the knowledge of their culture, but are taught by family and community (1993).

It has been argued by anthropologists that few aspects of the human experience are untouched by culture. This is particularly relevant to education, because the meanings of student beliefs must be understood within their specific cultural context. Students, however, who live in a culture distinct from the predominant society may perceive and communicate differently in the world. Culture, then, consists of the standards by which members of a society assign meanings, values, and significance to behaviors, events, and symbols.

Also unique to the cultural perspective is the existence, within the larger groups, of subcultures based on distinct social, religious, political, economic, generational, and educational views. The implications for the public schools are far-reaching, as various subcultures exist simultaneously and in combination with the national, state, and local cultures.

From PRESERVICE to PRACTICE

Critical Literacies

The world we live in—our social and political situation—is shaped by our abilities to communicate and represent. According to Kathryn Au and Taffy Raphael (2000), the more language proficiency individuals have, the greater their capacity to affect the world around them. Literacy (or, more accurately, a range of literacy skills) gives individuals not only the ability to understand the world but also, in Au and Raphael's terms, the ability to "rewrite" their world. In short, proficiency with literacy means power.

However, Au and Raphael argue, as the world changes, the literacy skills that bring power change as well. Students whose literacy education focuses only on the printed word will be limited. Au and Raphael emphasize the need for

"critical literacies." These critical literacies include such skills as the ability to decode, evaluate, and manipulate a wide range of communication media and technology. They also include the ability to communicate in a culturally and linguistically diverse community resulting from increasing globalization.

Questions for Reflection

1. How can students of all ages develop their abilities to communicate with one another using various technologies? Describe two or three examples.
2. In what ways can the development of "critical literacies" help to empower students in an increasingly diverse society? Explain.

Source: Au and Raphael (2000), retrieved from http://www.ncrel.literacy.smartlibrary.info/NewInterface/segment.cfm?segment=2355.

An individual's culture is at the heart of her or his identity. It serves to empower the individual by establishing a framework in which he or she can determine the purpose of life, set goals, and focus on achieving these goals. To degrade or reject an individual's culture is to damage the dignity and self-worth of that person.

Differences Are Not Deficits

Culture is basic to the human experience, but fully understanding how a set of people view life is an elusive goal, even for a member of such a group. No individual ever learns everything there is to know about a culture. In essence, each person's understanding of a culture is different from every other person's interpretation (Wolcott, 1991). We can, however, observe and examine the general characteristics of a culture that can help educators relate to diverse students and develop strategies to maximize student potential while meeting educational standards. These two concepts are not mutually exclusive.

For example, in American culture, the belief that hard work will lead to success is explicitly manifested in the ways we teach children about the importance of the work ethic. However, members of minority groups who do poorly in society and in schools are sometimes regarded as rebellious, ignorant, or lazy. Thus a school program that dispels such ignorant stereotypes by educating all students about diverse cultures both helps to maximize student potential and imparts understandings that benefit students and society. In this way, the predominant cultural norms, sanctioned, taught, and reproduced by such institutions as the public schools, often extend beyond the stated goals of education.

According to Sieber and Gordon (1981), instructional methods reflect teachers' beliefs and attitudes, and in the process of attending school, children are exposed to "a much broader 'hidden curriculum' of values, norms and social skills. A child's success in schools is as much dependent on his or her mastering the content of the hidden curriculum as it is on mastering the formal curriculum" (pp. 6–7).

Because culture persists as a driving force in human life and interactions, it is easy to assume that the predominant culture serves as the standard that individuals must meet to achieve acceptance and membership. Attitudes that focus on the superiority of one culture over another contribute to the perception that diverse groups who do not conform to the status quo are inferior, deprived, or irresponsible. Minority group characteristics, which often do not reflect predominant societal norms, are often regarded as idiosyncrasies, or even deficits, that must be corrected by the educational system. And yet, the **cultural deficit model** of viewing minority groups as inferior has been associated with the perpetuation of institutional racism (Baratz & Baratz, 1970).

The cultural deficit model has a serious impact on educational practices, because this view invites teachers to encourage students to adopt predominant cultural norms and to reject unique cultural practices that represent different, but equally valid, means of addressing basic human challenges and needs. (Cultural tolerance does not, however, mean sanctioning student behaviors that may be harmful to others or impede their educational success.) To celebrate and respect differences that enrich the human experience can only serve to challenge the prevailing view that some cultures exhibit "inadequacies" that must be remedied by the American educational system.

Certain cultures may practice actions that some educators feel are bizarre, but these activities may serve a problem-solving function. Each group maintains its particular standards to develop ways to resolve problems and address needs. Cultural change may reflect the level of success or failure in the group's effort to confront its unique challenges. And yet, the fact that a given culture has devised standards to address its problems does not establish that such standards meet all of the members' needs, nor does it suggest that such a framework is effectively transferable to another culture.

For example, say that on Saturdays, certain Japanese American students attend a school that teaches Japanese language and culture. This does not mean that these students will become "less American" or "more Japanese." The Japanese families who participate in such educational and social networks are introducing children to a particular cultural and linguistic heritage, because the families perceive a need. Other cultural or ethnic groups may share this need but prefer to teach children distinct variations of language and culture in the home.

In the end, it can be argued that individual and cultural practices continue to compete with the ideals of society. In a democratic society, cultural practices that limit freedom, undermine equal assess to opportunities, or exploit others cannot be defended because, ultimately, such restrictions undermine everyone's rights.

For Your CONSIDERATION

For an overview of the cultural deficit theory, read Donna Bolima's *Contexts for Understanding: Educational Learning Theories.* You will find it at **http://staff.Washington.edu/saki/strategies/101/new_page5.htm.**

The Enculturative and Acculturative Processes of Schooling

Every culture strives to reproduce itself through the methodical transmission of what it holds to be useful knowledge, beliefs, and behavioral expectations. Pai and Adler (2001) define education as the "deliberate transmission of culture" (p. 42). In various cultures, the process may be implemented informally as well as formally—for example, through cultural rituals and the intergenerational sharing of beliefs. In a more formal setting, such as in the schools, youths are taught specific types of knowledge and skills.

A father teaching an abacus lesson to his sons.

Various views regarding how culture is reproduced persist. One form of cultural transmission is known as **enculturation**, the process of learning one's own culture. When this process occurs formally in an institutional setting, it is called schooling. **Schooling** is a narrower concept than education because it involves specialists teaching in places established for that purpose. On the other hand, education does not always take place in an institutional setting. For diverse students, enculturation takes place in the home and in the community.

Education in the United States is also acculturative. As students in the schools are learning their own culture, diverse youth are simultaneously learning about the dominant culture. This process is known as **acculturation.** To acknowledge that the process of education in America is both enculturative and acculturative is to recognize that many of the students in the schools are learning two distinct cultures. This suggests that many learning and behavioral difficulties derive from the differences between the norms the school deems acceptable and those that diverse children see as appropriate in different settings.

In other words, one explanation for school failure among diverse students is a mismatch between school culture and home culture. Such incompatibilities derive from distinct goals, values, religious views, language, skills, and expectations. Nieto (2004, p. 235) puts it this way:

> The more consistent that home and school cultures are, the reasoning goes, the more successful students will be, in general terms. The opposite is also true: The more that students' experiences, skills, and values differ from the school setting, the more failure they will experience.

Keeping this perspective in mind, we realize that culturally diverse students who are often designated "at risk" are labeled in this way not only because of their behaviors, but also because of the interpretation that their behaviors are incompatible with the American school culture. Certainly, diverse students must acquire the knowledge and skills to negotiate between the dominant culture and their own. Different cultures do attach various meanings to specific actions. Therefore, educators need to consider carefully whether "disruptive" student behaviors may be responses influenced by their culture and/or language. For example, when English language learners speak their native language in class, a monolingual teacher may assume that these are off-task conversations. But in fact, the students may be translating—and clarifying to one another—instructional content or directions.

Society envisions other goals for education, including the promotion of social change. With the establishment of educational opportunities for a broader segment of the population, social, economic, and political action can now challenge the extent of educational inequities and economic disparity present in American society today.

Connecting to the Cengage Learning Video Cases

Diversity: Teaching in a Multiethnic Classroom
Watch the Cengage Learning video case entitled "Diversity: Teaching in a Multiethnic Classroom." Consider viewing questions 1, 2, and 4.

Video Case Study

1. In what ways do both teachers, Akiko Kawai and Jonathan Norwood, establish a positive learning environment for all learners?
2. How can the arts be integrated into a multicultural or culturally relevant curriculum?
3. Jonathan Norwood maintains that it is important for teachers to help students understand other cultures. Explain why.

Student Website

American Cultural Values

To understand why schools are generally more successful with Euro-American students than with students of diverse backgrounds, a good way to begin is to examine the mainstream culture. What exactly is American culture, and how does it differ from others? In the following paragraphs, we will examine some of the basic characteristics of the structure of American culture.

The population of America continues to grow in cities and towns located in diverse natural environments. Although the country has a strong agrarian tradition and still produces large yields of foodstuffs and fibers, the nation has become urbanized and dominated by cities. Extensive technology and the production of manufactured goods are also important. In fact, single-family American farms and ranches are declining and being replaced by corporations that contrast markedly with their pastoral roots. Daily life is generally urban, regulated by the clock and calendar. Many individuals are employees, living on salaries paid by large, complex institutions. Money is the primary medium of exchange, and the value of most property is expressed in terms of its monetary worth. The necessities of life are purchased, rather than produced for subsistence. Because of a high standard of living and advanced medical technology, Americans with health insurance generally live long lives. Although there is population growth in the United States, it is less rapid than in other developed nations.

Americans range widely in wealth, property, education, religious beliefs, and values. Nevertheless, despite the presence of a diverse population with various traditions and economic levels, there is, for the most part, conformity in language, diet, hygiene, dress, basic skills, community settlement, and recreation. Some social scientists would argue that Americans exhibit a narrow range of moral, political, economic, and social attitudes, being divided in opinion mostly by their religion, occupational interests, and, perhaps, age. There are regional differences, but they are less notable than the ethnic pluralism found in Eastern Europe, Asia, and Africa. The narrow opinion range of Americans may be a product of the relatively efficient educational system, in combination with the widespread mass communication system, in which all people get very similar messages.

Among Americans there are status differences, based mainly on occupation, education, and financial worth. Although in theory, everyone has equal opportunities, constraints based on one's ethnic background, gender, and physical abilities do exist. For example, an African American may be elected to the Senate, but it remains to be seen whether an African American or a woman will ever be elected president. Nevertheless, the possibility does exist, as demonstrated recently with the presidential candidacies of Senator Hillary Clinton and Senator Barack Obama. They were not the first woman and Africa American to run for president, but they certainly exceeded their predecessors in the millions of dollars they raised for their respective campaigns.

Changes in the composition of the "typical" American family unit continue. Although marital relationships are the heart of the culture, divorce is common. What constitutes family today has evolved, and we see children living in extended families, same-sex families, adoptive families, and blended families. In the United States, unlike some cultures, senior citizens and singles usually live apart from their families. Instead of being constrained by exclusive family ties, people are active in groups that revolve around common interests and along religious, social, recreational, and political lines.

The general level of education in America is high, although basic literacy is not universal. Between the ages of 5 and 18, children attend educational institutions, learning the culturally approved goals of character, citizenship, and health, as well as basic skills. Specialization generally takes place in college, although college attendance is not legally required.

The moral tone of American culture is driven by Christianity. Religious beliefs and practices focus on the worship of God and on morality, family relations, customs, civic responsibilities, and the search for understanding of the afterlife. Puritanical morality has become an integral part of the total American culture and is not bound to any one religious group. Religion plays a strong role in society, but it is not the unifying institution that it is in, for example, the Middle East or Latin America. This is not to say that Americans are antireligious but only that secular practices in America are not always dependent on religious views.

For Your CONSIDERATION

The First Amendment Center provides comprehensive research on First Amendment issues and topics, including a focus on religion and education for teachers. The webpage is maintained by the First Amendment Center, at Vanderbilt University. Visit the site at **http://www.firstamendmentcenter.org/rel_liberty/publicschools/Index.aspx.**

Judging Success: Material Well-Being

Economic growth, coupled with the nation's resources, makes America a comfortable place to live for those who can afford it. Such amenities as housing, transportation, electricity, clean water, abundant food, heating, air conditioning, entertainment, recreation, and electronics have become elements of an American life in which acquisition is paramount. Success is often measured by the amount one has accumulated; this indicates how much money an individual has acquired. Status is also reflected in one's educational level, occupation, and social activities, but again these factors are usually a function of one's earning power.

Middle-class Americans are not the only ones who value comfort and the conservation of labor. For the culturally diverse, the acquisition of material items not only represents economic success but also symbolizes a level of assimilation and acculturation into American society. However, the members of many diverse communities are unable to attain such status because of the effects of poverty. In their preoccupation with acquiring material wealth, Americans are quick to judge less successful individuals, who are often assumed to be wholly responsible for failing to scale the heights of economic opportunity. Without understanding all the influences involved, it is easy to characterize people in terms of binaries: moral-immoral, legal-illegal, sinning-virtuous, civilized-primitive, Christian-pagan, deserving-undeserving.

This kind of polarized thinking defines American values into fixed absolutes, and society often makes such judgments arbitrarily. Making judgments serves as a way to organize thought in America. Other cultures are more likely to grasp the complexity of lived experiences and spiritual beliefs (an example is the hybridity of religious beliefs among some Cubans who blend Santeria and Catholicism). Many diverse cultures do not necessarily elevate one perspective over the others, nor do they allow a single perspective to serve as a societal code of conduct.

Such rigid views entrench and separate Americans and affect their institutions. For example, in the U.S. educational system, students are seldom encouraged to maintain opposite or multiple perspectives within their knowledge base. This is not the case in other cultures. For example, Latina/o students may have knowledge about and accept Western approaches to remedying the common cold, but they may also be aware of and accept that the use of medicinal herbs by grandparents can serve the same function.

Judging people and their actions as right or wrong may have served its purpose in American history, but it has also caused problems in Americans' relationships with diverse communities. Every culture has its own code of behavior. Educators today are making efforts to understand cultural codes, despite the fact that acquiring such knowledge is especially challenging as cultures change. For example, for many Latin American cultures, individual dignity, personal honor, or compassion for and loyalty to others may be the ultimate evidence of having acquired knowledge and wisdom, not just successful participation in the American educational system.

On Work, Time, and Money

In American culture, work is perceived as a necessary activity. Recreation and play are seen as distinct from work. This distinction may not be made in the same way through the lens of a different culture. For some cultures, work and play coexist. It is not uncommon for students to miss school to assist in preparations for holidays, traditions, or festivities, such as Dia de Los Muertos or Chinese New Year.

Related to American culture's distinction between work and play is its perspective on time. When Americans interact with members of certain diverse groups, they quickly become aware that their views of time may differ. The term *hora Americana* refers to the American view of time—in other words, the view that meeting times are exact, events are scheduled, and people should be punctual.

American culture subscribes to the notion that "time is money." Employers actually buy their employees' time, so it is easy to see how society equates time with work and, ultimately,

An elementary student looks at the classroom clock and the class schedule for the day.

cash. Although this philosophy has contributed to American productivity, Americans do feel uneasy about the "tyranny" of schedules.

This view of time precision, associated with work, may be foreign to some diverse populations. Certain activities reflect, not hourly work output, but the needs for individual and social life, such as the honoring of and participation in family traditions, habits, and routines. It is not uncommon for individuals from diverse cultures not to keep hours or appointments precisely. Many are often surprised when they learn that Americans are perceived negatively, or even penalized, for tardiness or missed appointments.

On Effort

Americans believe that problems should be identified and solved. This national confidence in effort, coupled with the notion that "doing something" will bring quick resolutions, is unique to American society. This attitude reflects the growth of the American culture from its pioneer roots to industrialization.

Effort, achievement, and success are ever-present concepts permeating American society. Pragmatic, "black-and-white" values, rather than contemplative or mystical ones, are at the heart of the American culture. An all-out effort to achieve success in this culture is practically a requirement. The successful student is one who works hard to "get ahead." When a student is unsuccessful, it is usually assumed that it is her or his own fault—opportunities were overlooked or simply squandered.

This is a very rigid code. It reveals a culture in which effort is rewarded, competition is encouraged, and individual achievement is the ultimate goal. However, this concept does promote social conflict. Individuals who hold high-status positions are deemed successful, whereas those in low-status jobs are labeled "failures." American educators tend to evaluate students on the basis of this code. It is not difficult to understand how such a code contributes to feelings of resentment, frustration, and disillusionment in diverse groups because they may feel they did not have equal access and opportunity to achieve high-status positions. Ironically, both the dominant culture and minority cultures are resentful when they perceive an individual as having acquired a position or opportunity by means other than personal effort. On the other hand, Americans are unaware of the privileges they hold. Researcher Peggy McIntosh refers to this as the invisibility of white privilege. The term *white privilege* is often used to describe an advantage, immunity, or right enjoyed by or granted to white persons beyond the common advantage of all others. To explore McIntosh's examples of the presence of white privilege in society, visit the website Unpacking the Invisible Knapsack (http://seamonkey.edu.asu.edu/~mciaac/emc598ge/Unpacking.html).

PAUSE & REFLECT

How would you define *white privilege* after having read McIntosh's "knapsack"? Which of her examples do you think are valid? Which do you think could be challenged? Explain why. Why are the ramifications of white privilege for educational institutions? What can administrators and teachers do to ensure that all students have equal educational opportunities?

To the disenfranchised, a history of failure has been just as profound as the extent of American technological and economic successes. These negative outcomes contribute to counterproductive attitudes, including cynicism, passivity, resentment, and futility. Such responses persist not because diverse cultures refuse to pursue and achieve goals. They are the result of histories of segregation, deculturalization (the loss of one's culture and its replacement with a new one), exclusion, inequitable access to resources, and prejudice; they are the outcome of a lack of faith in America.

Various cultures have had periods of success in their histories, but it cannot be assumed that such progress will be sustained throughout a culture's existence. American society's zeal for development and technology does not come without negative consequences if preoccupation with those goals proceeds unchecked and obscures other values.

PAUSE & REFLECT

What do you feel are some other features of American culture? How are these features mirrored in the policies and practices evident in the public schools? Should educational practices change to accommodate different cultural experiences and perspectives? Explain your point of view.

American Culture and Egalitarianism

Americans do believe that everyone should have equal opportunities for success. However, this is more of an ideal of American culture than a reality. Social and political conditions dictate the true American attitude toward equal opportunity, and that is that people will be treated equally if they accept the basic beliefs and behaviors of the dominant culture.

Throughout American history, various subcultures have experienced inferior treatment and have been denied equal access to the educational and political systems. Limited access to privilege persists. But even though America's legal and institutional heritage emphasizes equal rights, disdains special privileges, and offers equal representation to every citizen, equal treatment for minority groups, for women, and for those with disabilities has been established only by protest and legal action.

Certain groups in contemporary American society are particularly disadvantaged educationally, economically, and politically. These groups include African Americans, Latinos, and American Indians. Anthropologist John Ogbu (2003) referred to such groups as **involuntary minorities**—groups who were brought into American society through conquest, slavery, or colonization. Involuntary minorities generally resent the loss of their culture and freedom, and they interpret the barriers to political, social, and economic empowerment as the outcomes of their oppression.

In contrast, Ogbu argues, **voluntary minorities** "have generally moved to their present societies because they believed that the move would lead to greater political and economic freedom." (p. 8) Voluntary immigrants tend to perceive the dominant culture less critically than involuntary minorities, because they feel that submitting to the treatment they receive is a sacrifice they must make to achieve their goals in America. Nevertheless, both groups experience prejudice. Voluntary minority groups generally have assimilated into American culture, whereas involuntary minority groups seek to maintain certain cultural patterns.

It is not unusual for involuntary minority students to behave in ways that reflect what Ogbu describes as "cultural aversion." Some students may resist learning certain behaviors and curricula that reflect the dominant culture. Activities, attitudes, and educational outcomes that symbolize "selling out" can result in being ostracized by peers of thier own culture. Such youth, according to Fordham and

Ogbu (1986) must deal with the "burden of acting white" (p.176). Diverse students may experience internal struggles as they strive to succeed in ways consistent with American culture, while coping with external pressures not to display that success in their community.

Ogbu also argues that involuntary minority parents, who have encountered prejudice and negative educational experiences, may hold similar views that can influence their children's attitudes about educational opportunities in America. In fact, some culturally diverse students may deliberately engage in behaviors and language that distinctly separate them from the dominant culture promoted in the public schools.

For Your CONSIDERATION

The Penn State University Graduate School of Education maintains the *Perspectives on Urban Education* website and journal. There you can read the essay "Contributions, Controversies, and Criticisms: In Memory of John U. Ogbu." Visit the site at **http://www.urganedjounral.org/archive/Issue4/ogbu_memorial.html**.

Bringing Cultures Together

To develop cultural understanding is a lengthy and formidable process that is especially challenging within the present structure and curricula of the American educational system. There is no established framework that models how we learn about other perspectives and ways of life. So how does one begin a journey to cultural understanding? We can consider the following three approaches:

- *A culturally sensitive educator must pursue personal transformation and reeducation.* This means that each person must focus on learning more about diverse cultures by reading, traveling, participating in community service and activities, or attending events that reveal diverse perspectives. It is important that we seek out learning opportunities that challenge us to go beyond the "comfort zones" of our own monoculture.

- *It is imperative that educators acknowledge and confront their own biases.* Because many of our contacts with others are limited to those who are "just like us," we continue to "self-segregate" and limit our interactions to those who are of the same ethnic background, socioeconomic class, religion, gender, physical ability, and sexual orientation. Because many of our biases are deeply embedded within our consciousness, we must identify and unlearn those internalized prejudices that cause us to judge and stratify those who are different from ourselves.

- *Cultural sensitivity requires that educators examine life from multiple perspectives and discourses.* The American educational system has provided students with curricula and standards that are largely one-dimensional (Banks, 2003). To acknowledge and examine an issue from the perspectives of "the diverse" invites us to enlarge our world view and learn about social contexts and practices that, although we may not ever completely comprehend or agree with them, have equal value in our global society and merit equal dignity and respect.

We can go even further in the quest for cultural understanding by identifying outcomes that are action oriented. These outcomes include developing tolerance, developing acceptance, and developing respect (Wink, 2004). There is no one panacea to manage bias, however. To develop acceptance is the ultimate goal of the process. Simply to be tolerant is not enough.

Being tolerant means having the capacity to "put up with" something that may be unpleasant (Nieto, 2004). To tolerate cultural differences means to endure them, but not necessarily to support them. This level of acceptance of differences is simplistic. What is tolerated at present can be rejected later. Tolerance represents the lowest level of human sensitivity. We may stress tolerance of other cultures, but this by itself does not result in our learning anything that brings us closer together. Strategies that support cultural learning, as opposed to trivializing or modifying cultural pluralism, can take us to the next level of understanding. For some, however, developing tolerance is the initial step.

Central to developing cultural sensitivity is promoting acceptance. Acknowledging that differences exist without ignoring or devaluing their presence gives educators the opportunity to act upon accepting those differences. For example, to acknowledge that English is not spoken in some students' homes requires that care-givers consult with bilingual educators, prepare bilingual documentation, and acquire a basic level of ability in a second language.

Respect is also critical to the development of cultural sensitivity. To respect another person is to hold her or him in high esteem. When we respect diverse cultures, we act in ways which support different lifestyles, while simultaneously empowering and embracing individuals within the larger American culture.

Contrary to popular opinion, promoting the affirmation of diverse cultures can serve to unite a community. To affirm a culture means to accept that culture and language as legitimate and symbolizes hearty support for diverse children and their families. This also means understanding that no culture is fixed or unchangeable. We can critique a culture, as long as that critique is constructive and founded on an informed knowledge base. After all, basic values of different cultures at times contradict one another, so conflicts are unavoidable. To provide affirmation in light of these conflicts requires that we not skirt or avoid issues.

Thus, we must develop an understanding of cultural differences by learning specifically about such fundamental issues as equitable employment, housing, access to health care, and educational opportunities. Conversely, to examine a culture without critiquing it romanticizes diversity. Cultures are then perceived as "exotic." The resulting absence of critical discourse denies and diverts our attention from the conflicts that must be resolved if our society is to achieve genuine cultural understanding.

Connecting to the Cengage Learning Video Cases

Integrating Internet Research: High School Social Studies

Watch the Cengage Learning video case entitled "Integrating Internet Research: High School Social Studies." Consider viewing questions 1, 3, and 4.

Video Case Study

1. How has teacher Elizabeth Sweeney's Internet research project on civil rights helped students understand how to address conflicts and become "people who can make a difference"?

2. How do you see the role of teachers changing as we use these new technologies?

3. In what ways can the study of primary documents, such as those focusing on the Montgomery Bus Boycott, help students better understand the long-term impact of cultural conflict?

Student Website

From PRESERVICE to PRACTICE

Cultural Teaching and the Tamalera

Following my move to Utah from California, my parents, Maria Luisa and George Sanchez Huerta, came to visit one snowy Christmas holiday. The purpose of this particular trip was for my mom to teach her "educated" daughter the ultimate of cultural and culinary Mexican traditions—the making of tamales. As a kid, I was quite content smearing tamale dough, known as "masa," onto a corn husk "hoja," spooning a dab or two of chile inside, folding it up sloppily, and rushing to the sofa to watch football with my dad and brothers. But now my mother wanted me to learn it all: how to make the dough, how to assess its consistency as the mixer blades spun in a dizzying whirl, and how to create, with great precision, the interior fillings of the tamales themselves: red chile, green chile, and sweet pineapple/raisin. And all of this completely from scratch—not from the line of scrimmage.

I was excited for my parents to see the growing Latina/o community in northern Utah. They had been skeptical. Yet there were signs of these changes all around the town. Latina/os worked at E. F. Miller, the beef-packing company (where immigration raids occurred in 2006), and Icon Fitness, where teens worked beside the adults in their families assembling, piece by piece, exercise toys in the dead of night.

When my parents arrived in Utah, they were initially exasperated. My mother took stock of our kitchen. There was not enough tamale-making gear. So we began making our shopping list, with my mother fretting all along, "Where are we going to find fresh chile serrano, fresh chile pasilla, fresh chile colorado, fresh chile jalapeño, in such a freezing place? And all of your pots are too small. Plus, you need a tamalera!"

A tamalera is a mandatory piece of tamale-making equipment that functions as a giant steamer, and I wasn't certain I could buy one in Utah. You are toast without one, especially if you are making mass quantities of tamales to give away to family and friends, which is the only reason my mom makes tamales. A tamalera resembles an aluminum trash can, including the handles and lid, but it is half the size. It is shiny, almost like silver, with a shelf inside. You fill it with a gallon or two of water, set it to slow boil, and rest and steam your tamales there for a couple of hours.

Soon we had dressed my 89-year-old father in practically all of the clothes he brought to Utah and ventured out into Cache Valley in search of the tamalera. Our first stop was a small Latino market called La Palma. We entered the small store, with the jingle of a bell tied to the door knob. Shelves were stocked with canned beans, chiles, chips, rice, tortillas, hojas, salsas, seasonings, menudo, Mexican CDs, magazines, movie rentals, blankets, dulces (sweets), candles with pictures of Catholic saints on them, vaquero hats, belts and boots (Mexican cowboy style), paletas (Mexican fruit popsicles), and Ibarra hot chocolate (Mexican style). I immediately decided that in the event of Armegeddon, this is where I would take shelter. But most important, in one corner of the room, tucked among crates of bottled Mexican sodas, was a stack of shiny tin tamaleras, giving off a silver glow. Most definitely Mexican style.

"There they are!" I shouted.

"It's a milagro! Tamaleras in Utah!" my mom exclaimed.

"Si, a miracle!" my father added. Once we arrived home, we began the roasting and peeling of chiles for the tamale filling.

"What this town needs next is a tortilleria, an authentic one," my mom added. "It's time. There are lots of Latino families here, que no?"

I said, "Sure mom, when I observe student teachers in the schools, I see more Latino kids every day. But I don't know how the community sees them. One school district administrator told me that there's only one problem with the Latino community—they just don't want to assimilate."

"So how do these teachers teach them?" my mom asked.

"Well, some of the teachers are very good and work with the kids closely. But others ignore them and leave them alone in the back of the room to teach themselves," I said.

"You don't have to have a college degree to see that kids get bored, do poorly in school, and act out if they are ignored or labeled as troublemakers," my mom explained.

My dad put down the chile he was peeling. "Kids need something useful to do and to feel good about themselves."

"Isn't it a teacher's job to draw that something special out of every child?" my mom wondered.

"Well, I think the educators here feel they are colorblind, so with that view, they can be insensitive to the cultures the kids bring to the classroom. That way, they don't have to identify strategies to help them be successful in school. Sometimes the teachers think the parents don't care about their kids," I said.

My mom scraped the masa from the edges of the mixer.

"That's ridiculous. If the people come here to work, and they probably work all sorts of long hours, their priorities are to make the rent, pay their utility bills, get a car, buy food, and avoid getting caught by the INS. Their pay isn't high and they don't have access to health care. Plus, I bet many don't speak English, so how would they feel welcome in the schools? Latino parents trust and respect teachers, in spite of what the teachers are doing and no matter if their children understand what is being taught."

"People aren't used to sudden cultural change in the community, Maria," my dad added.

Looking directly at me, my mother replied, "Well, the change is coming to them. Business in this community invites it. So mija, what are you doing about these problems?"

I couldn't answer her right away. In the world of education, it is one thing to answer to teacher education professors, school administrators, in-service teachers, student teachers, and students' parents. But it is completely intimidating to be held accountable to one's own mother—a mother who can hold a freshly roasted chili in one hand, while turning over another still hot on the griddle.

"Mom, I, I'm teaching my classes, preparing new teachers, and getting grants to help train ESL teachers," I stammered.

"But how are you working with the teachers and parents to learn about each others' cultures and traditions? Maybe then we wouldn't fight so much," she insisted. My mother was always good at finding my Achilles heel. Like singling out a stone from a pile of raw pinto beans before boiling.

"Well, mom, we've tried to have some parent outreach meetings at the high schools, but it is tough. The challenges of learning a new culture and a new language, the unfamiliar system of schooling, different economic and educational backgrounds, and different views about assimilation and acculturation make it tough. The parents are diverse. They're from China, El Salvador, Guatemala, Somalia, Korea, Eastern Europe—all sorts of places. But there are many community and faculty members trying to help, even though we don't always agree among ourselves about how to help."

My mom replied, "It still sounds like you need to be working harder. I don't see that many minority college students at your school. I think that's very important for this community to see. You have a lot of work to do here, mija. You need to get to it and stop wasting time. Now start filling up that tamalera."

Red chile tamales about to be steamed in a tamalera.

Understanding cultural differences means more than learning about cultural holidays and foods. Knowing about Cinco de Mayo in the Mexican American community or about health practices among the Chinese will do little to prepare educators and care-givers for day-to-day experiences with children. In addition, there is no one body of research that will tell educators all they need to know about the cultural groups they will serve.

To approach cultural learning in this static way is ineffective because cultures are always in flux. Culture cannot be taught as though it were a fixed entity. A more productive approach is for care-givers and educators to reflect on and investigate how cultural and linguistic differences may affect student learning—and to be open to changing their instructional strategies and curriculum accordingly.

Finally, if the purpose of education is to prepare all youth for productive and critical participation in a democratic and pluralistic society, then the activities, strategies, and approaches we use must reflect these goals. The cultural and linguistic differences students bring to school, and the ways those differences are perceived, are important factors that must guide teachers' instructional practices. As the student population becomes more diverse, we need to understand, respect, and accept the contributions that cultures bring to American society.

SUMMARY

This chapter offers a different approach to understanding culture. On the one hand, readers might expect this chapter to include a discussion of specific cultures represented in the K–12 classroom. On the other hand, that approach is problematic, given society's tendency to misleadingly collapse the understanding of culture into tangible artifacts, icons, symbols, foods, and stereotypes that are often superficially represented in the media. (For example, there is more to Latina/o cultural history than piñatas and Cinco de Mayo.)

Accordingly, this chapter discusses the shifting nature of all cultures and explores the influences that shape the ongoing cultural shifts that diverse communities experience. It also offers an overview of features relevant to America's own cultural perspectives insofar as they can be distinguished from other cultural perspectives and discourses. Finally, the chapter offers strategies that educators can use to increase cross-cultural understanding in their owns lives both in and out of the classroom.

DISCUSSION QUESTIONS

1. What is culture, and, in particular, what is its relationship to education? Why is the concept so difficult to pinpoint? How do cultures continue to change and shift?

2. Describe the concepts of enculturation and acculturation and their relationship to schooling. How can teachers help students reinforce their cultural identities through culturally relevant curriculum design and pedagogy?

3. What does John Ogbu mean by involuntary minority status and voluntary minority status? Explain. What are the ramifications of this theory for teachers? What are some limitations of this theory?

4. Compare and contrast the features of American cultural viewpoints and values and distinguish them from another cultural perspective.

5. In what ways do the public schools transmit American culture? Describe what you feel are the strengths of this approach. What can U.S. schools do to better educate students about culture diversity, given this age of technology in our global society?

ACTIVITIES

1. Discuss with two or three of your college education professors or public school teachers how they integrate cross-cultural perspectives within their philosophy, curriculum, and pedagogy. Describe your findings.

2. Investigate your own cultural heritage. What histories, traditions, languages, social networks, and institutional memberships have influenced who you are today? How do you think this knowledge will affect your educational philosophy and practice?

3. Learn more about the cultural deficit theory. Who are the key researchers behind the theory? What were their early findings? How have their views about cultural deficit theory been challenged today?

4. Create three or four concept maps in which you identify key themes or content-area-specific topics that reflect cross-cultural curriculum approaches. Also identify key websites and primary sources you will use to help your students expand their knowledge.

The First Amendment Center

http://www.firstamendmentcenter.org/rel_liberty/publicschools/Index.aspx

This webpage provides comprehensive research on First Amendment issues and topics, including a focus on religion and education for teachers. The site is operated by the First Amendment Center, at Vanderbilt University.

Multicultural Pavilion

http://www.edchange.org/multicultural/index.htm

This is another comprehensive website that offers lesson plans, classroom and community outreach strategies, ideas concerning social justice classroom projects, downloadable handouts, and links to other sites relevant to diversity education.

USC Center for Multilingual, Multicultural Research

http://www.usc.edu/dept/education/CMMR/home.html

This webpage provides a base for those interested in multilingual education, English as a second language, and foreign language instruction; multicultural education and related areas; and the opportunity to come together for research and program collaboration. The website includes research sources on diversity education, full text publications, teacher training information, and links to public service organizations and initiatives.

Utah State University, Department of Secondary Education, ELS/Bilingual and Diversity Education Websites

http://secondaryeducation.usu.edu/esl/resources.php

This site includes a number of content-area-based websites relevant to multicultural and diversity education. Ideas for instructional strategies in such areas as math, science, social studies, and language arts can be found at this site.

REFERENCES

Au, K. (1993). *Literacy instruction in multicultural settings*. Fort Worth: Harcourt Brace Jovanovich, 1993.

Au, K., & Raphael, T. E. (2000). Equity and literacy in the next millennium. *Reading Research Quarterly, 35,* 170–188.

Banks, J. (2003). *Teaching strategies for ethnic studies*. Boston: Allyn & Bacon.

Baratz, S., & Baratz, J. (1970). Early childhood intervention: The social science base for institutional racism. *Harvard Educational Review 40*(1), 29–50.

Fordham, S., & Ogbu, J. (1986). Black students' school success: Coping with the burden of acting white. *Urban Review 18*(3), 176–206.

Geertz, C. (1973). *The interpretation of cultures*. New York: Basic Books.

McIntosh, P. (n.d.) White privilege: Unpacking the invisible knapsack. Retrieved June 7, 2001, from http://seamonkey.ed.asu.edu/~mcisaac/emc598ge/unpacking.html

Nieto, S. (2004). *Affirming diversity*. Boston: Longman.

Ogbu, J. (2003). Understanding cultural diversity and learning. In J. Banks & C. Banks (Eds.), *Handbook of research on multicultural education*. New York: Simon & Schuster.

Pai, Y., & Adler, S. (2001). *Cultural foundations of education*. New Jersey: Prentice-Hall.

Sieber, R. T., & Gordon, A. J. (1981). *Children and their organizations: Investigations in American culture*. Boston: Hall.

Spindler, G. (1973). Anthropology and education: An overview. In G. Spindler (Ed.), *Cultural relevance and educational issues*. Boston: Little, Brown.

Spindler, G. (1993). Education in a transforming America. In F. A. J. Ianni, G. D. Spindler, & E. Storey (Eds), *Education and culture*. New York: Holt, Rinehart & Winston.

Wink, J. (2004). *Critical pedagogy: Notes from the real world*. Boston: Allyn and Bacon.

Wolcott, H. (1991). Propriospect and the acquisition of culture. *Anthropology and Education Quarterly, 22*(3), 251–273.

Teaching English Language Learners: Bilingual and English as a Second Language Efforts

FIRST PERSON

Success Story: Vicki and Ruben's Sixth-Grade Year

Ruben and Vicki were phenomenal students, but I didn't know it the first week of my first year teaching in San Jose, California. "This is just like *Dangerous Minds*!" (a 1995 movie about a white teacher who encounters challenges in an urban classroom) announced Vicki, a tall and outgoing student, to her fellow sixth-graders. I was struggling to gain the attention of the energetic class that was skillfully taking advantage of my inexperience. It was English Day, when everyone was to do their best to speak English in specific subjects. Some students were quiet, struggling to make sense of the unstructured classroom banter in English. Other students were speaking Spanish to their friends. I later learned that students who spoke Spanish during English time were usually translating for a peer who had just arrived from Mexico or another Spanish-speaking country.

Ruben, normally an intensely focused boy, was asleep with his head on his desk as I passed out materials and described a math activity. I was shocked and paralyzed into inaction. Why would a child fall asleep in the middle of a fun math game? At the end of the day, I asked Ruben why he was sleeping in class. He explained matter-of-factly that he wasn't sleeping much since his aunt's family moved into his family's small apartment. His space to sleep was the kitchen floor, which wasn't very comfortable. I soon came to understand that Ruben's Spanish was much stronger than his English, so on top of his new sleeping difficulties, English Day was quite taxing for him.

As Ruben continued to work hard in acquiring English, Vicki struggled to reclaim her Spanish. Just like Ruben, Vicki was born a native speaker of Spanish, but she had been placed in English-only classrooms in the primary grades and had not sufficiently developed her reading and writing skills in Spanish. Her

CHAPTER OBJECTIVES

- Readers will gain an introductory understanding of the variety of programs available to English language learners (ELLs) and their probable outcomes.

- Readers will identify and describe the major historical turns in language policy and practice in the United States.

- Readers will identify their own beliefs about English language learners.

- Readers will understand the difference between language learning and language acquisition and how students acquire language.

- Readers will identify the different strategies and aims of the major program types.

- Readers will gain an awareness of the strategies and challenges in assessment, identification, and placement of ELLs in school programs.

- Readers will understand the complexities and challenges that ELLs face related to their identities in schools.

This chapter was coauthored with Tricia Gallagher-Geurtsen of Cutting Edge Education.

goal was to be able to read the Bible fluently to abuela, her grandmother, when she visited her in Mexico next summer. Vicki, well liked by all and displaying high self-esteem, excelled in all academic areas in English and became student body president. She assisted the principal by translating from English to Spanish at school assemblies.

As the school year progressed and students developed both their Spanish and English literacy skills, I encouraged students to teach their peers about their real lives outside of school. This aspect of the classroom curriculum helped students learn about one another's heritage and changing cultures. One assignment asked students to create a Culture Bag. On the outside of the bag, they were to paste pictures that represented "who they were" that people knew about them. Then, inside the bag, they were to bring objects from home that showed "who they were" that people probably didn't know about them and symbols representing where they came from. The Culture Bag presentations were special because only one student presented each week, and a book was compiled and bound for the presenter, each page a response from one of the presenter's peers about what that person had learned about the presenter.

I remember Vicki's presentation well. She stood in front of the class with a bag on which she had pasted pictures and written the names of rock and mariachi bands that she liked, family members and friends, and foods she enjoyed. Vicki opened her bag and uncharacteristically hesitated before pulling out a leather hair barrette with her full name, Victoria, branded into the leather. Vicki found her voice and explained that she got the barrette in Mexico when she visited her abuela, whom she missed very much. She said that it reminded her of her family and the fun they had each summer when she visited and that she couldn't wait to return this summer. The class listened attentively and then asked Vicki where her family was from in Mexico. This started a discussion of the different Mexican states of origin of many of the students in the class.

Ruben's presentation was one of the most powerful moments I have experienced in a classroom. Ruben explained the pictures and words on the exterior of his bag in English and then asked if he could speak Spanish to describe the inside of his bag. Although it was an English Day, I said that it would be fine. Ruben placed both hands over his heart, looked up to the far corner of the ceiling, his thin, small body now more apparent, and began to sing. The class was spellbound, and a few students began to smirk in slight sixth-grader-style embarrassment and recognition of the Mexican ballad. It was a long song about love, betrayal, and heartache. As the students warmed up to the event, a few called out gritos (emotional cries) at appropriate moments, in response to the song. When Ruben finished, the students applauded enthusiastically and, all pre-teen embarrassment temporarily transformed into cultural pride, gave him an uproarious standing ovation.

Both Ruben and Vicki finished the year with an A in both Spanish and English. They enrolled in honors courses in junior high. On a sunny afternoon the following year, Vicki returned to my classroom to catch me up on her family, to recount her accomplishments in junior high, and to thank me for being her teacher.

Ruben and Vicki's successful journeys in school as English language learners (ELLs) are examples of the positive educational outcomes that can be achieved with particular programs designed for ELLs. Given research-based program designs and teaching strategies, students have the opportunity to enjoy the benefits of becoming bilingual, bicultural, and biliterate, as Vicki and Ruben did. There are many routes to follow when educating students who may want and need to learn another language. Each of those paths leads to different educational outcomes. And to complicate the issue, there are myriad different programs and variants within each type of program.

PAUSE & REFLECT

What surprised you about Vicki's and Ruben's stories? Explain why.

How often and under what circumstances should teachers break their own rules about teaching (such as allowing Ruben to speak Spanish on English Day)?

Different Roads to Different Outcomes: Choices in Language Education

How did schools get to the point where there are so many options for English language learners (ELLs)? This chapter will help to unravel the different programs. As a starting point, consider three drastically different cases:

- Your grade school teacher locks you in a classroom closet or asks you to kneel on the floor as punishment for speaking your first language, the language your parents taught you (Soto, 1997).

- Your parents came to the United States from Vietnam, speaking only Vietnamese, when you were 10 years old. You worked hard in your **sheltered English** classes from fourth grade through high school. You now speak, read, and write English very well and even understand a little bit of spoken Vietnamese, although you can't read or write it (Crawford, 1991; Krashen & Biber, 1988; Ramírez, Yuen, Ramey, & Pasta, 1991).

- You finish the sixth-grade reading, writing, and speaking English and another language at or above the sixth-grade level. And, as a bonus, on tests you outscore your classmates who speak only English (Hakuta & Diaz, 1985; Ramírez et al., 1991).

The scenarios above reflect the results of widely divergent strategies that educators have utilized over time when teaching ELLs in our nation's schools. This chapter will introduce the complex and highly controversial story of the schooling of speakers of minority languages in our country. You will learn a bit about the history, politics, law, and classroom approaches related to the educating of ELLs.

It may surprise you to learn that, although such abuse may not occur often anymore, the children in the first scenario were punished for not speaking English in our country's schools in contemporary times (Soto, 1997). Although there are many excellent and decent school programs for minority-language speakers (MLSs) that I will discuss later, there are weaker programs that include deficit model programs, linguistic and cultural assimilation, untested programs, and, unfortunately, outright linguicist treatment (Genesee, 1994; Skutnabb-Kangas, 1991). As you will see, the strategies and programs developed to support the linguistic and cultural needs of ELLs have vastly improved. However, there is much work to be done to make exemplary programs available to all ELLs.

The second scenario describes the probable outcome if, as an ELL, you took most of your classes from teachers who knew how to specialize, or *shelter,* their curriculum and to teach in such a way that it would make sense to you in English. For example, in kindergarten, a teacher might teach you the seasons by singing a song and holding up pictures of weather in different seasons. Or, your high school history teacher might introduce a reading assignment in your history textbook by teaching you difficult vocabulary and then, after you had read the material, might review the lesson with you by comparing it to a film with the same topic. These teachers would be *sheltering* the English language for you but still teaching you the same subjects as your native-English-speaking peers. That way, you wouldn't get behind in your school subjects as you were learning English. The downside of this type of program is that without a bilingual Vietnamese-English program, you would probably lose your ability to speak Vietnamese and not learn to read or write it unless your parents were able to find the time to teach you at home or had the means to send you to a special Vietnamese-language school. Some families are satisfied with this option, because they are most concerned about their children learning English and less concerned about their remaining familiar with their native language.

Finally, the third scenario described above is what researchers have shown results for youth who are students in a well-designed **dual-language** or **two-way bilingual program**. This means that if you were a native Spanish speaker, then from kindergarten through sixth grade you spent a large portion of your day reading and learning in Spanish and another smaller, but progressively larger, portion of your day learning in English. By the end of the sixth grade, you were considered a *balanced bilingual* and gained the benefits of balanced bilingualism: scoring higher on tests than monolingual peers and being bilingual, biliterate, and bicultural.

Why, then, don't we have more well-designed dual-language or two-way bilingual programs in our country? There are a variety of reasons: lack of funding, lack of or insufficient numbers of well-trained bilingual teachers who speak the needed languages, small populations of ELLs in less common languages, and policies that prohibit such programs. But, as we will see in the next section, the larger roadblocks stem from particular ideologies, tumultuous politics, and inattentiveness to research-based information.

PAUSE & REFLECT

Why do you think there are so many different programs for English language learners in schools? How do public perceptions of these programs blur our understanding of these distinct educational approaches to the process of language acquisition?

The Story: History, Politics, and Law

In order to imagine how multilingual this land used to be, a starting point is precolonial times in what is now the United States, when it is estimated that 250 to 1,000 Native American languages were spoken (Sherzer, 1992, & Grosjean, 1982, in

Ovando, Collier, & Combs, 2003). Due to the process of **language extinction,** whereby languages die with the last speaker because more aggressive language groups have imposed their language and culture on the minority-language group, there currently are only 187 Native American languages, with a half million speakers in the United States and Canada. Only 20 percent of those remaining languages are being learned by children (Ovando et al., 2003; Nettle & Romaine, 2000; http://www.native-languages.org/).

One example of an **endangered language** is Cherokee. In other words, Cherokee is in danger of becoming extinct. The story of the Cherokee language is typical of the story of all Native American languages (*Native Languages of the Americas,* 2005). Whatever gains Native Americans made in transmitting their language and culture, Europeans in power repeatedly thwarted their efforts. For example, in 1828 the Cherokee people published the first newspaper prepared in a Native American language. However, President Andrew Jackson's policy forced the Cherokees to leave their land in the 1830s. One-third died on their way to Oklahoma in what came to be known as the Trail of Tears.

Those Cherokee who resettled began **bilingual education** (teaching in two languages; see Table 11.1) and achieved a higher level of English literacy level than surrounding populations of whites. But in 1871, the U.S. Bureau of Indian Affairs mandated that all Indian school instruction be conducted in English only. In 1879, federal officials began taking Native American children away from their parents and forcing them to live in boarding schools, where they were punished for speaking their native languages and were taught exclusively in English. Also during this time period, campaigns led by the Bureau of Indian Affairs promoting Americanization and "civilization" began. Much later, in 1934, Indian Commissioner John Collier overturned the English-only policy and tried to institute teaching in native languages, but teachers in these schools defied his order and continued to forbid the children to speak languages other than English.

A Surprisingly Multilingual History

Gradually, as European colonists began populating this land and imposing their cultural and linguistic systems on Native Americans, European languages such as English, German, and French began to dominate in the governing classes. Although we may imagine that English has always been our nation's predominant language of communication, this has not always been the case. In the 1740s, because of anti-British sentiment, Congress urged the *banning of English* and called for replacing it with Hebrew, German, French, or Greek as the official language of the colonies (Crawford, 1991). However, it is true that our government has time and again encouraged and even mandated English instruction and the assimilation of "American values" for English language learners in public schools.

Although bilingual schools and foreign language classes were offered in the United States throughout the nineteenth century, "linguistic assimilation was the ultimate goal for immigrant students" (Crawford, 1991, p. 21). **Linguistic and cultural assimilation** meant that new immigrants were expected to learn and speak English and learn to act "American" even if it meant losing their native language and culture. There was a fear that if Americans spoke different languages and held on to their different cultures, it would tear our country apart.

This sentiment was shared by William Torrey Harris, St. Louis school superintendent in the 1870s and later the U.S. Commissioner of Education, who thought that schools should "Americanize" ELLs. Further, in a surge of nativism in the late nineteenth century, the American Protective Association succeeded in having English declared the sole language to be used for instruction in public and private schools. Although this measure was repealed, after the recommendation was made German-language schooling and bilingual education declined. Policymakers believed that by controlling the language of people who did not speak English, they might "Americanize" them.

In 1900, with new groups of immigrants arriving, fear of difference, or *xenophobia*, reigned. "In 1906, Congress passed the first federal language law of any kind, an English-speaking requirement for naturalization" (Crawford, 1991, p. 22). Similarly, in an effort to bind Americans together, English was presented as a naturally superior language after the Spanish-American War. The United States began mandating English-only instruction in its colonies of Puerto Rico, Hawaii, and the Philippines.

The same colonial treatment was applied to immigrants, as then President Theodore Roosevelt exhorted, "We have room for but one language in this country and that is the English language" (Crawford, 1991). During and following World War I, restrictions were placed on the teaching and speaking of the German language; one town even fined its residents for speaking German on the street. By the 1930s, bilingual education was almost nonexistent, and the study of foreign languages had declined.

Students march for immigrant and language rights at Bayfront Park in Miami.

Although based on the seemingly benign intent of building a single American identity, this discouragement of the use of other languages resulted in inequitable treatment of English language learners throughout U.S. history. The following are two recent examples. Soto (1997) tells the story of "Steel Town," Pennsylvania, where an award-winning bilingual program was dismantled by the school board in 1993 and replaced with an English-only, "sink or swim" program. A city ordinance was also proposed that would allow local merchants to post a "Blue E" in their windows and charge extra for customers who spoke with an accent or used poor English. It was claimed that the extra charge was justified by the extra paperwork or expense supposedly involved. In her ethnography, Soto (1997) documents the regular and pervasive discrimination and hostility directed at the Puerto Rican Americans living in this community, who made up the majority of the participants in the bilingual program.

Similarly, the history of the education of ELLs in New York City is marked by inequities. "In 1963, the city's public schools awarded 331 academic diplomas to Puerto Ricans, representing no more than *one percent* of the total Puerto Rican enrollment" (emphasis added) (Crawford, 1991). In 2001, the New York City Board of Education (BOE) revised its policy for ELLs to focus more intensely on learning English. The policy requires all ELLs not enrolled in **dual-language programs** (see Table 11.1 for a description of dual-language programs) to develop English proficiency in three years and exit their bilingual and **English as a second language (ESL)** program. This policy ignores the research that says it takes five to seven years to develop **Cognitive Academic Linguistic Proficiency (CALP)** (the ability to speak about abstract concepts) in a second language (Cummins, 1989). The BOE ignored research and implemented a policy that pushed ELLs to learn English too quickly, effectively providing them with an inferior education.

Changing Policies but an Unchanging Focus on English

United States federal educational policymakers have also ignored research and have inconsistently supported children in learning two languages. Although many Americans, when considering increasing global interdependence, believe that children should be taught to communicate in two or more languages and cultures, the United States government has not mandated or supported such efforts on a wide scale. It is inequitable that there is consistent support of bilingualism or multilingualism for native speakers of English but not always for English language learners.

Since the writing of the National Defense and Education Act (NDEA) in 1958, U.S. education policymakers have consistently funded foreign-language classes that largely serve *native English speakers*. This contrasts sharply with bilingual education funding and policy goals for ELLs that vacillate between focusing on monolingual English fluency and targeting bilingual fluency in the child's native language and English (Gallagher-Geurtsen, 2001).

One of the most challenging periods in the story of educating ELLs took place in the 1960s and 1970s when **deficit model programs** were used to teach ELLs. Basically, researchers began to tell teachers that ELLs were genetically and linguistically inferior. ELLs were said to come from homes where there was a lack of language, structure, and morals. Of course, deficit models have a racist and linguicist foundation and serve only to devalue children who grow up with rich life experiences that are different from—not lesser than—those of white, middle-class, native English-speaking children (Genesee, 1994; Ovando et al., 2003). For example, a student who recently arrived in my classroom from Mexico may come to my classroom knowing how to raise, care for, and sell sheep, knowledge acquired while working on a ranch in Mexico, but may be less familiar with how to choose a film to see and then pay for an afternoon at an American movie theater. There is no reason for this child's funds of knowledge to be devalued.

The Law: What We Must Provide English Language Learners

Although the story of the education of ELLs may seem to change as the political winds shift, educators must now follow laws that aim to protect ELLs in schools. There are various federal laws and many court cases that address the education of ELLs, but there is one law you should know about and one court case as well: the Bilingual Education Act (BEA) and *Lau v. Nichols*, which was argued before the Supreme Court in 1974. The BEA of 1968 was the first time that our nation recognized that ELLs have special educational needs. The federal funding that the BEA offered schools was to be spent on programs and teachers that were helping children living in poverty who spoke little or no English (Ovando et al., 2003). As we have noted, over the years the BEA policy changed, sometimes funding programs that developed two languages and sometimes funding programs that only helped to develop English.

Similar to the original goals of the BEA, *Lau v. Nichols* established that a group of native Chinese-speaking children in San Francisco schools were not receiving equal educational opportunity because they were given their lessons in English, a language they (unlike their native English-speaking peers) did not understand. A whole series of regulations followed that ultimately gave the Office of Civil Rights (OCR) the power to check up on schools to make sure they were providing ELLs an education equal to that provided to their native English-speaking peers (Ovando et al., 2003). Basically, the regulation says that schools may not discriminate against ELLs and must meet their educational needs. Schools can provide an equal education to ELLs by providing programs, materials, and teachers that help ELL overcome any language barriers. There are many different ways to do this, and we will consider some of them later. Before talking about programs, however, it is important to examine how we think and feel about ELLs.

PAUSE & REFLECT

How do you think our current policies about educating ELLs might be different if, after Europeans had arrived here, our government leaders had consistently promoted the use of Native American languages? How do you think newly arrived immigrants felt in English-only classrooms in the 1870s and how do you think they feel today?

Ideologies: How Do We Think About English Language Learners?

For educators to work toward a just society that treats all linguistic groups equitably, we must understand the privileges we have. Because standard English is seen as a cultural norm in schools (that is, without really thinking about the benefits and costs, we expect all schoolwork to be in English), a student's human worth may be inadvertently measured by how much standard English he or she can produce (Gallego & Hollingsworth, 2000). For example, a teacher may unconsciously think a student who speaks better English than her classmates is smarter than her classmates. However, her classmates may speak Spanish at more advanced levels than she is able to speak English. Ignoring the meaning of language—and the social norms and practices that educators may not recognize that language carries—can translate into real damage to student self-esteem and success in school. That's why it's important to imagine "walking in the shoes" of ELLs.

It's impossible to fully understand what it's like to be someone else, much less someone who grew up speaking a language and living a culture that's different from those of most people around them. But one powerful way to begin to understand the lives of ELLs is to try to recognize and acknowledge the privileges that you have if you grew up speaking standard English. Linguistic and cultural privileges may be tucked away in the unconscious assumptions of native speakers of standard English. It is important to locate and think about some of the **linguistic privileges** we have. For example, most native speakers of standard English can confidently make the following statements:

- I do not feel the need to make my name more like "everyone else's" by, for example, anglicizing Beatriz to Betty or Estalex to Stanley.

- I can go to my child's school and be clearly understood when I express myself about the needs of my child.

- I can speak my native language and interact using my native culture at school and at work without being considered suspicious or secretive.

- I can easily take classes in my native language and culture while I learn a second language and culture.

- I can learn my first language and culture first and my second language and culture second, and so on.

- I can go to a job interview and not worry that my accent will work against my being hired.
- I do not feel the need to eliminate my accent.
- My friends and family are in awe of my bilingualism or biculturalism.
- Most of the time, I feel that I understand what my teacher says and does.
- Learning a second language and culture will be an asset to my identity and economic future.
- When I take a standardized test, I can take it in my stronger language and feel confident that my score will fairly represent what I know.

ELLs do not always have these privileges in school and society. These students daily enter and engage in classrooms that are geared to the instruction of native speakers of standard English. The cost of ignoring the extra hurdles that ELLs must jump can be devastating.

Considering that high school dropout rates are higher for those 16- to 24-year-olds who spoke a language other than English at home than for those who spoke English at home, educators need to be deeply concerned (*The Condition of Education 1997*, 1997). One way to help students achieve is to assist them in learning the dominant language and culture of schooling (English), while maintaining their own native languages and cultures.

However, providing a high-quality and equitable education for ELLs requires more than a focus on language learning. It is important to understand our belief systems and how we act unconsciously toward students who are learning standard English. Lisa Delpit reminds us, "We do not really see through our eyes or hear through our ears, but through our beliefs" (1995, p. 46). Therefore, our beliefs about standard English and ELLs are implicated.

Educators need to be aware of their belief systems about the linguistic and cultural ways of knowing of different groups and must not privilege one over another. There are real consequences when educators do not become aware of the linguistic privileges of native speakers of standard English. For example, a teacher may unconsciously judge students less academically competent because their test scores represent their efforts in their weaker, second language. Students may malign or disregard their home language and culture. Teachers may punish students because they did not understand what the teachers said or what they meant to say. Students may lose their first language and become monolingual English speakers instead of bilingual speakers. A parent may not come to a parent-teacher conference because there are no translators provided by the district. A teacher "without an accent" (we all have accents depending on who's listening) may get hired in preference to a teacher "with an accent."

Just like racism, **linguicism** is a pervasive problem in schools and in society. Skutnabb-Kangas (1991) defines linguicism as "ideologies and structures which are used to legitimate, effectuate and reproduce an unequal division of power and resources (both material and non-material) between groups which are defined on the basis of language" (p. 383). An example of linguicism is native speakers of English acting as though non-native English speakers' languages are of less value (Skutnabb-Kangas, 1991). When educators recognize the worth of all languages and acknowledge that all students' cultures are a valuable part of our country's linguistic and cultural mosaic, all students in schools benefit. They will have positive attitudes toward their own and their peers' diverse languages and cultures as we can begin to eradicate linguicism.

PAUSE & REFLECT

What is linguicism? How does linguicism inform people's beliefs about English-only movements? In what ways do you have linguistic privileges? Name at least two ways in which you benefited from your knowledge of standard English today.

The Theories: How Should We Teach English Language Learners?

How do people learn a second language? If we can answer this question, we will know how to best teach ELLs. However, the answer is complex and changes as researchers learn more and more. Different theories have been proposed about how we actually learn our first (L1) and second languages (L2). A powerful way to think about how people acquire a language in school is the Prism model (Thomas & Collier, 1997). The Prism model takes into consideration our linguistic, social and cultural, academic, and cognitive worlds in describing how we learn a first and second language. Each of these worlds plays an important role in how we learn language: Am I accepted or teased by classmates? Am I comfortable learning in a group setting? Do I know my first language well enough to begin learning a second language effectively? Does my teacher teach academic subjects through the second language or teach language isolated from academic subjects? When working with ELLs, educators need to carefully consider all of these questions in the context of the different "worlds" identified in the Prism model.

When considering the linguistic world, it is important first to understand the difference between language *learning* and language *acquisition*. Language learning is what we do when we study a bilingual dictionary, repeat isolated sentences in our second language, or copy vocabulary from a book. Language acquisition occurs when we actually gain more language (be it our first or our second language). What would you rather do: *learn* a language or *acquire* it? To acquire a language, you have to *understand* the messages given to you in that language. Here's an example that should help you see the difference: If we had lunch together and I held up an apple in front of you and said with a smile, "*Me gusta la manzana*" [I like the apple], then when I said "la manzana," you might acquire the word *apple* in Spanish and know what it meant.

On the other hand, if I gave you a piece of paper and had you write *la manzana*, and repeat *manzana*, you might learn how to spell it and maybe even what it meant, but you would not have *acquired* the word, nor would you be likely to be able to use it in daily life. Thus the goal for teachers is to get children *acquiring* language by giving students meaningful messages. If students don't understand what their teachers are telling or showing them, they will not acquire language. Therefore, when schoolchildren understand what is going on around them, they are gaining more and more language (first and/or second) every day at school, without necessarily being aware that they are doing so. Children are able to speak their first language because they have *used* it in meaningful settings (such as sitting at lunch with their dad and talking about and looking at an apple), not because it has been explicitly taught to them.

Another important aspect of understanding the linguistic world of language-minority (LM) speakers is to consider the crucial role of their L1 in learning their

L2. Students who have a strong foundation in speaking, reading, and writing in their L1 before they begin to learn English will learn English more rapidly and will achieve better academically than students who have a weak foundation in their first language and/or are exited into English-only settings prematurely. Finally, to learn a second language, students must be motivated to learn it, must have many opportunities to interact socially in the target language, and must receive high-quality teaching for 5 to 10 years as they learn the new language (Ovando et al., 2003).

Just as important as the linguistic world of ELLs are their social and cultural worlds. Included in these worlds are influences such as socioeconomic status, past schooling, attitudes of school and community toward languages (which can range from racism and linguicism to acceptance of different backgrounds). All of these factors and more help to determine how well and how quickly, for example, newly arrived immigrants, war refugees, second-generation immigrants, and migrant workers will learn English and whether they will retain their native languages and cultures. Therefore, it is imperative that educators get to know their students and their families well through home visits, interviews, parent classroom visits, and surveys. We cannot meet the needs of the wide variety of ELLs who populate our classrooms without knowing who they are and recognizing the rich knowledge and experiences that they bring to our schools and communities.

And finally, we have to consider the cognitive world of ELLs—what happens in the brain. Among the research findings most applicable to language learning for ELLs is that when acquiring an L2, we use our L1 to compare linguistic features to help us. We also acquire language by using learning strategies that we are taught. These strategies can help us acquire an L2 faster and more effectively (Ovando et al., 2003). The cognitive world of students, as well as their linguistic, social, cultural, and academic worlds, should be taken into consideration when designing programs for ELLs. There are many programs available to ELLs in our country, but few of those programs consider all the needs of ELLs.

Connecting to the Cengage Learning Video Cases

Bilingual Education: An Elementary Two-Way Immersion Program
Watch the Cengage Learning video case entitled "Bilingual Education: An Elementary Two-Way Immersion Program." Consider viewing question 1.

Video Case Study
1. How do the teachers Sarah Bartels-Marrero and Sheila Donehan work together closely to provide the students with content-area instruction (in this case, mathematical concepts) in two different languages?
2. What are the strengths of the two-way bilingual method?
3. What might be some of its shortcomings?

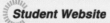
Student Website

The Programs: A Largely Monolingual Tale

Although in the present day there are a variety of programmatic choices for ELLs, the majority of these programs have a specific target: English language acquisition (see Table 11.1). Only a small percentage of ELLs attend programs that target bilingualism as a goal. Grinberg and Saavedra (2000) explain that although the early goals of bilingual education were to demand civil and educational rights for ELLs, both bilingual and ESL (English as a second language) programs now focus largely on English language development "in order to justify [bilingual/ESL programs'] existence as legitimate in a political climate reluctant to support diversity, multiculturalism, and different points of view" (p. 430). Snow and Hakuta (cited in Crawford, 1991) concur: "The bilingual education initiatives that were taken in the sixties have certainly made the transition easier for [ELLs]. But the bottom line of all these programs has been an almost single-minded interest in the extent and the efficiency of English proficiency development" (p. 164). Although English-only acquisition is the goal for most of the programs, a variety of programs are being utilized in schools. Table 11.1 offers an overview of the differences among them.

Sheltered Programs

Sheltered English, briefly introduced in the manzana example above, is known by many names (such as SDAIE, structured immersion, and content-based ESL) but is basically a classroom where the teaching and the classroom materials are in English but are "sheltered" through language that is made meaningful with props, graphic organizers, demonstrations, body language, drama, and the like. For example, a sheltered high school science lesson on photosynthesis might include actual experiments comparing plants that are grown on the windowsill in the sun with plants that are grown in the closet. Discussing the appearance of each plant, the teacher might speak slowly but naturally, reviewing vocabulary and referring to a chart that describes with drawings the process of photosynthesis. In sheltered classrooms, academic content is taught in a meaningful context—something that should happen in *all* classrooms.

Teachers in true sheltered classrooms either have received special preparation in how language is acquired or team-plan and teach with an ESL teacher. Sheltered classrooms are appropriate for all children, although they are sometimes inappropriately treated as remedial classrooms where ELLs are segregated. When presented correctly, sheltered content is not watered-down or remedial and is appropriate and high-quality instruction for *all* students (Ovando et al., 2003).

Pullout ESL Programs

The term **pullout ESL** refers to the practice of removing, or *pulling out*, ELLs from their regular classroom(s) and bringing them to a special classroom for part of the day with other ELLs to receive instruction in English. What happens in this special room varies widely. But pullout ESL classes have the worst track record in teaching students English and are only one step above schools doing absolutely nothing (which is illegal) to teach ELLs English. Troublingly, ESL pullout is the most widely used model in the United States *and* the most expensive (Chambers & Parrish, 1992; Crawford, 1997; Thomas & Collier, 1997). Usually pullout ESL teachers are not able to plan their lessons to match what is happening in the mainstream class(es), so students get behind in their subjects. Recently, there have been efforts in some schools to *push-in* ESL teachers so that they can help make what the mainstream teacher is presenting meaningful to students learning English.

TABLE 11.1 Characteristics of the Major Program Models for English Language Learners

Language(s) of Instruction	Typical Program Names	Native Language of Language-Minority Students	Language of Content Instruction	Language of Arts Instruction	Linguistic Goal of Program
A. English and the native language	1. Two-way bilingual education or Bilingual immersion or Dual-language immersion	Ideally, 50% English-speaking and 50% limited English proficiency (LEP) students share same native language.	Both English and the native language	English and the native language	Bilingualism
	2. Late-exit bilingual education or Developmental bilingual education	All students speak the same native language.	Both. Mostly the native language is used at first, and instruction through English increases as students gain proficiency.	English and the native language	Bilingualism
	3. Early-exit bilingual education or Transitional bilingual education	All students speak the same native language.	Both at the beginning, with quick progression to all or most instruction through English	English. Native-language skills are developed only to assist transition to English.	English acquisition and rapid transfer into English-only classroom
B. English	1. Sheltered English or 2. Specially designed academic instruction in English (SDAIE) or 3. Structured immersion or 4. Content-based ESL	Students can share the same native language or have different language backgrounds.	English adapted to the students' proficiency level and supplemented by gestures and visual aids	English	English acquisition
	5. Pull-out ESL	Students can share the same native language or have different language backgrounds; students may be grouped with all ages and grade levels.	English adapted to the students' proficiency level and supplemented by gestures and visual aids	English. Students leave their English-only classroom to spend part of their day receiving ESL instruction.	English acquisition

Source: Antunez (2001).

Bilingual Education

English acquisition is a primary goal in much of the three major approaches to teaching ELLs in public schools (sheltered, ESL, and bilingual programs), as well as in the multitude of variations that fall under each of these umbrella terms. For example, under bilingual education, there are both subtractive and additive programs. The goal of subtractive programs, or *transitional bilingual education*, is for the ELLs to learn English, subtracting their L1. The less common approach is the additive program, which intends to *add* an L2 (English in the United States) to the L1, while supporting literacy in both. Some additive programs are combined with other programs to meet the perceived needs of the ELLs. For example, most bilingual programs include an intensive English instruction period classified as ESL. These programs focus on a particular language focus, without including an orientation to the *cultures* of ELLs.

An exception is a two-way or dual-language bilingual program where ELLs and native English speakers are designated linguistic and cultural models for one another in the same classroom. In this model, both groups engage in both languages and cultures. The benefits of a two-way program extend beyond producing bilingual, biliterate, and bicultural youth. In one such two-way program, both the native speakers of Spanish and the native speakers of English reported (Center for Applied Linguistics, 1994) that they

- Feel confident about their ability to teach both English and Spanish to their peers,
- Apply no ethnic or linguistic bias in their choice of close friends,
- Perceive [Latinos] as they would other Americans, and
- Favor bilingual classes over monolingual classes.

However, two-way programs are small in number. The majority of programs orient ELLs to the English language *and* to white, middle-class values and neglect the child's personal lived realities. The majority of these bilingual programs fall under the category of **transitional bilingual education**.

The goal of transitional programs is to *transition* students from their L1 to English. *Early-exit* bilingual programs are designed for students to exit from the bilingual program "early," which usually means sometime between the first and third grades—not nearly enough time for students to learn a second language. In *late-exit* bilingual programs, the goal is for students to exit from the bilingual program in the upper elementary grades (between the fourth and sixth grades). Students are more academically successful in late-exit programs than in early-exit programs because they have had more time to build, in their L1, a foundation for learning effectively.

However, ELLs are most academically successful when they participate in well-designed two-way or dual-language programs (Ramírez et al., 1991; Thomas & Collier, 1997). When parents, researchers, youth, and community members are better informed about the benefits of bilingualism and strong models of bilingual education, they may be able to convince policymakers to focus funding on exemplary programs such as the two-way model.

PAUSE & REFLECT

If you had to send your children to one of the programs described above, where would you send them? Explain why. What do you think are the strengths and shortcomings of each of these approaches?

From PRESERVICE to PRACTICE

Language Gains, Language Losses

Being bicultural and bilingual has affected my life tremendously, in spite of my English-only educational background. Although I experienced a certain amount of success in school, that success entailed a sense of cultural loss. And I have come to recognize, over the years, the impact that **linguicism** had on my parents and grandparents as they tried to establish a life for my generation. At the heart of this process has been the struggle of our family to keep the Spanish language at the center of our lives.

The Los Angeles community of the 1960s and 1970s, where my family settled, had a burgeoning economy and was a safe haven for the growing number of Latinos. A Mexican social network flourished there, as well as products, restaurants, and Catholic churches. People could speak Spanish, they were not afraid of policies established in the workplace, and social services were readily available.

While my three brothers and I were growing up in Los Angeles, however, speaking and writing Spanish were things that we did only inside our sun-dried rented house or outside with the kids down the street. Spanish was certainly not welcome in the schools. Although I attended a public school whose student population was exclusively Latina/o and African American, we students never learned about who we were, what languages we spoke, how our cultures had evolved, or what role models existed in our history or community. To speak Spanish at school resulted in harsh warnings from our monolingual teachers.

When we did speak Spanish in the hallways, on the athletic field, or during spare moments in the classroom, the content of those conversations was not intended to antagonize the teachers. Most of the time, the topics ranged from "What's for lunch?" and "Who's the new boy in room nine?" to "When do we turn in our homework?"

It soon became apparent that Spanish was not welcome at school and that my teachers did not admire skill in speaking Spanish. When we visited my Spanish-speaking grandparents, I began to resist speaking to them in their language. At home, I would devastate my mother by declaring, "I don't want to speak that language anymore. We're not supposed to." I

can still see the tears spring into my mom's eyes and her face redden with anger. I missed out on learning from my grandparents, who spoke only Spanish.

In high school, my Mexican friends sneaked around the classroom to speak Spanish, even though our parents used both languages at home. In fact, now our parents spoke Spanish to discuss taboo topics, parent stuff that we kids tried to decipher. What I did begin to decipher was the written word in English.

Eventually, I was admitted to a university. Being the first in my family to attend college resulted in added pressure to succeed in a world my family knew little about. Many sacrifices were made as my parents financed the purchase of a beat-up Rambler station wagon so I could commute to USC.

When I made it through my freshman year, I felt pretty good. By my sophomore year, I was getting confident. That year's courses included the foreign language requirement: Spanish. Thinking that I could easily resurrect my oral Spanish skills, I began to realize that maybe I did need "that language." I didn't take a foreign language class in high school. So I quickly enlisted my mother to serve as my in-house tutor. What could be more convenient?

Soon I met my instructor, a serious Spaniard whose Castilian was unlike the Spanish I had heard while growing up in L.A. She quickly ushered us through conjugating verbs to translating short stories by Gabriel García Márquez. I remember getting increasingly frustrated as the course became more difficult, despite the fact that I never missed a class.

Finally, I looked to my mom for guidance with my major writing assignments. She was exasperated by the translation complexities of the Marqúez works, whose stories were like the Spanish versions of William Faulkner's writings. With only an eighth-grade education, and having had no opportunity to study Spanish formally, she struggled to help me with my homework. Her late-night sighs as we worked together showed me that this wasn't something she could resolve quickly, like so many of the obstacles she faced in stabilizing and nurturing our familia.

And my response? I was angry. I was disappointed that my mom could not do my work for me. I knew she was quietly fighting the temptation to deliver the "I-told-you-so-you-should-have-practiced-your-Spanish" lecture. Perhaps she held back because she felt some responsibility for not requiring us to speak more Spanish at home and for listening to all of the rhetoric (including the words of her daughter) that essentially said, "Speaking Spanish is unacceptable in America."

Stubbornly, I refused to seek out other assistance or Spanish tutoring. I was ashamed that I, a Mexican, was about to earn a poor grade in Spanish. I began to feel resentment toward my instructor, who critiqued my compositions relentlessly.

That entire semester ended miserably. My frustration continued to fester, as I berated myself with thoughts like "What kind of Mexican am I?" My sophomore grades were pathetic. By the middle of summer, I was notified by a supporting organization, the USC Mexican American Alumni Association, that it was not going to renew my scholarship, and I was being placed on academic probation.

I was devastated. How would I tell my proud parents, who, after all, saw me as the "smart" one in the family who was such a success in high school? In my mind, I began to blame Spanish. I blamed my mother for not being educated enough. I blamed my father for having to work too much. I blamed my grandparents' not speaking English. I blamed my entire sweep of K–12 teachers for dismissing my bilingualism. But it certainly wasn't my fault, I "reasoned."

Finally, I told my parents about the grades and the loss of my scholarship. They held their disappointment squarely in, only to release it in diffuse ways. My father said he could work more overtime. My mother added that there were some emergency savings that could be used, although there was not much. "We'll manage," she reassured me. Then she added dryly, "You'd better get yourself together and study harder. Especially your Spanish skills." I expected a tongue-lashing but ended up with a body blow—a challenge, a goal, and a new direction.

I decided to take additional Spanish coursework at East L.A. College. I applied for a new work-study job tutoring elementary students in the barrio, where I could practice my Spanish reading and writing skills. I encouraged the kids to speak Spanish, even if it meant only speaking it at home.

I resolved that in grad school, I would take courses in Latin American literature. I practiced my Spanish with my family.

After a year of work in the community and the college classroom, I was able to renew my scholarship and complete my senior year. I continued to work on my Spanish and ended up teaching hundreds of limited-English-proficient students. Of course, over my 9 years of teaching in Los Angeles county secondary schools, the bicultural/bilingual issues of the day have changed. These issues are no longer limited to Spanish. Double-digit numbers of languages are the watercolors that teachers must create with today. And I often wonder if Cantonese students, Vietnamese students, Armenian students, and Korean students (to name a few) ever consider just who they are in America or ever challenge their parents with "I don't need that language." I wonder whether their teachers ever help them to address or reflect on these questions?

That is not a treatise advocating bilingual education, well, at least not entirely. For language-minority students to become empowered in this society, they must learn English. Bilingual educators do not reject English. They reject the ineffectiveness of English-only education and lament the alienation it inflicts. They advocate developing literacy in one language quickly in order to mainstream students into the courses where, perhaps, one teacher will empower them to persist, maybe even to persist biculturally. As an associate professor today, I still work to maintain my culture and language. For I am bicultural, moving within both worlds in hopes of arriving at a place where all students will recognize that to "make it" in America, it is not necessary to become who you are not.

Questions for Reflection

1. In what ways does an English-only approach affect families? How can educators balance the cultural and linguistic needs of diverse families with students' acquisition of the English language?

2. How can teachers design classroom instruction in ways that build on student's skill in their native language to foster the development of English language comprehension?

3. In what ways can an English-only approach to language instruction be alienating and disruptive to family cohesion across generations?

Curriculum: What Should We Teach English Language Learners?

The curriculum in all programs for ELLs must be specially adapted. Language is learned best when it is presented in a way that is meaningful and responds to the cultures of ELLs. The following guidelines (Center for Research on Education, Diversity, and Excellence, 2005) can help teachers build on student strengths when they design curricula and teach.

- Listen to student talk about familiar topics such as home and community.
- Respond to student talk and questions, making "in-flight" changes during conversation that directly relates to students' comments.
- Assist written and oral language development through modeling, eliciting, probing, restating, clarifying, questioning, and praising in purposeful conversation and writing.
- Interact with students in ways that respect students' preferences for speaking that may be different from the teacher's, such as wait-time, eye contact, turn-taking, and spotlighting.
- Connect student language with literacy and content-area knowledge through speaking, listening, reading, and writing activities.
- Encourage students to use content vocabulary to express their understanding.
- Provide frequent opportunity for students to interact with each other and the teacher during instructional activities.
- Encourage students' use of first and second languages in instructional activities.

This list is only a short overview of basic pedagogical modifications that teachers of ELLs can make to help students develop language across the curriculum. Educators can access a wide body of research and many pedagogical strategies that cater to the needs of students who are learning a second language in our public schools.

For Your CONSIDERATION

The Mora Modules website by Dr. Jill Kerper Mora offers techniques for instructing English language learners in bilingual, sheltered immersion, and mainstream classrooms. This site provides ideas for core curriculum design, thematic unit planning, and lesson planning for L2 learners. Visit the site at **http://coe.sdsu.edu/people/jmora/MoraModules/Default.htm.**

Assessment: How Do We Know What English Language Learners Know?

One of the most hotly debated issues in education is standardized testing. The federal government, under the No Child Left Behind Act of 2001 (NCLB), requires each state's public schools to test students annually in grades 3 to 8; any state that does not comply is denied its annual federal funding. This raises a number of issues for English language learners and their teachers: Does testing students on one standardized test actually measure what students have learned? Do the test results help teachers teach better and students learn more? Can *one* test score really capture all a student knows? If NCLB requires that each school improve its scores each year (thus demonstrating "adequate yearly progress," or AYP), but it takes from five to seven years for ELLs to acquire academic English, is this a reasonable expectation? Beyond these larger questions, can students who are learning English really show how much they know in what may be their weaker second language?

Most important, we need to think about the purpose of assessment. *Why* do we assess students? Mostly, we want to know what students are learning so that we can make good decisions about our teaching. We can also collect information about *how* students learn best so that we can teach them using those effective strategies. When assessing ELLs, we need to pay special attention to language and culture.

Some school districts recognize that giving ELLs who are just beginning to learn English a standardized test in English does not measure all that they know and puts children in the uncomfortable position of taking a test that they can't read well or at all. Compounding the problem, those ELLs who do have to take the test may

Students greet their teacher in the schoolyard.

encounter testing bias. As an example of cultural bias, consider a math word problem that referred to counting firecrackers on the Fourth of July. A student from another country might not be familiar with our national holidays and might have trouble understanding the question without the culturally based experience of the Fourth of July. In other words, embedding a math question in a context that may distract and confuse some test takers, but will be familiar to others, imposes cultural bias and undermines the validity of the test.

Another important issue in assessment is the tests that are used to identify which students qualify as linguistic-minority speakers, how their placement is determined, and when they are ready to learn in all-English classes. Individual states have come up with their own definitions of an ELL student, and not all states have even created a definition. Also, states use a variety of different tests to determine the student's level of reading, writing, and oral language in English. To fully understand how much literacy students have, they should also be tested in their L1. Knowing the literacy level of students in their own language would help educators understand the foundation they have on which to build English literacy (Ovando et al., 2003). Testing students on their knowledge of reading, writing, and speaking in their L1 also can prevent the overrepresentation of minority-language students (MLSs) in special education and their underrepresentation in programs for the gifted and talented and advanced placement classes. Research has shown that difficulties with English are often misidentified as disabilities and that consequently, MLSs are sometimes placed in special education programs when they should be in ESL or bilingual programs. And although it seems paradoxical, many ELLs who *do* need special education services are not identified at all (Ochoa, 2003)—in other words, not only too many MLSs but also the wrong MLSs are placed in special education.

The problems with testing, identification, and placement of minority-language students are complex. To imagine how high the stakes of one placement test might be, just imagine you are a recently arrived native Korean speaker and you are given a test in English to determine whether you should be in a mainstream classroom, a "gifted classroom," or a special education program. How do you think you would do? Finally, when English language learners have been part of a program designed to meet their language needs, a variety of assessments that measure language and content-area achievement should be utilized to determine whether they are ready for a classroom without special support for ELLs.

Once students have been appropriately placed in the best program available to them, their classroom teacher(s) should be guided by five principles in designing assessment to determine what they are learning day by day (Harp, 1994; O'Malley & Pierce, 1996; McTighe & Ferrara, 1998—all in Ovando et al., 2003):

- Such assessment must be based on what we know about how language learners learn, in particular, how they acquire reading and writing processes.
- It should be integral to instruction, inform teaching, and improve learning.
- It should use multiple sources of information on a regular and systematic basis.
- It should be culturally and developmentally appropriate.
- It should provide valid, reliable, and fair measures of learning.

It takes a great deal of thought and expertise to design appropriate assessments for ELLs—right down to how the assessment takes place. For example, if your English language learners don't value competition, they may need to take a test in pairs, in groups, or in some other manner that does not highlight competition.

PAUSE & REFLECT

Which of the assessment issues described in this section are the most troubling? Explain why. How might you find out about your students' culturally based assessment preferences?

Karen: Hybrid Identity

By this point, you may be wondering if the story of the education of ELLs in our country could be any more complicated. We've talked about the history, politics, law, theories, programs, and assessment of ELLs. But we have yet to individualize the story, and doing so does indeed make it even more complex. Because of the incredible diversity of ELLs—their countries of origin, their generation in the United States, their reasons for immigration, the programs offered, and the attitudes of those around them—each individual story will be just that: individual. I chose to share part of Karen's story with you because now, as a bilingual teacher, she has been able to reflect in a poem upon her experiences as an ELL herself in school and to show how she has taken two often opposing linguistic and cultural worlds into her life.

Karen Garcia was a Latina graduate student and a Spanish-English bilingual teacher. Karen, a native speaker of Spanish who has "always lived in New York [City]," wrote the following three-stanza poem (translated by Tricia Gallgher-Geurtsen). Her poem is a response to reading Luis Alberto Ambroggio's (1994) poem "Aprender el ingles" ("Learning English"), which describes the struggle between Spanish and English identities that occurs in learning English. Here is Karen's poem:

> Spanish shouldn't be spoken in America
> To be American
> You have to speak English
> No accents
> You are in America
> Don't you want to be American?
>
> To be Latina
> You have to speak like a Latina
> Speak it proudly
> Don't speak like you're not Hispanic!
> Do you want to be a disgrace to the Latin community?
> Don't you want to be Latina?
>
> I'm Latina
> Soy Americana   (I am American)
> Hablo en Inglés   (I speak English)
> I speak Spanish
> ¿Por qué no me tratas de conocer?   (Why don't you try to get to know me?)
> Before you decide not to accept me.
> ¡Soy parte de dos mundos!   (I am a part of two worlds!)
> Why can't you just accept me?

The first stanza, Karen explained, describes her experience of learning English in school, where she felt she had to speak English and speak it without an accent to be seen as wanting to be "American." Karen says, "By the third grade, I was placed in a monolingual English classroom" (e-mail communication, November 11, 2001). Her father, who taught her Spanish at home, helped her to keep learning Spanish. The second stanza is an analysis of what Karen calls her "biggest problem" in her language-learning history (e-mail to the author, November 11, 2001):

> The biggest problem I had (in middle school and high school) was being accepted because I didn't fit [the] "Hispanic" criteria that most of my other peers felt I should have. It was mostly the way that I spoke (they thought that I wanted to sound "proper").

Karen not only was struggling with having no choice except to learn English in school, but also felt a need to adopt community language that might oppose school language. In this instance, Karen felt pressured to adopt a community language driven by what she called "Hispanic criteria" in the form of speaking English with a *Latina* accent. This particular accent did not come naturally to her and was not consistent with speaking English without an accent, as required in school. Thus, she was perceived by her peers as speaking English as though she were trying to "sound proper." Karen resolved this conflict in a way that upholds the legitimacy of both her school language and her community language, while also critiquing them both.

In the language of the last stanza of her poem, Karen comes up with a creative solution that allows the contradictions between the school requirement of speaking English without an accent and the community requirement of knowing Spanish and speaking English like a Latina to remain in tension. In her personal life, too, she made some adjustments (e-mail to the author, November 11, 2001):

Because I felt that they [her Hispanic peers] would not accept me I befriended the Greeks in my high school who for the most part knew that I was Latina but thought I couldn't speak Spanish.

Karen's joining a different peer group that accepted her unaccented English, and the fact that today Karen speaks English with a Latina accent—the community language that she resisted in high school—illustrate how she uses her personal agency to manage the contradictory languages in her life. By expressing an identity that is neither purely English nor purely Spanish, Karen critiques both school and community languages, illustrates that they exist in tension, and comes up with her own personal expression of her identity, which is presented in the last stanza.

In this last stanza, she juxtaposes her school and community literacies by using English to claim her Latina identity and ability to speak Spanish, while using Spanish to claim her American identity and ability to speak English. She "messes with" her target reader—the typical American who is a white, middle-class, mono-lingual English speaker—by denying a translation that would allow the reader to see her affinity to an American English identity, while proclaiming her Latina identity loudly in English. This juxtaposition and tension form an integral part of Karen's personal agency; by utilizing her school and community languages in a strategic way, she also critiques and celebrates them. Gallego and Hollingsworth (2000, p. 15) explain:

Personal literacies [agency] reflect[s] both the ways students believe they should join in socially accepted discourse communities and the private ways they know they can and would like to be able to participate across communities, as well as the tensions between these views.

Karen ends the poem claiming that she is neither purely a Latina Spanish speaker nor purely an American English speaker. She is a hybrid of the two. In Spanish, she claims that she is part of two worlds: "¡Soy parte de dos mundos!" Karen expresses herself with a combination of her school, community, and personal worlds, refuses to be pigeonholed, and remains a hybrid of two worlds. Recognizing that there is pressure to remain purely of one or the other world, she makes it clear that the issue is one that her readers, as well as she herself, must address: "Why can't you just accept me?"

Perhaps Karen's struggle and resulting hybrid identity will help you think in more complex ways about the lives of ELLs. How do you think Karen's life might have been different if she had been enrolled in a late-exit transitional bilingual program or a two-way bilingual program? The educational decisions that we make have an enormous impact on individuals' lives.

PAUSE & REFLECT

How will you address issues of student identity in your own classroom? What are ways in which you can get to know about your students' personal, community, and school languages?

SUMMARY

This chapter provided you with an introduction to the story of teaching language-minority (LM) students in the United States, beginning in precolonial times and ending in a complex and shifting present. You are now familiar with the challenges that are part and parcel of the historical, political, legal, theoretical, and curricular aspects of teaching English language learners (ELLs) in schools. The English-language centrism evident in all aspects of this educational arena can be described as misguided—and even dangerous given increasing political, economic, and environmental global interdependence among cultures. It is imperative that policymakers, educators, and community members move toward producing a multilingual and multicultural citizenry as our world grows ever smaller. If we hope to maintain our way of life and improve our relationships with other nations, we must embrace one another's languages and cultures. When we think about the three scenarios near the beginning of the chapter, it is important to recognize that although we have come a long way in how well we educate ELLs in this country, all three situations still occur in the present day. It is up to all of us to learn more about the languages and cultures of people around us and how we can strive to provide excellent and equitable educational programs for all ELLs in public schools.

DISCUSSION QUESTIONS

1. Talk with your classmates about what it means to be an American. Write down a definition of an American. Can one definition apply to everyone? Should language be a part of that definition? Should all Americans be bilingual or multilingual?

2. "We have room for but one language in this country and that is the English language" (President Theodore Roosevelt). Do you agree or disagree with President Roosevelt's opinion? What are the benefits and costs of multilingual schools and a multilingual country?

3. Is the history of language education in the United States a monolingual or a multilingual one? Explain.

4. Look at the chart of programs for linguistic-minority speakers in Table 11.1. Talk with your classmates about which program you think is the most appropriate for English language learners. Support your choice with information from the chapter.

5. A new student in your classroom is learning English as a second language. You have a hunch that she might have a learning disability. What should you do?

ACTIVITIES

1. Ask a teacher to help you identify a student in her or his classroom who is new to learning English. Observe the student over time, and take note of the curriculum, the teaching strategies employed, and the nature of the interactions between the student and teacher(s) and between the student and peers. How are instruction and assessment being adapted to meet the student's needs? How is the student's culture included in the curriculum and instruction? With whom does the student interact and what is the nature of those interactions? Judging on the basis of the guidelines outlined in this chapter, what could be done to improve the educational experience for the student?

2. Review the list of privileges on page 247. If you are a native English speaker, take some time to think about and make notes on how the things you do during your day would change if you were an English language learner (ELL). What privileges are denied such students on a daily basis? If you are an English language learner yourself, add to the list of the privileges enjoyed by the native speaker of English.

3. Research the history of language education in a nearby school district. Talk with district personnel to discover the current program designs for English language learners (ELLs). Then trace back as far as you can (to the creation of the district, if possible) what kinds of programs or policies were created for ELLs. Make a timeline that represents the changing programs over time.

4. Interview someone whose native language was not English about his or her schooling. Create a list of questions that will help you put together a brief linguistic and cultural biography of the person. Try to determine the extent to which they feel bilingual or monolingual, bicultural or monocultural.

5. Make a video documentary about the languages and cultures represented in your community. You might include short interviews with business owners, educators, community leaders, and local government leaders.

Note any issues that are related to the variety of languages and cultures in the community, and ascertain how much importance is attached to these issues.

6. Review the section on how English language learners (ELLs) learn language. Create a plan indicating how you would teach a lesson on plant growth and gardening to elementary or middle-school science students, in English, utilizing sheltering strategies.

WEBSITES

Cutting Edge Education
http://www.cuttingedgeeducation.com/index
This site provides information about professional development, curriculum development, and instructional resources based on recent educational research into the needs of linguistically and culturally diverse learners.

The Mora Modules
http://coe.sdsu.edu/people/jmora/MoraModeuls/Default.htm
The site was developed by Dr. Jill Kerper Mora at San Diego State University. The links and modules available here offer theories, methods, and techniques for instructing English language learners (ELLs) in bilingual, sheltered immersion, and mainstream classrooms. There are several modules for curriculum design, thematic unit planning, and lesson planning for L2 learners to guide and assist educators in improving second-language, literacy, and content-area instruction.

National Clearinghouse for English Language Acquisition
http://www.ncela.gwu.edu
This site provides information and resources on language instruction educational programs. There are many resources and frequently asked questions (FAQs) regarding all types of programs for ELLs. The site is funded by the U.S. Department of Education.

National Association for Bilingual Education (NABE)
http://www.nabe.org
NABE is a nonprofit professional development and advocacy group for English language learners. It has a variety of research publications and links to organizations that research and advocate for ELLs.

Native Languages of the Americas
http:www.native-languages.org
This is the official website of the nonprofit organization. Here you will find information about Native languages, number and location of speakers, and cultures of Native groups.

Teachers of Speakers of Other Languages (TESOL)
http:www.tesol.org/s_tesol/index.asp
TESOL offers a number of comprehensive links relevant to language acquisition research, professional development, language policy, and teaching standards for early childhood to adult populations.

Ambroggio, L. A. (1994). "Aprender el ingles." In L. M. Carlson, *Cool salsa: Bilingual poems on growing up Latino in the United States* (pp. 17–18). New York: Fawcett Juniper.

Antunez, B. (2001). *What program models exist to serve English language learners?* Retrieved from http://www.ncbe.gwu/askncbe/faqs/22models.htm

Center for Applied Linguistics. (December 1994). *Two-way bilingual education programs in practice: A national and local perspective.* Available at http://www.cal.org/resources/digest/ed379915.html

Center for Research on Education, Diversity, and Excellence. (2005). *The five standards for effective pedagogy.* Available at http://crede.org/standards.html

Chambers, J., & Parrish, T. (1992). *Meeting the challenge of diversity: An evaluation of programs for pupils with limited proficiency in English.* Volume 4, *Cost of programs and services for LEP students.* Berkeley: BW Associates.

The Condition of Education 1997. (1997). Supplemental Table 1. Document available at http://nces.ed.gov/pubs/ce/c9704d01.html

Crawford, J. (1991). *Bilingual education: History, politics, theory, and practice* (2nd ed.). Los Angeles: Bilingual Education Services.

Crawford, J. (1997). The campaign against Proposition 227: A post mortem. *Bilingual Research Journal, 21*(1), 1–29.

Cummins, J. (1989). *Empowering minority students.* Sacramento: California Association for Bilingual Education.

Delpit, L. (1995). *Other people's children: Cultural conflict in the classroom.* New York: New Press.

Gallagher-Geurtsen, T. M. (2001). *A comparison of funding for bilingual education and foreign language education.* Unpublished paper.

Gallego, M. A., & Hollingsworth, S. (2000). *What counts as literacy: Challenging the school standard.* New York: Teachers College Press.

Genesee, F. (Ed.). (1994). *Educating second language children: The whole child, the whole curriculum, the whole community.* Cambridge: Cambridge University Press.

Grinberg, J., & Saavedra, E. R. (2000). The constitution of bilingual/ESL education as a disciplinary practice: Genealogical explorations. *Review of Educational Research, 7*(4), 419–441.

Hakuta, K., & Diaz, R. (1985). The relationship between the degree of bilingualism and cognitive ability. In K. E. Nelson (Ed.), *Children's language.* Hillsdale, NJ: Erlbaum.

Krashen, S. D., & Biber, D. (1988). *On course: Bilingual education's success in California.* Los Angeles: California Association for Bilingual Education.

Native Languages of the Americas: Cherokee (Tsalagi). (2005). St. Paul: Native Languages of the Americas. Available at http://www.native-languages.org/Cherokee.htm

Nettle, D., & Romaine, S. (2000). *The extinction of the world's languages.* New York: Oxford University Press.

Ochoa, T. A. (2003). Bilingual special education. In C. J. Ovando, V. P. Collier, & M. C. Combs (Eds.), *Bilingual and ESL classrooms: Teaching in multicultural contexts* (3rd ed.) (pp. 358–378). New York: McGraw-Hill.

Ovando, C. J., Collier, V. P., Combs, M. C. (2003). *Bilingual and ESL classrooms: Teaching in multicultural contexts* (3rd ed). New York: McGraw-Hill.

Ramírez, J. D., Yuen, S. D., Ramey, D. R., & Pasta, D.J. (1991). *Longitudinal study of structured English immersion, early-exit and late-exit transitional bilingual education programs for language minority children* (Final report to the U.S. Department of Education, Executive Summary). San Mateo, CA: Aguirre International.

Skutnabb-Kangas, T. (1991). Swedish strategies to prevent integration and national ethnic minorities. In O. Garcia (Ed.), *Bilingual education: Focusschrift in honor of Joshua A. Fishman* (pp. 25–40). Philadelphia: John Benjamins.

Soto, L. D. (1997). *Language, culture, and power: Bilingual families and the struggle for quality education.* Albany: State University of New York Press.

Thomas, W. P., & Collier, V.P. (1997). *School effectiveness for language minority students.* Washington, DC: National Clearinghouse for Bilingual Education.

CHAPTER 12

Globalization and Schooling: Education at the Crossroads

CHAPTER OBJECTIVES

- Readers will understand why it is important to understand educational approaches and initiatives beyond the United States borders.

- Readers will examine the different perspectives that inform the definition of globalization.

- Readers will be introduced to global education Web resources to find model lesson plans and to help guide curriculum development and project planning.

- Readers will compare and contrast education responses in international settings, including Japan, Mexico, and Iraq.

FIRST PERSON

Computer Labs, School Cafeterias, and the Global Economy: A Healthy Mix?

Today, my work continues as a teacher educator. Each semester I supervise secondary student teachers, whose target classroom populations range from sixth grade to twelfth grade. The student teachers deliver instruction in a variety of content areas, such as the arts, sciences, mathematics, language arts, social studies, and agricultural education. Depending on the needs of the students, the student teachers, and the cooperating teachers, I observe each student teacher in the classroom, on average, three to four times a semester. Sometimes I visit student teachers and their students because I've been invited to observe their projects and presentations. These invitations result in some of my best school visits, as I take in wonderful collaborations among the students, the teachers, and (on occasion) families.

However, some of my visits to high school campuses feel strange and heavily commercial. When I enter a school, I sometimes see racks of student newspapers with Domino's pizza advertisements edging out between the pages. Promotional posters advertise such products as class rings and video yearbooks. During passing periods, candy and soda machines lure their young customers away from class. Although some schools maintain that they are provide healthy lunch meals, Taco Bell and Pizza Hut dominate many student cafeterias.

Inside the classrooms are TV monitors that show the teen-targeted news program Channel One. Often, the student teachers don't question the time allotted for viewing these segments. In fact, new teachers seem to enjoy having the moments to breathe, take attendance, and prepare for class. While watching "the news," students are exposed to 12-minute profiles of national and world events, segments punctuated with fast-food, clothing, and soda commercials. This emphasis on consumer markets on high school campuses is hard to ignore.

The emphasis on commercial markets continues as I observe my student teachers lead their classes into a school's computer lab. The new teachers guide students through various software programs and Internet sites, and suddenly, the images the students just viewed on Channel One reappear on the World Wide Web. At the students' fingertips are Internet links to international communities and information, but they have few skills to sort and critique the information they are immediately exposed to. With a single click of a mouse, students become consumers of a vast landscape called information technology in a global society. Do technology and the marketing that drives technology contribute to students' accurate knowledge of the world? Or does technology represent yet another virtual community whose language and images we can simply turn on, turn off, or passively accept without interrogation or critique?

As I complete my semester observations in the public schools, I feel thrilled for the new teachers and their students, especially for those who are collaborating, learning, and growing together. At the same time, I wonder about the powerful commercial forces now present on the campuses and in the classrooms. Are we truly enabling our students, through technology, to understand the larger global society and to consider problem-solving strategies? Or are we just exposing them to new marketing schemes?

Considering Education Beyond Our Borders

The students attending public school classrooms reflect the increasing diversity of contemporary American society. As immigration, transportation, labor needs, and political strife contribute to the changing demographics of the United States, it is not uncommon to see immigrant student populations increasing in schools, not only on the East Coast and the West Coast, but also in such states as Iowa, North Carolina, and Arkansas. To illustrate this point further, it has been estimated that in the year 2000 one in ten U.S. residents was born in another country (Lollock, 2001).

In response, we see educators striving to address the needs of their diverse student populations, although the nature and extent of schools' responses differ tremendously, depending on the availability of resources and trained faculty. To prepare new teachers to have an understanding of their students, and, in turn, to help students to have a better understanding of one another, it is imperative that educators be aware of the features and challenges that characterize today's global community.

Coming to such an understanding requires teachers to ask questions and seek knowledge about the political, economic, and cultural perspectives held by other nations. This content is often referred to as **global education** and encompasses the interconnected topic of **globalization**. Equipped with such knowledge, educators are not basing their cross-cultural instruction on uninformed opinions and assumptions. Instead, teachers who research and design a global education curriculum that includes a discussion of such complicated issues as globalization are providing students with authentic content about the world they live in and its future sustainability. In this way, teachers can help the next generation gain knowledge about the lived experiences, environments, and viewpoints of other cultures that may differ from their own. In the following chapter, I discuss globalization and global education and how together they impact our understandings of educational policy and practices across continents today.

Understanding the Global Community

What Is Globalization?

A common definition of globalization invokes the interactions among cultures, corporations, and governments across the world, interactions motivated by international investments and trade agreements facilitated by information technology (Scholte, 2000). These interactions have major consequences for national cultures, government and political policies, global economies, and the environment. Globalization affects the health and well-being of all citizens in our global community. As a result, some critics consider it extremely problematic, especially given the ongoing tensions, war, and violence occurring in numerous parts of the world.

From a historical perspective, international trade has occurred for thousands of years. Nations, and more recently corporations, have bought and sold goods from Asia, Europe, and the Americas. With the backdrop of such ventures as those of Christopher Columbus and the atrocities of the slave trade, nations have supported international enterprise for the purpose of profit. In contemporary times, dramatic changes in free-market trade agreement policies and technological advances continue to influence domestic and international trade and investment.

New technologies help major stakeholders, such as governments, corporations, and consumers, to quickly analyze economic trends, sell products to buyers worldwide, and easily access and transfer assets. Globalization, according to *New York Times* reporter and author Thomas Friedman, continues to move farther, faster, cheaper, and deeper (2000). And yet, globalization has its negative consequences and passionate detractors. They are concerned that rampant, unregulated globalization can have an adverse impact on local cultures, markets, and laborers and on the environment. On the other hand, proponents maintain that globalization can assist developing countries by helping them generate investment and capital. Therefore, it remains critical that when educators introduce the topic of globalization to their students, those teachers be well informed about its costs as well as its benefits.

Other Meanings That Circulate in the Public Discourse Regarding Globalization

The public often embraces the topic of globalization in the classroom because of its association with technology. However, as the next generation of teachers enters the classroom, it is imperative that these professional educators grasp what globalization, and its ramifications, mean to other nations and to the diverse cultures living within their borders.

On one level, globalization is referred to in education as part of an increasingly borderless society brought ever closer by the Internet. What is often not included in the discussion is the role globalization plays within the larger society and its influence and impact on political and economic institutions across the world. Certainly, the international society, with its wireless access to immediate multimedia news and information, is served by this technology. But how? Is technology the ultimate medium for global cultural transmission? Does it draw attention to worldwide human rights and to democratic processes? Or is globalization simply a vehicle for international commerce and market exchange? What is the role of American teachers as they seek to help their students understand globalization? These are important questions for all educators to consider, regardless of grade level and content-area emphasis.

While educators emphasize the democratic process in the classroom, any individual—anywhere—who is equipped with a computer and a network connection can transcend national sovereignty literally in seconds. Suddenly, international alliances are blurred and complicated, as new world economies are created and recreated faster than any emergent government can forge out a plan for peace or the safeguarding of human rights. Thus, students' understanding of shifting world events is no longer easily presented in the curriculum or in a textbook. With this broad, global perspective come new possibilities for problem solving, as students' eyes are opened to concerns of other countries. At the same time, globalization can also generate tensions and cause us to close our eyes, as nation–states are blurred and rendered borderless by market exchanges, deregulation of environmental and tax policies, and the exploitation of labor, all of which can corrupt and inhibit cross-cultural interactions, understanding, and the promotion of human rights.

Students dressed as Colonel Sanders (Kentucky Fried Children's symbol) promote egg tarts in a Shanghai KFC restaurant.

How else can globalization be described? Globalization has also been defined as "the intensification of worldwide social relations which link distant localities in such a way that local happenings are shaped by events occurring many miles away and vice versa" (Held, 1991, p. 9). A predominant feature of these social relations is the growth of global economies whose powerful forces now redefine and obscure international identities, alliances, and world affairs.

Why Should Teachers Be Concerned About This Perspective on Globalization?

While educators teach students in the schools, the world outside their classroom is an uncertain place. As technology brings information to us second by second, our understandings of nations and their governments can no longer be essentialized and stereotyped. Our assumptions about other nations are now challenged regularly, as regional differences, religions, cultural and ethnic traditions, languages, historical conflicts, gender roles, shifting loyalties, and rapid social movements are informed by the use of technology. Therefore, educators have the responsibility of keeping up with this "information superhighway" and giving students the skills to help them become discerning consumers in search of credible and authentic information about the world today.

Globalization also drives the production of goods, including technology, that captivate contemporary youth culture. For some youth and their families, the lure of inexpensive goods is far more important than where those goods come from, what workers made them, and under what conditions. Nike shoes, X-Boxes for computer gaming, iPods, and cheap fuel for sports utility vehicles represent highly prized commodities in an increasingly borderless world—a world whose institutions are less concerned with human rights and equal educational opportunities for its citizens and more concerned with how institutional cultures can reinvent themselves to become more marketable and profitable.

How, then, can educators take a stand on behalf of a democratic education, when the pressures of globalization and the production of new market economies require students to become competitors for schooling and goods in this fragile world?

These complex questions continue to emerge as globalization gains momentum. Is *globalization* simply another term for global capitalism? Is technology, globalization's vehicle, bringing about the homogenization of cultures, as some critics maintain? Will the proliferation of powerful, multinational corporations, such as McDonalds, spread capitalism around the world, obliterating rich facets of diverse cultures? Or will globalization contribute to the blending of cultures that represent the diversity of a new contemporary society whose members accept responsibility for each other through "environmental action, democratization, and humanization" (Torres, 2002, p. 365)?

These issues are not easily resolved. Ultimately, globalization is complicated, with numerous layers, dimensions, and demands that can empower citizens and, at the same time, can also exploit them. Today's teachers must help students to explore those layers, as countries generate their own constantly evolving perspectives on sovereignty, economics, sustainability, and human rights.

PAUSE & REFLECT

Consider the description of globalization at the beginning of this section. What forms of globalization do you see emerging in ways that benefit, as well as challenge, contemporary society? How do you imagine that globalization will affect educational institutions in your state? How are college and public school students responding to globalization?

What Is Global Education?

How can teachers explore global concerns with their students without perpetuating stereotypes and assumptions? One response has been the study of global education. **Global education** is often referred to as an approach to curriculum development that focuses on cross-cultural knowledge construction, including the study of cultural, ethnic, religious, and gender diversity. William Kniep (1989) has identified four categories, or domains, that can frame the development of global education in the curriculum):

- **Human values:** Universal values shared by all of humanity, including those held by diverse cultures.
- **Global systems:** This includes an understanding of how all parts and all aspects of the world are interdependent and linked through the economy, environmental sustainability, political interactions, and technology.
- **Global issues:** Worldwide problems that include environmental concerns, human rights, and national security.
- **Global history:** This traces the historical background of diverse cultures, examines their values, and explores the history of international conflicts.

With this framework, teachers can target a range of age-appropriate instructional approaches while developing a global curriculum in a variety of content areas, including social studies, literature, journalism, government, mathematics, and science.

For example, using the *global history* domain, teachers can design a curriculum that addresses colonialism. *Human values* can be explored with a discussion of child labor and sweatshops. Environmental issues, such as global warming, can be introduced from a *global systems* perspective. Global issues, such as the war in Iraq, can also be analyzed from a variety of journalistic perspectives.

For Your CONSIDERATION

Who benefits and who suffers from the World Trade Organization's version of "free trade" is seen most clearly in the WTO's rulings. Consider the following cases. Go to the text's website and **http://www.rethinkingschools.org** for scenarios from the International Forum on Globalization publication "Invisible Government: The World Trade Organization: Global Government for the New Millennium?" by Jerry Mander and Debi Barker.

Such news events illustrate the interconnectedness of nations and their citizens. Sadly, the attacks of September 11, 2001, have resulted in an increasingly difficult and violent period across the globe. Conflicts in Afghanistan and Iraq and tensions in Iran, Israel, North Korea, and the Palestinian territories illustrate the kinds of shifts in government policies and commitments that will continue to affect families in the years to come. To help societies understand these complex and ongoing events, educators can build a curriculum that informs students about international cultures, histories, and politics.

Some other interdisciplinary, age-appropriate instructional topics are world hunger, poverty, health care, women's and girls' rights, indigenous peoples' rights, immigration, community-based service, international industry, and environmental issues. This content, of course, also requires educators to have an understanding of approaches to education in countries beyond the U.S. borders.

Specific resources to help guide the development of curriculum addressing these topics, along with project models and sample lesson plans, can be found at the following comprehensive websites:

- The Discovery Channel's Global Education Partnership
  http://www.discovergyglobaled.org
- The American Forum for Global Education
  http://www.globaled.org
- The National Council for Social Studies
  http://www.socialstudies.org
- National Geographic Education Guide
  http://www.nationalgeographic.com/education
- United Nations CyberSchoolBus
  http://www.un.org/Pubs/CyberSchoolBus

Eleven-year-old Aliyah (*left*) studies at a private English lesson in Kabul. Aliyah's family returned to Afghanistan from Pakistan several months before.

For Your CONSIDERATION

Visit one of the websites listed above. Identify a topic relevant to global education. Select a sample lesson and/or project, and describe how you would modify and present such a lesson in a manner appropriate to your target grade level and relevant to your content area.

Understanding Comparative Education

Given the increased momentum of globalization, and the ongoing educator interest in global education, it is imperative that educators also become familiar with diverse educational systems as they seek to explore commonalities and to subject to scrutiny any assumptions they may have about international schooling. By examining school systems in other parts of the world, American educators can study what philosophies, instructional methods, and curriculum content other nations are working with. International schools are often grappling with a number of issues similar to those U.S. teachers confront: limited resources, meeting testing standards, serving the needs of diverse learners, teacher shortages, and gaining adequate access to technology.

At the same time, however, many international schools are threatened by even more serious and immediate issues, such as war, poverty, health concerns, gender bias and exclusion, and culture clashes. In the next section of this chapter, we will briefly explore how such nations as Iraq, Japan, and Mexico structure their approach to education. The countries discussed here were selected because of their compelling associations with the United States, including the competitive nature of the U.S. relationship with Japan, immigration concerns regarding Mexico, and the ongoing tensions associated with the Iraq and Afghanistan wars.

Japanese Schooling and Structure

Japan is well known for its education programs and has a strong, worldwide reputation in mathematics instruction and testing outcomes. Japanese students also maintain a high rate of literacy, with percentages climbing over 95 percent (Ellington, 2005). In addition, Japanese secondary school students have a 95 percent graduation rate, compared to the 85% graduate rate of American high school students. However, Japanese and American secondary students attend colleges or universities at comparable percentages (Ellington, 2005).

The Japanese schooling structure is regulated by the *Monbukagakusho*, the National Ministry of Education, Culture, Sports, Science, and Technology. Students are required to attend school through the ninth grade. The majority of these students attend publicly funded schools, although approximately 29 percent of them are enrolled in private schools. Ironically, the National Ministry is not the main source of funding for the public schools. Local municipalities or private entities generally fund schools. Japanese teachers generally enjoy higher status and salaries in a competitive job market, whereas American educators, with specific areas of expertise and lower salaries, have more options in a market that is experiencing teacher shortages.

Japanese students attend school approximately six weeks longer than U.S. students, although the six-day school week has been phased out (Ellington, 2005). As in American schools, the classrooms have enrollments that reflect the mixed abilities of the students. The grades range from first to sixth with a student-teacher ratio of 20:1, then move into the middle-level grades of seventh to ninth, and conclude with the secondary level of tenth to twelfth. For families who can afford it, many students attend after-school enrichment, or *juko*, classes two or three times a week in the arts, athletics, or specific academic content areas in preparation for upper secondary admission tests (Wu, 1999).

The stereotype of Japanese education is that it is extremely "lock-step," or regimented. And yet, although some rote instruction occurs in most educational systems (including that of the United States), Japanese teachers offer students puzzles, or problem-solving approaches, in their instruction in mathematics (Desmond, 1996). The curriculum is similar to that of the United States, although Japanese students take English courses beginning in the seventh grade. Secondary schools are identified as college preparatory, vocational, or industrial. "Character education" is also a part of the curriculum, and students are encouraged by their teachers to invest rigorous effort in their studies and to care for their schools (as illustrated by the students and teachers who help clean the school buildings each week).

However, the notion that Japanese schools are better and more competitive than American schools belies the fact that they are simply different. Japanese students must compete for admission to upper-level secondary schools by taking examinations. Students compete for available slots; it is not necessarily enough to get a passing score (DeKoker, 2002).

Since 2002, the Ministry of Education has also proposed educational reforms. The curriculum now includes hands-on, project-driven instruction in the social studies or "integrated studies. This reform is controversial because some maintain that the Japanese curriculum is being "watered down." Nevertheless, Japanese schools face challenges to their efficacy similar to those that American schools face, including funding issues, equitable access to an elite curriculum, and the identification of effective instructional practices.

Mexican Schooling and Structure

Understanding the educational structure of Mexico begins with understanding its educational history and the development of its primary and secondary schools.

In 1867, Mexican president Benito Juarez, the first and only indigenous leader of the country, declared that elementary education would be free to all. Education would also be secular, and school attendance would be mandatory. Fifty years later, in 1917, the federal government was granted even greater powers in the area of education, as outlined in Mexico's Constitution, which added federal guidelines for private schools, as well.

Rural students in Chiapas, Mexico.

By 1992, the federal government mandated new educational standards that required all students to attend secondary school through grade 9. The curriculum was also revised at that time and stressed a renewed emphasis on the core curriculum. In addition, P–12 administration was decentralized and granted more local autonomy. Despite these reforms, the difficult economic conditions that prevail in Mexico today weigh heavily on the educational outcomes of its students. Nevertheless, the country strives to develop and maintain educational facilities for all students attending school through the ninth grade.

Mexico, however, is still challenged by "rezago," or educational collapse. The country is plagued by high dropout rates not only of secondary students but of primary students as well. Students from rural communities experience high levels of poverty, especially indigenous children for whom Spanish is a second language (McLaughlin, 2003). Many of these students leave school to seek employment so that they can help support their families.

Mexican schools consist of federally funded preschools (*pre-escolar*) for four- to five-year-olds, primary (*primaria*) schools for grades 1 to 6, one-room multigrade (*multigrados*) schools for grades 1 to 6, middle-level schools for grades 7 to 9, secondary (*secundarias*) or *prepartorias* schools for college-bound students in grades 10 to 12, and technical (*tecnicas*) schools for vocational students not bound for college. Rural students may have access to *telesecundarias*, distance-education school sites that provide televised instruction curricula, via satellite.

Mexican schools follow a nationalized curriculum. The federal government offers free textbooks to students in primary schools, but secondary students must pay for their books. In first and second grades, an interdisciplinary approach to the social sciences and environmental studies is offered. Also in the primary grades, Spanish, mathematics, and geography are emphasized. In general, primary students are not ability-grouped in the classroom, a practice very different from that in U.S. schools. Students are taught geometry and algebra in grades 7 and 8 and are introduced to trigonometry in grade 9. Secondary students are required to take science, although lab facilities are often limited. By the time students enter high school, grades 10 to 12, they must indicate whether they will pursue college, a vocational career, or business education.

Tests on the national curriculum are administered five times a year and graded on a scale of 1 to 10. Students who score less than a 6 on the end-of-the-year national exam are retained at the same grade level in the following year.

Much as in U.S. schools, Mexican students take part in patriotic and character education exercises such as singing the national anthem, while learning to be respectful, serious students who honor their teachers (*maestros/as*). Class schedules differ greatly from American schools, where lessons, recess, and breaks are tightly scheduled. In contrast, the Mexican school day may last up to four hours. Secondary students may work in the morning and go to school later in the day.

Finally, it is important to note that there are major differences between the schooling of Mexican urban and rural children. Rural communities are often isolated and extremely poor. Therefore, Mexican schools located in remote places face many challenges, such as the difficulty of finding teachers willing to live in or travel to such communities, the students' compromised ability to attend school due to a lack of reliable transportation on undeveloped roads, and the need for children, particularly indigenous children, to work or care for younger siblings. McLaughlin (2003) found that "Rural students may have to leave their communities after elementary school to attend school in a nearby town, and some families cannot afford to pay for travel, textbooks, uniforms, and other school costs after sixth grade. The same is true of poor urban students, although they have more school choices where they live (p. 1)." In essence, access to education in Mexico is something not to be taken for granted.

Iraqi secondary students receiving book bags funded by the United States.

Iraqi Schooling Post-9/11

Since the 1990s, Iraqi teachers had taught history from the perspective of Saddam Hussein's Baath Party. According to this ideological and politicized version of history, the United States was an invader to be challenged, Israel threatened the world at every turn, and all Iraqi wars were driven by noble causes from which Iraq emerged as the victors. And now, with Saddam Hussein having been executed for war crimes in 2006, some Americans feel that Iraqi teachers will be free to present history more accurately. But can they?

New textbooks arrived in 2003. They were revised to meet the needs of Iraq's 5.5 million schoolchildren in 16,000 schools

(Asquith, 2003). The textbooks were edited by a team of American-appointed Iraqi educators, and images of Hussein and his Baath Party have been eliminated. In addition, the Iraqi Ministry of Education, influenced by the United States coalition government, has edited out content deemed propaganda and/or controversial, such as information about Israelis, Americans, Kurds, the 1991 Gulf War, and the war between Iran and Iraq. These revised textbooks are just one example of the political and educational challenges that the U.S.-supported government of Iraq faces.

Numerous private, nongovernment organizations (NGOs) and nonprofit agencies now assume a wide range of responsibilities relevant to education, including the reconstruction of schools and an overhaul of the national curriculum. As the *Christian Science Monitor* reporter Christina Asquith explained, "While US advisers don't want to be seen as heavy-handed in influencing the way Iraqis interpret history, neither do they want to be in the position of endorsing texts that could be anti-American, anti-Israeli, or radically religious. As a result, some charge, in a matter of months Iraqi education has gone from one-sided to 'no-sided'" (November, 2003).

As the Iraq war continues, the Iraq/United States coalition has focused its energies on the reconstruction of school infrastructure and, specifically, the hundreds of buildings damaged in battle or by vandalism. However, a spokesman for the League for the Defense of the Rights of the Iraqi People, Muzhir al-Dulaymi, maintains that NGO contracts for rebuilding Iraqi schools are not enough to improve facilities for teaching and learning. "Companies are winning bids worth millions of dollars to reconstruct schools, but in fact schools have only been painted. [There has been no] improvement to the infrastructure, and no new equipment has been bought" (Janabi, 2004).

Yet, Iraq did not construct new schools during the period of United Nations sanctions, 1990 to 2003. Consider, for example, 1980, when about 500 students attended a single school. By 2003, 4,500 pupils attended school in one building (Asquith, 2003). The impact of the 1991 Gulf War and the UN sanctions sent school funding plummeting. Teachers were paid $6 a month. In addition, U.S. government officials hold Saddam Hussein responsible for embezzling educational funds for his luxuries. It has been estimated that school enrollment had fallen to 53 percent in 2002 because of dropouts and children seeking employment to assist their families (U.S. Agency for International Development, 2002).

From PRESERVICE to PRACTICE

USAID in Action

The United States has a long history of extending a helping hand to people overseas who are struggling to make a better life, recovering from a disaster, or striving to live in a free and democratic country. This caring stands as a hallmark of the United States around the world—and shows the world our true character as a nation.

U.S. foreign assistance has always had the twofold purpose of furthering America's foreign policy interests in expanding democracy and free markets, while improving the lives of the citizens of the developing world. Spending less than one-half of 1 percent of the federal budget, USAID works around the world to achieve these goals.

USAID's history goes back to the Marshall Plan reconstruction of Europe after World War II and the Truman Administration's Point Four Program. In 1961, the Foreign Assistance Act was signed into law, and USAID was created by executive order. Since that time, USAID has been the principal U.S. agency to extend assistance to countries recovering from disaster, trying to escape poverty, and engaging in democratic reforms.

Such assistance has helped Iraq move away from unrelieved rote learning in decrepit, unsanitary classrooms to interactive learning in rehabilitated buildings. Since 2003, USAID has rehabilitated nearly 3,000 schools. Over 20 million new textbooks have been supplied by USAID (8.6 million) and UNESCO (12 million). By mid-2006, more than 120,000 primary school teachers—nearly a third of Iraq's educators—will have received training and technical assistance.

As a result of two decades of wars and economic hardship brought on by misrule, Iraqi schools fell into disrepair, enrollment dropped, and literacy levels stagnated. Iraq's adult literacy rate is now one of the lowest in all Arab countries; UNESCO estimates literacy rates to be less than 60 percent, or 6 million illiterate Iraqi adults. Rural residents and women have been hit hardest; only 37 percent of rural women can read, and 30 percent of Iraqi girls of high school age are enrolled in school, compared with 42 percent of boys.

USAID and the Ministry of Education are working together to improve access to quality education in Iraq at the primary, secondary, and university levels. Programs have provided essential supplies and training to support schools nationwide. A series of model schools have been established where Iraqi educators implement new and innovative teaching methods, while giving students access to improved equipment. USAID also developed partnerships between U.S. and Iraqi universities, a collaborative venture that has helped reequip and revitalize Iraq's higher-education system.

USAID Accomplishments

- 2,962 schools have been rehabilitated in full or in part since 2003.
- Hundreds of thousands of desks, chairs, cabinets, chalkboards, and more than 3 million school kits have been distributed throughout the country.
- 55,000 teachers and administrators have been trained. By the end of the 2005–2006 school year, more than 120,000 educators had received in-service training supported by USAID since 2004.
- Eighty-four primary and secondary schools are being established to serve as model schools. Teachers will receive specialized training, and schools will be equipped with computer and science laboratories.
- An accelerated learning program, targeting 14,000 out-of-school youth, is being implemented during the 2005–2006 school year.
- To improve resource management, a comprehensive Education Management Information System is being developed, and Ministry of Education staff are being trained.
- Satellite Internet access and computers have been installed at the Ministry of Education and in all 21 Directorates of Education.
- More than 8.7 million math and science textbooks have been edited, printed, and distributed throughout Iraq.
- Partnerships have been established between 5 American and 10 Iraqi universities. Through these partnerships, more than 1,500 Iraqi faculty and students have participated in workshops, training, conferences, and courses in Iraq, the Middle East, Europe, and the United States.
- University facilities, such as libraries, computer and science laboratories, lecture halls, and buildings, have been rehabilitated at colleges of law, engineering, medicine, archeology, and agriculture. In addition, books and electronic resources have been provided to university libraries.

Source: Adapted from USAID Assistance in Iraq (2005), http://www.usaid.gov/iraq/accomplishments/education.html.

Iraqi schools also face ongoing pressures regarding the current curriculum. There is fear that the U.S. government will attempt to westernize the curriculum. Certain factions, such as the Muslim Awareness Association, maintain that schools and teachers should instruct students primarily in Islamic law. For this reason, there is some resistance to the role of the United States in Iraqi schools.

The American perspective on this situation is a sensitive balancing act. Gregg Sullivan, spokesman for the Near Eastern Affairs Bureau of the State Department, explained, "We will strongly recommend concepts of tolerance, and be against anything that is anti-Semitic or anti-West—content that would only sow the seeds for future intolerance. . . . We'd hope it's only an advisory role, but if something develops that's disadvantageous to the Iraqi people, we'd weigh in on a stronger level" (quoted in Asquith, 2003).

Author James Loewen, who wrote the book *Lies My Teacher Told Me* (1996), argues that all countries teach a form of propaganda, even the United States. Loewen feels that the best strategy to address imbalances of content is to ensure that multiple perspectives are included in texts, such as the historical perspectives of other Middle Eastern countries: Saudi Arabia, Jordan, and/or Turkey. Then, he maintains, the students can reflect on the content and form their own interpretations regarding its meaning.

SUMMARY

New teachers today must be cognizant of the diversity that exists both within and outside U.S. borders. With the international world being brought closer through advanced technology and information systems, educators can address globalization from a variety of perspectives. Whether the global community is examined in the classroom through the lens of human values, global issues, or history, teachers and students today have access to new forms of knowledge that enable them to think critically think about the privileges, responsibilities, challenges, and problem-solving approaches we must all confront.

DISCUSSION QUESTIONS

1. What is globalization? In what ways is it a controversial topic for teachers to address in the classroom? Why is it important to discuss globalization with students, especially in terms of such issues as international economies, environmental concerns, human rights, and poverty?

2. Describe how global education can be incorporated with various target grade levels and content areas. How can cultural values and history be presented in the classroom to illustrate the interconnectedness of nations and people?

3. How are technology, globalization, and schooling interrelated? What are some strategies that teachers can employ in the classroom that utilize Web resources for core curriculum instruction? Describe two or three websites that you can envision yourself using as part of curriculum design.

4. As you reflect on other international educational systems, describe the social, cultural, and political issues that influence the teaching and learning experiences of educators and their students. What obstacles do teachers across the globe face? What issues are important to all educators?

ACTIVITIES

1. Compare and contrast the educational systems and practices of two or more nations. What are their educational priorities, curriculum features, and pedagogical approaches? How does the cultural, political, and economic climate affect teachers, students, and the community?

2. Develop a global education unit in a content area of your choice. Refer to and cite some of the links noted in the chapter. Integrate core curriculum objectives, hands-on strategies, photo and video galleries, and podcasts. Include as part of the unit how your own

students will utilize and demonstrate multimedia as part of their knowledge construction.

3. Visit with two or three diverse community members in your community. Discuss with them their perspectives on globalization and global education. What do they feel students should know about other countries and their cultures, religions, languages, and history? Do they believe this knowledge is important even if controversial? Give them an opportunity to explain at length, if they want to do so.

WEBSITES

Campaign for Labor Rights
http://www.clrlabor.org
This site offers an e-mail listserv of alerts on sweatshop and solidarity issues. The Campaign for Labor Rights (CLR) website includes past updates, links, and resources. It also features a document library on the Nike campaign, Disney in Haiti, Guess jeans, child labor issues, teachers' rights in Mexico and Central America, farm worker issues, and youth and campus activism. CLR publishes a useful newsletter filled with audiovisual resources, fact sheets, and updates on campaigns to support workers organizing around the world.

The Center for Commercial-Free Public Education
http://www.ibiblio.org/commercialfree
The Center is the main national organization that opposes the increasing commercialization of public schools. It helps communities organize against Channel One, cola contracts, and other infiltration of public space by private interests. The Center publishes the newsletter *Not for Sale!* and offers information about its various campaigns on its website.

Rethinking Schools
http://www.rethinkingschools.org/publication/rg
This website offers lesson plans and resources from the book *Rethinking Globalization: Teaching for Justice in an Unjust World,* by Bill Bigelow and Bob Peterson. The topics addressed include colonialism, the global economy, global sweatshops, child labor, agriculture, consumption, the environment, and culture.

Schools for Chiapas
http://www.schoolsforchiapas.org
Visit this website for an overview of rural education programs for Mayan families living in the mountains of Chiapas, Mexico. The site provides background on community-run centers that focus on democracy, literacy, language maintenance, cultural traditions, health education, and ecology.

United Nations Children's Fund (UNICEF)
UNICEF produces educational materials and distributes funds to children's programs throughout the world. Its annual report, *The State of the World's Children,* provides useful statistics.

REFERENCES

Asquith, C. (2003, November 4). Turning the page on Iraq's history. *The Christian Science Monitor.* Retrieved June 7, 2007, from http://www.csmonitor.com/2003/1104/p11s01-legn.html

DeCoker, G. (2002). *National standards and school reform in Japan and the United States.* New York: Teachers College Press.

Desmond, E. (1996). The failed miracle. *Time, 147*(17), 60–64.

Ellington, L. (2005). *Japanese education.* Bloomington, IN: National Clearinghouse for U.S.-Japan Studies. Available online at http://www.indiana.edu/~japan/digest5.html

Friedman, T. (2000). *The Lexus and the olive tree.* New York: Anchor Books.

Held, D. (1991). *Political theory today.* Stanford: Stanford University Press.

Janabi, A. (2004, May). Iraq's education setback. *The World Press.* Available online at http://www.worldpress.org/Mideast/1864.cfm

Kniep, W. (1989). Global education as school reform. *Educational Leadership 47*(1), 45.

Loewen, J. (1996). *Lies my teacher told me.* New York: Touchstone.

McLaughlin, H. (2003). *Schooling in Mexico: A brief guide for U.S. educators.* ERIC Digest. Available online at http://www.ericdigests.org

Lollock, L. (2001). The foreign born population in the United States: Population characteristics. Washington, DC: U.S. Department of Commerce, Economics and Statistics Administration, U.S. Census Bureau. Available online at http://www.census.gov/prod/2000pubs/p.20-534.pdf

Scholte, J. A. (2000). *Globalization: A critical introduction.* London: Palgrave.

Torres, C. (2002). Globalization, education and citizenship: Solidarity versus markets? *American Educational Research Journal, 39*(2), 363–378.

U.S. Agency for International Development. (2002). U.S. aid for Iraq. Available online at http://www.usaid.gov/iraq

Wu, A. (1999). The Japanese education system: A case study and analysis. National Institute on Student Achievement, Curriculum and Assessment, Office of Educational Research and Improvement, U.S. Office of Education. Available online at http://www.ed.gov/pubs/ResearchToday/98-3038html

acculturation The process of cultural learning as groups encounter a dominant culture other than their own. To acknowledge that the process of education in America is both *enculturative*, as students first learn their own culture, and *acculturative*, as students in schools learn about a second, dominant culture, distinct from their own firsthand, lived experiences.

alternative licensure programs Education licensure programs for teaching candidates with bachelor's degrees in fields other than education who have not completed traditional, state approved teacher education programs. Such programs help relieve some of the pressure schools districts face as they aim to meet the specific needs of schools in such fields as English as a second language, mathematics, and science.

authentic and performance assessment A strategy that seeks to determine students' content area knowledge and skills. *Performance assessment* refers to those assessments that measure how well a particular skill is completed, whether it is rebuilding a car engine or writing a formal letter. *Authentic assessment* refers to assessments that emulate real-world experiences, such as through problem solving and analyzing, as opposed to the reporting of facts.

assimilation The process whereby individuals or groups of differing ethnic heritage are absorbed into the dominant culture of a society through contact and participation in the larger culture, gradually give up most of their former culture traits, and take on the new traits.

behaviorism A philosophy grounded in the belief that human actions are influenced by environmental factors rather than by human free will or agency.

Bilingual Act of 1974 A federal law that requires the involvement of parents in the educational and instructional planning for English language learners.

bilingual education Instruction that is provided to students in English and in a second target language or native language.

Bracero program (Emergency Farm Labor Program) The U.S. guest-worker program that ran for twenty-two years (1942 to 1964) and that brought some 4.5 million guest workers (temporary agricultural, railroad, and other workers) into the United States from Mexico. It began as an emergency measure to meet the labor shortage of World War II. The Bracero (from the Spanish *brazo*, which translates as "arm") program, also referred to as the Mexican Farm Labor Supply Program and the Mexican Labor Agreement, was sanctioned by Congress through Public Law 45 of 1943.

breach of contract A failure to meet a commitment set forth in a contract. Either a teacher or a school district can breach a contract. For example, a teacher might not complete a teaching assignment based on the terms of the contract, or a school district might refuse to pay a teacher compensation for services such as extracurricular activity coaching or advisement.

Brown v. Board of Education of Topeka, Kansas A 1954 U.S. Supreme Court case that found that the desegregation of students because of race was unconstitutional. This decision laid the foundation for equal educational access for all public education students in the United States.

Bureau of Indian Affairs A U.S. governmental agency whose primary responsibility is the administration and management of 55.7 million acres of land held in trust by the United States for American Indians, Indian tribes, and Alaska natives. There are 561 federal recognized tribal governments in the United States. Developing forestlands, leasing assets on these lands, directing agricultural programs, protecting water and land rights, developing and maintaining infrastructure and economic development are all part of the agency's responsibility. In addition, the Bureau of Indian Affairs provides education services to approximately 48,000 Indian students.

career ladder A program of incentives, such as pay increases, for teachers who have demonstrated specialized skills.

certification The state recognition of teachers who have met basic professional standards for classroom instruction.

charter school A specialized, independent school that can be either privately or publicly funded. Charter schools are often free from regulations that impact the curriculum, budget, and hiring restrictions faced by the public schools.

Chinese Exclusion Act The 1882 federal legislation that stopped the Chinese immigration to the United States.

classroom management Curriculum design and classroom structure that ensures the maximum effectiveness of instruction and time management for teachers and students.

collective bargaining Negotiations of groups of teachers, usually in a union, regarding professional rights, salary, health care, and retirement policies.

common schools The tax-supported colonial schools that provided boys and girls with three years of education.

cooperative learning An instructional approach where teachers place students in specialized groups to work together and meet learning objectives.

constructivism A concept that contends learners construct their own understanding of the world around them. Thus, teachers access students' background or prior knowledge and then design their instructional strategies, activities, and questions in ways that guide the learners to the next level of content area knowledge or skills.

culture A pattern of knowledge, skills, behaviors, attitudes, and beliefs, as well as material artifacts, produced by human society and transmitted from one generation to another. Culture is the whole of humanity's intellectual, social, technological, political, economic, religious, moral, and aesthetic accomplishments.

culturally relevant pedagogy An approach to meeting the academic and social needs of culturally diverse students that, according to Geneva Gay (2000), uses "the cultural knowledge, prior experiences, frames of reference, and performance styles of ethnically diverse students to make learning more relevant to and effective [for students]. . . . It teaches to and through strengths of these students. It is culturally validating and affirming" (p. 29). An additional, and some would argue the most important, goal of culturally relevant pedagogy is to increase the academic achievement of culturally diverse students.

cultural deficit model Instruction and policies that view minority groups as inferior intellectually, culturally and socially. Cultural deficits are generally associated with the perpetuation of institutional racism. For example, English language learners were said to come from homes where there was a lack of language, structure, and morals. Such deficit models have a racist and linguicist foundation and devalue children who grow up with life experiences that are different from those of white, middle-class, native English speaking children.

discourse A dialogue between speakers. The concept holds different discipline-specific meanings. For example, Michel Foucault saw discourse as a system of ideas or knowledge, inscribed in a specific vocabulary (e.g., psychoanalysis, anthropology, cultural/literary studies) given certain historical, social, and cultural systems of knowledge in a society. According to Foucault, such discourses are used to legitimate the exercise of power over certain persons by categorizing them as particular "types."

deculturalization Society's attempt to disregard and eliminate the cultures of conquered peoples and replace them, through education, with European American culture.

dual-language or two-way bilingual program Instructional programming where students receive as much as 50 percent of the content instruction in a second language other than English. The remaining percentage of instruction is provided in English.

due process The requirement that teachers' and administrators' rights are protected in legal disputes; the criteria and evaluation data used for employee notification, hearings and dismissal proceedings.

Elementary and Secondary Education Act of 1965 A federal law that requires all states to provide a free and equal public education to all children. The act provides funds for instructional programming, instructional materials, remedial instruction, counseling, and health services.

enculturation The process of learning one's own culture. When this process occurs formally in an institutional setting, it is called *schooling*. Schooling is a narrower concept than education because it involves specialists teaching in places established for that purpose. On the other hand, education, although planned as well, does not always take place in an institutional setting. For diverse students, enculturation takes place in the home and in the community.

essentialism A philosophy that maintains there is a single body of knowledge that each person must learn to function in society.

existentialism A philosophy that acknowledges the individual in the process of learning, choice, and creativity as well as the subjective nature of each human's lived experience.

Family Educational Rights and Privacy Act (FERPA) A federal law that ensures that students' records—such as grades, test scores, teacher and counselor reports, and letters of recommendation—must be made accessible to students and their guardians and cannot be released without parent and guardian permission.

formative assessment Ongoing evaluation of knowledge through the use of observation, discussion, and practice as students build and develop skills.

Homestead Act of 1863 A federal law that allowed any American citizen to file for a quarter-section of free land (160 acres). The land could be owned at the end of five years if a house was built on it, a well was dug, 10 acres were plowed, a portion was fenced, and the homesteader actually lived there. Additionally, the homesteader could claim a quarter-section of land by "timber culture" (commonly called a "tree claim"). This required that you plant and successfully cultivate 10 acres of timber.

Individuals with Disabilities in Education Act (IDEA) A federal act that ensures that children with disabilities have the opportunity to receive a free appropriate public education, between the ages of 3 and 21 (Part A) and from birth to age 2 (Part B), regardless of the severity of the disability. The law has been revised many times over the years. The most recent amendments were passed by Congress in December 2004, with final regulations published in August 2006.

individualized education program (IEP) A plan approved by families that outlines what teachers must do to meet a student's individual learning needs.

Interstate New Teacher Assessment and Support Consortium (INTASC) Knowledge and performance standards that guide state teacher licensing requirements. Superintendents of public instruction representing 17 states and educational researchers developed the INTASC standards. These standards introduce beginning teachers to essential concepts they need to be familiar with when entering the profession.

involuntary minorities Groups that compare their chances of success in America with the dominant white group and conclude that they are worse off because of their minority status. They often attribute their economic and other difficulties to institutionalized discrimination, which cannot be eliminated by hard work and education alone.

land grant initiatives Public schools and land acquired, funded, and developed through federal law beginning in 1785.

language extinction The disappearance of languages that are no longer used. Sometimes this occurs when cultures no longer use their native language because more aggressive language groups impose their language and culture on the minority language group. There currently are only 187 Native American languages, with a half-million speakers in the United States and Canada. These languages are also known as *endangered languages*.

licensure The process of meeting standards and requirements to become a professional teacher.

linguicism A form of prejudice that makes judgments about people's wealth, education, social status, and other traits based on their use of language (including accents, size of vocabulary, and sentence structure or syntax). It may also involve a person's ability or inability to use one language instead of another. The word is attributed to the linguist Tove Skutnabb-Kangas, who may have coined the word in her writings in the mid-1980s about prejudice in education.

linguistic privileges Unseen privileges given to those whose utilize a language preferred by a dominant society over another.

Massachusetts Act of 1642 A law that stated that the parents or guardians of children and servants were required to ensure that their wards adequately understood the basic principles of religion and the laws of the commonwealth. They also had to ensure that their wards were competent in reading and writing, thus paving the way for one of the nation's first educational policies. If the government decided that the parents were not abiding by this law, they would remove children from their home and place them in another home where they could receive adequate education.

merit pay Incentive pay provided by school districts for superior teaching or school performance, as demonstrated by students' test outcomes, administrator observation, curriculum and portfolio development, or instruction in underperforming schools or in high-need subjects (such as ESL, bilingual education, math, and science).

multiple intelligences The eight independent dimensions of overall intelligence that include linguistic intelligence, logical-mathematical intelligence, musical intelligence, bodily-kinesthetic intelligence, spatial intelligence, interpersonal intelligence, and intrapersonal intelligence.

National Educators Association (NEA) and American Federation of Teachers (AFT) Teachers' organizations that represent specific disciplines, offer conferences, committee activities, professional development, and research journals to its members.

These teachers' unions negotiate and supervise collective bargaining for the rights and interests of teachers specific to salary, health benefits, tenure, and other employment concerns.

normal school An educational program established in the 1800s to train teachers according to specific standards.

parochial schools Schools supported by religious groups to transmit certain beliefs and curricula to students.

pedagogy The art of being a teacher. The term generally refers to the strategies, decisions, and social contexts relevant to one's instruction or a style of instruction. The word comes from the Greek—literally, "to lead the child." However, according to Paolo Freire and Ira Shor, *critical pedagogy* challenges teachers' own habits of thought, reading, writing, and speaking, which must go beneath surface meaning, first impressions, dominant myths, institutional pronouncements, traditional clichés, received wisdom, and mere opinions to understand the deep meaning, root causes, social context, ideology, and personal consequences of any action, event, process, organization, experience, text, subject matter, policy, mass media, or discourse.

perennialism A philosophy that ascribes great value to historical knowledge and thought.

portfolio A specific and purposeful collection of a teacher's or student's work that chronicles and demonstrates content area knowledge, skills, and progress.

progressive tax A tax rate that generally increases with an individual's income. Federal income tax formulas are generally progressive in nature and are often viewed favorably by the public, while regressive tax formulas are perceived negatively.

property taxes The taxes that are determined by the assessed value of a home or property and the amount of tax revenue to be raised by a community to provide services, particularly education.

proportional taxes Specific state sale taxes imposed on everyone equally, regardless of income. For example, a person with an income of $100,000 may pay $10,000 or 10 percent income tax. A person with an income of $10,000 would also pay 10 percent or $1,000 in income tax.

pullout ESL The practice of removing or *pulling out* English language learners (ELLs) from their regular classrooms and bringing them to a special classroom for part of the day with other ELLs to receive instruction in English.

reduction in force The layoff or termination of (primarily) untenured teachers.

remittances Transfers of money by immigrant workers to their home countries. Remittances contribute to economic growth and to the livelihoods of people residing in developing nations.

regressive tax A tax plan that serves high-income citizens by providing them with a lower tax percentage rate, while low-income citizens pay a larger percentage of their income tax dollars. For example, an individual earning $10,000 and facing a 5 percent income tax rate would pay $500. In contrast, an individual earning $100,000 could pay 3 percent income tax or $3,000.

rubric An assessment instrument that provides information guidelines or criteria that are scored holistically.

scaffolding A metaphor that describes an instructional approach presented by a teacher or peer to guide and support learning when the student cannot do it alone. Through this process, the instructor provides the student with assistance only when those skills are beyond the learner's ability.

school choice The belief that families should be free to choose schools for their children, using, generally speaking, public funding or vouchers.

schooling A narrower concept than education because it involves specialists teaching in places established for that purpose. Education, although planned as well, does not always take place in an institutional setting.

sheltered instruction An instructional approach for English language learners where the teaching and the classroom materials are in English but are "sheltered" through language that is made meaningful with props, graphic organizers, demonstrations, body language, drama, and so on. An example of a sheltered high school science lesson on photosynthesis might include actual experiments with plants that are grown in the window sill in the sun compared with plants that are grown in the closet.

segregation The forced separation of people of different ethnicities, race, gender, language, or physical abilities in daily life when both are doing equal tasks, such as when seeking employment, housing, health care, attending school, eating in a restaurant, drinking from a water fountain, or using a rest room.

social reconstructivism A philosophy based on the belief that people are responsible for their social conditions and can improve their standing by challenging and changing the current social order.

teacher induction or mentoring programs Programs that support the retention of teachers within the profession. They generally include the following features—mentoring, professional development, evaluation, and opportunities for ongoing collaboration and remediation. These programs focus on meeting the unique needs and challenges new teachers face when beginning their careers.

Title I The section of the federal Elementary and Secondary Education Act of 1965 that established programs to support the academic achievement of low income students in need of instructional remediation.

Title IX The section of the federal Education Amendments of 1972 that guarantees students may not be excluded from federally funded educational programs and initiatives based on gender.

tenure A permanent contract, generally offered after a probationary teaching period where new teachers demonstrate their teaching skills through formative, observable evaluation.

tracking The segregation of students in classrooms based on ability.

transitional bilingual education The goal of transitional programs is to *transition* students from their L1 to English. *Early-exit* bilingual programs intend to *exit* students from the bilingual program "early," which usually means sometime between first and third grade—not enough time for most students to learn a second language. *Late-exit* bilingual programs have the goal to exit students from the bilingual program in the upper elementary grades.

tuition tax credit A federal and state provision that allows a taxpayer to deduct educational costs from taxable income before computing taxes.

voluntary minorities Immigrants who move voluntarily to the United States because they believed this would result in more economic well-being, better opportunities, and/or more freedom. These groups are, for example, Chinese and Punjabi immigrants.

voucher A credit scrip or certificate that is used for student tuition and that is provided by the state.

TEXT CREDITS

Chapter 1

Pages 6–7: Adapted from World Wide Learn, http://www.worldwidelearn.com/education-timeline/education-timeline.htm.

Pages 26–27: Reprinted courtesy of The American-Arab Anti-Discrimination Committee (ADC).

Chapter 2

Page 56: From Faculty and TA Development (FTAD), The Ohio State University.

Chapter 3

Page 65: The Interstate New Teacher Assessment and Support Consortium (INTASC) standards were developed by the Council of Chief State School Officers and member states. Copies may be downloaded from the Council's website at http://www.ccsso.org. Council of Chief State, Model standards for beginning teacher licensing, assessment, and development: A resource for state dialogue (Washington, DC, 1992), http://www.ccsso.org/content/pdfs/corestrd.pdf.

Page 66: Reprinted by permission.

Page 68: PRAXIS materials are reprinted by permission of Educational Testing Service, the copyright owner. However, the test questions and any other testing information are provided in their entirety by Houghton Mifflin Company. No endorsement of this publication by Educational Testing Service should be inferred.

Page 71: Reprinted by permission.

Page 74: National Education Association, Rankings and estimates: Rankings of the states 2005 and estimates of school statistics 2006 (Figure 3.1, Average salaries ($) of public school teachers, 2004–2005). Reprinted with permission of the National Education Association © 2006. All rights reserved.

Page 75: Reprinted by permission.
Page 77: Reprinted by permission.

Chapter 4

Page 97: Martha Floyd-Tenery, La visita, in L. Moll, C. Amanta, & N. Gonzalez (Eds.), *Funds of knowledge: Theorizing practices in households and classrooms* (Mahweh, NJ: Lawrence Erlbaum, 2005), p. 125. Reproduced with permission of Lawrence Erlbaum Associates Inc., in the format Textbook via copyright Clearance Center.

Chapter 5

Pages 108–109: Reprinted with permission of the Sexuality Information and Education Council of the United States (SIECUS), 130 West 42 Street, Suite 350, New York, NY 10036, www.siecus.org.

Page 113: Used with permission. Copyright 2007 National School Boards Association. All rights reserved.

Page 118: Reprinted by permission.

Chapter 6

Page 135: Copyright © 2000 CQPress, a division of Congressional Quarterly Inc.

Chapter 7

Pages 146–147: Used with permission. Copyright 2007 National School Boards Association. All rights reserved.

Page 148: Reprinted with permission from NSBA Legal Clips, a weekly e-newsletter of the National School Boards Association. Free subscriptions available at www.nsba.org/legalclips.

Page 154: Reprinted with permission from NSBA Legal Clips, a weekly e-newsletter of the National School Boards Association. Free subscriptions available at www.nsba.org/legalclips.

Page 157: Reprinted by permission.

Page 161: Reprinted with permission from NSBA Legal Clips, a weekly e-newsletter of the National School Boards Association. Free subscriptions available at www.nsba.org/legalclips.

Page 166: Reprinted with permission from NSBA Legal Clips, a weekly e-newsletter of the National School Boards Association. Free subscriptions available at www.nsba.org/legalclips.

Chapter 8

Page 176: Reprinted by permission of Stephen Holtrop.

Page 183: From M. J. Larkin, Providing support for student independence through scaffolded instruction, *Teaching exceptional children, 34*(1) (2001), pp. 30–34. Copyright © 2001 by The Council for Exceptional Children. Reprinted with permission.

Page 184: Reprinted by permission of Stephen Holtrop.

Page 186: Alison Kreider, 1968 blow outs! Chicano students in East Los Angeles mobilize for quality education. Reprinted by permission.

Page 194: Reprinted by permission.

Chapter 9

Pages 202–203: Reprinted by permission of Jon Mueller.

Page 209: Reprinted by permission of Jennifer Thill.

Pages 211–212: Reprinted courtesy of Blackstone Valley Tech High School.

Page 214: Reprinted by permission.

Chapter 10

Page 226: From K. H. Au & T. W. Raphael, Equity and literacy in the next millennium, *Reading Research Quarterly, 35* (2000), 170–188. Copyright 2000 by International Reading Association. Reproduced with permission of International Reading Association in the format Textbook via Copyright Clearance Center.

PHOTO CREDITS

Chapter 1

Page 2: Library of Congress LC-DIG-ppmsc-02459

Page 12: Chris Detrick/The Salt Lake Tribune

Page 20: © Corbis

Page 22: Center for American History, University of Texas, Austin, CN Number 07207a, b. Lee (Russel) Photograph Collection, 1935–1977. June 1949. Courtesy of lulac.org

Page 23: Library of Congress LC-USZ62-42810

Chapter 2

Page 31: Cleve Bryant/PhotoEdit, Inc.

Page 33: © Martin Jenkinson/Alamy

Page 35: © Bettmann/Corbis

Page 42: Courtesy of Grace Huerta, used with permission of Beth Kennedy

Page 49: © Corbix

Chapter 3

Page 60: Pam Francis/Photographer's Choices/Getty Images

Page 63: Digital Vision/Getty Images Royalty Free

Page 72: Joe Raedle/Getty Images

Page 77: Courtesy of Grace Huerta, used with permission of Dan Coffin

Chapter 4

Page 81: © Lee Celano/Reuters/Corbis

Page 85: AP Images/Steven Senne

Page 88: © Will & Deni McIntyre/Corbis

Page 96: Courtesy of Grace Huerta, used with permission of Martha Perea-Ewer

Chapter 5

Page 104: David McNew/Getty Images

Page 114: Dave Einsel/Getty Images

Page 115: Courtesy of Grace Huerta, used with permission of Frank Schofield

Page 121: Amy Etra/PhotoEdit, Inc.

Chapter 6

Page 124: © Sonda Dawes/The Image Works

Page 133: © Jeff Greenberg/Alamy

Page 141: © Bob Daemmrich/The Image Works

Chapter 7

Page 144: AP Images/David Duprey

Page 155: Michael Newman/PhotoEdit, Inc.

Page 160: Michael Newman/PhotoEdit, Inc.

Page 163: AP Images/Science

Page 165: Kayte Deioma/PhotoEdit, Inc.

Chapter 8

Page 170: AP Images/Douglas C. Pizac

Page 173: Blend Images/Getty Images Royalty Free

Page 174: Jonathan A. Nourok/PhotoEdit, Inc.

Page 185: AP Images/Akron Beacon Journal, Bob DeMay

Page 186: © George Rodriguez Photography

Page 192: © Steve Skjold/Alamy

Page 193: PictureIndia/Getty Images Royalty Free

Chapter 9

Page 199: © Charles Gupton/Corbis

Page 201: Michael Newman/PhotoEdit, Inc.

Page 210: Kayte Deioma/PhotoEdit, Inc.

Chapter 10

Page 222: © Michael J. Doolittle/The Image Works

Page 228: © Ariel Skelley/Corbis

Page 231: © Ellen B. Senisi/The Image Works

Page 237: Courtesy of Grace Huerta

Chapter 11

Page 240: © Bob Daemmrich/The Image Works

Page 245: Jeff Greenberg/PhotoEdit, Inc.

Page 257: Richard Hutchings/PhotoEdit, Inc.

Chapter 12

Page 264: AP Images/Rick Bowmer

Page 267: © Hu Sheng/epa/Corbis

Page 269: UNHCR/N, Behring

Page 271: With permission of Schools for Chiapas (www.schoolsforchiapas.org)

Page 272: USAID/Thomas Hartwell

Abernathy, S., 190

Abilities, understanding differences in, 173–184

Ability grouping, 90–91, 179
effects of, 95

Abington School District v. Schemp, 160

Abstinence-only programs
curriculum policy on, 163
medical inaccuracies in, 108–109

Abuse
child, 156–158
physical, 158
sexual, 158

Academic freedom, 159–160

Accountability, standards-based, 131

Acculturation, 12, 228

Actions, controlling own, 190–191

"An Act Relating to Common Schools," 10

Acuna, R., 186*n*

Adeed, P., 24

Adequate yearly progress (AYP), 131, 218

Adler, Mortimer, 35, 43, 44

Adler, S., 225, 228

Advanced placement (AP), 179
open-access, 180

Affective domains, 206, 207

African Americans
admission to common schools, 11
creation of NAACP and, 49, 51–52
early education for, 18–20
exclusion of, from schools, 10
support for voucher plans, 120

African American Zion School, 18

African Methodist Episcopal Church, 18

Afrocentric curriculum, 52–53

Age of Reason, 8, 9

Agricultural Adjustment Act (1935), 128

AIDS/HIV education in public schools, 163–164

Alexander, K., 138

Al-Hazza, T., 24, 25, 26

Al-Khatah, A., 26

Alternative lesson plans, 190

Alternative licensure programs, 64, 69, 141

Amanti, C., 97, 195

Ambroggio, Luis Alberto, 258

American Civil Liberties Union (ACLU), 113

American cultural values, 229–233

American education
European influences on early, 8–9
Greek influences on, 5–8

American Federation of Labor-Congress of Industrial Organizations (AFL-CIO), 72–73

American Federation of Teachers (AFT), 64, 72–73, 140, 206

American Indians
early education for, 20–21
exclusion of, from schools, 10

Americanization, 20

American Missionary Society, 19

American Protective Association, 245

Americans with Disabilities Act (ADA) (1990), 130

Amrein, A., 72

Analysis, 206

Analytic rubrics, 202, 203

Anti-Arab discrimination, 26–27

Anzaldúa, Gloria, 32, 53–55

Application, 206

Arab Americans
education of, 26
immigration and changing demographics, 25
stereotypes and, 24–26

Archer, J., 63

Aristotle, 8, 31, 35, 37, 43

Armstrong, Samuel, 49

Army academy, 106

Arouet, François Marie, 8

Asian Americans
early education of, 22–24
segregation of, 23–24

Asquith, C., 273

Assessment(s). *See also* Standardized tests
alternative strategies in, 218–219
authentic, 201, 202–203
for English language learners, 256–258
history of student strategies, 200–201
identification of goals and objectives, 201–202, 204
performance, 201, 202, 203, 219
politicization of national and state standards, 204–206
strengths and weaknesses of instruments, 208–213
teachers union's position on, 214

Assessment instruments, 208–213
paper and pencil tests as, 208
portfolios as, 209–213
rubrics as, 208–209

Assimilation
early resistance to, in schools, 13–14
of immigrant children, 12–13
linguistic, 244
process of, 12

Au, Kathryn, 225, 226*n*

Authentic assessments, 201, 202
tools for, 202–203

Authentic tasks, 202

Babyak, S., 64

Back-to-basics teaching, 33

Bagley, William, 33, 43, 44

Balfanz, R., 92

Banks, C., 187

Banks, J., 14, 187, 234

Bankston, C., III, 17

Baratz, J., 227

Baratz, S., 227

Batzle, J., 210

Becker, C., 9

Behavior
dealing with off-task, 188–189
decreasing incidence of, 190
responsibility for classroom, 188–191

Behavioral theory, 181–182

Behaviorism, 36–37, 43

Berlin, I., 19

Berliner, D., 72, 125

Berrol, S., 14

Bethel School District No. 403 v. Fraser, 165

Bhagat Singh Thind, United States v., 23

Biber, D., 242

Bible, 19

Biddle, B., 125

Bilingual education, 15, 21–22, 244, 246, 252–253
transitional, 252–253
two-way, 243

Bilingual Education Act (1968), 246

Bilingualism, 246

Bill for Establishing Religious Freedom (1779), 9

Bill for the More General Diffusion of Knowledge (1779) (Jefferson), 9

Block grants, 130

Bloom, Benjamin, 206–207

Board of Education of the Westside Community School v. Mergens, 160

Bodily kinesthetic intelligence, 175, 177

Bonds, 135

Borderland theory, 53–55

Borich, G., 201

Bracero Act (1943), 15

Bracero Program, 15

Breach of contract, 149–150

Brimley, V., 119

Brookfield, Stephen, 56

Brophy, J., 172, 173, 180

Brown, 118

Brown v. Board of Education II, 130

Brown v. Board of Education of Topeka, Kansas, 106–107

Brumberg, S. E., 13

Bruner, Jerome, 183

Bruning, Robert, 63, 172

Buckley Amendment, 165

Bullock, H. A., 18, 19

Burghart, Mary Silvina, 49

Burnout, 77–78

Bush, George W., 32, 69–70, 108, 131–132, 205

Butcher, Susan, 187
Butler, M., 44

California Achievement
    Tests, 205
Cambron-McCabe, N., 156
Cameron, J., 189
Cangelosi, B., 170, 189, 190,
    191, 198
Cangelosi, J. S., 189, 190, 191
Canter, L., 190, 191
Canter, M., 190, 191
Caplan, N., 17
Capotorto, Patrick J., 154
Career Education Implementa-
    tion Incentive Act (1977),
    130
Carlisle Indian School, 20
Carlton, Gay, 161
Carter, James G., 10
Carter, Jimmy, 106, 130
Castro, Sal, 186
Catholic schools, 21–22
Center for Applied
    Linguistics, 253
Center for Research on
    Education, Diversity,
    and Excellence, 256
Certification, 64
    effect of No Child Left Behind
      Act on, 213–215
    process of, 67, 69
Chadha, Y., 46
Chambers, J., 251
Chang, M., 89
Charles, C. M., 189, 191
Charter schools, 117–119
    funding of, 139
Chavez, Ben, 36
Chavez, Cesar, 47
Checkley, 175
Checklists in assessing
    performance, 219
Chicano students, East Los
    Angeles blowouts and, 186
Child abuse, 156–158
Chinese Exclusion Act
    (1882), 23
Chinese Primary School,
    opening of first, 23
Choy, M. H., 17
Christianity, American culture
    and, 230
Civilization Fund Act, 20
Civil rights movement, 21

Classroom
    dealing with size of, 94–95
    funds of knowledge in,
      98–99
    responsibility for students'
      behavior in, 188–191
Classroom management, strate-
    gies of, 188–191
Clinton, Bill, 205
Clinton, Hillary, 230
Coast Guard Academy, 127
Coates, L., 193–195
Cognitive Academic Linguistic
    Proficiency (CALP), 245
Cognitive domain, 206
Cole, K. B., 211, 212
Coleman, J., 16
Coles, A., 163
Coles-Ritchie, M., 13
Colleagues, utilizing help of, in
    dealing with disruptive
    behavior, 190
Collective bargaining, 148
Collier, V. P., 244, 246, 249–251,
    253, 257, 258
Combs, M. C., 244, 246, 250,
    251, 257, 258
Common schools, 10, 18
    English-only, 13
    Mann's role in development
      of, 12
    in New England, 19
Communities
    bringing together, 95–96
    engaging, 96–99
Comparative education,
    270–275
Competency testing, 67, 69
Comprehension, 206
Comprehensive sex education
    approach, 163
Constitution, U.S., 126
Constructivism, 182
Contemporary context,
    immigration in, 14–17
Content, 212
Content-area standards,
    202–203
    national organizations
      generating, 205–206
Contracts
    breach of, 149–150
    securing, 147–153
    terms of, 148
Cooper, Patricia, 161
Core curriculum, 33
Corporal punishment, 20

Corporate income tax, 135
Corporation for Public Broad-
    casting educational televi-
    sion programming, 129
Counts, George, 41, 43, 44
Crain, R. L., 89
Crawford, J., 242, 244, 245, 251
Creationism, 162
Criteria, 203
Critical analysis, 187
Critical literacies, 226
Critical pedagogy, 187
Cubberly, E., 126
Cultural assimilation, 244
Cultural aversion, 233
Cultural deficit model, 227
Cultural identity, maintaining,
    16–17
Culturally relevant curriculum,
    185, 187, 222–224
Cultural practice, 98
Cultural sensitivity, 234
Cultural teaching, 236–237
Cultural tolerance, 227
Cultures
    American, and egalitarian-
      ism, 233–235
    American values and,
      229–233
    bringing together, 234–235,
      237–238
    defined, 224–228
    differences in, 226–227
    relationship between
      education and, 225
Cummins, J., 245
Cunningham, N. E., 10
Curriculum
    Afrocentric, 52–53
    core, 33
    culturally relevant, 185, 187,
      222–224
    engaging families, with,
      through funds of
      knowledge, 195–196
    for English language learn-
      ers, 256
    Eurocentric, 52–53, 184–187
    inclusive, 184–187
    policy on abstinence-only
      programs, 163
    students' test scores and
      changes in, 213

Declaration of Independence
    (1776), 9, 126
Deficit model programs, 246

DeKoker, G., 271
*Delgado v. Bastrop Independent
    School District*, 22
Delpit, Lisa, 248
Democratic society, role of
    teachers in, 61–63
Demographics, impact of
    changing, on school
    finance, 140–141
Demonstration schools, 20
Descriptors, 203
Desegregation
    of schools, 106–107
    social and educational out-
      comes of, 89–90
Desmond, E., 271
Detracking, 180. *See also*
    Tracking
    challenges to implementa-
      tion of, 181
Dewey, John, 39–40, 41, 43, 44
Dickens, C., 35
Discourse, 35, 55, 76, 159, 222,
    234, 235, 238, 260, 266
Discrimination, anti-Arab,
    26–27
Dismissal, contributing factors
    regarding, 153–154
Disruptions, controlling time
    and place for dealing
    with, 189
Diverse learners
    impact of standardized test
      outcomes on, 215–218
    impact of tracking on, 180
Diversity, regional, in public
    schools, 86–88
Doe, Mimi, 194
Domains
    affective, 206, 207
    cognitive, 206
    of knowledge, 98, 195–196
    psychomotor, 206, 207
Douglass, Frederick, 18
Dropouts
    empowerment of, 93
    poverty, segregation, and
      race as factor in, 92–93
Dual-language programs,
    243, 245
Du Bois, Alfred, 49
Du Bois, Nina, 52
Du Bois, W. E. B., 19, 32,
    49–54, 185
Due process, 154, 158
Duty of care, 156–157

East Los Angeles Blowouts, 186
Economic and Social Research Council (ESRC), 109
Education. *See also* School(s)
  achievement of immigrant students, 15–16
  for African Americans, 18–20
  for American Indians, 20–21
  for Arab Americans, 24–26
  for Asian Americans, 22–24
  bilingual, 15, 21–22, 243, 244, 246, 252–253
  comparative, 270–275
  European influences on early American, 8–9
  global, 265–275
  in Greece, 5–8
  of immigrants, 12–14
  job market in, 76–78
  for Mexican Americans, 21–22
  relationship between culture and, 225
  religion and, 160–161
  sexuality, 109–110
Education, Bureau of, 106
Education, Office of, 106
Education, U.S. Department of, 115
  political contexts and, 106–107
Educational equity, No Child Left Behind Act (NCLB) (2001) and, 94
Educational exclusion, legacy of, 18–24
Educational outcomes of desegregation, 89–90
Educational philosophies, 31–56
  of Anzaldúa, 53–55
  behaviorism, 36–37, 43
  in the classroom, 36
  composing own, 56
  of DuBois, 49–53
  essentialism, 33–34, 43
  existentialism, 41–44
  of Gandhi, 46–49
  idealism, 37, 43
  making time to care about, 31–32
  perennialism, 35–36, 43
  progressivism, 39–40, 43
  realism, 37–38, 43
  role of, in teaching profession, 32–44

social reconstructionism, 40–41, 42, 43
  student-centered, 38
  teacher-centered, 33–38
  of Wollstonecraft, 44–46
Educational practice, intersections between socioeconomic status and, 90–93
Educational reform, impact on teaching profession today, 69–72
Education Consolidation and Improvement Act (1981), 130
Education for All Handicapped Children Act (1975), 106, 107, 128, 129
Education for All Handicapped Children Act (1990), 130
Education for Economic Security Act (1984), 130
Education funding, 124–141
  changing demographics and, 140–141
  of charter schools, 130
  contemporary finance systems, 128–129
  Education of Mentally Retarded Children Act and, 128–129
  Elementary and Secondary Education Act and, 129
  equitable, 136–141
  federal education initiatives, 127
  historical overview of, 125–126
  impact of No Child Left Behind Act on, 131–132
  of private schools, 130
  public funds in, for private schools, 140
  of public schools, 132–136
  social needs and federal policy responses and, 130
  standards-based accountability and, 131
  state, of public schools, 132–136
  taxes generating, 134–136
  unequal, 124–125
Education initiatives, federal, 127–128
Education of Mentally Retarded Children Act (1959), 128–129

Effort, 232
Egalitarianism, American culture and, 233–235
Eggan, P., 173
Elam, S. M., 205
Elementary and Secondary Education Act (1965), 106, 107, 128, 129, 131
  Title I of, 204–205
Elenes, C. A., 55
Ellington, L., 270
Elmandjra, M., 24
Employment
  making decisions about, 94
  securing, 147–153
Enculturation, 228
Endangered language, 244
English, changing policies on, 246
English as a Second Language (ESL), 14, 17, 245
  pullout program in, 251
  push-in program, 251
English language learners (ELLs), 179, 218
  assessment for, 256–258
  characteristics of major program models for, 252
  curriculum for, 256
  ideologies on, 247–248
  legal requirements on instruction for, 246–247
  sheltered programs for, 251
  standardized test outcomes in, 216–217
  theories on teaching, 249–250
English-only common-school classroom, 13
English-only instruction, 14
English-only laws, 21–22
Enlightenment, 9
Enthusiasm of caring teachers, 173
Epstein, J., 193–195
Equal opportunity, 83–84
Erasmus, 31
Essentialism, 33–34, 43
Essentialistic Education Society, 33
Eurocentric curriculum, 52–53, 184–187
European influences on early American education, 8–9
Evaluation, 206
Evaluation portfolios, 209, 210

Evolution, 162
  teaching, 162–163
Excise taxes, 135
Existentialism, 41–44
Expectations, maintaining high, 173
Extracurricular religious clubs, 160

Face-saving way, leaving students to terminate incident, 189
Falco, M., 45
Families, engaging, 96–99
  with curriculum through funds of knowledge, 195–196
Family Education Rights and Privacy Act (FERPA) (1974), 165
Federal and Administrative Services Act (PL 81-152) (1949), 128
Federal education initiatives, 127–128
Federal funding, 131
Feistritzer, E., 64
Ferrara, 258
Fifteenth Amendment, 19
First Amendment, 159–160, 165
Fiscal equalization, 138
Fiscal neutrality, 138
Fischer, L., 153, 156, 163
Foreign Assistance Act (1961), 273
Fourteenth Amendment, 19, 23, 150–151
Fourth Amendment, 165
Franklin, Benjamin, 9
Freedmen's Bureau schools, 19
Freed slaves, 19
Free speech, 165
Friedman, Thomas, 266
Fugitive Slave Act, 11
Fundamental philosophical positions, 33
Funding. *See* Education funding
Funds of knowledge, 96–97
  engaging families with the curriculum through, 195–196
  using, in classroom, 98–99

Gallagher-Geurtsen, Tricia, 246, 258
Gallego, M. A., 247, 260
Gallup, A. M., 205
Gambling, 135
Gandhi, Karmachand, 46
Gandhi, Mohandas, 46–49
Gandhi, Puthabai, 46
Gardner, Howard, 174–175
Garfield, R., 119
Garrett, Maggie, 113
Garrison, William Lloyd, 19
Gay, Lesbian, and Straight Student Alliance, 112
Gay-Straight Alliance Club, 161
Gay teachers, termination of, 159
Geertz, Clifford, 225
Genesee, F., 242, 246
Gerald, D., 62
Gewertz, C., 140
Ghandi, Mohandas, 32
GI Bill, 128
Gibson, Kurt, 166
Gibson, M., 14, 16
Gifted and talented, 179
Glickman, J., 64
Global education, 265–275
  defined, 268–269
  Iraqi schooling post-9/11, 272–273
  Japanese schooling and structure, 270–271
  Mexican schooling and structure, 271–272
Global history, 268
Global issues, 268
Globalization, 265
  concerns of teachers on perspective on, 267–268
  defined, 266
  public discourse regarding, 266–267
Global systems, 268
Goals, 203
  identification of, 201–202, 204
Goals 2000: Educate America Act (1994), 131, 205
Godse, Vinayak, 48
Gonzalez, G., 22
González, Norma, 96, 97, 195, 216
Good, T., 172, 173, 180
Gordon, A. J., 226
Graham, Shirley, 52
Grant writing, 131
Greece, education in, 5–8

Greek influences on American education, 5–8
Greek society, makeup of, 5
Greene, J., 119
Gresham, A., 118
Grinberg, J., 251
Grosjean, 243
Grutter v. Bollinger, 89
Guadalupe Hidalgo, Treaty of (1848), 21
Gutek, G. L., 12, 18, 48, 50

Hager, K. D., 218
Hakuta, K., 89, 251
Haladyna, T. H., 201, 204
Harp, 258
Harris, William Torrey, 244–245
Hauser, R., 84
Hawkins, H., 51
Hawkins-Stafford Elementary and Secondary School Improvement Amendment (1988 and 1993), 130
Hawley, Willis, 89
Hazelwood School District v. Kuhlmeier, 165
Head Start, 95
Health, Education, and Welfare, U.S. Department of, 106
Hegel, Georg, 50
Held, D., 267
Hess, F., 118
Hidden passage, 19
Higher education, merging social justice and, 49–53
High stakes testing, No Child Left Behind Act (NCLB) (2001) and, 70–72
High tracking, 180
Hirsch, E. D., Jr., 33, 43, 187
History
  sample lesson plan reflecting multiple intelligence, 176
  sample lesson plan reflecting scaffolding, 184
HIV education in public schools, 163–164
Holidays, celebration of, 222–224
Holistic rubric, 203
Hollingsworth, S., 247, 260
Holtrip, Stephen, 184
Homer, 35
Home school movement, 120–121
Homestead Act, 25

Honors courses, 180
Hovey, H., 135
Hovey, K., 135
Howard, T., 141
Huerta, Dolores, 47
Huerta, G. C., 13
Human values, 268
Hussar, W., 62
Hussein, Saddam, 272
Hutchins, Robert Maynard, 35, 43
Hybrid identity, 258–260

Idealism, 37, 43
Ideologies on English language learners, 247–248
Illinois High School Association, 166
Immigrants
  assimilating children, 12–13
  education of, 12–14
  outreach strategies for parents, 15
Immigrant students
  educational achievement of, 15–16
  maintaining cultural identity in, 16–17
Immigration
  complexities associated with, 15
  in contemporary context, 14–17
Immigration Act (1990), 15
Immigration Reform Act (1965), 14
Improving Academic Achievement of the Disadvantaged, 218
Inclusive curriculum, 184–187
Income taxes, 134–135
  corporate, 135
Incompetence, 163
Indian Affairs, U.S. Bureau of, Office of Indian Education programs, 107
Indian Self-Determination and Education Assistance Act (1975), 21, 106, 107
Individualized Education Plan (IEP), 11, 217
Individuals with Disabilities Education Act (IDEA) (1997), 130
Inequalities, 131
Inner cities, poverty in, 85–86

Institute of Democracy, Education, and Access, 92
Instructional methods, 226–227
Instructional portfolios, 209–210
Integrated academic core curriculum design, 15
Intelligence
  bodily kinesthetic, 175, 177
  interpersonal, 175, 178
  intrapersonal, 175, 178
  linguistic, 176
  logical-mathematical, 175, 176–177
  musical, 175, 177–178
  naturalist, 175
  spatial, 175, 177
Interactional patterns, 98
Interpersonal intelligence, 175, 178
Interstate New Teacher Assessment and Support Consortium (INTASC) standards, 64, 65, 69
Intrapersonal intelligence, 175, 178
Involuntary minorities, 233
Iowa Tests of Basic Skills, 204, 205, 216
Iraqi schooling post-9/11, 272–273

Jacobson, D., 15
James, William, 50
Janabi, A., 273
Japan, schooling and structure in, 270–271
Japanese immigrants, influx of, 23
Jefferson, Thomas, 9, 61–63
  vision of, 9–10, 11
Jim Crow segregation laws, 51
Jobim, Antonio Carlos, 3
Job market in education, 76–78
Johnson, Lyndon Baines, 204–205
Jones, J., 89
Jorgenson, L., 13
Juarez, Benito, 271

Kaeser, L., 163
Kaestle, C., 12, 13
Kao, G., 16
Karnasiewicz, S., 86
Kauchak, D., 173
Keating, Ana Louise, 55
Keller, B., 163

Kelly, C., 153, 156, 163
Kennedy, John F., 20
Kierkegaard, Søren, 41, 43
Kinder, D., 211, 212
King, Martin Luther, Jr., 47
King, R., 135
Kish, C. K., 211, 212
Kniep, William, 268
Knights of America, 22
Knowledge
    domains of, 98, 195–196
    engaging families with cur-
        riculum through funds
        of, 195–196
    funds of, 96–99, 195–196
    measurement of, 206–207
Kohn, A., 201, 205, 213, 218
Kozol, Jonathan, 85, 131
Krashen, S. D., 242
Kreider, Alison, 186n
Ku Klux Klan (KKK), 51
Kurlaender, M., 89

Ladsen-Billings, Gloria, 4
Land grant colleges, 106, 127
Land Ordinance (1785), 127
Landry, D., 163
Language(s). See also English as
        a Second Language (ESL)
    dual programs for, 243, 245
    endangered, 244
    Native American, 243–244
Language education, choices
    in, 242–243
Language extinction, 244
Language-minority (LM)
    speakers, 249–250
Larkin, M., 183
Lau v. Nichols, 246
Laws. See also Public school laws
    English-only, 21–22
    Jim Crow segregation, 51
    teachers and, 146–148
League for the Defense of
        the Rights of the Iraqi
        People, 273
League of Latin American
        Citizens, 22
League of United Latin
        American Citizens
        (LULAC), 22
Learners. See also English lan-
        guage learners (ELLs)
    impact of standardized test
        outcomes on diverse,
        215–218

impact of tracking on
    diverse, 180
    remedial, 179
Learning disabled, 179
Learning process, parental in-
    volvement in, 192–196
Lee, C., 85, 87, 89
Lee, S. J., 16
Lee, V., 173
Lee v. Weisman, 160
Legters, N., 92
Lesson plans, alternative, 190
Levin, J., 189
Lewis, D. L., 49, 50, 51
The Liberator (Garrison), 19
Librera, William, 154
Licensure, 64, 67
    alternative routes to,
        64, 69, 141
Lincoln, Abraham, 19, 25
Linguicism, 248, 254
Linguistic assimilation, 244
Linguistic intelligence, 175
Linguistic privileges, 247–248
Lipton, M., 179
Literacies
    critical, 226
    personal, 260
Locke, John, 9
Loewen, James, 275
Lollock, L., 265
Losen, D., 92
Love for children in teachers,
    174
Low-income status, free lunch
    and, 88–89
Lucking, R., 24, 25, 26
Lunch, low-income status and
    free, 88–89

Makanji, Kasturbai, 46
Mancha, Robert, 156
Mancha v. Field Museum of
    Natural History, 156
Mandela, Nelson, 47
Manera, E., 190
Mann, Horace, 18
    emergence of public schools
        and, 10–12
Maranto, R., 118
Marginalization, 14
Marquéz, Gabriel García, 254
Marx, Karl, 50
Massachusetts Act (1642), 126
Massachusetts Board of
    Education, 10
Massachusetts Law (1647), 133

Material well-being, 230–231
Mathews, J., 121
McCarthy, Joseph, 52
McCarthy, M., 156
McGuffey readers, 19
McIntosh, Peggy, 232
McKenney, Thomas, 20
McLaughlin, H., 271, 272
McNabb, Devin, 88
McNergney, J., 164
McNergney, R., 164
McPherson, Christopher, 19
McTighe, J. 258
Medical inaccuracies in
    abstinence-only programs,
    108–109
Mehlig, L. M., 208
Memory-level skills, 206
Mentoring programs, 141
    as antidote to early burnout,
        77–78
Merchant Marine Academy,
    127
Meritocracy, 84
Mertler, C., 201, 217
Messerli, J., 10, 11, 12
Mexican Americans, early
    education of, 21–22
Mexican Farm Labor Supply
    Program, 15
Mexican Labor Agreement, 15
Mexican schooling and struc-
    ture, 271–272
Millman, S., 118
Mills v. Board of Education in
    Washington, 129
Minorities
    involuntary, 233
    myths in communities,
        81–83
    poverty and, 84–85
    in teaching profession, 62–63
    voluntary, 233
Minority-language speakers
    (MLSs), 242
Mix, Charles, 20
Model schools, 10
Moll, Luis, 96, 97, 195
Monbukagakusho (National
    Ministry of Education,
    Culture, Sports, Science,
    and Technology), 270
Montejano, D., 21
Moraga, Cherríe, 55
Morality, puritanical, 230
Morrill Act (1862), 106, 127

Morrison v. State Board of
    Education, 159
Multilingualism, 246
    history of, 244–245
Multiple intelligences, 173–184
    bodily kinesthetic, 175, 177
    interpersonal, 175, 178
    intrapersonal, 175, 178
    linguistic, 176
    logical-mathematical, 175,
        176–177
    musical, 175, 177–178
    naturalist, 175
    sample lesson plan for
        United States history
        reflecting, 176
    spatial, 175, 177
Multiple Intelligences inven-
    tory, 176–178
Musical intelligence, 175,
    177–178
Muslim Awareness Associa-
    tion, 274
Muzhir al-Dulaymi, 273

Naff, A., 25
National assessment, politiciza-
    tion of standards, 204–206
National Assessment of Educa-
    tional Progress (NAEP)
    Assessment Authoriza-
    tion, 131
National Association for the
    Advancement of Colored
    People (NAACP), 49
    creation of, 51–52
National Campaign to Prevent
    Teen Pregnancy, 163
National Center for Educa-
    tional Statistics (NCES),
    62, 63, 76, 87, 88, 89, 92,
    93, 111, 139, 140
National Child Abuse Preven-
    tion and Treatment Act
    (1974), 156
National Council of Social
    Studies, 206
National Council of Teachers of
    English, 206
National Council of Teachers of
    Mathematics, 64
    "Principles and Standards
        for School Mathemat-
        ics," 205
National Council on Measure-
    ment in Education
    (NCME), 206

National Defense Education Act (1958), 107, 128–129, 246

National Defense Education Act (1962), 106

National Education Association (NEA), 63, 64, 72, 76, 108, 119, 140, 206
  challenge of No Child Left Behind Act (NCLB) (2001) by, 132
  Health Information Network of, 108

National organizations, generating content-area standards, 205–206

National Parent-Teacher Association, 193, 194

National Science Teachers Association, 206

"A Nation a Risk: The Imperative for Educational Reform," 205

Native American languages, 243–244

Native English speakers, 246

Natural consequences, allowing students to recognize, 190

Naturalist intelligence, 175

Naturalization Act (1790), 22

Naval Academy, 106, 127

Neff, D., 97

Negligence, 156–157

Nettle, D., 244

Newcomer programs, 15

New England common schools, 19

New Jersey teacher tenure law, 154

New Jersey v. TLO, 165

New teacher induction as antidote to early burnout, 77–78

Nieto, S., 228, 235

Nietzsche, Friedrich, 41, 43

No Child Left Behind Act (NCLB) (2001)
  alternative assessment and, 218–219
  curriculum changes and, 213
  detractors of, 71
  dropout rates and, 92
  educational equity and, 94
  education reforms and, 69–70
  effect on teacher certification and, 213–215

English language learners and, 216, 256–257

essential curriculum and, 187

focuses of, 108

funding for, 133, 138

high stakes testing and, 70–72

impact of, on school funding, 131–132

multiple intelligence and, 175

as outcomes-based initiative, 32, 33

parent involvement and, 195

programs funded through, 107

school choice programming and, 117, 119

school district responsibility and, 111

standardized testing, 138

Title I testing and, 205

Noddings, N., 173

Nontenured teachers, termination of, 152–153

Norby, M., 172

Normal schools, 10

Norm-referenced standardized tests, 204

Northwest Ordinance, 127

Oakes, J., 90, 179

Obama, Barack, 230

Objectives, 203
  identification of, 201–202, 204

Ochoa, T. A., 257

Off-task behavior
  dealing with, 188–189
  determining disruptiveness of, 189
  as part of habitual patter, 189
  working, to decrease incidence of, 190

Ogbu, J., 15, 26, 233–234

Oliva, P. F., 190

Olneck, M., 13–14

O'Malley, 258

Ongoing teacher training, 15

Open-access advanced placement, 180

Options, maintaining your, 191

Order of the Sons of America, 22

Orfalea, G., 25

Orfield, G., 85, 87, 89, 92

Outcomes, 203
  educational, of desegregation, 89–90
  impact of

on diverse learners, 215–218
  on teachers, 213–215

Ovando, C. J., 244, 246, 250, 251, 257, 258

Pager, D., 84

Pai, Y., 225, 228

Paige, Rod, 64

Pan-Africanism, 54

Parental involvement in learning process, 192–196

Parkhurst, Helen, 43

Parochial schools, 8
  enrollment in, 13

Parrish, T., 251

Pasta, D. J., 242, 253

Patel, M., 48

Pawlas, G. E., 190

Pennsylvania Association of Retarded Citizens v. Commonwealth, 129

Perennialism, 35–36, 43

Performance assessments, 201, 202, 203, 219

Personal literacies, 260

Personal traits of effective teachers, 172

Phillips, Wendell, 49

Physical abuse, 158

Physical neglect, 158

Piaget, Jean, 182–183

Pierce, W. D., 189, 258

Plato, 8, 31, 35, 37, 43

Play, distinction between work and, 231–232

Political contexts, U.S. Department of Education, 106–107

Politicization of national and state assessment standards, 204–206

Popham, J. W., 213

Portes, A., 16, 17

Portfolios, 203, 209–213, 218, 219
  electronic guidelines, 211
  evaluation, 209, 210
  instructional, 209–210
  planning and evaluation of, 212–213
  student night, 211

Poverty
  dropout rates and, 92–93
  free lunch program and, 88–89
  in inner cities, 85–86

minority students and, 84–85
  standardized test outcomes and, 217–218

Poverty threshold, 84

Powers, Regina, 174

Praxis, 68, 187

Principals
  role of, 115
  in transition, 116

Prism model, 249

Private lives of teachers, 158–159

Private schools, 21–22
  funding of, 139, 140

Privatization of public schools, 117–119

Process standards, 203

Progressive tax rates, 134

Progressivism, 39–40, 43

Property taxes, 134

Proportional taxes, 134

Psychomotor domain, 206, 207

Public Broadcasting Act (1967), 129

Public discourse regarding globalization, 266–267

Public funds in funding public schools, 140

Public school(s)
  emergence of, 10–12
  privatization of, 117–119
  regional diversity in, 86–88
  sex and AIDS/HIV education in, 163–164
  state funding of, 132–136
  teaching of evolution in, 162–163

Public school laws, 144–167
  breach of contract, 149–150
  categories of information, 146–147
  free speech, 165
  pending issues, 166–167
  search and seizure, 165
  securing employment, 147–153
  sex and AIDS/HIV education, 163–164
  student records, 165
  teacher rights, 159–162
  teachers and law, 146–148
  teachers' private lives, 158–159
  teachers' rights and liability issues, 155–158
  teaching evolution, 162–163
  tenure, 150–151

Public-sector collective-bargaining rights, 148
Pullout English as a Second Language (ESL) programs, 251
Punishment, 36
Puritanical morality, 230
Push-in English as a Second Language (ESL) teachers, 251

Race, dropout rates and, 92–93
Racism, 21
Ramey, D. R., 242, 253
Ramírez, J. D., 242, 253
Raphael, T. E., 226n
Rationale in planning and evaluation of portfolios, 212
Ravitch, D., 40
Reagan, Ronald, 205
Realism, 37–38, 43
Regressive taxes, 134
Rehabilitation Act (1973), 130
Reliability, 203
Religion, education and, 160–161
Remedial learner, 179
Resources, competition for, 133
Reynolds, Ruth, 11
R-ICE method, 213
Richards, C., 163
Roblyer, M., 172
Romaine, S., 244
Ronning, R., 63, 172
Roosevelt, Theodore, 24, 245
Rose, L. C., 205
Rosenwald, Robert, 161
Ross, G., 183
Rothstein, R., 86
Rousseau, Jean-Jacques, 8, 45
Rubrics, 203, 208–209, 219
   analytic, 202, 203
   book review, 209
Rumbaut, R., 16, 17
Ruskin, John, 47

Saavedra, E. R., 251
Salaries, teacher, 73–76
Salazar, Ruben, 3
Sales taxes, 135
Salinas, K., 193–195
Salmon, R., 138
Sanders, J. W., 13–14
Sanders, M., 193–195
San Juan Board of Cooperative Educational Services (BOCES) alternative licensure program model, 66

San Miguel, G., 22
Santayana, George, 50
Sartre, Jean-Paul, 41, 43
Saunders, John, 116
Savage Inequalities (Kozol), 131
Scaffolding
   defined, 183
   points to consider when implementing instructional, 183–184
Schaw, G., 172
Scheider, B., 16
Schimmel, D., 153, 156, 163
Schlossman, S. L., 13
Scholte, J. A., 266
School(s). See also Education
   Catholic, 21–22
   charter, 117–119, 139
   common, 10, 12, 13, 18, 19
   demonstration, 20
   desegregation of, 106–107
   early resistance to assimilation in, 13–14
   emergence of public, 10–12
   establishing, in new country, 126
   Freedmen's Bureau, 19
   funding of, 124
   governance of, 106
   model, 10
   normal, 10
   parochial, 8
   private, 21–22, 139
   segregation of, 22
School board
   role of local, 112, 114
   role of state, 108, 110–111
School choice, 139–140
   initiatives in, 119–120
   programs in, 116–117
School districts, 111
   structure of, 116
School finance, impact of changing demographics on, 140–141
Schooling, 228
   enculturative and acculturative processes of, 228
   Iraqi, 272–273
   Japanese, 270–271
   Mexican, 271–272
School prayer, 160
Schraw, G., 63
Schwartz, M. W., 24
Scopes "Monkey Trial," 162
Search and seizure, 165
Second Treatise on Government (Locke), 9

Segregation
   charter schools and, 120
   dropout rates and, 92–93
Self-fulfilling prophecy, 91
Servicemen's Readjustment Act (PL 78-346) (1944), 128
Severance taxes, 135
Sex education, 109–110, 163–164
Sexual abuse, 158
Sexuality Information and Information and Education Council of the U.S. (SIECUS), 108
   Advocates for Youth, 163
Shakespeare, William, 35
Shakir, E., 25
Shanken-Kaye, J. M., 189
Sheehan, J. K., 211, 212
Sheltered English, 242, 251
Sherzer, 243
Sieber, R. T., 226
Simmons, S., 84
Simon, B., 193–195
Sin taxes, 135
Skinner, B. F., 43, 181, 201
Skutnabb-Kangas, T., 242, 248
Slocum, T. A., 218
Smith, P., 24
Smith-Bankhead Act (1920), 128
Smith-Hughes Act (1917), 128
Snow, C. 251
Social justice, merging, and higher education, 49–53
Social outcomes of desegregation, 89–90
Social reconstructionism, 40–41, 43
   in action, 42
Socioeconomic background, advantages of students with high, 91
Socioeconomic status, intersections between educational practice and, 90–93
Socrates, 8, 37
Socratic method, 37
Sorting, 179
Soto, L. D., 242, 245
Spatial intelligence, 175, 177
Special needs students, standardized test outcomes in, 217
Speech, free, 165
Spindler, G., 224, 225
Spring, J., 20

Standardized tests, 175. See also Assessment(s)
   impact of outcomes on diverse learners, 215–218
   impact of outcomes on teachers, 213–215
   norm-referenced, 204
Standards, 203
   accountability based on, 131
   content, 202–206
   politicization of national and state assessment, 204–206
   process, 203
   value, 203
Standards for Teacher Competence in Educational Assessment of Students, 206
Stanford Achievement Test (SAT), 201
Stanford-Binet Intelligence Test, 215, 216, 217
Stanton-Salazar, R., 192
State assessment standards, politicization of, 204–206
State board of education, role of, 108, 110–111
State funding of public schools, 132–136
State lotteries, 135
State office of education, 111
Stern, S. 203
Stereotypes, Arab Americans and, 24–25
Steroid testing, 166
Stipek, D., 172, 173
Stowe, Harriet Beecher, 19
Strategizing household, 98
Strip-searches of students, 165
Struyk, L. R., 208, 211, 212
Student(s)
   ability grouping and tracking of, 90–91
   advantage of, with high socioeconomic background, 91
   changes in curriculum and test scores, 213
   educational achievement of immigrant, 15–16
   knowing, 191
   maintaining cultural identity in, 16–17
   minority, 84–85
   records of, 165
   responsibility for classroom behavior, 188–191

Student(s) (cont.)
special-needs, 217
strip-searches of, 165
Student-centered
philosophies, 38
existentialism, 41–44
progressivism, 39–40. 43
social reconstructionism,
40–41, 42, 43
Suleiman, M., 24
Sullivan, Gregg, 274–275
Sumptuary taxes, 135
Superintendent, role of, 114
Support staff, 115
Surplus Revenue Deposit Act
(1836), 127
Swanson, A., 135
Swanson, C., 92
Sweetland, S., 135
Sylanski, Cheryl, 4
Synthesis, 206

Takaki, R., 10, 23
Tamalera, cultural teaching
and, 236–237
Tape, Mamie, 23
Tasks, authentic, 202
Taxes
corporate income, 135
education funding and,
132–134
excise, 135
income, 134–135
property, 134
sales, 135
severance, 135
sin, 135
sumptuary, 135
Teacher(s)
burnout of, 77–78
certification of, 64, 67, 69
characteristics of caring,
172–173
characteristics of today's, 62
concerns of, on globalization, 267–268
expectations of, 90–91
impact of standardized test
outcomes on, 213–215
law and, 146–148
licensure of, 64, 69
losing job, 153
love for children, 174
negligence of, 156–157
No Child Left Behind Act
(NCLB) and, 213–215

personal traits of effective,
172
private lives of, 158–159
rights and liability issues,
155–158
rights of, 159–162
role of, in democratic society,
61–63
salaries of, 73–76
tenure for, 67, 150–151
termination of tenured,
152–153
Teacher-centered
philosophies, 33
behaviorism, 36–37, 43
essentialism, 33–34, 43
idealism, 37, 43
perennialism, 35–36, 43
realism, 37–38, 43
Teachers' unions, position on
assessment, 214
Teaching
characteristics, theory, and
strategies of effective,
171–173
composing philosophy of, 56
cultural, 236–237
impact of educational reform
on, 69–72
minorities in, 62–63
role of philosophy in, 32–44
theories on, for English language learners, 249–250
women as, 62–63
Tenery, Martha Floyd, 97, 98,
195, 196
Tenth Amendment, 106, 108
Tenure
earning, 151
importance of, 150
law on in New Jersey, 154
statutes on, 150
teacher's achievement of,
67, 150–151
Tenured teachers, termination
of, 152–153
Termination, causes for,
153–154
Testing. See also Assessment;
Standardized tests
competency, 67, 69
high stakes, 70–72
paper and pencil, 208
standardized, 175
steroid, 166

Thill, J., 209n
Think-alouds, 184
Thomas, S., 156
Thomas, W. P., 249, 251, 253
Thoreau, Henry David, 47
Thorndike, Edward L., 201
Tienda, M., 16
Tinker v. Des Moines Community
School District, 165
Title I funding, 129, 204–205
Title II funding, 129
Title III funding, 129
Title IV funding, 129
Title V funding, 129
Todd, J. M., 44, 45
Tolerance, cultural, 227
Tolstoy, Leo, 47
Tombari, M., 201
Torres, C., 268
Tracking, 90–91, 179. See also
Detracking
impact of, on diverse
learners, 180
Transitional bilingual educa-
tion, 252–253
Two-way bilingual program,
243
Tyack, D., 13

Uncle Tom's Cabin (Stowe), 19
Unions, 72–76
American Federation of
Labor-Congress of In-
dustrial Organizations
(AFL-CIO) as, 72–73
American Federation of
Teachers (AFT) as, 64,
72–73, 140, 206
National Education Associa-
tion and, 72
position of, on assessment,
214
teacher salaries and, 73–76
U.S. Air Force Academy,
106, 127
U.S. Military Academy, 127
U.S. Task Force on Indian
Affairs, 20
Upward Bound, 95
USAID, 273–274
Utah Performance Assessment
Systems for Students
(U-PASS), 214

Valdes, Guadalupe, 15, 216
Valdez, G., 192
Valencia, R., 21
Valenzuela, A., 16, 17
Validity, 203
Values
American cultural, 229–233
human, 268
Value standards, 203
Vélez-Ibáñez, C. G., 97
Vertical equity, 138
Viadero, D., 71
Virginia, University of, 10
Vocational Rehabilitation
Act, 128
Voltaire, 8
Voluntary minorities, 233
Vouchers, 119, 140
Vygotsky, Lev, 182–183

Wald, J., 92
Wallace v. Batavia, 157
Washington, Booker T., 19, 48,
50, 51
Weber, Max, 50
Well-being, material, 230–231
Wells, A. S., 89
Wheatly, David, 116
White privilege, 232
Whitmore, J. K., 17
Williams, A., 114
Witt, D., 89
Wolcott, H., 226
Wollstonecraft, Mary, 32,
44–46, 55
Women in teaching profession,
62–63
Wood, D., 183
Work, distinction between play
and, 231–232
Wright, R., 190
Wu, A., 270

Xenophobia, 245

Ye Olde Deluder Act (1947), 126
Yuen, S. D., 242, 253
Yun, J., 89

Zirkel, P., 165
Zone of proximal development
(ZPD), 182–183